At Stalin's Side

AT STALIN'S SIDE

His Interpreter's Memoirs
From the October Revolution
to the Fall of the Dictator's Empire

Valentin M. Berezhkov

TRANSLATED FROM THE RUSSIAN
by Sergei V. Mikheyev

A Birch Lane Press Book
Published by Carol Publishing Group

A Birch Lane Press Book
Published by Carol Publishing Group
Birch Lane Press is a registered trademark of Carol Communications, Inc.
  Editorial Offices: 600 Madison Avenue, New York, N.Y. 10022
    Sales and Distribution Offices: 120 Enterprise Avenue, Secaucus, N.J. 07094
In Canada: Canadian Manda Group, P.O. Box 920, Station U, Toronto, Ontario M8Z 5P9
Queries regarding rights and permissions should be addressed to Carol Publishing Group,
  600 Madison Avenue, New York, N.Y. 10022

Carol Publishing Group books are available at special discounts for bulk purchases, sales
promotion, fund-raising, or educational purposes. Special editions can be created to
specifications. For details, contact: Special Sales Department, Carol Publishing Group,
  120 Enterprise Avenue, Secaucus, N.J. 07094

Manufactured in the United States of America
10 9 8 7 6 5 4 3 2 1

Library of Congress Cataloging-in-Publication Data

Berezhkov, V. M. (Valentin Mikhaïlovich), 1919-
    At Stalin's Side : his interpreter's memoirs from the October Revolution to the fall of the
dictator's empire / by Valentin M. Berezhkov: translated by Sergei M. Mikheyev.
      p. cm.
    "A Birch Lane Press Book."
    ISBN 1-55972-212-6
    1. Berezhkov, V. M. (Valentin Mikhaïlovich), 1919-   . 2. Stalin, Joseph,
1879-1953—Friends and associates.   3. Soviet Union—History—1917-1936.   4. Soviet
Union—History—1936-1953.   5. Translators—Soviet Union—Biography.   I. Mikheyev,
Sergei M.   II. Title.
DK268.B38A3   1994
947.084 ' 2—dc20   94-19044
                                                                    CIP

To my grandson, Daniel

CONTENTS

PREFACE

I address this book to readers of different ages. Those who are closer to my generation may find much here that speaks to their own experiences. Young people, just venturing out on their life's journey, may learn lessons to take along.

The twentieth century has seen some ugly dramas—two bloody world conflicts, revolutions, civil wars, and ethnic strife. Empires have fallen; idols have come on the world's stage and have made their exits. This century has seen the countries of the anti-Hitler coalition, representing different social systems, join forces and triumph over a heretofore unknown evil.

I have had the good fortune to be witness to some of the events that helped shape our century. I have written about them in my book. But I also wanted to show how those history-making developments played a role in the lives of ordinary people. That is why I am also telling a personal story about myself and my family.

Thus the flight from the hungry Petrograd to the Ukraine after the October 1917 revolution. The journey across the country devastated by the Civil War. The famine and repressions of War Communism. A brief breather of the New Economic Policy. A new wave of expropriations of private property by the Bolsheviks. Elimination of private farms. More famine and repression. My father's arrest. Abandoned corpses of people dead from hunger or disease. My incredible peregrinations from the Pacific navy in Vladivostok to the factory of Germany's cannon king Krupp, from my office inside the Kremlin to Hitler's Imperial Chancellery in the company of the People's Commissar for Foreign Affairs, Molotov. After Hitler's declaration of war on the Soviet Union, work for Stalin as his interpreter at his talks with Churchill and Roosevelt. My parents' mysterious disappearance from Kiev during the German occupation. A brush with death after being denounced by Beria and my banishment from the Kremlin.

All this and much more compacted into one life. And the fears I felt and the dreams I lived were shared by my countless compatriots.

I am especially pleased that this book is coming out in the United States. My life has been particularly and intricately linked with this country. From my childhood passion for the stories about American Indians, through my years of work as assistant to the people's commissar for foreign affairs, assigned to the Soviet-American desk, editor of a Soviet periodical devoted to the study of the United States, my parents' discovery of America the hard way, teaching in U.S. colleges, and—a recent raw wound—the tragic death of my twenty-six-year-old son Andrei, who participated in a joint venture with a Texas oil company, I have always felt America's presence.

It is my hope that this book will give my readers a better insight into the life of a country and its people, who for three score and ten years were living out a fantasy, trying to build a perfect society, "man's heaven on earth." Today they are having a rude awakening, their dreams shattered.

Yet I believe that the reader will have an optimistic feeling after reading my book: The people who have survived such a horrendous experiment will endure and rise again to build a free and democratic country that will take up a worthy place in the world community of nations.

I am grateful for the help and encouragement I received during the work on this book from my wife Valeria and my sons—Sergei, Alexei, and Andrei.

In conclusion I would like to acknowledge Mr. Sergei Mikheyev, who translated my book and acted as my agent on this project, Mr. James Walls, who provided invaluable editorial assistance, and Ms. Lee Ann Elliott, who offered insightful comments on the draft English text.

Claremont, California
1994

At Stalin's Side

CHAPTER ONE

I have this feeling that stored in my memory are events that happened long before I was even aware of what was going on around me. Later in my life, my mind must have pieced together these images, which seem so real, out of actual events, conversations of adults around me, stories I heard, broken-off sentences, old portraits and photographs in Grandma's family album, and maybe even my childhood dreams, all those things that memory had unconsciously registered without assigning any meaning to them. Today, looking back over my life, I not only get flashbacks of events I could have witnessed when I was still a boy, but also amazingly vivid pictures of things that happened even before I was born.

How It Began

I SEE AN ELEGANTLY FURNISHED LIVING ROOM with crimson velvet, shirred draperies and lace curtains on the windows, high-back chairs, and end tables covered with cream-colored cloths with long tassels. There is a thick carpet and the skin of a white bear lying on the floor. The head of the bear looks almost alive, and its teeth are bared. The logs are crackling in the fireplace. Mother and Grandmother come in. They are accompanied by a young officer decorated with the Cross of St. George. This is Mother's brother, my uncle Leonid, who has just come back from the front. His face is handsome and well proportioned. His well-trimmed hair is parted in the middle, and it looks as if a thin crack were running over his head. He sits down at the grand piano, and the living room fills with melodious sounds that envelop me with their magic. Gradually, the picture grows dim and fades away. . . .

The dining room is bright and sunny. At the head of the table is a big, shining copper samovar that resembles a barrel. The carved chairs are Viennese. The tea set has a bright flower pattern. Father and Mother are having tea with homemade cookies that give off a delicious aroma. Suddenly, Mother's mother, my grandmother, rushes in. She has on a white lace dress and is carrying an umbrella to match. She is wearing a light, wide-brimmed hat. Her passion is horse racing. She is back from the racetrack and is all upset.

"Lost again?" Mother asks her.

Grandma slumps into a chair, tired. She looks guilty and distraught.

"Please do not scold me, kids. Someday I will win. But this time, I had to give everything away. I pawned the rings, chains, and bracelets. Even Grandpa's gold watch . . ."

Father tries to calm her down. Mother pours Grandma tea and, moving the cup toward her, kisses her on the cheek.

"Don't get upset. This is not the first time this has happened to you. However, we have to get Grandpa's watch back fast. Misha, dear"—Mother turns to Dad—"we have to redeem it right away."

"Oh, no," Grandma objects. "It's my fault. I will do it."

Father smiles and nods to Mother. His hair is thick and raven, and he sports a little mustache of the same color. He is elegantly dressed. His long brown suit snugly fits his muscular body. His white shirt is starched stiff, and his striped tie is made into a bow.

Great-grandpa—my great-grandfather on my mother's side—is revered in our family. He is our pride. In his time, he was known as the Grandfather of Russian Romantic Song. Nikolai Alekseyevich Titov, born in 1800 (he died in 1875), was a contemporary of Pushkin's and his great admirer. He put many of Pushkin's poems to music. We particularly liked and often played Grandpa's song "Talisman," based on the poem of the same name, a poem written on the night of November 6, 1827, when the great poet was visited by inspiration:

> Where the sea forever dances
> Over lonely cliffs and dunes,
> Where sweet twilight's vapor glances
> In a warmer-glowing moon,
> Where with the seraglio's graces
> Daylong toys the Mussulman,
> An enchantress 'mid embraces
> Handed me a talisman.*

*Alexander Pushkin, *Collected Narrative and Lyrical Poetry*, translated by Walter Arndt (Ann Arbor, Mich.: Ardis, 1984), 81–82.

N. A. Titov composed over one hundred romantic songs, marches, quadrilles, and waltzes. Some of his works are still popular today, such as "The Song of the Coachman," "The Icon Lamp," "Mother, My Dear," "My Dear and Fickle Friend."

Right until the beginning of World War II we kept his portrait, which showed a brave officer with fluffy sideburns and a mustache, wearing epaulets and decorated with the Star of St. Andrew.

And another vision: a summer house made of logs in Kolomyagy, outside Petrograd, on a clear spring day. On a spacious veranda overgrown with wild vines, two women are sitting in wicker chairs: Grandma in a white blouse and a long black skirt with a book by Lermontov in her hands, and Mother in a wide pink gown. Mother is sewing a lace band to a baby's vest. She is getting ready for an increase in the family. I am going to be born soon. Father arrives in a carriage from the railway station where he gets off the train from Petrograd. Always calm and reserved, today he is visibly agitated.

"What happened?" Mother asks, taking note of his condition.

"I have to talk to you," Father replies, and, turning to Grandma, excuses himself.

"Lyudmila, darling," Father says, "don't get worried. Nothing bad has happened. It's just that I have been offered the job of head of the Procurement Commission. The Commission is leaving for America to monitor purchases of naval and merchant ships. It is going to take a while, and you will be coming with me."

"Oh!" Mother exclaims. "What bad timing! I am going to go into labor soon. And then again, the war is going on."

"It's quite all right. We will be sailing on a big ship. There will be physicians on board. They will help if anything should happen. And then you still have two months to go. By that time, we will be in New York."

That was in the spring of 1916. And I was born on July 2.

They go back out on the veranda.

"So what happened?" Grandma is eager to know.

Father explains.

"By no means!" Grandma objects categorically. "How can she sail over the ocean in her present state? The war is raging. There are German subs in the Atlantic. And what is it like out there in America? Let her have her baby first, let the child grow up a little, and then you can leave."

Father tries to dissuade Grandma, but all in vain. Mother also begins to have her doubts.

"Maybe, Misha, you should go without me."

"No, I won't. Only together."

"How can you, Mikhail Pavlovich?" Grandma sounds unusually official. "How can you subject Lyudmila and the baby to such trials?"

Grandma, who comes from a family that always lived in comfort, is convinced that only at home in Petrograd are conditions all in place to bring her new grandchild into this world.

Grandma points out that Lyudmila, a woman raised genteelly, a graduate of the Smolni Institute of Maidens of Noble Origin, is not suited for such dubious adventures as traveling to America in the last few months of her pregnancy. Maybe Misha, the son of a provincial teacher, an orphan, is used to all kinds of tribulations. But as for Lyudmila, Grandma will not let her go anywhere.

"Then I also stay," Father says firmly. "I will turn down the offer."

If only they had known the ordeals our family was to go through during the years of the Civil War and beyond, the transatlantic voyage, even with the threat of German subs, would have seemed a pleasure trip to them. Chance, which played such a major role in my life, had its first joke at my expense while I was still in my mother's womb. If my grandma had not been so stubborn, I would have been born in the United States. And maybe I would have ended up by becoming an interpreter not for Stalin, but for Roosevelt.

Working Late at the Kremlin

IT IS QUIET IN MY SMALL ROOM in the northern wing of the Soviet of People's Commissars building in the Kremlin. Only the chimes of the clock on the Spasskaya Tower break the silence every quarter of an hour, marking the march of time. The windows are blacked out with dark blinds. It is late in July of 1941. An air alert can sound at any minute, warning of the approaching German bombers. It is the middle of the night, but the vast government bureaucracy continues to function. Stalin is still busy in his office, and every ranking official, be he a member of the Politburo or a people's commissar, stays put waiting for a possible order to report to the "boss" or for the ring of the green phone, which only Stalin uses. An hour ago, People's Commissar for the Defense Industry Dmitri Ustinov called me on the government line to find out whether Molotov had gone home. In the spring of 1940, Ustinov and I had worked together at the Krupp factory in Essen, Germany, and he is frank in telling me that he has finished up in his office and is ready to leave. But the "boss" doesn't like it when he is unable to reach his subordinates in their offices. If Molotov had left, that would be a telltale sign that Stalin would not need anybody any more tonight.

"Please let me know when your chief leaves." I hear a tired voice. "I have to get up early to go to the shooting range. Wish I could snatch at least a couple of hours' sleep."

However, Molotov, as far as I know, is not yet ready to leave. Today, Stalin has had a lengthy talk with Harry Hopkins, Franklin Roosevelt's personal representative, who has just arrived in Moscow. Stalin has high expectations for this visit. The lightning advance of the Germans in the first weeks after the invasion had pressed him to look for allies, and the United States is unquestionably the most desired one of them all. Stalin did all he could to convince the U.S. president's envoy that the Soviet Union would not capitulate and would fight fascism until the final victory. He promised to provide Hopkins with detailed information about the Soviet Union's military needs at their next meeting, and Molotov, together with Mikoyan and military experts, are now busy preparing the necessary documentation.

What was said at this first talk with the American envoy—the first high-ranking U.S. official to arrive in Moscow after Hitler's invasion—is to be reported to the members of the Politburo in the morning. I have been instructed to verify the text of the memorandum of conversation prepared from the notes hastily taken by Maxim Litvinov, who interpreted at the meeting.

One passage in the memorandum really bothers me. Stalin told Hopkins that Germany's attack on the Soviet Union was unexpected. Stalin had not expected Hitler to strike at that particular moment. Even though for all of us Stalin is the unquestioned authority, I find it hard to accept his assertion. How could it be? In our embassy in Berlin, we had accurate information about the invasion being prepared. We even knew the precise date—the night of June 22. The embassy had sent all this information to Moscow. Could it be that it had not been reported to Stalin? The information came not only from Dekanozov, the ambassador in Germany, but also from the military attaché, Tupikov, and the naval attaché, Vorontsov. Each of them had his own reliable sources, and all the information tallied.

Indisputable facts that have since become public indicate that Stalin was fully informed about the preparations for the invasion. In addition to the tip-offs from Berlin, a warning had come from Churchill, and reliable information had been received from Soviet agent Richard Sorge in Tokyo. Stalin had detailed reports that German forces were completing their concentrations along the borders of the Soviet Union, and that Wehrmacht units were fully mobilized and poised for the attack.

Immediately after Hitler's deputy in the National Socialist Party, Rudolf Hess, landed in England, Stalin had one more confirmation of the impending danger to our country. Kim Philby, who held a ranking position in the British secret service, reported to Moscow that the attack on the Soviet Union was imminent, and that Hess, after breaking this information to the authorities in London, had tried to secure Britain's commitment to stay out of this conflict.

Finally, on the night of June 21, a report was placed on the boss's table about German defectors who had risked their lives swimming across the Bug and the Dniester rivers to give a last-minute warning to the Soviet command about the invasion scheduled to begin in a few hours. Stalin refused to believe any of this. But because he had been warned of what was to happen, he was deeply embarrassed when the invasion actually occurred. The all-knowing and all-seeing helmsman of all peoples had turned out to be a blind man.

Stalin, of course, understood that Hopkins was aware, at least in general terms, of the warnings that had been coming to Moscow. With his statement about the "unexpected attack" he probably wanted to forestall any possible disconcerting questions from his American visitor. But what could a shrewd man such as Hopkins make of this ploy? He could not have believed that officials in the government that Stalin ran with an iron hand would have dared conceal such vital information from him. Hopkins should have asked about it. But he chose to be polite and did not pursue the subject.

The episode casts an important light on the way Stalin felt about Hitler.

They had never met. However, Stalin was in a way drawn to the Nazi dictator and kept waiting for a meeting to be scheduled. According to Hitler's pronouncements, he also thought much of Stalin. They had a lot in common, and their ways of controlling people were similar in many respects.

Stalin and Hitler

WHEN I WORKED IN NAZI GERMANY in 1940, I was struck by what I saw around me. The same idolization of "the leader," the same mass rallies and parades where the participants carried portraits of the Führer and little children presented him with flowers. Very similar, ostentatious architecture, heroic themes depicted in art much like our socialist realism. Having eliminated all opponents or sent them off to detention camps, Hitler, just like Stalin, persuaded the crowd to idolize him through massive ideological brainwashing. I watched the Victory Parade along Siegesallee in Berlin after victorious Wehrmacht divisions returned from defeated France. Standing close to the podium, I saw people reach out to Hitler as he drove by in an open convertible Mercedes. Women lifted their babies for him to touch. While despising his people, he knew how to flatter them by calling them "a master race."

Stalin was like that. I could see him smiling paternally at the crowds of marchers filing past the Lenin mausoleum, flattering them by hailing them as "builders of communism," while at the same time calling them fools under his breath as they praised him loudly. However, at the time I could not make such comparisons—even to myself. In those days, there were many things I did not know, and I was unable to understand the sinister significance of the many similarities between Germany and the Soviet Union. After all, the stated goals of the two countries were fundamentally different. Stalin urged the Soviet people to build a socialist society where all people would be equal and happy. Hitler, on the other hand, was proclaiming the "millennium of the empire of the master race." At the same time, he was hurling the best of the German nation into the carnage of the war.

The first time I saw Hitler up close was on November 12, 1940, when, together with Molotov, I walked into his office in the Imperial Chancellery in Berlin. At that moment, the Führer was at the peak of his power and glory: all of Western Europe was at his feet. France was defeated. The British, finding refuge in their island, were preparing for an invasion that never came.

Aware as he was of the might of the German war machine, Hitler was haughty and arrogant. In this respect he was the complete opposite of Stalin, who amazed everyone with his ostensible modesty and total lack of desire to impress. Unlike Hitler, Stalin thought that if his limitless power over millions of his subjects was evident, there was no need to advertise it.

As we entered his office, Hitler was alone. He was sitting at a huge desk, bent over some papers. He immediately raised his head, got up quickly, and walked over to his visitors taking little steps. We met him in the middle of the room, we being Molotov, his deputy Dekanozov, as well as Pavlov and I, the two interpreters. The Führer shook everyone's hand. His palm was cold and damp, giving me an unpleasant sensation, as if I were touching a reptile. His handshake was limp and expressionless. In this he resembled Stalin. Stalin's handshake was flat and indifferent. He would, as it were, slide it into the hand of the person he was shaking hands with. Through the skin of his small hand one could easily feel the bones.

I must be one of a few people alive today who shook hands with every major political figure of the period of World War II: Stalin, Hitler, Churchill, Roosevelt, Chou En-lai. A more glib writer could perhaps spin off an entire novel just about those handshakes. They were indeed each different and unique. And they certainly reflected each individual's character. Churchill's hand was big, yet soft and warm, enveloping and comforting, as it were. Roosevelt greeted people by energetically putting out his hand, which had that special strength that is quite typical of people who have problems with their legs. Chou En-lai's handshake was fairly firm yet delicate and friendly. Perhaps these were my subjective responses, but that is how I remember them.

In the Imperial Chancellery

THE FÜHRER BESTOWED a compliment of sorts upon me. When I began interpreting Molotov's words that he was happy to meet the Reich chancellor, Hitler, probably unprepared for my Berlin accent, looked at me carefully and suddenly asked: "Who are you, a German?"

"No," I replied, and hastened to explain to Molotov what this was all about. I thought the two leaders would then resume their conversation, but the Führer would not give up:

"Are you German by nationality?"

"No, I am Russian."

"It can't be," Hitler said in amazement.

He turned to Molotov and invited him over to a low, round table that had a sofa and chairs placed around it.

When the conversation between Molotov and Hitler was officially over, Hitler walked his visitor to the door of the Imperial Chancellery. I was following along interpreting their conversation, which was general in content. The other members of the delegation had fallen behind us. Before parting, Hitler shook the people's commissar's hand and said:

"I consider Stalin to be a historic personality. I also flatter myself with the thought that I will also go down in history [*Ich bilde mir ein, dass ich auch in die Geschichte eingehen werde*]. That is why it is natural for two political leaders like us to meet. Please, Mr. Molotov, transmit to Mr. Stalin my greetings and my proposal that we hold a meeting in the not too distant future."

After returning to Moscow, Molotov, of course, relayed Hitler's proposal to Stalin, and it probably played a considerable part in Stalin's miscalculations of the timing of Germany's attack on the Soviet Union.

There is no doubt that the "helmsman of the peoples" was flattered by the praise he had received from the Führer. He had also been prepared for quite some time to sing Hitler's praises.

When, in 1934, Hitler eliminated his comrade-in-arms Ernst Röhm, together with other commanders of the storm troopers, Stalin spoke highly of the bloodbath. Mikoyan told me that at the very first meeting of the Politburo after Röhm's execution, Stalin said:

"Did you hear what happened in Germany? Hitler, what a great man! This is the way to deal with your political opponents."

That was the summer of 1934. And in December, Stalin's comrade-in-arms Sergei Kirov was murdered. We now know that Stalin was implicated in this crime. That was followed by severe repressions of Lenin's Old Guard, the elimination of the top commanders of the Red Army, white-collar workers, and intellectuals. Thousands, millions, of innocent people were engulfed in bloody purges.

In this respect Stalin and Hitler acted in similar ways. Röhm was declared an enemy of the people, a traitor, and was publicly disgraced. Erwin Rommel, whom Hitler forced to commit suicide, was buried with honors. Stalin eliminated Bukharin, who was "the darling of the Party," to use Lenin's expression. On the other hand, he forced his friend Sergo Ordjonikidze to commit suicide and then made a moving speech at his bier and carried his coffin on his shoulders to the grave, just as he carried the urn with Kirov's remains.

All that was going on in the Soviet Union in the 1930s could not but provoke a very negative reaction among the leaders of the Western democracies. Their rejection of the October Revolution in Russia found further support in Stalin's repressions. Hitler, however, had two reasons for liking them. First, they provided additional justification for blackmailing Western politicians with the threat of Bolshevism. Second, they weakened the protests against Nazi prosecutions of Communists and dissidents in general, leading a number of Western politicians to the conclusion that Hitler's National Socialism was preferable to Stalin's communism. At the same time, Hitler admired Stalin's ruthlessness, cruelty, and mercilessness. He identified with these traits.

In the late 1930s, when it became evident that Britain and France were evading a serious agreement with the Soviet Union to stem fascist aggression, Stalin began to look toward Berlin more often. The experience of the civil war in Spain—where no country except the Soviet Union provided assistance to the legal government of the Republic, and where Hitler and Mussolini, capitalizing on the policy of noninterference by the Western powers, were able to provide unhindered military aid to General Franco and, ultimately, to install him in Madrid—demonstrated to Stalin who was exercising real power in the West. And he respected power. The anschluss that absorbed Austria and the Munich deal that gave Hitler parts of Czechoslovakia provided further proof that Western politicians were prepared to let Hitler get away with anything so long as he delivered on the promise he made in his bible, *Mein Kampf*, to eliminate Bolshevism. It was probably at that time that Stalin began to entertain the idea of an amicable agreement with the Führer.

Litvinov, because of his Jewish origin and his passionate speeches in the League of Nations, was deemed not suitable for concluding deals with Nazi Germany, and he was removed as foreign minister. Molotov became the people's commissar for foreign affairs. At that time, he was the man closest to Stalin.

Hitler, in his turn, had also come to the conclusion that he had a better chance of winning in the West than in the East. In 1939 it was no secret to him that France, as sometimes happens with victorious nations, had completely lost its combative spirit. True, the powerful Maginot line had been erected along the Rhine border, but it could be bypassed if the attack was launched through the Netherlands and Belgium. Having taken care of France, the Führer would be in a position to come to an agreement with Britain, which was also not too eager to engage in battle. Furthermore, the meetings Hitler had had with Neville Chamberlain in Bad Godesberg and Munich helped him form an opinion of the British prime minister as a man who would yield to blackmail. The neutralization of Great Britain would finally make it possible to take on Russia. In the meantime, he should try to establish a common language with Stalin.

The Kremlin, however, decided to make one more attempt to reach an agreement with Great Britain and France. Negotiations got under way, but from the very start held out no promise of success. The British and French delegates lacked authority, and their level of representation was too low.

By early August 1939, Stalin had come to the conclusion that it was futile to hope for a serious agreement with London and Paris. This conclusion was confirmed by negotiations with the British and French military delegations that arrived in Moscow on August 11 to talk about taking joint actions to repel the German aggressor. When People's Commissar for the Defense of the Soviet Union Marshal Voroshilov asked if there was an agreement with Poland to let Soviet forces through its territory in case of war with Germany, General Doumain, who headed the French delegation, replied that he did not know Poland's plans. When Voroshilov asked what contingents

Britain could provide to reinforce the French Army, the British general Heywood stated that in the first stage of the war with Germany, Britain would supply sixteen divisions, and subsequently a further sixteen divisions. But at that time the British were deploying in their islands only five regular and one motorized division. These figures looked ridiculous in comparison with a Germany, which already had 140 divisions under arms. Nor could the British forces be compared with the 120 divisions that, as London and Paris believed, the Soviet Union was to provide from the very start of military operations. In response to the question raised by the Soviet side concerning Allied plans for Belgium, the French representatives stated that they could cross the territory of that country only if Belgium requested it, but that they did not know whether such a request would be forthcoming. All this induced Voroshilov to make this statement on August 14:

"Without clear and unambiguous answers to these questions, further negotiations are pointless. The Soviet military delegation cannot recommend that its government participate in an undertaking so clearly doomed to failure."

Against this backdrop a proposal came from Berlin regarding the advisability of improving German-Soviet relations. On August 2, in his conversation with the Chargé d'Affaires Georgi Astakhov of the Soviet embassy in Berlin, Joachim von Ribbentrop, undoubtedly on direct instructions from Hitler, expressed the wish to establish a "new kind" of relation between Germany and the Soviet Union. He stated that there were no problems in the area stretching from the Baltic to the Black seas that could not be resolved to their mutual satisfaction. When Astakhov requested the Reich minister to be more specific, Ribbentrop expressed readiness to engage in negotiations on outstanding problems, provided the Soviet government reciprocated that readiness. The cable that the Reich minister sent to the German ambassador in Moscow, Schulenburg, to brief him on the content of his conversation with Astakhov had an interesting addition. The Soviet chargé d'affaires was given to understand that Germany was prepared "to reach an agreement with Russia regarding the future of Poland."

Exodus From Petrograd

I REMEMBER WELL our flight from hungry Petrograd. The Civil War is raging in the country. The once resplendent "Northern Venice" looks cold, bleak, and disconsolate with its sepulchral stone buildings looming over the miserable, blanket-wrapped inhabitants of the former imperial capital. The Soviet government has moved to Moscow, and the "proud city on the Neva" is turning into the provincial town that it remains to this day. Mother is dragging me along by the hand. My face is wrapped in a kerchief, with only my eyes showing, I am trying hard to keep up with her. The wind down Nevsky Prospekt is driving scraps of newspapers, proclamations, and the husks of sunflower seeds. A detachment of sailors is marching toward us, their rifles over their shoulders with bayonets attached.

Mother was given our week's food ration at Father's factory—half a loaf of black bread, two dried salted fish, and four potatoes. She is in a rush to get home, where Father is laid up in bed, delirious with typhoid fever. Always so strong and full of energy, he is completely helpless.

Father had no interest in politics, especially when he was younger. However, he hailed the February Revolution, and whenever he set off for town, he would wear a red button in the lapel of his jacket. He believed that the liberation of Russia from the shackles of the czarist autocracy would open up prospects for the country's rapid industrial development, and he dreamed of being a part of this. That is why he saw the havoc caused by the October Revolution and the fratricidal Civil War that followed as a personal tragedy. Having come from the family of a poor provincial teacher and having lost both his parents early in life, he was a self-made man. After graduating summa cum laude from the gymnasium, as we call our secondary schools, he traveled from Chernigov to St. Petersburg. There he completed a course of studies first at the Gatchina school and then at St. Petersburg Polytechnic. Since he was an honors student at the Polytechnic, his name is etched there in golden letters on an honorary marble plaque. Yet throughout his college years he lived from hand to mouth. He would tell us how, together with other students from poor families, he would walk into restaurants where there would always be a pitchers of water and thick slices of bread placed on the tables—free of charge. Current newspapers were available on the rack, and he could read without ordering. He would sit there pretending to be reading while furtively eating bread and washing it down with the water. Father also taught privately in order to make it through his years of study. Immediately after his graduation he got a job as a senior engineer at the Putilov shipyard, where he began making good money. He married a girl from a well-known if somewhat impoverished St. Petersburg family. Life seemed to promise happiness and prosperity. And suddenly all those hopes were dashed. The great efforts he had made and the hardships endured as an orphan all proved in vain.

Grandma sells her family jewelry to buy food from black marketeers. We are able to give better food to our bedridden father while somehow managing to get by ourselves. The apartment is not heated, and we all stay in one room. We have no wood for the fireplace, but we are lucky to have a tin stove, called a *burzhuyka*, "a bourgeoise." It sits with its four legs on a sheet of metal placed in the middle of the living room. Its flue, looking like a water pipe, angles across the ceiling and out the window. We have already burned a dozen chairs as well as Grandpa's desk. The dining-room china cabinet is next in line. Some entrepreneurial craftsmen launched the production of such stoves. They are used for warmth by the bourgeoisie, the people living in the once prosperous neighborhoods that used to have central heating. The stove gets its name from them. It gets red-hot in a matter of minutes and it takes only a few minutes more for the water in a kettle to come to a boil. However, the *burzhuyka* cools down just as quickly, and at night the temperature in the apartment drops below freezing.

In 1942–43, when there was no heating in Moscow, those *burzhuyka* stoves made a comeback. Such a stove saved us in the Petrov Street apartment I was given after my oldest son, Sergei, was born in 1942.

Father is gradually improving. He begins to take walks out in the street. The Putilov shipyard where he worked is closed down: no fuel, no metal, no orders. Most of the workers have been called up to the front. Life in the city is getting harder and harder. The family meets to discuss the situation. Father's sister, Lyubov Pavlovna, lives in the Ukraine. She is an obstetrician in a village hospital about sixty miles from Chernigov, father's hometown.

"Maybe we should go there," Father suggests. "That part of the country has always been rich and hospitable."

"How will you make a living there?" Grandma is doubtful.

"I'll find work. In any case, it's easier there than here. Look how thin your grandson is. He's not going to last long here. He needs milk, vegetables, fruit. There is plenty of that in the Ukraine."

Listening to them argue, I begin picturing myself lying in a little casket. Over the last weeks I have seen many caskets. Mournful figures drag them along the icy pavements of Petrograd, just as they did later, during the siege of the 1940s. I am lying motionless in the little casket and they stand bent over it crying their hearts out. I start bellowing myself.

"What's your problem?" Mother turns on me sternly. "Stop this. It's bad enough as it is."

"Don't be so hard on him, Lyudmila," Grandma intervenes. "See how feeble he is. His nerves are no good."

I begin howling even louder. I totally lose control when someone feels sorry for me. The moment someone says jokingly, "Oh, you poor thing!" I burst into tears.

My breakdown and my emaciated appearance must have provided an additional argument in favor of our departure. But now Grandma balks.

"You go, and I'll stay here."

And no matter how much my parents tried to persuade her, she stood her ground.

"Alone, I'll make it," she assures us. "I'll sell everything, and I don't need much, you know. Anyway, it's not long before it's going to be all over for me. I've lived my life. Father, Grandpa, Great-grandpa, are all buried here. I'll stay here, too."

In the end, we decide to leave without her.

It didn't take us long to get ready to go. Mother packed our clothes, blankets, and linen into wicker trunklike baskets. She talked Grandma into giving us our family album. I added a few samples from an illustrated magazine, the *Golden Childhood*. It had beautiful pictures, like today's comics. Later, I would use them to learn to read.

The time came to say goodbye. All that day Grandma clutched me in her arms. She treated me to a sweet mousse she herself had made from some pre-Revolutionary recipe. For the first time I saw her in tears. Maybe she knew we would never see each other again.

Grandma died of starvation one year after we left.

The journey south was long, arduous, and difficult. We crossed the fronts of the Civil War, traveling now in packed railroad cars, now in horse-drawn carriages, and sometimes footing it, with Father pushing the cart with our personal belongings to our next resting place. I was four years old, and the ordeal must have been too much for me. I remember I would get this pain in my chest similar to the one that pierced me many years later when I had a heart attack. I could not walk or even move my hand. Father, exhausted by the endless journey, would get angry at me, thinking I was feigning. Once he even spanked me. Mother stepped in and suggested we take a rest. But he again tried to keep me walking on. I felt that another step would be my last. I fell down and did not move. They had to put me on the cart. I understood it was hard for Dad to push it even without my being on it, but I couldn't do anything about it. I even began to think they would be glad if I disappeared. Of course, it was not fair and not right to think that way. But when the pain came, I wished I were dead so they could be free of me.

Some episodes are firmly etched in my memory. A huge crowd is milling around in front of a freight train at a small station, people with knapsacks, bundles, baskets, and bags. They are shoving and pushing and shouting. The whistle has already blown. The train is about to leave. We have to hurry to get inside the freight car in time. Father, a basket on his head, squeezes through the door and stretches out his hand toward Mother. She is pulling me behind her with her other hand. People are crushing me so hard that it hurts. Just as I am about to set foot on the car step, a powerful shove hurls me to the side. I am torn loose from Mother's hand, and I fall back on the platform. The crowd presses on, and I see Mother being pushed farther and farther into the car. Father is trying to elbow his way out, but the people close in around him like a wall. The train begins to move and I remain alone on the platform. Mother cranes her head from behind somebody's shoulder and is calling, but nobody is paying attention. The cars are rolling by one after another, faster and faster, and the thoughts in my head are moving even more quickly: I will never see them again, I will become homeless like those droves of shabby, hungry kids I see at railroad stations.

It was all so sudden that I didn't even cry. I calmly resigned myself to my fate. Suddenly, a strong hand swept me off the platform. A huge sailor in a striped vest and an unbuttoned pea jacket standing on the step of the last car places me on the car platform. Why did he do it? Maybe he saw me pushed away from the car, maybe he heard Mother call out. I still don't have the answer. The shock totally blanked my memory after that point. The only thing I knew for sure is that I was reunited with my parents.

Another thing that stuck in my memory from those years of wandering around the ravaged country is the constant, gnawing pangs of hunger. Unfortunately, ever since I was a kid, I wake up early, around five o'clock in the morning. I remember crouching in some unfamiliar cold room or in some windswept freight car, my hands pressed to my stomach, waiting for my parents to wake up and give me something to eat.

A rickety house on the outskirts of a village already somewhere in the Ukraine. A Jewish family has given us shelter here. It is a winter evening, not too late yet already dark. Water in a cast-iron pot is being heated on the stove. Mother is getting ready to wash my hair. In the corner, the owner of the house, his head covered with a striped fabric, is mumbling a prayer. His two adolescent sons are hunched over their textbooks. Father whispers to Mother:

"Look how diligent they are. The school must be closed now. But they keep on studying on their own. They will certainly be somebody someday."

Our hostess puts an old washbasin on a stool. She pours boiling water into it. Mother adds some cold water and bends my head over the basin. I see swarms of yellowish little creatures creeping out of the cracks—they wiggle in the boiling water and then become still.

"Look!" I cry out. "Lice!"

"*Oy vay, mir!*" the hostess exclaims. "I'm sorry. I washed the basin and I thought there weren't any. They are everywhere now. There is no soap, people don't eat right. So you get lice."

"It's all right." Mother tries to calm her down. "They are indeed all over the place. We are going to pour the water out, splash the basin with boiling water one more time, and it will be all right. And here are two bars of soap for you, from our stock."

"Oh, thank you!" says the hostess.

Recalling this distant episode, my thoughts turn to Moscow 1990, where, due to the shortages of shampoo and detergents and also probably because of poor diet, lice are again found in schoolchildren's hair.

In the morning, together with our hosts' sons I set out for a walk in the village. It is half-deserted. We walk into the local store. Its owner, Uncle Josef, an opulent man who is no longer young but is unmistakably a Semite, gives us a container of kerosene—the most effective lice-killer. I got a clay whistle from him as a present.

We are awakened in the middle of the night by the sound of shots, the clatter of hooves, and loud shouts. The mistress of the house whispers to us to stay still.

"Zeleny's band is terrorizing the neighborhood," she explains. "Here they are now."

Suddenly, a knock on the door.

"Open up, you stinking Jews, you!" comes a drunken voice with a thick Ukrainian accent.

"What Jews? We are Ukrainians, Orthodox Christians," Father calls out in the Ukrainian he has not forgotten.

"All right then . . ."

We hear a horse neigh and a clatter of hooves. Then a few more shots.

In the morning, we look out the window and see people running toward the store. We hurry after them. Beside the door, which is hanging from only one hinge, there is Uncle Josef, lying in a pool of blood. His shirt is pulled off his big paunch. His wife is kneeling by his side, sobbing.

Respite in Kiev

THE TRAIN STOPS AT DARNITSA. It can't go any farther. All the bridges across the Dnieper leading to Kiev have been blown up. It's an early morning on a frosty day, still totally dark. There are no lights or fires. Passengers, hardly distinguishable in the dark, get out of the cars, carrying their belongings with them. We also get down onto the icy platform. The wind is blowing low, driving sharp needles into our faces. The railway terminal has been destroyed, its windows smashed. One-half of the entrance door, still hanging by its hinges, bangs against the wall from time to time, sounding like gunshots. Hoping to find shelter from the piercing wind, we enter the terminal. It is drafty here, too, but in one corner, where there used to be a ticket window, it is not so bad. Here we sit down right on the floor to wait for dawn. Mother places a blanket on the floor, covers me up, and I sink into sleep right away.

"Get up," I hear Mother calling me through my sleep. "Daddy's found a coachman. We have to move on."

The small, snow-covered square near the terminal is deserted. All the passengers have dispersed. Father is standing next to a sleigh drawn by a skinny little horse. The coachman is also here, wearing a torn, dirty sheepskin. The basket and the bundles have already been loaded. I am squeezed between them. My parents settle down on each side and we set off. The Dnieper is just a few miles away, but the horse is barely moving. For the first time I become aware of this strange feeling: the moment I close my eyes, it feels as if we were moving backward. And maybe we are? Isn't this why we can't make it to the other bank? I am fighting drowsiness and trying to keep my eyes open so we will be moving only forward. The well-beaten road runs through a forest. The road is bumpy, and the sleigh jumps up every now and again and skids sideways. I find this so much fun that it even takes my breath away.

At last we reach the Dnieper. Close to the bank the river has frozen solid and a dark path runs across the ice. But halfway across the river is a narrow strip of water. Here, lying between the stone piers, we can see the bridge girder that fell when the bridge was blown up. Beyond that point more snow-covered ice, all the way to the steep bank on top of which we can see the domes of the Kiev-Pecherskaya monastery.

"How shall we get to the other bank?" There is despair in Mother's voice.

"Don't worry, ma'am, you'll get there," the coachman says calmly, helping Father unload our things in the snow. "Everybody gets there. First you follow the path, then go over the girder. But be careful, go slowly so you don't fall off into the water."

Some people come up to us; they have crossed from the other side. They confirm that the girder is safe. The coachman turns his sleigh around, picks up the new passengers, and leaves us standing alone on the bank.

Dragging our things over the ice, we finally reach the girder, which is made of steel beams held together by rivets. Somebody has strung a thick cable over them, which serves as a handrail. First Father helps Mother get to the other side. Then he travels there and back twice to carry our belongings. Then my turn comes. Holding me firmly by the hand, he leads me along the beam, which is lying somewhat askew. The beam is slippery, and I am trying to walk sideways, holding on to the cable with my free hand.

Gusts of icy wind push me toward the water. It feels as if we will never make it to the other side where, standing on the ice, Mother is waiting for us impatiently.

Another blank in my memory, and the next thing I see is a room in Podol, the section of downtown Kiev that is populated primarily by Jews. The family we are staying with is getting ready to leave for America, and then we will have the entire apartment to ourselves, consisting of two rooms, a kitchen, and a bathroom. After our long ordeal, this is a wonderful prospect. Father is hoping to find a job here, and then we will have to wander no more. Despite his expectations, however, food in Kiev is also in short supply. Our staple diet consists of slimy, watery oatmeal, bread that is three-quarters dried beet tops, and, rarely, a stale herring. Father manages to get hired as a guard at a warehouse. Early each morning, mother leaves for some offices where she cleans for a bag of oatmeal. I stay home alone, not knowing what to do to amuse myself. I already know by heart the pictures in the *Golden Childhood* and have learned to read their captions. I have no toys. I am not allowed to go out in the street because there are bandits out there. Rumor has it that they snatch children and turn them into soap. My favorite game is "driving the train," sitting on top of our metal bed. I use the metal bars of the headboard and footboard as the locomotive's controls. The space between them is also a window for the engineer to look out of. It seems to me there's a man straight ahead on the tracks. I squeeze my head through the bars. But there is no one there. It was just my imagination. But now I can't pull my head back in. I somehow forced it through, but now my ears get in the way. No matter how hard I try to push the bars apart, I can't do it, and finally I fall asleep. This is how my parents find me in the evening, with my head dangling between the bars and my ears red from rubbing. Of course, it is no problem for Father to pull the bars apart, but I have to kneel in the corner for two hours as punishment.

Kiev, under constant siege, passes from hand to hand: the Germans with hetman Skoropadsky, Petlyura, the Whites, the Reds, the Poles, the Reds again. Everything has been plundered, pillaged, and burned. Even oats are hard to find. A horse collapsed on the Vladimir hill. It was carved up on the spot. We also got a piece of the horse meat. What will happen next?

"We can't stay here any longer," Father says. "We'll have to get to Lyuba in the country. We'll manage there somehow until the Civil War is over."

Father did not know, of course, that War Communism would follow and totally devastate the village.

We are in a large cabin in the hull of a ship. Long benches are placed all along the walls, and passengers are sitting on them. We are sitting in a corner. A round porthole is above my head. I stick my head out and see the spray from the ship's paddle wheels form a shimmering rainbow in the rays of the sun. Waves are running back along the ship's sides, with many whirlpools and white froth. I spend hours watching this mesmerizing sight. We are sailing north toward Lyubich, one of the ancient centers of Kievan Rus. En route there is Stanetskoye, a small village on the river. The ship does not usually stop there. But Father got the captain to agree to drop us off there. Kiev is not too far away—a little over a hundred miles as the crow flies. But the river winds and turns, and sometimes after making a sharp U-turn, we are sailing south again, meandering on and on. On top of that, the ship is going slowly and we are sailing upstream. So the trip will be at least twenty-four hours.

I spend most of my time on deck. It is packed with passengers who have not been assigned a place in the cabins. They are crowding around the funnel that is spitting out black smoke. Here it is warm and not so windy. As for me, I like staying on the open deck swept by the winds from all sides. Walking around the deck, I see two machine guns in the stern and a small gun in the bow. The gun is covered with a canvas, its barrel sticking out. Father explains that this is in case we are attacked by bandits. And of course, I want us to be attacked.

In the morning, I am back on deck. The sun is high above the fields and it's getting quite warm. The ship is sailing close to the steep bank, skirting a shoal. Most of the deck passengers are still asleep on the benches. Others have placed their food on pieces of cloth and are having breakfast. Suddenly, a shot rings out from the bank, followed by another. A number of people riding horseback emerge from behind the bushes. They are waving sawed-off shotguns and shouting. The passengers crawl under the benches, and those who are closest to the ladder go down inside the hull. I am hiding behind the funnel. The captain on the deck shouts out an order: "Full speed ahead!"

Our machine guns begin spitting out fire, and then the ship's gun booms. Mother peeps out through the opening of the ladder and beckons to me. The captain notices her:

"Let the boy stay where he is, madam. He is safe behind that funnel. But you, please go below."

I am happy I can watch the battle. Quite suddenly, the ship is speeding ahead. But the men on horseback are keeping up. They are riding parallel to our ship and continuing to fire at random. Bullets ricochet off the funnel. Our machine guns mow down one of the attackers. The horse under another stumbles and throws him off. Farther upstream, around the bend, I can see a thick oak grove. This is our way to safety. The horses will have to slow down there. The bandits fall behind and don't appear again.

Cat-and-Mouse Game

BERLIN WAS NOT WRONG in its assumption that Moscow would view its readiness to address the Soviet-Polish problem as a sign of serious intentions on the part of the German government. In the evening of August 3, 1939, Molotov received Count Werner von Schulenburg. The ambassador reiterated Ribbentrop's statement that there were no insoluble problems in the area between the Baltic and Black seas and went on to say that Germany wanted "to reach an understanding regarding spheres of interest." Molotov, however, questioned the sincerity of the German initiative and cited a number of unfriendly actions by Germany: the anti-Comintern pact, support for Japan's actions directed against the Soviet Union, exclusion of the Soviet Union from the Munich agreement. I would note in passing that, under the terms of an existing treaty, the Soviet Union and France were to assist Czechoslovakia jointly in case of an act of aggression against her. When in the fall of 1938 the threat became real, Moscow was ready to fulfill its commitment.

Mobilization orders were issued in the western part of the Soviet Union. France, on the other hand, did not live up to its part of the agreement and struck a deal in Munich without even consulting

Moscow. The Munich agreement itself was clearly anti-Soviet. How can all this be reconciled with Germany's announced readiness to normalize relations with the Soviet Union, Molotov asked Schulenburg, adding that, for the time being, he saw no evidence of a shift in the German position. After the meeting, Schulenburg stated: "At present the Soviet government has decided to conclude an agreement with Britain and France."

He recommended that Berlin make new efforts to interest the Kremlin. In the meantime, Stalin was leaning more and more toward an agreement with Hitler.

Berlin acted on Schulenburg's suggestion, and thanks to the efforts of both sides, things began happening fast. On August 12, Astakhov visited Envoy Julius Schnurre and informed him that Molotov was prepared to meet the Germans in Moscow to discuss the questions that had been raised, including the Polish problem. During the conversation, Schnurre mentioned, among other things, the possibility of a nonaggression treaty. Astakhov said that the Soviet side would rather engage in phased negotiations, without undue haste. But Hitler, who had already set the invasion of Poland for September 1, was not thrilled with the idea of a "phased" discussion. On August 14, Schulenburg was instructed to inform Molotov that, in Berlin's view, "German-Russian relations have reached a turning point," that "there is no real conflict of interest between Germany and Russia," and that "in the past, both sides have profited from friendship and suffered from enmity." The ambassador was further instructed to declare that "Britain's policy of incitement created a situation which made it imperative to bring clarity into German-Russian relations." Without that, it was emphasized, both governments "could find it impossible to reestablish German-Russian friendship nor could they jointly clarify the territorial issues of Eastern Europe."

Hitler, of course, was holding out both the stick and the carrot: promising Stalin friendship and new territories while threatening him with an irreparable rift. But the Great Leader stayed with his game plan: at that stage Moscow's reaction to the German proposals was cool. Molotov stated to Schulenburg that although the Soviet government welcomed Germany's intention to improve relations with the Soviet Union, it didn't want to rush. The people's commissar explained that Ribbentrop's visit to Moscow "would require appropriate preparations to ensure a fruitful exchange of views." At the same time, during that meeting, Molotov manifested an interest in a nonaggression pact between Germany and the Soviet Union. Other issues were also addressed. In particular, the people's commissar asked whether Berlin was ready to use its influence with Japan to get it to improve its relations with the USSR and whether it was prepared to discuss the issue of guarantees to the Baltic states. This last issue was probably raised because during the recent negotiations with Britain and France, it became clear that London and Paris had no intention of providing guarantees to the Baltics like those they had provided to Poland. Moscow viewed this position as a sort of a hint to Hitler as to which route he could take to attack the Soviet Union without provoking any hostile response from Britain and France. Now Stalin wanted to get Hitler himself to confirm the impossibility of going through the Baltic states.

As it proceeded with its plans for the attack on Poland, the German government had a stake in eliminating any threat from the Soviet Union. For its part, Moscow probably believed that a nonaggression pact would protect the Soviet Union, at least temporarily, from the threat of a Nazi invasion. On August 16, Hitler's reply came: Germany was prepared to conclude a nonaggression treaty with the Soviet Union, as well as to exercise its influence with Japan to get it to improve Russian-Japanese relations. The Baltic states were not mentioned specifically, but Schulenburg was instructed to inform Molotov that, in the Führer's opinion, "given the present situation and the possibility of its becoming more complicated, since Germany did not intend to put up forever with the Polish provocations, it was desirable to clarify thoroughly and without delay Soviet-German relations in the context of the current issues." It was also stated that, starting on August 18, Ribbentrop would stand by to fly to Moscow at any time, authorized by the Führer to discuss the entire range of issues and to sign appropriate documents, if need be. Stalin, of course, was impressed by this eagerness. He didn't forget that the British and French missions had arrived in the Soviet Union on a passenger-cargo ship and without authorization from their governments to sign any documents.

At the same time, perceiving Hitler's haste, the Great Leader decided to haggle a little longer. Acting on his instructions, Molotov informed the German ambassador that prior to the Reich minister's arrival in Moscow it would be necessary to undertake "a number of important practical steps": sign a treaty on commerce and credits and prepare a draft nonaggression pact, including a protocol spelling out, inter alia, the substance of Germany's earlier proposals. Here, for the first time, a document was mentioned that was subsequently referred to as the "additional secret protocol" and that to this date has been the subject of fierce debate.

At this stage of the negotiations, Astakhov disappeared from the diplomatic stage, his mission accomplished. But, as Stalin liked to say, "he knew too much," and that decided his fate. Later it became known that Astakhov had been shot. The truth of the medieval maxim that Stalin liked so much was borne out again: "A dead man cannot bite."

Moscow keeps putting off the start of the negotiations. Molotov informs the German ambassador that Ribbentrop's visit requires "thorough preparation," and that, in general, it should not be publicized. Schulenburg's report with this information reaches Ribbentrop in Berchtesgaden, the Führer's Alpine retreat. The Reich minister, who always tries to please his boss, is aware that this time he has to carry out an unpleasant mission. And sure enough, Hitler reacts vehemently to Schulenburg's report. He thought he would persuade Stalin without much difficulty, but now that procrastinator was upsetting all his plans. Ribbentrop's trip to Moscow cannot be delayed any longer. Hitler wants an agreement with Stalin before the Polish campaign. Putting off the date of the invasion, when his war machine was fully charged up and especially when bad fall weather was about to set in, means jeopardizing the entire plan. And Hitler makes another move. On August 19, Schulenburg gets new instructions: arrange a meeting with Molotov immediately and inform him that, although Germany would also prefer to conduct the negotiations "under normal circumstances" and through regular diplomatic channels, the unusual situation of the moment makes that impossible. The ambassador was further instructed to say that German-Polish relations were deteriorating rapidly, and that a confrontation could develop any day that would lead to an open conflict. In the Führer's opinion, this conflict should not be allowed to create problems for clarifying Soviet-German relations, particularly since "the Russian interests should be taken into account" in that conflict. The ambassador's instructions placed special emphasis on this last point.

After receiving these instructions, Schulenburg immediately set off for the Kremlin. Molotov, however, received the information rather coolly. He repeated again that signing and announcing a commercial treaty remained top priority. Only after that could work begin on the nonaggression treaty.

But suddenly events took an unexpected turn. The ambassador had barely made it back to his residence when he was called again to the Kremlin. Molotov had reported to Stalin on his meeting with Schulenburg, and Stalin has sensed that Hitler's message contained the tantalizing possibility of concluding an advantageous deal with the Führer. He gave orders to summon the German ambassador immediately. Totally unperturbed by the fact that only some half an hour before he was saying something completely different, the people's commissar graciously explained to Schulenburg that, after reporting to the Soviet government, he was now in a position to make the following statement: "If the signing of the commercial treaty takes place on August twentieth, the Reich minister may arrive in Moscow on August twenty-sixth or twenty-seventh."

To add more emphasis to the new Soviet position, Molotov handed Schulenburg a draft nonaggression treaty.

Berlin interpreted these developments as Stalin's readiness to meet German requests. Concluding that an understanding was emerging between Stalin and himself, Hitler decided to make the best of a favorable situation. The German delegation at the economic negotiations was instructed to show flexibility, and on August 20 a Soviet-German trade agreement was signed. But the Führer cannot accept that Ribbentrop's visit to Moscow be delayed until August 26–27: these dates are too close to the day of the projected invasion of Poland. In a dramatic move, he dictates his first personal letter to Stalin, the hated leader of the hated "world Bolshevism":

August 21, 1939
Moscow

His Excellency Mr. Joseph Stalin:

1. I sincerely welcome the conclusion of the German-Soviet trade agreement, which represents the first step on the road to transforming German-Soviet relations.
2. For me, the conclusion of a nonaggression pact signifies codification of German policy for a long-term period. Germany thereby reverts to the political course that over centuries bene-

fited both states. That is why the German government is determined to draw all the conclusions from such a radical change.

3. I accept the draft nonaggression treaty proposed by the chairman of the Soviet of People's Commissars and the USSR people's commissar Mr. Molotov; however, I deem it necessary to clarify the issues related to it at the earliest possible date.

4. I am convinced that we can very quickly clarify the substance of the additional protocol, as requested by the USSR government, if a ranking German official is allowed to discuss these matters personally in Moscow. Without that, the German government cannot imagine how that additional protocol can be clarified and drafted within a short period of time.

5. The tension between Germany and Poland has become intolerable. Poland's conduct toward a great power is such that a crisis can develop any day. In any event, from now on Germany is determined to use all and every means to protect its interests from such encroachments.

6. I believe that if both states intend to establish new relations with each other, it is not advisable to lose time. That is why I am proposing for a second time that you receive my minister of foreign affairs on Tuesday, August 22, but not later than Wednesday, August 23. The minister of foreign affairs has full and unlimited authority to draft and sign both a nonaggression treaty and a protocol. In view of the international situation, the minister of foreign affairs cannot stay in Moscow longer than one or two days at most. I would be pleased to receive your early reply.

Adolf Hitler

Origins of the Pact

WHAT WERE THE OPTIONS of the Soviet leadership in that situation? Some scholars now believe the USSR should not have signed the nonaggression pact, and if it had to sign, it should at least have rejected the additional protocol, which has been qualified as intrinsically "immoral" and "illegal." Even though this became the official

Soviet position, I believe that today's standards have been applied in evaluating what happened then. Let us not forget that much of what progressive people throughout the world today qualify as immoral was considered normal in international relations half a century ago. Today, for instance, the U.S. military invasion of a sovereign country, Panama, just because Washington did not like its president, appears to be fully justified for many Western moralists. By today's standards, the policy of noninterference in Spain, where, with the help of Hitler and Mussolini, the legitimate government was overthrown, as well as the Munich deal with Hitler, which gave him Czechoslovakia, are unquestionably qualified as immoral. But the present British and French leaders are in no hurry to condemn the policies of their predecessors of the 1930s. And this is not the whole point. It is also necessary to consider the situation in Europe by the fall of 1939.

What happened at the time was, of course, a deal struck between two dictators who did not trust each other all that much. Each of them was guided by his own considerations, which happened to converge at that particular moment. In his cable to Stalin, Hitler implied that he was prepared to accept far-reaching Soviet demands. At that stage, concessions to Moscow did not have major significance for him. He was not giving up his ultimate objective—the elimination of Bolshevism—and thought that in the years to come he would be able to make up for any losses incurred at this moment and end up with much, much more. His current top priority was meeting the deadline for the attack on Poland. And he was clearly giving Stalin a hint about the date when he mentioned the two days beyond which Ribbentrop could not stay in Moscow.

From his perspective, Stalin interpreted Hitler's message as a statement of his intention to cooperate with Moscow over a long period of time. He liked the vigorous, businesslike style of the letter, the concrete and specific proposals of its author. A politician he could do business with! And his cable was so different from the dull, amorphous, and vague messages he had been getting from London and Paris. The Nazi leader had always appealed to him. Even before Hitler came to power, Stalin believed that the main threat emanated not from the National Socialists, but from the Social Democrats, whom he contemptuously called "social traitors." His attitude is easy to understand: the ideas of social democracy could undermine the command system he had installed in the USSR and could lead to questioning of the legitimacy of his unlimited personal power. The

Nazi approach, on the other hand, was something he could identify with. That is why he thought it was desirable to improve cooperation with Hitler's Germany. In Germany, the word of the Führer was law. In the Soviet Union, the word of the Great Leader was just as sacrosanct. Neither country had any problems with public opinion, "that product of rotten bourgeois liberalism."

After sending his dispatch to Moscow, Hitler was depressed. Impatiently waiting for an answer, he counted the minutes, unable to stay in one place. He still believed, however, that he had chosen the right approach with Stalin and that he would get the answer he wanted.

At that fateful hour, the ruler in the Kremlin was making the final assessment of the options before him. If he rejected the agreement, who could guarantee that the Soviet Union would not be the next target of Nazi aggression? France and, prior to her, Poland had signed nonaggression pacts with Germany. Chamberlain, after his return from Munich, had declared that "peace in our time" had been achieved and had stated that one could do business with Hitler. Now Berlin was proposing a nonaggression pact to Moscow. A rejection would give Hitler an opportunity to announce to the whole world that the Bolsheviks were the ones who had rudely spurned his olive branch. He would allege that by repudiating the idea of nonaggression, the Communists showed that they themselves were preparing an act of aggression. European civilization was in grave danger, he could say. All the nations of Europe had to unite to repel this danger, and Germany was prepared to accept the difficult mission of eradicating "the plague of Bolshevism." And while "the Munich dealers" were still in positions of power in Britain and France, such calls would indeed be heeded. The Soviet Union could not count on their support since their minds were set on bringing about a confrontation between Germany and the Soviet Union.

On the other hand, the signing of a nonaggression pact could avert war between Germany and the Soviet Union, at least for some time. Stalin did not rule out the idea that eventually he would have to confront Hitler. However, he wanted to put off the conflict for as long as he could. A pact appeared to offer a prospect of that. Furthermore, it could lead to a long period of Soviet German cooperation. Perhaps this was also what Hitler was thinking when he wrote in his letter that from now on Germany "reverts to the political course that over centuries benefited both states." In any event, Stalin was reasoning, Germany's readiness to sign the pact clearly showed that its government had decided to attack not the East, but the West. This conflict could turn out to be quite protracted, which would enable the Soviet Union to stay out of it until Stalin concluded it was time to get involved. In terms of that time and place, this was all a logical way of thinking. Every country that was potentially a target for Nazi aggression was reasoning roughly along the same lines.

Against this background, the secret additional protocol does not look to be the fiendish scheme it appears to us today. It clearly followed from Hitler's letter that an attack on Poland was a foregone decision. There was no doubt that the Polish army would not survive an assault by the Wehrmacht tank army. After that, the German troops would gain access to our border, running very close to Minsk and Kiev, and the people of western Byelorussia and western Ukraine would find themselves living under German rule. Along with many others in the Soviet Union at the time, Stalin believed that the Soviet border with Poland was not "just" and had been imposed upon the country when it was going through a difficult time. However, he himself was largely responsible for that "unjust" border. When, after the October Revolution, an independent Polish state emerged, its border with Soviet Russia was defined by a decision of the Supreme Allied Council of the Entente and became known in history as the Curzon Line (named after the then British foreign minister, Lord Curzon). This line was established on the basis of an ethnic principle: the areas populated primarily by Ukrainians and Byelorussians were given to the Soviet Union. In the hostilities that soon broke out between Soviet Russia and Poland, the Red Army was at first successful. Its units under the command of Tukhachevsky laid siege to Warsaw. Lenin attached great importance to this campaign, believing that the defeat of Poland would demolish the entire Versailles system. That is why he ordered the Red Army divisions, advancing on Lvov under Yegorov's and Stalin's command, to march on the Polish capital to join Tukhachevsky's army. That operation would have ensured Warsaw's fall. But Stalin, dreaming of laurels for his military exploits, decided to take Lvov first. He disobeyed Lenin and did not carry out his orders. As a result, the Polish troops, reinforced by French units and equipped by the Entente with modern weapons, dealt a devastating blow to Tukhachevsky's army, rolling it far back to the east. At that same time, the units conducting operations in the Lvov area also had to retreat. The Polish forces occupied vast areas of Byelorussia and the Ukraine, took Kiev and other major cities, and, in 1921, compelled the Soviet government to sign the Treaty of Riga, forcing upon Soviet Russia a new border which was far to the east of the Curzon Line. That episode gave Stalin another reason for being pleased with this agreement with Hitler. He would be able to rehabilitate himself in his own eyes, as it were, and reestablish the country's western border roughly along the Curzon line.

And the agreement with Hitler opened up other prospects as well. If the 1991 publication *One Hundred and Forty Conversations with Molotov* accurately reproduces the words of Stalin's comrade-in-arms, then many events of 1939–45 present themselves in a new light. Speaking to his interviewer Feliks Chuyev on November 29, 1974, Molotov, already many years in retirement, made the following confession:

"As minister of foreign affairs, I saw it to be my duty to expand the borders of our country as far as possible. I believe Stalin and I did a pretty good job."

Stalin had reason to be pleased with what he acquired after the war. One day, a newly printed school map of the USSR, showing the new borders, was brought to his dacha. As was his wont, the leader of all times and peoples pinned it to the walnut paneling in his living room and said smugly:

"Well, let's see what we've got here now. . . . Everything looks all right in the north, fine. Finland has been very naughty to us, so we moved our border away from Leningrad. The Baltics—these traditional Russian lands—belong to us again. The Byelorussians are all living together now, the Ukrainians, together, and the Moldovans, together. Looks all right in the west."

Tracing the eastern borders of his empire with his pipe, he went on to say:

"Now, what do we have here? The Kurils now belong to us. All of Sakhalin belongs to us—look, that's good! And Port Arthur, and Dalny and the Chinese Eastern Railroad—all belong to us. China, Mongolia—everything seems in order."

And then, moving his pipe south of the Caucasus, he added:

"Don't like our border here."

Stalin failed to recapture Kars, which Lenin had given to Turkey in 1921.

Stalin acquired the territories he mentioned partly through his deal with Hitler and partly as a result of the victorious, if bloody, war, which won him the consent he needed from his allies in the anti-Hitler coalition.

Stalin was obsessed by his imperial ambitions. He wanted to re-possess all the territories that had ever been part of czarist Russia. He made public statements about this. After the victory over Japan, he declared that the people of his generation had waited forty years to see Port Arthur, Dalny, and southern Sakhalin become part of the country again. Our prewar maps had designated Bessarabia a disputed territory. He also dreamed of annexing the Baltics to the Soviet Union. The secret protocol made implementation of those designs feasible. His plans were probably in line with the mentality of the period between the two wars. But even if they are judged by today's standards as immoral and expansionist, it should at least be admitted that the secret protocol of August 23—and the protocol of September 28, 1939—can be viewed as documents that helped establish the frontline area where the German-Soviet armed conflict began. A buffer zone was created that moved the border away from Leningrad, Minsk, Kiev and Odessa by about 150–200 miles. It is not difficult to guess what Leningrad's fate would have been had the invasion begun not outside Vyborg, but almost at the city limits.

Maybe today, this Venice of the North would be no more, with nothing but waves dashing on the rocks where Hitler planned "to drown this cradle of the October Revolution." A more balanced view of historical realities is called for, since in the period between the two World Wars, using force to solve international disputes was still considered to be a "legal" political recourse. Few people questioned von Clausewitz's definition of war as a continuation of diplomacy, a carrying out of the same by other means.

In the evening of August 21, Schulenburg was handed Stalin's reply to Hitler:

August 21, 1939
Reich Chancellor of Germany

Mr. Adolf Hitler:

Thank you for your letter.
I am hopeful that the German-Soviet nonaggression agreement will mark a shift toward a major improvement in the political relations between our two countries.
The peoples of our two countries want peaceful relations between them. The agreement of the German government to con-

clude a nonaggression pact forms a basis for the elimination of political tension and helps promote peace and cooperation between our two countries.

The Soviet government has instructed me to inform you that it agrees to Mr. Ribbentrop's arrival in Moscow on August 23.

                                                               J. Stalin

That same night, soon after eleven P.M. Central European time, the German radio interrupted its regular broadcasts and an announcer solemnly read out the following statement:

"The Imperial government and the Soviet government have agreed to conclude a nonaggression pact. The Reich minister of foreign affairs shall arrive in Moscow on August twenty-third to finalize the negotiations."

Hitler was in a hurry to tell the world about the agreement reached with Stalin. He wanted to make going back on it impossible.

Svarichyovka

THE CLOCK ON THE SPASSKAYA TOWER is striking again, reminding me of the relentless passage of time. I have to finish up this memorandum of conversation. But my mind wanders back to the distant past where the road starts that has eventually led me to this little room in the Kremlin.

We prepared well in advance for our landing at Stanetskoye. We have brought our belongings to the lower deck and are waiting for the ship's bow to ram into the sandy bank. Because this is an unscheduled stop, we have to hurry. But since no one except us gets off here, the whole thing doesn't take more than five minutes. Aunt Lyuba is waiting for us at the ladder. Despite the muddle in the country, Father had somehow managed to notify her that we were coming. She looks so unlike Father to me that it is hard to believe they are

near kin. Dark-skinned, lean, with a nervous, long face, she is taciturn and, it seems to me, not very happy to see us descend upon her
like this. But my first impression proved to be misleading. She was
like a mother to us, to these refugees from Petrograd, and made
every effort to make our new life in Svarichyovka easier. As I see it
now, she appeared austere because she was grieving for her husband,
who had left her, and because it was really hard for her at that difficult time, left alone with a child to raise. But above all, jealousy was
gnawing at her heart: her former husband had married a much
younger woman, "a treacherous and dishonest seductress," my aunt
would remind us at every opportunity. Father had known Aunt
Lyuba's former husband since before the Revolution. He lived in
Chernigov and came to see us a few times in Svarichyovka with his
new wife, a beautiful blonde. When that happened, Aunt Lyuba
would lock herself up in her room, showing her contempt for her
rival from behind the blind.

My ten-year-old cousin, Sergei, sat in the two-horse carriage holding the reins. I had, of course, heard about him, but now saw him for
the first time. He looked mischievous with his shock of unruly red
hair and freckled face. I knew right away that we would be friends.
My parents and Aunt Lyuba kissed. She gave me a pat on the head.
After we loaded our belongings on the carriage, we made ourselves
comfortable for the ride.

The road went through a thick pine forest, then came out onto
potato fields. From there we could see a long row of Lombardy
poplars.

"That's Svarichyovka," Aunt Lyuba said. "We used to have poplars
like that all around the place. But we had to cut down some of them
to heat hospital wards and our houses."

After crossing a bridge over a small river, we found ourselves in
front of an open gate leading into an inner yard overgrown with
thick grass. Two red-brick, three-story buildings were on the right.
Aunt Lyuba explained that one was the outpatient clinic and the
other an inpatient section that could accommodate forty people.
The Svarichyovka country hospital was built at the end of the last century by an enlightened local landowner who gave it its name. Designed to provide medical care to the people of the five neighboring
villages, it was setting standards when it opened. The Civil War and
the German and Polish occupation had not touched it directly, and
it was still almost in its original condition. Most of the hospital staff

also stayed: the head doctor, Konstantin Konstantinovich Vasilyev, the obstetrician, Aunt Lyuba, and the doctor's assistant, Prokofiy Fyodorovich Ushach. Almost all service personnel also remained.

Behind the hospital buildings, along the yard, stood the stables and the coach house. In addition to the carriage we had arrived in, there was also a light carriage and a sleigh. The cowshed was now empty, but animals owned by the hospital and staff used to be kept there. They once supplied dairy products for both the staff and the patients at the hospital. A little farther away stood a shed with a hayloft and a pigsty. The living quarters were on the other side of the yard—the house of the head doctor and a wing for the obstetrician and the doctor's assistant. Behind the living quarters was a fruit garden, with a vegetable garden next to it. A swift river wound around the garden with ivy-covered trees growing along its banks. A place had been set up for swimming in a spot where the river ran deep. The garden must have been here long before the hospital. The branches of the Antonov apple trees hung over the roof of the wing, and we could pick apples from the very top of the trees by climbing up on the roof. And the pear trees were so large that they looked more like oaks.

We first moved in with Aunt Lyuba, only to find out quickly we were too big a crowd for her place. There was enough space for her and Sergei in her two-room flat, but our arrival made their lives more complicated. She was forced to sleep in the same room with her son. The three of us were also cramped in one tiny sleeping room. On top of that, Aunt Lyuba would have pregnant women stay with her if they developed complications. There would be a new patient almost every week. She would be lodged in the kitchen. At night, when she would start having contractions, groans and screams could be heard. My aunt would jump out of bed, run to the kitchen, and the house would be in turmoil. And we would be there, getting in the way. We had to look for another place to stay.

Father went from village to village but couldn't find anything suitable. Eventually, help came from the doctor's assistant, Prokofiy Fyodorovich. He had a three-room flat all to himself and invited us to stay with him. We moved into two joined rooms and for our meals gathered all together in a large kitchen with a Russian stove. The flat also had a storage room with a window, where Father later set up a shoe-repair shop. Prokofiy turned out to be a kind and considerate man. We soon became close and in fact lived as one family. Later, when we returned to Kiev, Uncle Prokofiy stayed with us for three years while he was finishing medical school.

Father began looking for a job, but nothing came up. At first, we lived off Mother's dresses, which she would give to country girls in exchange for any food. Before long, however, Father, ingenious as always, had set up a business to meet local needs. He began making soap by mixing fish fat, ash, and some other stuff. The product did not smell too good, but it served its purpose quite well. Then he visited his hometown, Chernigov, about a hundred kilometers from Svarichyovka, and brought back shoe-repair tools and, for me, fairy tales by the Brothers Grimm and a few books by Karl May in German and by Walter Scott in English with beautiful color illustrations. That was what first kindled my interest in foreign languages. Before long Father became a past master shoesmith. Leather was no problem, and he was swamped with orders for boots and even more elegant shoewear for the village belles. He made me a beautiful pair of red, soft-leather boots, which I liked so much I wouldn't take them off even to go to bed.

Our food situation naturally improved. Despite the fact that War Communism was sweeping the country clean of food, village people, especially in our area, were able to stash some food away. We began to get eggs, cereals, milk, country cheese, homemade Ukrainian sausage, and sometimes even meat. For Easter, father painted eggs with great mastery. They were also popular with our neighbors. At Eastertime, villagers would amuse themselves by playing this old game of crack-an-egg. One person would be clenching a hard-boiled painted Easter egg in his fist while another would knock his egg against it. If your egg cracked, you lost and had to give your egg to the winner. In order to get hens to lay strong eggs, all kinds of supplements were given to them. But success was far from guaranteed. Father came up with a better idea, one that admittedly stretched the rules. He would mix together country cheese, lime, and the white of an egg and place the mixture on the pointed end of an egg. He would then paint these reinforced eggs different colors, which completely concealed the extra layer. These eggs were fully crackproof, and Sergei and I, using them to play crack-an-egg, would bring home a lot of trophies for our festive board.

The people who lived near the hospital got along well. Similar groups of intelligentsia, both local and those fleeing from starvation, lived near the forest ranger's station, located in a large green forest a few kilometers from Svarichyovka, and by the church in Stanet-skoye, on the bank of the Dnieper River. The chief ranger, Uncle Yegor, together with some of his mounted guards and huntsmen, lived in a big house surrounded by century-old pine trees. Every one of them had a family with kids about Sergei's and my age. We loved the parties they held there to celebrate Easter, Holy Trinity, Christmas, and the New Year. Many people came, some quite talented. In the beginning there would be an amateur concert. Someone would play the piano, guitar, mandolin, or violin. Then dinner would be served, followed by dessert. Children would run away into the forest to play hide-and-seek and, in winter, to ride the sled. Grown-ups would dance to a gramophone. On such occasions, people temporarily forgot that just outside that oasis of joy, there was want, hatred, and bloody conflict, with brother killing brother.

We spent our free hot summer days on the Dnieper in the same noisy and cheerful company. Early in the morning, we would harness the horse, load up the carriage with all kinds of snacks, and set off for our meeting place on a country road leading to Kapachev. Before the Revolution, there was a large stud farm here that belonged to Count Miloradovich. Nothing remained now but abandoned stables with their roofs fallen in and the vast pastures stretching along the river. The Miloradoviches had fled, their horses requisitioned by the new rulers of the Ukraine, and the huge estate was left without a master. Scattered in the tall grass were bright red beads of poignantly fragrant wild strawberries. Their aroma, blended with the scent of blossoming grass, floated over the fields. Here the river made a sharp curve creating a shallow bank on its other side where the sand was so soft your feet would sink right into it. A small elevation overgrown with shrubs and sweetbrier divided the shallow area into two separate beaches, as it were. Women would swim on one side, men on the other. This made it possible for both to go skinny-dipping. After taking a swim, the grown-ups would return to the camp where they would make a fire and cook food, while the young people stayed on to sunbathe and splash around in the river. On our very first picnic Uncle Yegor's elder son, Vladimir, called Sergei and me over to him. Vlad was already seventeen. He was surrounded by his friends.

"Listen, guys," Vlad spoke to us, "run over to the women's side and take a look at the girls to see what they look like. You're just kids. They won't pay any attention to you. And then you'll tell us what you saw."

I tried to refuse, recalling a warning I had heard from adults: if you look at a naked woman, you'll go blind.

"Well, risk one eye," Vlad insisted. "You'll see it'll be fun for you, too."

Since I had never seen women except in long dresses, I had this idea that they had to have short legs, not much longer than what could be seen below the skirt. Then, I thought, a long body followed. Now I had a chance to find out whether this was the case. Finally, we decided to do it. I might add that Sergei, who was three years my senior, did not really object.

Scratched all over from getting through the sweetbrier, we got to the other side of the beach and walked up to the water. Peeping out of the corner of my eyes at the graceful naked bodies, I had to admit that I had a totally wrong idea about their shape. We wanted to get a better look, so we began pacing up and down by the edge of the water, looking askance at the girls. At first, they paid no attention to us, but seeing that we continued our saunter, one of them swung her body around to face us and called out scornfully:

"Hey, kids! Stop churning the water here! Come on, beat it!"

Flushed with shame, we ran back to the bigger boys, who were waiting for us behind the bushes and who asked very detailed questions.

Maybe it was that experience, at that early stage in life, that kindled a certain special interest in us. At one time Mother hired a seventeen-year-old girl, Paraska, from a neighboring village to help her about the house. In the fall, everyone in the house would help make preserves for winter—marinating tomatoes, pickles, mushrooms, and apples. That day Paraska was deftly chopping cabbage on a big oak board. Sergei and I were loitering behind her back.

"Let's pinch her little behind," Sergei whispered.

We tiptoed closer, and reaching out, I tried to pinch her. But her body was so firm and she wore so many skirts, as was customary among all country girls, that I couldn't get a grip. My fingers slipped while Paraska just wagged her behind, as a filly would when brushing off flies. We retreated, but soon crawled back again, and this time Sergei tried his luck. He didn't do any better, however. But this time Paraska got mad and decided to teach us a lesson in her own way. She turned around toward us, picked up her numerous skirts, and with a quick movement raised them over her head. From waist down she was completely naked. We froze in our tracks, staring at the black, curly triangle right before our eyes.

After this shock treatment we left Paraska alone.

A yard was set up at Stanetskoye to repair river ships. It was also used to convert ships for the Red Army Dnieper River Fleet. When father learned about this, he offered his services. He used his expertise to determine whether a deck was strong enough to support the artillery pieces to be mounted on it. For this work he got two bags of oats a month. At that time, that was a fortune, because country folk would give almost anything for oats.

In the village of Grekovka there lived an old man called Onyshchuk. It turned out he could make wonderful boats, like the dugouts the Dnieper Cossacks had sailed here since time out of mind. A little boat with a pointed bow and a blunt stern would be chiseled out of the thick trunk of a pussy-willow tree. Then a few thick layers of a special substance were applied both inside and outside the cream-colored wood, and this made the boat waterproof and durable. Such boats could last a hundred years, and quite a few of them were on the Dnieper in those days. The preparation of the waterproofing, which resembled today's plastic, was also a peculiar process. Birch bark would be distilled for tar. Then resin, fine sand, ash, and ground coal were added to it. All this was thoroughly mixed into a viscous paste. When this mixture dried, it turned into a rock-solid coating that never washed away. The boat would be outfitted with small seats. Such a boat was incredibly light, and steering it from the stern with one oar, one could easily sail fast while keeping it highly maneuverable. The Dnieper Cossacks, like a swarm of bumblebees, attacked big ships in these dugouts, and in case of danger, they could quickly retreat into small channels.

Father, being a shipbuilder, got interested in these small boats. Together with Uncle Onyshchuk, he made a small boat for me. I had so much fun with it! It was fast and mobile, and skimming in it over the surface of the river, I was able to get over any shallows. Perched on the stern with the bow high up in the air, I would sail our river to the world's end. Effortlessly working the oar, I would glide between white and yellow lilies and huge burdocks. I spent all my time on the river. I would dock in a quiet backwater at a rushy bank and would swim and bask in the sun in a green meadow. I still had no toys. I used twigs, weeds, shells, and pine bark to make entire armadas of sailboats, peopling them with pirates, abducted princesses, and knights out to rescue them or off on their next crusade. After I learned to read, a local priest gave me a little copy of the Old Testament, and this became my favorite reading. On my boat trips I would act out scenes from the Bible, undergoing a transformation from a pharaoh's son, who stumbles in the bulrushes upon a basket with Moses in it, to Noah sailing his ark in the flood.

Rumors about the New Economic Policy traveled around. Father went to Kiev and soon informed us that the situation was improving. He was promised a good job at one of the factories and wanted us to go to the city. Mother was happy, and we began getting ready to leave.

"Among Old Party Comrades"

RIBBENTROP ARRIVED IN MOSCOW AS PLANNED, on August 23, 1939, and immediately headed for the Kremlin. Armed with Hitler's instructions to wrap up quickly the nonaggression treaty and the additional secret protocol, the Reich minister did not bargain long. In fact, he accepted all the major Soviet demands, and that same night the documents were signed at a solemn ceremony in Stalin's presence. The cocktail party that followed went on until dawn. Only after that was Ribbentrop able to inform Hitler that his mission had been a total success. All this time, the Führer didn't have a wink of sleep. Like a caged animal, he paced up and down the balcony of his villa in Berchtesgaden, afraid to believe that everything would go according to his plan. Ribbentrop's silence was becoming intolerable. Hitler even declared to the people around him that if his minister failed to reach agreement with Stalin, he would immediately leave for Moscow himself.

Meanwhile in the Kremlin, Molotov and Ribbentrop are signing and sealing the agreements. Waiters bring in the champagne. Toasts are made, niceties are exchanged, glasses clink, smiles flash, and jokes crackle—all this warms up the atmosphere. Those present review an exhibition set up right there with drawings of new and ostentatious buildings planned for the capital of the Third Reich. They were created by Hitler's favorite architect, Albert Speer, an unsurpassed master of grandiose construction projects and lighting effects intended to impress the public imagination. An awed Ribbentrop explains that Hitler himself suggested the concepts for these structures, and his sketches are displayed on separate stands. Stalin likes the drawings. They are in line with his own ideas about the architecture of a time of great achievement. In Moscow after the war, on instructions from Stalin, high-rise buildings would go up designed similar to Speer's—the same towers and classical columns. But, ironically, the ground floors of these buildings would be faced with granite taken from the ruins of Hitler's Imperial Chancellery.

The reception in honor of Ribbentrop continues. A lively discussion brings the hosts and their guests closer together. Later, when briefing Hitler on the reception, the Reich minister, impressed by the hospitality of the Great Leader, will complacently add, "Stalin and Molotov are very nice. I felt as if I were among old party comrades" (wie unter alten Parteigenossen). The comrades came, of course, from different political parties, but how quickly our leaders established a common language! That night Stalin turned on all his charm. In that atmosphere of "camaraderie," Ribbentrop decided to brush aside—in passing, as it were—the anti-Comintern pact.* He remembered that Molotov had qualified that pact as incompatible with the new relations between Germany and the Soviet Union. Talking to Stalin, the Reich minister said half in jest that "the anti-Comintern pact was essentially directed not against the Soviet Union, but against the Western democracies." Although that was an absurd statement, Stalin played along and replied to Ribbentrop in the same vein:

"In reality, the anti-Comintern pact scared the City of London mostly—and the small shopkeepers in Britain."

Pleased with this unexpected meeting of minds, the Reich minister hastened to second his interlocutor's opinion:

"You, Mr. Stalin, were of course less scared by the anti-Comintern pact than was the City of London and the British shopkeepers."

That brief exchange proved to be a prelude of a sort to the subsequent negotiations on the accession of the Soviet Union to the tripartite treaty, signed soon thereafter by the participants in the anti-Comintern pact—Germany, Italy, and Japan.

---

*The anti-Comintern pact was signed in 1936 by Germany, Italy, and Japan. It was directed against Bolshevism, communism, and the Soviet Union. In 1940, Germany, Italy, and Japan renegotiated the pact and called it the "Tripartite Treaty," which was now proclaimed to be directed against "American warmongers." Moscow was invited to join that treaty.

The reception is still going on. Stalin raises his glass to toast Hitler. Molotov toasts the health of Ribbentrop and Schulenburg. All drink to a new era in German-Soviet relations. Saying goodbye, Stalin assures the Reich minister:

"The Soviet Union is very serious about the new pact. I give you my word of honor that the Soviet Union will not cheat on its partner."

Stalin expected that Hitler would reciprocate.

After the Polish campaign and the meeting between the Red Army and the Wehrmacht at a line agreed on in the secret protocol of August 23, 1939, it became necessary to formalize the new situation. Ribbentrop arrives in Moscow again. Under the circumstances, a border convention or a demarcation-line agreement would have sufficed. But Stalin, who wanted to continue developing the relationship with Germany, went much further. On September 28, 1939, Molotov and Ribbentrop signed the Treaty on Friendship and the Border, also accompanied by secret protocols. In the first protocol each party pledged not to allow "Polish propaganda." This commitment resulted in actual cooperation between the secret services of the Soviet Union and Hitler's Germany. They not only exchanged information about "Polish propaganda" but also turned over to each other people whom their respective countries wanted for various reasons. By the summer of 1941, the Soviet secret service had extradited to Germany some four thousand people, among them family members of German Communists who had been arrested and shot in the Soviet Union (during the Stalin years, 242 German Communists were eliminated in the Soviet Union, including a considerable number of members of the Central Committee of the German Communist Party), as well as German workers who had moved to the Soviet Union during the economic crisis in the West. Most of them were immediately sent to concentration camps by the Gestapo, where many were shot or died from starvation. On their side, the Nazis deported to the USSR people wanted by the NKVD, the security police.

The second secret additional protocol contained a provision to amend paragraph 1 of the secret protocol of August 23. In the earlier protocol, the Soviet sphere of influence embraced Finland, Estonia, and Latvia. Now Lithuania was also included in the sphere of Soviet interests. At the same time, the Lublin and Warsaw regions were transferred to the German sphere of interest, and the necessary adjustments were made to the demarcation line. It was also stipulated that the existing economic relations between Germany and Lithuania would not be affected by movements to be undertaken by the Soviet Union in that region.

Again champagne was served. Toasts were made. Stalin did not hide his satisfaction with the new agreements with Hitler. In one of his toasts he said:

"I know how the German people adore their Führer. That is why I would like to drink his health."

When a map was brought in with the newly agreed border between German possessions and the Soviet Union, Stalin spread it on the table, took one of his big blue pencils, and, giving free rein to his emotions, signed his name in large letters with a flourish that ran over into the newly acquired territories of western Byelorussia and western Ukraine. Ribbentrop also put his name down, using Stalin's red pencil.

In 1989, when there was a discussion in Moscow of the secret protocol of August 23, 1939, many of its participants, for some reason, overlooked the protocol of September 28 of the same year. This created a confusion that resulted in President Gorbachev's becoming misinformed. Probably acting on the advice of his experts, he questioned the authenticity of the August 23 protocol, pointing out that in that protocol Lithuania was included in Germany's sphere of interest, and that the border did not correspond to the actual line of demarcation. Had the experts taken a look at the protocol of September 28, that embarrassing situation would not have occurred.

The praise Stalin sang to Hitler at the Kremlin banquets did not go unnoticed. In the second half of December, the Führer sent a message to the Great Leader congratulating him on his sixtieth birthday. The telegram expressed "best wishes of well-being and prosperity to the friendly Soviet Union." Stalin immediately replied: "The friendship between the peoples of Germany and the Soviet Union, cc mented by blood, has every chance of lasting longer and getting stronger."

The mention of "friendship . . . cemented by blood" sounds somewhat strange. Was he making a reference to the recent events in Poland or to the manifestation of "camaraderie" at military parades conducted jointly with the Germans in Brest and other cities after the Wehrmacht and the Red Army met at a previously agreed line?

Or was he hinting at the heavy losses suffered by the Soviet troops in the snow-covered expanses of Finland? Or maybe he was already thinking about future actions to be launched together with Hitler to divide up spheres of influence in the world.

It may well be that the Great Leader entertained such ambitions. After Britain and France declared war on Germany, Stalin breathed with relief. Now Hitler was bogged down in a protracted conflict in the West. It could last years. And even if, ultimately, Germany won, it would emerge weakened, and great opportunities would present themselves to Moscow. The stage could be set for "a world proletarian revolution." At the present juncture, however, it was important to preserve the relations with Hitler that had so recently taken shape.

The blitz campaign of the Nazi hordes in Western Europe, the unexpectedly quick fall of France, the inability of the British forces to stop the Wehrmacht's advance to the Channel and their panicked retreat from Dunkirk—all of this puzzled and frightened Stalin. He began to fear his own confrontation with Germany and was ready to make concessions to please Hitler. In which direction would the German war machine move now? Molotov's trip to Berlin in November 1940 offered a chance to feel out the intentions of the Nazi leadership. Hitler also knew he was getting Stalin worried. In an effort to allay Stalin's fears, he launched an all-out misinformation campaign to convince Moscow that he was engaged in major preparations for an invasion of the British Isles. Hitler was pursuing this objective when during his talks with the Soviet people's commissar he suggested that the Soviet Union participate in the division of "no one's British property," that is to say, in divvying up Britain's colonial possessions among Germany, Italy, Japan, and Russia, assuring Molotov that soon Britain would be occupied by German forces and would cease to exist as a great power. Hitler also proposed that the USSR join the tripartite pact, which had been signed by Germany, Italy, and Japan on September 27, 1940, in other words, a month and half before Molotov arrived in Berlin. The people's commissar was cautious and did not get involved in discussing Hitler's proposals. He emphasized, however, that the German troops that had been massing along the Soviet border over the last few months had to be moved back.

Pact of Three or Four?

ON THE EVENING OF NOVEMBER 13, the eve of the return of the Soviet delegation to Moscow, Ribbentrop, acting on instructions from the Führer, was to wrap up the Soviet-German negotiations. Just as at the meetings with Hitler, I attended these talks as an interpreter.

A luxurious study, perhaps somewhat smaller than Hitler's own. Antique gilded furniture. Tapestry covers the walls from floor to ceiling, pictures hanging in heavy frames, porcelain and bronze statuettes on high stands placed in the corners. The first few minutes are taken up by a photo opportunity for reporters. Ribbentrop is smiling pleasantly, holding his head high. He is shaking the hand of the Soviet guest. He looks haughty and dignified.

As I am writing this, I recall the same study but a different Ribbentrop on the night of June 22, 1941, when he declared war on the Soviet Union, delivering his message to the Soviet ambassador to Germany, Dekanozov, whom I was accompanying. Before making that statement, so fateful to the Third Reich, he had a drink to muster up his courage. But then again, Ribbentrop had just arrived from Hitler's headquarters, where they were celebrating the launch of a new blitzkrieg. His face was flushed and his hands were trembling. He stated that two hours earlier German forces had crossed the Soviet border. The Soviet ambassador jumped to his feet. He said that Germany's leaders were committing a criminal act of aggression for which they would be severely punished. Turning his back on Ribbentrop and without another word, Dekanozov headed out. I followed. At that point, something quite unexpected happened: Ribbentrop hurried after us and began whispering his assurances that he personally had been against the Führer's decision to declare war on Russia. He had even tried to talk Hitler out of that madness. But Hitler would not listen.

"Please inform Moscow that I was against the attack," were the last words from Ribbentrop I heard when, having crossed the outside hallway, I was already hurrying down the stairs in pursuit of the ambassador.

What could have been the meaning of such a strange statement from the minister of foreign affairs of a country that had just declared war on another country? Perhaps Ribbentrop had premonitions of a disgraceful end on the gallows. At the Nuremberg trial, he tried to make the judges more sympathetic to his case by reminding them of his opposition to Hitler's decision to attack the Soviet Union. But that did not help him.

At the earlier meeting, the reporters and photographers at last withdraw. The two ministers begin their conversation, seated at a round table that has as its centerpiece a lamp with a thin leather lampshade decorated with colored prints. The tapestries and the old masters in the Reich minister's study must be recent trophies from France. But that lampshade? Now I wonder—was it not one of those infamous gifts from Himmler? The skin was too thin, as if it were human.

"In accordance with the Führer's wishes," Ribbentrop begins the conversation, "we should take stock of the negotiations and reach an agreement on principle."

The Reich minister takes a piece of paper out of his pocket and continues, "Here is an outline of some of the proposals of the German government."

He begins expounding the same idea, previously formulated by Hitler, about the division of "no one's property" after the end of Britain and its spheres of influence in the world, but is unable to finish his sentence. An air alert sounds. Bombs can be heard exploding nearby, and the glass jingles in the high windows of the minister's study.

Aware of Molotov's presence in Berlin, the British command had mustered all its available air power to launch a fierce attack on the capital of the Third Reich to demonstrate that Britain still had the capacity to fight. Later, Stalin would jokingly scold Churchill for this: "Why did you bomb my Vyacheslav?"

But at the time it was, of course, no joke for us.

"It is not safe to stay here," Ribbentrop said. "Let's go down to the bunker. We'll be more secure there."

He led us down a long corridor to an elevator. We descended deep underground and came into a spacious study, also rather elegantly appointed.

When Ribbentrop resumed the exposition of his idea about Britain's imminent defeat and the need to do something about its possessions, Molotov interrupted him with his famous phrase: "If Britain is defeated, why are we sitting in a shelter? And whose bombs are falling so close their explosions can be heard even here?"

As can be seen from this episode, assertions that Molotov had no sense of humor are not altogether accurate. On occasion, his tongue was very sharp. He would just hold it in Stalin's presence, which earned him a reputation for being tongue-tied.

Ribbentrop was a little disconcerted but quickly regained his composure and stated categorically that, one way or another, Britain would be defeated.

"In the opinion of the German government," he went on to say, "the time is coming when it will be necessary to take practical steps to divide the former British Empire. That is why it is important that the Soviet Union accede in time to the pact of three, to which Germany, Italy, and Japan are parties, to turn it into a pact of four."

The Berlin-sponsored draft treaty between Germany, Italy, and Japan, on the one hand, and the Soviet Union, on the other, declared that the four states shared the desire to cooperate "in ensuring their natural spheres of interest in Europe, Asia, and Africa." Furthermore, Germany, Italy, Japan, and the Soviet Union were "to respect each other's natural interests." The treaty was to enter into force at the time of its signing and had a duration of ten years with a possible extension with the consent of the parties. Two secret protocols were also provided. One of them defined the parties' primary spheres of interest. The southern direction "toward the Indian Ocean" was set aside for the Soviet Union. The second protocol concerned relations with Turkey and the replacement of the Montreux Convention with a new regime for the Straits to take account of the interests of the Soviet Union.

Meeting With Schulenburg

AFTER HIS RETURN TO MOSCOW, Molotov, reporting to the Politburo the results of his talks with Hitler and Ribbentrop, concluded that there was no reason to fear Germany's attack in the near future. I do not think Molotov believed Hitler's story that the German troops assembled along the Soviet border were there to relax before invading the British Isles. In fact, he repeatedly and categorically demanded that they be moved back. At the same time, the proposals relating to the pact of four and the detailed conditions elaborated by Germany in this connection seemed to support the view that the government of the Third Reich intended to continue developing German-Soviet cooperation for some time yet to come. And perhaps more important—and Molotov informed only Stalin about this—Hitler was prepared to meet him face-to-face.

Stalin always considered Hitler to be a shrewd politician who carefully calculated his moves. He thought he could read the Führer's mind and penetrate his schemes. Berlin's current proposal on the pact of four appeared to him a logical evolution of those designs. Hitler saw that the Soviet Union scrupulously fulfilled its commercial commitments, even after Germany had considerably reduced the supplies of military equipment it was sending to the Soviet Union in return. The Soviet Union had rid Germany of its fear of a British sea blockade by purchasing goods from the colonies and shipping them to Germany through its territory. He, Stalin, gave Hitler his word of honor that he would not cheat on his partner. And now Hitler was proposing that Moscow join the pact of four and was prepared to take Soviet interests into account, including a change in the regime of the Black Sea Straits. They would discuss all this at a tête-à-tête that Hitler was offering to hold. Molotov, that blockhead, is evading any discussion of that interesting proposal and wants to procrastinate. But why wait? Surely, we must act fast in this favorable situation.

This or something like this probably went through the mind of the Great Leader. It took him a little over a week to draw up an answer for Hitler.

On the morning of November 25, that is to say, only ten days after Molotov's return from Berlin, the people's commissar called me to his office.

"Tonight at nine," he said, looking at me with some special intensity, "I'm going to see Schulenburg. Please advise him about this in advance. It'll be a very serious talk. You will be interpreting."

I called the German embassy and informed the ambassador's secretary that the people's commissar was expecting the ambassador at his Kremlin office at nine o'clock that evening.

Some ten minutes before nine I was outside the front door of the building of the Council of People's Commissars to meet the ambassador and take him to Molotov. I had met Count Werner von Schulenburg on previous occasions. More than once I had accompanied People's Commissar for Foreign Trade Mikoyan to the German embassy in Stanislavsky Street (formerly Leontyevsky Place) and to the ambassador's private residence in Chisty Place (this building is now occupied by the Patriarch of All Russia). The last time I saw Schulenburg, it was on the platform of the Byelorusky Railway Station where he had come to greet Molotov on his return from Berlin. On that occasion, the ambassador was wearing a shiny top hat, a tailcoat, and a cloak. This time he had on a long, dark gray overcoat and a felt hat with its brim bent upward, as dictated by the latest fashion. He got out of a black Mercedes followed by a counselor of the embassy, Gustave Hilger, who had an excellent command of Russian and acted as an interpreter.

Leaving our overcoats at the cloakroom, we went up to the second floor in a mahogany-paneled elevator and headed for the office of the Chairman of the Council of People's Commissars of the USSR. The ambassador always dressed with the utmost elegance. Tonight, his suit had a barely noticeable stripe, a snow-white handkerchief was stuffed in his breast pocket, the cuffs of his shirt were heavily starched and were fastened together by large gold links, and the shirt collar, also rigid with starch, made him hold his head up high. Because of that, a wide, black, loosely knotted tie with a blue pearl pin was clearly seen. With his closely cropped head, dark skin stretched tight over his jowls, and his well-groomed, small mustache, there was something oriental about his face. Maybe that was because he had stayed so long in the Middle East. For many years, Schulenburg had represented Germany in Teheran. He obviously had a soft spot in his heart for Iran. His residence presented a lavish display of marvelous Isfahan carpets covering the walls, old weapons, shields with intricate inlaid designs, sabers, and swords. Persian miniatures hung all over the place, many of them erotic, which was quite shocking in those days but which also proved that this aristocrat by birth was a man with an "open mind."

Schulenburg strode confidently ahead of us down the Kremlin corridor—tall, elegant, knowing his worth. Who would have thought that in only a short while the Gestapo would execute him for his part in the failed assassination attempt on Hitler?

Both ambassadors—Schulenburg in Moscow and Dekanozov in Berlin—were destined to a tragic end. They were the envoys for their countries on the eve of a terrible bloodbath, and both were later condemned and executed by their respective governments—Schulenburg in 1944, Dekanozov, as a member of the Beria group, in 1953.

After greeting his visitors and inviting them to sit down at the long, green-cloth-covered table along the wall, Molotov said:

"I have invited you here, Mr. Ambassador, to make the following statement. The Soviet government has carefully studied the proposal made by the German foreign minister, Ribbentrop, on November thirteenth and is prepared, under certain conditions, to take a positive view of the idea to conclude the pact of four on political and economic cooperation."

The people's commissar then went on to spell out those conditions: immediate withdrawal of German forces from Finland, conclusion of a Soviet-Bulgarian treaty on mutual assistance to ensure the safety of the USSR Black Sea borders, a long-term lease to establish Soviet military and naval bases in the area of the Bosporus and the Dardanelles, recognition of the Soviet Union's special interest in the area south of Batum and Baku, stretching toward the Persian Gulf, Japan's renunciation of its concession rights to the coal and oil of northern Sakhalin.

"In light of these suggestions," Molotov went on to say, "amendments should be made in Mr. Ribbentrop's proposals for the protocols. We believe that if Turkey objects to the establishment of Soviet bases in the Straits, the three powers—Germany, Italy, and the Soviet Union—should devise and take appropriate diplomatic and military action. The Soviet government therefore believes that the quadripartite treaty should be accompanied by five secret protocols and not by two, as suggested by the Reich minister."

After a brief statement on the contents of these protocols, the people's commissar asked the ambassador to forward the Soviet considerations on the pact of four to Berlin on an urgent basis.

"We are looking forward to an early reply from the German government," Molotov concluded.

As I was accompanying Schulenburg out, I was overcome with emotions. Soviet bases in the Bosporus and the Dardanelles! Unbelievable! My mind recalled the words from Pushkin's poem "The Song of Oleg, the Prophet": *Your shield shall be on the gate of the Czar's City.* That is to say, on the gate of Constantinople-Istanbul.

I also recalled that during World War I, Britain and France promised that after the defeat of Turkey, which sided with Germany in the conflict, Russia would get Constantinople and the Straits. It did not happen then. It could well happen now.

Could Stalin make the eternal dream of the Russian imperial rulers come true? He would then indeed deserve to be called a wise and great man. I was seized with a sort of a fit of great-power chauvinism. I didn't even think about how much suffering, tears, and blood the realization of these plans would cause.

When in 1988 the secret protocol of August 23, 1939, became the subject of a controversy, I feared that Stalin's agreement to join the pact of three and all the related developments might result in an unnecessary confrontation or an attempt to conceal or obfuscate the actual facts. So I wrote a letter to the then USSR foreign minister Shevardnadze where I expressed my readiness to describe events as they had happened. Some time passed, and I got a call from an assistant to Deputy Foreign Minister Leonid Ilyichev, who eventually received my letter. What Ilyichev essentially had to say was that the time was not right to make these facts public. I could not expect any other comment from Leonid Fyodorovich, whom I knew well. His response was typical of the mind-set of that period of stagnation in the country. I prepared an article for *International Life* magazine, where I traced the entire history of the pact of four. It was accepted for publication and appeared in the August 1989 issue.

Today, some Russian historians hold that when Stalin agreed to sign the pact of four, he only wanted to feel Hitler out, as it were, and never had any serious intention of concluding such an immoral deal with him. If this were true, why wasn't this suspicious and cunning man concerned when Hitler didn't respond despite his wish—relayed by Molotov to Schulenburg—to get an early answer from Berlin? Nor was there any reaction from Berlin when the Soviet side repeated this request. Why didn't Stalin draw the necessary conclusions? In my opinion, the truth of the matter is that Stalin believed that Hitler thought, just as he did, that it was to Hitler's advantage to expand cooperation with the USSR at that stage.

The following six months did not bring any significant developments in Soviet-German relations if we disregard the deal involving a piece of Lithuanian territory apportioned to Germany under the secret protocol of September 28, 1939. The two governments reached an agreement under which Germany would renounce its claims to that part of Lithuania's territory, and the government of the USSR would pay the German government 7.5 million gold dollars (equivalent to 31.5 million deutsche marks) in compensation for it. On January 10, 1941, without any fanfare, Molotov and Schulenburg signed the secret protocol in Moscow.

A Cruel Romance

WHEN THE NEW SOVIET AMBASSADOR, Vladimir Georgiyevich Dekanozov, arrived in Berlin in December 1940, the head of the Imperial Chancellery, Otto Meissner, quickly became his friend. The friendship was clearly approved by Hitler himself, who had met Stalin's envoy when he accompanied Molotov on his trip to the Reich capital to attend talks in the Führer's office. A short, stocky man with a barrel chest, balding head, and thick, red eyebrows, Dekanozov kept his post of deputy people's commissar for foreign affairs despite his new job, a sign that the Great Leader held him in special regard. When in late December I was assigned to the USSR embassy in Germany as its first secretary and began my work there, Vladimir Georgiyevich was very nice to me. He would often invite me in to dinner and take me along on important negotiations, even though there was a staff interpreter at the embassy. Dekanozov not only allowed me to read all cables pertaining to relations with Germany but also documents he was receiving from Moscow as a member of the Party's Central Committee. Over a bottle of good Georgian wine, he enjoyed telling the story that he and Stalin came from the same part of the country, both being Cartelians (an ethnic group in the Caucasus). But he was Beria's man first—he came to work for the Commissariat of

Foreign Affairs directly from State Security. All this must have been taken into account at the Reich Chancellery, when blessing was given to the special relationship between Dekanozov and Otto Meissner.

Meissner, also short and stocky, regularly joined the ambassador for lunch a few times a month and, slouching in a chair over cognac and coffee, would tell his host "in confidence" that the Imperial Chancellery was working on important proposals for the upcoming meeting between Hitler and Stalin. These proposals, he would intimate, were intended to promote German-Soviet cooperation and largely accommodated Molotov's concerns expressed to Schulenburg at their November meeting. This was pure and simple disinformation. Dekanozov naturally reported his conversations with Meissner to Moscow, where Stalin, increasingly fearful of a confrontation with Germany and eager to preserve "friendly" relations with Hitler, believed these reports instead of the warnings reaching him from everywhere else about an imminent and inevitable invasion.

And as time went by with no signs that the Germans were getting ready to land in the British Isles, Stalin formed his own interpretation of the situation: As an experienced politician, Hitler is, of course, leery of becoming engaged in a conflict with the USSR while the question of Britain remains unresolved. The continuing concentration of German forces along the Soviet border can be explained by the Führer's desire to have a powerful bargaining chip in dealing with the Soviet government. However, it cannot be ruled out that the German generals were advocating an early attack on the USSR. New top Red Army commanders had not yet been trained to replace those who had been dismissed, nor had the production of modern military equipment yet been launched. The winter war with Finland showed that the Soviet Union was not ready for a major conflict. In view of this, the German General Staff is demanding that the invasion not be postponed. A fierce struggle is under way among the top German leadership. The balance tips one way, then the other. And Stalin concludes: We must exercise caution. We must not respond to the provocations of the German military while trying to win Hitler over to our side. If we show restraint and ignore the provocateurs, Hitler will understand that Moscow does not want any problems with Germany. He will then take his generals in hand. After arriving at this conclusion, Stalin rejects all proposals to stop the overflights of Soviet territory by German aircraft and disregards reports of flagrant violations of the Soviet border by German soldiers. Even when our border guards are killed by the Germans, there is only an oral protest from the embassy to Ribbentrop's deputy, Weizsäcker.

The Wehrmacht's campaign in the Balkans, which lasted over two months, and the flight by the Führer's deputy, Rudolf Hess, to England totally convinces Stalin that there will be no war in 1941. Even if Berlin decides to attack after all, it will not happen earlier than the spring of 1942, because valuable time has been lost on the operations in Yugoslavia and Greece. Hitler, a careful politician, will not start an invasion of Russia in the middle of summer, especially since the German army, as Stalin knows, is not prepared for a winter campaign. Hess must have been instructed to come to an agreement with London. But so long as Churchill remains in power, such an agreement is unlikely. It will take months to reshuffle the British government. If, on the other hand, Hess's mission fails altogether, Hitler may decide to proceed first against England with Operation Sea Lion. We must give Hitler the right signal and support him in his face-off with the generals.

And so, on June 14, 1941, a week before the Nazi hordes smash over the Soviet border, Moscow makes public a statement via Tass. It declares that "according to Soviet information, Germany complies with the terms of the Soviet-German nonaggression pact as scrupulously as does the Soviet Union, in light of which, in the opinion of the Soviet Union, rumors about Germany's intentions to annul the pact and to launch an attack on the Soviet Union are completely baseless." After making this startling statement, Stalin probably expected to hear something similar from Hitler. But Berlin responded with complete silence. Hitler was not perturbed by the Tass statement. The German press did not even mention the Soviet declaration, which was surely giving the wrong message to the Red Army and to the Soviet people. And Stalin was still trying to engage the Führer in negotiations.

During one of his meetings with Feliks Chuyev, Molotov touched upon the Tass statement of June 14, 1941, and the way I treated it in my book *With a Diplomatic Mission to Berlin*.

"Berezhkov reproaches Stalin for the Tass statement," Molotov says, "claiming there was no reason for it."

Justifying the Great Leader, Molotov explains that Stalin had carefully thought the statement through:

"It was a game of diplomacy. Of course, it was a game. Didn't work out. You don't get good results every time you try, but there was nothing bad about it either. Berezhkov writes that it was so naive. Not naive but a certain diplomatic move, a political move. In that particular case, it didn't work out, but there was nothing unacceptable or inadmissible about it. And it was not a dumb move. It was an attempt to help clarify the issue, so to speak. And the fact that they refused to react only showed they were playing a double game with us."*

If this was the case, then why didn't Stalin put our forces on heightened alert on June 15 or 16, when it had already become clear that there would be no reaction from the Germans? Why did he persist to the very last day in rejecting any proposals from the Soviet command to do this? Why didn't top Red Army commanders at least initiate steps to camouflage our tanks, artillery, and aircraft in the border areas? Why did they permit the Germans, on the night of June 22, to destroy twelve hundred combat aircraft on the ground as well as other equipment?

The fateful Tass statement disarmed the entire country. A game of diplomacy indeed!

Starting in May, family members of German embassy personnel began leaving Moscow en masse. Only the most essential staff stayed on. On June 19–20, German ships left Soviet ports, some sailing off half-loaded. Stalin was getting reports about all this. But he clung to his ideas, becoming hostage to his stubborn faith in Hitler. Not only was the Soviet embassy staff not being reduced in Berlin, but more and more families were arriving, many of them with children. Not a single Soviet ship was recalled from German ports. More than that, Stalin saw to it that the flow of supplies into Germany continued uninterrupted. The last train carrying oil, manganese, and grain crossed the German border one hour before the invasion. As camouflaged German officers and soldiers, expecting the signal for the attack at any moment, were watching the freight train roll by, they could only have been amazed at how poorly informed the Soviet authorities were.

Even on June 21, on the very eve of the invasion, Stalin was still hoping to engage in a dialogue with Hitler. That Saturday, our embassy in Berlin received a cable from Moscow instructing the ambassador to see Ribbentrop immediately and to inform him that the Soviet government was prepared to engage in negotiations with the Reich top leadership and "to hear Germany's grievances." This was in fact a hint that the Soviet Union would not only listen but would satisfy Germany's demands. But nothing could stop Hitler at that point.

*Reported in *One Hundred and Forty Conversations with Molotov,* 41–42.

Stalin, on the other hand, continued to believe in the fantasy he had created. At the break of dawn on June 22, German planes bomb Minsk, Brest, Lvov, Rovno; bombs are exploding at our airports and tank depots, turning military hardware into scrap metal. Fuel and ammunition depots are going up in smoke. The German armada crosses the Soviet border from the Baltic to the Black seas. Stalin continues to hesitate. He refuses to sign orders to repel the attack. He says to his marshals and to the Politburo members around him:

"Maybe all this is a provocation by the German military? Let Molotov summon Schulenburg. He has a hot line to Hitler. Let him ask him what is going on."

War is raging outside. But inside Stalin's office all is quiet. Everyone is waiting for the results of the talks with the German ambassador. Molotov goes back to his office and orders that a call be put through to Schulenburg, who is in no rush to come to the Kremlin. Valuable time is being lost. Finally, the ambassador arrives and says in reply to Molotov's question:

"It's war. The German forces crossed the border of the Soviet Union on orders from the Führer."

"We have not deserved this." That was all the people's commissar could think of to say to the ambassador.

Molotov's words "It's war!"—repeating the words of the German ambassador—explode like a grenade to everyone assembled in Stalin's office. They had all believed Stalin until the very last moment. Finally aware of the situation, they still hoped that the Great Leader knew something that had allowed him to disregard all warnings. Now they know: wise Stalin has miscalculated. The country has been plunged into war—the expected has unexpectedly happened. Stalin was so profoundly shocked that he was speechless. After a long, heavy pause he signs orders to repel the aggressor. The members of the Politburo ask him to address the nation over the radio.

"I can't," he replies. "Let Molotov speak."

Calling for his car and without another word, Stalin leaves for his nearest dacha at Kuntsevo. For almost a week he does not see anybody. He has been shamed by Hitler, who fooled him. Not until July 3 does he muster up enough strength to speak on the radio.

It is interesting that even while the war is raging Stalin is trying to speak to his adversary across the fronts and over the battling armies. In his conversations with foreign political leaders he never lets an opportunity pass to say something personally offensive about the

Führer. On one occasion, comparing Napoleon and Hitler, he called Bonaparte a lion and Hitler a kitten. He could have called him a hyena or a jackal or some such other offensive word. Why a kitten? Our cartoonists had a hard time trying to portray this gentle, homely creature as a frightening monster. And Stalin had enough mastery of the Russian language not to make a mistake in choosing this expression. Maybe he wanted to let Hitler know that he was not even worthy to be called a jackal, and thereby to offend him even more and to soothe his own smarting pride a little.

Incidentally, during the war, Hitler never lost interest in Stalin. The people in the Führer's inner circle testify that he usually spoke respectfully of Stalin, especially praising his restraint and fortitude. The following paradoxical statement he made half in jest during a dinner conversation illustrates this point:

"After the victory over Russia it would be a good idea to get Stalin to run the country, with German oversight, of course. He knows better than anyone else how to handle the Russians."

In the spring of 1945, Hitler was already in a hopeless situation but was still pinning his hopes on Stalin. On March 4, Goebbels writes in his diary that Hitler wanted to reach an agreement with Moscow: "The Führer is right in saying that it is easy for Stalin to make a radical turn because he doesn't have to take public opinion into account." One of Hitler's biographers writes that during his last days Hitler "felt an even closer affinity to Stalin," hailing him as "a man of genius" worthy of "vast respect." Comparing himself with Stalin, "the Führer did not hide his feeling of admiration" and stated repeatedly that the "grandeur and unshakable resolve" that both of them shared "are essentially free of vacillations and concessions typical of bourgeois politicians."

It remains to be said that this view of Stalin is similar to the statements by some of today's staunch Stalinists.

After beating Stalin at the game of diplomacy on the eve of the war, Hitler ultimately lost. And Stalin finally triumphed. Celebrating his victory, he decided to be magnanimous to his fallen adversary. Stalin knew quite well that the burned bodies of Hitler and Eva Braun were identified in the bunker of the Reich Chancellery. The Führer's dentist testified that the artificial teeth of the body and those of his patient were identical. However, when the Great Leader arrived at the Potsdam Conference, he declared that the Führer's body had not been found, giving rise thereby to unending speculation that Hitler had managed to escape. Rumor had it that he had hidden away in Spain or South America. Over the years, stories came to light again and again claiming that the Führer had found refuge on an uninhabited island that he had reached in a submarine. Someone even saw him in a secluded monastery in the Pyrenees. Others claimed to have seen him at an Argentine rancho. Stalin gave Hitler a gift of many years of semimythical life after death.

Thus ended the cruel romance between Stalin and Hitler that cost the peoples of the USSR and Germany countless lives and indescribable suffering.

The Red Director

ON A SUNNY AUGUST DAY in 1923, the ship *Koltsov*, after passing the gray granite piers of the railroad bridge blown up during the Civil War and still not rebuilt, was approaching Kiev. The sandy shallows of the Chertoroi and Trukhanov islands stretched on its port side. The aroma of sun-drenched red vines was floating in the breeze. From the deck, the city's towers stood out against the sky—the golden domes of the churches, the green parks, and the smokestacks of the factories in Podol in the lower part of the city. The paddles were splashing against the water slower and slower. The ship was coming to a halt and turning around—the bow against the current. We were approaching White Pier, the place for landing passengers at the Kiev river port.

I saw Father from a distance, standing on the pier. He had on an off-white tussah suit and a cap to match. I noticed that in the time since we had parted, Father had gained some weight, looked more fresh, and was standing more erect. At long last his knowledge and experience were being put to use. He did not have to make a living anymore by making boots or soap; now he could do what he was good at in his job as technical director and chief engineer at the Bolshevik factory, by the standards of that day a large manufacturer of agricultural machinery and equipment for sugar refineries.

The ship is moored quickly. A wide gangway is lowered onto the pier. Father is running toward us, pushing his way through a crowd of passengers. After the long separation, Mother glues herself to him, her arms around his neck, and I can't wait to get my turn to hug him. Now he is lifting me up, kissing me, enveloping me in his tobacco smell and tickling me with his well-trimmed, small, black mustache. The porters are hauling our belongings—wicker chests, boxes, plywood cases, parcels. We come out on a spacious, stone-paved square in front of the pier. Carriages are lined up here. Among the old, beat-up carts are a few elegant coaches. These holdovers of the old regime had mysteriously survived the Revolution, the Civil War, the plunder and pillage by the authorities in Kiev succeeding each other many times over: the Germans, hetman Skoropadsky, Petlyura, the Whites, the Poles, and finally the Reds. Portly coachmen are sitting in their boxes in dark green vests and corduroy hats of like color that look like top hats. Farther out, passengers are haggling with draymen. Their stalwart horses and huge carts equipped with hooks can deliver even the most bulky cargo to any part of the city. Covered with canvas and tied with ropes, a cartload will safely reach its destination rain or shine, without delay. Our luggage is modest but is nonetheless loaded on one such platform. Father gives the address to the coachman and he sets off at once. Mother is worried:

"He'll not disappear with our things, will he?"

"Impossible." Father calms her down. "Draymen are proud people. They set great store by their reputation."

I had not yet seen such standards of decency. After the life in the village, ravaged by the Civil War, where everyone was ready to pick up anything lying around unattended, I was puzzled by father's unconcern. There are then people in this big city one can depend on, people who will not cheat or steal. I recalled the stories I found hard to believe that my parents told me about pre-Revolutionary St. Petersburg where relations among people were based on trust.

We went up to a beautiful carriage drawn by two dapple-gray, well-groomed horses. Father explained that his factory owned this outfit. Bolshevik had inherited the stables, horses, and carriages from the former Czech owners, industrialists Greiter and Krivanek. Coachman Uncle Ivan got down from the box, nice, courteous, yet dignified. Later I made friends with him and would spend hours on end at the stables, trying to help him take care of the horses. I was fascinated by the carriage with its glittering black body painted over with gold filigree, the red spikes in the rubber wheels, the velvet cushions, and the two carbide lamps sparkling with polished copper. Uncle

Ivan helped Mother and Father settle down in the backseat and placed me on a collapsible little bench facing them.

The carriage rolled down the cobblestone streets smoothly and noiselessly, rocking nicely on its bouncy springs. Their rubber-inlaid shoes made the horses' trot barely audible. Uncle Ivan clicked his tongue and, from time to time, called out to the gaping pedestrians, "Out of the way!"

Today, it is hard to believe that in my childhood the principal means of city transportation for the individual was still the horse, the animal that has served man over many thousands of years! Cabs made their appearance in Kiev only in the early 1930s, and draymen competed with trucks right up to the beginning of the war.

After climbing the steep rise of the Vladimir Hill, we drove into Kreshchatik. The sun was going down in the west, lighting up the left side of the street. A lot of well-dressed people were around. Some city folk were sitting comfortably at tables in the outdoor coffee houses located along the sidewalks, sipping cool drinks. An especially large crowd was milling around Bessarabka, the central marketplace built in the old Russian style. Watermelons and melons are piled up right on the roadway. All around the place are stands with all kinds of fruit, ice cream vendors, roasting grills giving off fragrant odors of mutton shish kebab. Here we turned right and began going up Bibikov Boulevard (Shevchenko Boulevard today), lined with tall Lombardy poplars. On the left, over the cast-iron fence of the Botanical Garden, acacia trees were spreading their branches with bunches of unseasonable white flowers giving off a heady fragrance. Then followed the Jewish Bazaar, or Jewbaz as it was called for short, and we were immediately sucked into the noisy, motley whirlpool of the flea market. Vendors blocked our way, offering their goods, praising their quality in every imaginable manner, calling out their prices, which they reduced on the spot. This bright and colorful vision is invariably conjured up in my mind whenever, on a trip to Kiev, I drive over the barren asphalt of Victory Square, which later went up in place of the joyful and garrulous Jewbaz.

Once on the Brest-Litovsk Highway, we rolled on faster and three kilometers later reached our destination. On the left behind a wall we could see the towering buildings of the Bolshevik factory. Right next to it was a mansion that had belonged to the factory owners. Our carriage stopped in front of a tall, double-doored gate painted white. Uncle Ivan nimbly jumped down from the box, flung the gate open, and led the horses in by the bridle. The carriage rolled smoothly over a threshold and we found ourselves in a little cobblestoned yard. About thirty meters to the left, the factory grounds began. To the right, a light wire fence with a similar gate blocked off an alley leading to a one-story house with a green roof. The panes in the windows were rounded at the top. The columns at the front door and the spacious open veranda made it look as if it were a landowner's country house. Father led Mother away on a tour of the house, and I immediately ran out into the garden. It was huge, with many little nooks and crannies, thickets of some exotic plants similar to bamboo, and arbors overgrown with ivy. Decorative shrubs and fruit trees, giant walnuts, raspberry, black and red currant, grew here. Pools with water lilies and little fountains, flower beds, and rosariums made the garden even more beautiful. Opposite the veranda overgrown with wild vine was a cone-shaped grotto built out of slag blocks with little beds bedecked with lilies of the valley. In the spring, this fragrant miracle resembled a sugarloaf. Paths strewn with yellow sand branched off in different directions from the grotto. The place was still tended by a gardener, a bearded, imposing man who put his heart into his work.

Deeper into the garden was an outbuilding where, as I learned later, lived the chief accountant, Schechter, and the factory fire chief, former czarist officer Perekrestov. We shared the house with the factory's political manager, Vladimirov, also known as the Red director. Our part was somewhat smaller and comprised five rooms—which was more than we needed. Mother said that three would have sufficed: two bedrooms and a living room. We barely found enough furniture for three rooms since over the years of anarchy all the furniture inside the house had disappeared. The rooms were left absolutely bare. Later, when I made friends, we organized an amateur theater in the two empty rooms. We also had a bathroom and a small kitchen from where a long corridor lined with chests led to the veranda. Having learned her lesson over the hungry years, Mother immediately filled the chests with groats, flour, sugar, potatoes, marinated foods, and other edibles. But there was really no need for this. Kiev under the New Economic Policy had everything galore.

When the chervonets—the large ten-ruble note with a picture of a ploughman and a hammerman—came into circulation, the ruble became a respected convertible currency. My parents, who had ruined their teeth in the years of wandering around the country, bought czarist ten-ruble gold coins for tooth crowns, paying two chervontsi for three coins.

The convertibility of the ruble made it possible for our industrialists, writers, and performers to travel abroad without any financial problems. The chervonets was welcome anywhere, even more welcome than the dollar. And people in the street used to sing this ditty:

Oh, chervonets, my chervonets, you are like pure gold
So, of course, it is no wonder you're liked by young and old . . .

Every week Mother and I would take the train to the Jewbaz to stock up on food. I was mesmerized by the colorful sight of its unbelievable abundance, enveloped in the fragrance of vegetables and fruits. For two rubles we would fill up two large baskets that we could barely manage to lug home. Often I would be sent to buy food from the local grocer, Paremsky. Going down Mother's list, he would weigh me out meat, fish, butter, cheese, etc., and putting everything in the basket, would make a note in a thick notebook lying on his desk. I would have no money with me, and Paremsky, thanking me for the purchases, would usually say, "You'll pay when your dad gets paid."

All the people in the neighborhood would buy his food on credit, and at no time had there been any problem. Sausage maker Zhuk followed the same procedure. I enjoyed my trips to his place. I could sniff the tantalizing smells of his curing shop from a long way off. Inside, hams, sausages, links of wienerwursts, were hanging from the beams in the ceiling. There was another reason for my frequent visits to Zhuk's curing shop—I was secretly in love with his redheaded daughter, Svetlana, already a mature girl. She would often help her dad behind the counter.

My memory registered the first two weeks in Kiev as a wonderful dream. It must have rained and the sky must have clouded over, but all I recall are warm, mild, sunshiny days with the soft palette of early fall as the leaves were just beginning to turn. After the lean and crude life in the country, with no electricity or running water, and only the first signs of revival after the devastation of War Communism, everything in the city left a profound impression on me—streetlights, asphalt sidewalks, trams running along their tracks by some magic. Not to mention the few automobiles! Everything here seemed incredible and fantastic. Left alone in the flat, I would at first spend hours turning the light switch on and off, unable to understand what made the lamp light up right away. I thought it should take some time for the stuff that lights the bulb to reach it. And I wanted to catch that moment. I was equally amazed by a loaf of white bread, the likes of which I had never seen in my life, a red round of Dutch cheese, and a watermelon. Prior to that I had only seen pumpkins. And I was totally flabbergasted by the glass box sitting on Father's desk in the living room. A wire ran from it to a headset and a little knob stuck out on top, which was connected by a little lever to a crystal at the bottom. By putting the headset on and turning the little knob so that the little lever scratched the crystal, you could hear a human voice or music. That was a crystal-set radio, a marvel of the time created by engineering genius.

From the very first days I liked our neighbor, the Red director Vladimirov. He won me over by treating me like an adult, talking to me as an equal and lending me an attentive ear while my parents thought I was still a silly kid and would not let an opportunity pass to show it, as it seemed to me.

Of course, the Red director had no idea about production. His job was to provide "political guidelines" and to ensure control over the technical expert, that is to say, my father. I saw right away that they had established good, confidential relations. Vladimirov delegated all decisions to the chief engineer and did not interfere in the affairs of the factory. During the Civil War, Vladimirov had been a commander in the Kotovsky division that conducted guerrilla warfare in Bessarabia and was subsequently absorbed into the Red Cavalry. Later, Vladimirov's unit was redeployed to the Far East to fight the Japanese invaders. He crowned his feats there, which were acknowledged by the Order of the Red Banner, by bringing back a wife, a beautiful diminutive Japanese woman, smiling and hardworking. From dawn till dusk, she was busy around the house—hanging out linen in the garden after her daily laundry or making delicious meat dumplings with fantastic stuffing. They had a three-year-old daughter, Zoya, who for some reason fell for me right away. Sometimes in the evening after her bath she would slip out of her mother's arms and run, completely naked, over to our part of the house, shouting, "You are my fiancé, you are my fiancé!" chasing me all around the house. I would be terribly embarrassed—with the exception of the sausage maker's daughter I had a pretty skeptical view of all members of the opposite sex.

In reality, my father ran the Bolshevik factory and was responsible for all that happened there. He would not even assign to anyone else questions relating to security at the factory. Particularly the security, since he understood perfectly well, being a pre-Revolutionary expert, that in case of an accident he could be charged with sabotage with all the ensuing consequences. Not long before Father got the job, there was a fire at one of the three huge oil tanks for the boiler house. For this, the then chief engineer, also an old-regime specialist, was arrested and sent to a labor camp even though the cause of the fire was not clearly established. The burnt-out, rusty, and twisted tank was a constant warning about a possible act of sabotage. The factory fire chief, Perekrestov, used every opportunity to show his diligence, briefing Father on the situation every morning. Even on Sundays, when our family would be having breakfast out on the open veranda, he would invariably show up, holding his hand to his cap in a military salute and marching straight across the flower beds and lawn. Walking right up to us, he would bellow out his report:

"Reporting the situation at the factory to be quite normal, sir. Fire Chief Perekrestov, sir."

"Come on, Konstantin Konstantinovich," Father would tell him. "You don't have to be so official. Come in and sit down and have a cup of tea."

"I can't, sir. Official business. May I go now, sir?"

He would then turn on his heels and march off the property, walking as rigidly and strictly straight as if following a stretched thread. This scene would repeat itself every Sunday. Not once did Perekrestov accept father's offer of a cup of tea, and Father called him a typical workaholic. Yet Father did not fully trust him and would regularly walk around the factory grounds at night, checking the guards and night watchmen on duty at the entrance gate. One night I was awakened by Mother's voice, unusual noise, and a commotion outside my bedroom door. It was pitch-black outside. It had to be a long time until dawn. Why then are my parents not asleep? I got out of bed, walked barefoot to the door, and opened it a crack. A terrible scene was before my eyes, Father, fully dressed, was half-lying in a chair, with bloody marks on the open collar of his shirt and his neck. Mother, her gown thrown over her shoulders, sat beside him, applying a wet towel to his face. I burst out crying and ran toward them.

"Don't cry," Father said, calming me down. "It's not that bad. I was walking the grounds and saw a man near the tanks. I called out to him, but he took off. So I ran after him. I didn't see a metal bar in the dark and crashed into it. It's going to be all right after I hold a cold towel to it."

Early next morning, as usual, he went off to the office and gave Perekrestov a dressing-down. After that the fire chief beefed up the night detail, but father would still continue his nightly rounds, and the scar on the ridge of his nose remained forever.

I enjoyed walking around the factory. I was allowed to do that. The guards soon knew me and paid no attention when I walked past them. I didn't dare go in the shops but was a frequent visitor in the administration building. The offices of the Red director and the chief engineer were close to each other, behind tall oak doors that separated them from a spacious room filled with desks for the employees of the factory administration. Behind a glass partition was a typing pool. Demure ladies sat there, wearing white lace blouses and ankle-long dark skirts. The way their hair was styled high reminded me of the pictures in Mother's family album. Their virtuoso staccato performance on the Underwood keyboards impressed me as much as the radio crystal set. The ladies treated me to strong tea and *boubliks* (round-shaped rolls). We became friends, and I was initiated into the mystery of typing. To this day, that special smell of carbon paper brings back those long-gone days. In the years of the Civil War, these ladies worked at the Red Army battalion command posts; they typed and edited orders, reports, and instructions by poorly educated and sometimes totally illiterate division commanders. Those romantic years were a thing of the past, and they were now engaged in the day-to-day process of socialist reconstruction.

One day, I looked in on my father to find the Red director in his office. He was wearing a military-style jacket, dark blue riding breeches, and tall, shiny boots. I wanted to make myself scarce, but Vladimirov beckoned me toward him, sat me in his lap, and began to ask questions. I proudly informed him that I had learned to type.

"It is not a man's business to be around women's skirts," said the director. "Better go to the shops, meet the working-class people. You'll learn something more interesting there."

Father supported this idea, and the next day he took me around the main shops of the factory. I liked the steam engine that was turning a huge flywheel from which a wide leather band ran to a hole in the wall and disappeared into it. Behind the wall, in the lathe shop, it was placed over a smaller wheel attached to a long transmission shaft with a multitude of little cogs. They rotated narrower pulleys connected to lathes. Similar transmission mechanisms were in the other shops. And this entire complex system was driven by the steam engine. I would spend a lot of time with the patternmakers and the foundry people. They were friendly and would let me tinker at something on a vacant workbench, lending me a handsaw, a plane, and other tools. I would use leftover pieces of lumber to make railroad engines, automobiles, and planes. In the foundry I was captivated by the molding process, when sieved black earth would be compacted into flasks, and then a wooden casting pattern would be taken out and melted metal poured into it. I also liked the work of the electricians. I would be only too glad to fetch them wires, breakers, switches, and I generally tried to make myself useful. All this prepared me for my future work as a lineman at that same Bolshevik factory.

The Death of Lenin

GREITER AND KRIVANEK had had a fair number of highly qualified Czech workers employed at the factory. Almost all of them stayed on at the Bolshevik after the Revolution. Working conditions remained the same as under the former owners. They were given work clothes: for lathe operators they were made of leather, for all others out of thick canvas. The workers came to the factory in suits and changed into overalls. After the shift, they would shower and change back into their street clothes. There was no canteen, though. They would bring their food with them in aluminum containers. Not only the Czechs but workers of other nationalities mostly lived in their own houses with a garden in a small compound located behind a brick wall, opposite the entrance gate. A tiny brewery operated close by, and people from all around the area enjoyed excellent Czech beer. There was a club with a movie projector and a stage upon which plays on Revolutionary themes were produced with shots fired from rifles and the Reds invariably defeating the Whites. The factory hospital with a small inpatient section also provided services for the employees' family members. I would think that today the workers at the Bolshevik factory also enjoy fairly good working conditions, but it is unlikely that all of them live in separate houses or regularly drink fresh Czech beer. Admittedly, Greiter and Krivanek were quite cozy in their mansion. But they also deserve credit for taking good care of their workers.

When the theater season began, my parents would go to the theater almost every Sunday, and when they went to the opera, they often took me along. The architecture of the opera house, the rich interior, the purple seats, the shining gold, the fanciful candelabra, the solemn hall—all of this left a profound impression. The first opera I went to see was Rubinstein's *Demon*, based on a poem by Lermontov. The dreamlike story, the unusual dresses, the fairy-tale-like set reproducing the austere landscapes of the Caucasus mountains, the seduction by the Demon of the beautiful Tamara, grief stricken over the death of her betrothed, caught my fancy so much that I wanted to replicate all this in our home theater. Together with my school buddies we cut out the sets from pasteboard and colored paper, patched dresses together from pieces of mother's handiwork, and reading Lermontov's poem again and again, added our own episodes to the libretto. At last, everything was ready and the show was scheduled to premiere on January 22, 1924.

In the night of January 21, the air was suddenly split by the long, endless sound of the Bolshevik factory horn. It was echoed by horns from the neighboring factories, which, when combined, struck a disturbing chord. Suddenly all became quiet; the silence was eerie. But a few minutes later the Bolshevik's powerful voice led again, inviting others, as it were, to join in the mournful song. This was repeated again and again. Interrupting our last-minute preparations for the show, we gathered around Mother.

"What happened? Why are they hooting?"

Mother looked lost. Everything was falling from her hands.

"Something terrible must have happened," she said in a trembling voice. "Maybe it's a war again. What's keeping Father so long?"

He should have been back from the factory a long time ago, but he was still not home. My friends got dressed quickly and hurried to their homes. Putting our coats on, Mother and I went out on the veranda. Here, out in the open, the sound was even more frightening. We went back in, filled with worry. We perched on the corner of the sofa and sat there waiting, listening to the hoots. Flashbacks flick through my mind. Terrible pictures of the Civil War: soldiers with bayonets attached, machine-gun fire. Mother hides me in some gateway. People are running by. Someone falls, mowed down by a bullet. Screams of women and children. Can this be war again?

Father walks into the room, gloomy, his face sunken. We jump up to meet him. He sees the question in our eyes and replies: "Lenin is dead."

What did a seven-year-old feel at that moment? I had no interest in politics whatsoever. But I had known two names since I was a baby: Lenin and Trotsky. This two-liner stuck in my head:

> I am sitting on a barrel, trying not to make a fuss,
> Lenin-Trotsky have declared Russia will belong to us!

Nobody had heard of Stalin at that time. His name became predominant only in the late 1920s.

People associated Lenin's name with the New Economic Policy, which almost overnight had changed life for the better. The emergence of the chervonets and the disappearance of the zillions of worthless ruble notes that people began using as wallpaper was also credited to Lenin. These developments generated a feeling of safety, a belief that the worst was behind us and that only good things were in store. I did not even know that Lenin was sick, that he had already been incapacitated for a number of months, and that other people were running the country. Lenin's constant presence, even somewhere far away in Moscow, was something I took for granted and thought to be invariable, something that protected me and made the life of our family prosperous. And all of a sudden, Lenin was no more. I had seen a lot of people die in my short life. But the death of people, fighting each other, seemed inevitable, even natural. War was raging, there was shooting all around, and those who survived were lucky. But watching over it all from the far-away Kremlin was Lenin, and his closest comrade-in-arms, Trotsky. And while they were there, what went on made some sense. Nobody taught me this; Father had never discussed politics with me. Somehow, I had the smarts to get this myself. And now Lenin was no more. When Father said "Lenin is dead," something snapped inside me. I burst into tears and ran off to my room, where I couldn't calm down for a long time.

Through the half-open door I heard Father tell Mother in a low voice that Lenin's death was a terrible loss.

"Lenin understood," I heard Father whisper huskily, "that the experiment with War Communism had plunged the country into an abyss. And he had enough common sense to turn the country around. Will his followers stay the new course? They are all fanatics. They will again start ramming dubious ideas down people's throats. But first there will be a power struggle. They will start slitting each other's throats."

I couldn't understand why Father spoke so badly about Lenin's comrades. Lenin surely had followers, people who would continue his work.

Still sobbing, I came out into the living room. Father placed me next to him on the sofa and asked about our premiere scheduled for tomorrow.

"The theater is closed. It's in mourning," I declared categorically.

I immediately set about to write a notice in black paint over a red cloth: "The presentation of the opera *Demon* has been canceled due to the death of Lenin."

Vladimirov came. He did not conceal his grief. His eyes were filled with tears. He hugged my father, put his head on his chest, and cried like a baby.

"We've been orphaned," he kept on saying. "Completely orphaned. There is no one to replace Ilyich. We have lost our leader. What's to become of us?"

"We have to be brave," Father said, trying to calm him down. "Life goes on. We mustn't lose heart."

Vladimirov wiped off his tears and asked Mother to forgive him for his weakness. Then, after listening to the hoots for a while, he said, "Time to go to the mourning rally."

I asked to come along and Father took me with him. A big crowd was at the factory square. Despite the snow and the cold wind, peo-

ple's heads were uncovered. Some people were standing on a platform made out of boards draped in black and red crepe. Vladimirov
climbed up to join them. Father and I stood close by. The hooting
stopped. An amateur wind ensemble began playing a funeral march.
Again I felt a lump in my throat and tears welled up in my eyes. Father, noticing the state I was in, squeezed my hand till it began to
hurt, and I felt a little better. First the people on the platform spoke.
Then one after another workers mounted it. Everyone was grief-
stricken. Funeral melodies were played again and again. The grief
was sincere. The meeting went on well past midnight. For a whole
week, Kiev, just like the rest of the country, mourned the irreplaceable loss. People were numb with grief, sorrow, and fear for the future. The leaders in Moscow were committing themselves to continue Lenin's work. And people believed them. They didn't know yet
that the man who had deluded them with the utopia his mighty mind
had generated had already primed the diabolic machine of repression that would send to their graves tens of millions of their fellow
countrymen.

Gradually, life got back to normal. The Red director of the Bolshevik still felt his work was a bore. He would usually show up at the
office only in the first half of the day. Then, transferring the reins
of management to the chief engineer, he would sneak off to Uncle
Ivan and the horses, his obsession since the days of the courageous
cavalry charges in Kotovsky's division. The object of his special ado-
ration was a young filly called Aida, a bay beauty with fiery hazel
eyes, an arching neck, and a pitch-dark mane. He would personally
saddle her and walk her on the drill ground. Then he would wrap
a white felt cloak over his shoulder, tie his combat saber to his waist,
a gift from Simeon Budienny,* dashingly mount his horse, and ride
out of the gate and over on the other side of the road. Here he
would spur Aida up into a gallop and ride off down the field toward
the horizon. Pulling the saber out of the sheath and swishing it
around, as if chopping off the heads of invisible enemies, he would
tear down the boundless field, raising clouds of dust, riding all the
way to Svyatoshino, Kiev's aristocratic suburb of yore. A few hours
later he would reappear on the foaming horse, happy and bubbling
with energy.

This man, a committed soldier of the Revolution, was not spared

*Simeon Budienny, commander of the Red Cavalry during the Civil War in Russia, later Mar-
shal of the Soviet Union.

the fate of many of his fellow countrymen. Sometime later, he was transferred to the then capital of the Ukraine, Kharkov. Here he was given the job of director of the institute designing heavy-engineering enterprises.

In the early 1930s he was denounced, arrested, and shot. His Japanese wife was enough incriminating evidence to declare him a Japanese spy.

CHAPTER TWO

On the Procurement Commission

THE PROCUREMENT COMMISSION, which was to leave for Germany in early February 1940, comprised prominent economists, experienced designers of military hardware, generals, admirals, and managers of large enterprises. Many of them later became well-known politicians, as was the case, for instance, with Dmitri Ustinov. At that time, he was director of a defense-industry factory in Leningrad. A talented engineer and a good manager, Ustinov caught the eye of the people's commissar for the shipbuilding industry, Tevosyan, who headed the Procurement Commission, and who later recommended him to Stalin. At the beginning of the war, Ustinov was appointed people's commissar for the defense industry and played a major role in organizing the production of modern armaments that were superior even to corresponding German types. He ended his career as a member of the Politburo and as the USSR defense minister and was among those who made the infamous decision to send Soviet forces into Afghanistan in December 1979.

Because of the secrecy that shrouded everything in Stalin's time, everyone on the Commission, myself included, was listed as a "merchant" on his passport. A funny episode resulted from this.

Sometime after our arrival in Berlin, our group was received by the commander of the German Navy, Grossadmiral Erich Räder. As I entered the admiral's office, following Tevosyan, I saw our host seated at a large desk. He was thin, already fairly advanced in years, with the face of a man of strong will. He was wearing an admiral's black uniform, his chest adorned with numerous decorations and service ribbons. Räder slowly rose from his chair, stood straight up, towering tall, and reaching out his hand toward Tevosyan, said in a loud voice:

"Greetings, distinguished admirals and generals!"

Unprepared for these words of welcome, Tevosyan began explaining that his delegation members were mere "merchants." But Räder stopped him short with a gesture of protest. He went back to his desk and picked up a copy of *Pravda* that happened to be lying there. He opened it so that we could see the entire front page. The Party newspaper carried a decree by the Presidium of the USSR Supreme Soviet establishing new top military ranks and awarding them to leading generals and admirals. A number of photos followed, among which it was not difficult to recognize the "merchants" on our Procurement Commission.

Our cover blown, we stood there looking embarrassed. Tevosyan could only spread his arms and flash a disarming smile at our host.

We left Moscow by an overnight train that departed from the Belorussky Railway Station. The next morning, we arrived in Riga, the capital of capitalist Latvia, where late that night a German train would take us to Berlin via Königsberg. We checked our bags in the luggage room and spent the whole day touring the city. In those days, the stores in Moscow were much better stocked than in the 1980s, let alone the 1990s; but still they paled compared to what we saw in Riga. The abundance of food and goods was staggering. We had been told by accounts in our newspapers that life was hard for the farmers and workers in capitalist Latvia, that the German barons, who had settled in the Baltic region a long time ago, were getting fat sponging on the simple folks, who, of course, lived from hand to mouth. We could not possibly imagine that life there would be better than in Moscow, the capital of the vast Soviet Union. But what we saw at the market near the railway station, and in other stores throughout the city, was beyond our wildest dreams. More importantly, we could afford all of it even on our shoestring budgets. A great variety of footwear, fur coats and jackets, suits and pullovers—plus gramophones, records, radios, heaps of fruits and vegetables, whole carcasses hanging from hooks in meat stores—we couldn't believe our eyes.

If Germany is this bountiful, I thought to myself, I'd better be smart with my money. I'll buy wonderful presents for my family—and for me, a renewed wardrobe. Therefore, I concluded, I have to start saving. The dollar advance we had received suddenly became much more important. I was already sorry I had spent fifty cents to buy a bar of Swiss chocolate after we crossed the Soviet-Latvian border.

When we returned to the railway station after our tour of the town, we decided to have a snack at a local restaurant. There were five of us—the others were still in town and hadn't come back yet. The waiter, who spoke fluent Russian, handed us menus in Latvian, English, and Russian and began rattling off the house specialties: fried piglet with buckwheat porridge, lamb served with potatoes baked in their jackets, turkey stuffed with apples, and many other things that made my mouth water. But recalling that I had made a vow to hold on to my hard cash, I said I wasn't hungry and ordered a cup of clear broth with an egg. The others were obviously suffering no such compunctions, and before long next to my modest cup of broth there appeared fried piglet, turkey, carp monastery-style, and, to top it all off, an ice-cold bottle of vodka and coffee with cream. I tried to keep my eyes on my meager broth, sipping it slowly to make it last through the awful orgy that was going on around me. At last, the waiter came back to us, notepad in hand, ready to give us our bill.

Before I was able to open my mouth, engineer Valentin Petrovich Seletsky, seated next to me, called out merrily, "One check, please!" And, turning to the rest of the party, added, "And we'll all chip in, right?"

"Of course!" answered a somewhat discordant chorus of voices.

I mumbled my agreement as it dawned upon me what a terrible mistake I had made. Of course, I couldn't admit that I had decided on the broth to save money. Everyone had heard me say I wasn't hungry. I had to pay up like everyone else.

At first I was angry at Seletsky, but then I said to myself, "Serves you right: Don't be a miser, don't be so stingy with your money."

Later Seletsky and I became very good friends.

At the Krupp Factory

IN FEBRUARY 1940, when I went to Berlin for the first time, I didn't find it as clean as I'd imagined it to be from the stories told by my colleagues who had visited it earlier. Dirty snowbanks were melting in the streets, the wind drove litter along them, and the air was filled with the smoke from the brown coal that was used to heat the Reich's capital. Signs of the war that had started six months earlier were everywhere. It was quickly obvious that mass mobilization had created a huge shortage of labor. When we checked in at the Saxenhof Hotel near Nollendorfplatz, the desk clerk handed each of us a round fluorescent pin. We were to wear it in plain view so that during blackouts, which were strictly enforced, people could see a glowing spot and wouldn't bump into each other. When night fell, the city sank into darkness. There were no bright neon lights, no shining shop windows. Double-thick felt canopies covered entrances to shops, cafes, and office buildings, forming narrow passageways. Only when you were inside the first canopy were you allowed to open the second one that led into the lighted interior. Automobile headlights were covered with black hoods with slits in them to let narrow beams of light pass through.

That was what we saw in the capital of the Third Reich.

Recently, much has been written about Soviet shipments to Germany, and Stalin has been rightly blamed for supplying Hitler with grain, oil, and rare metals and for helping the Nazis accumulate strategic reserves that they subsequently used in the war against the Soviet Union. But at the same time, it should be pointed out that in return we also obtained much that we needed in the way of equipment and modern military hardware. Only on those terms did the Soviet government agree to supply to Germany the resources it was requesting. Among our acquisitions from the Germans was the *Lutzov*, a state-of-the-art cruiser of the same class as the cruiser *Prinz Eugen*. Both ships were built by Germany for its own fleet. The Germans also gave us the shop drawings for their newest battleship, the *Bismarck*, for thirty different combat aircraft, including Messerschmitt 109 and 110 fighters and Junker 88 dive bombers, samples of field-artillery pieces, modern fire-support systems, tanks together with the formulas for their armor, and a variety of explosive devices. In addition, Germany undertook to supply us with locomotives, turbines, diesel motors, merchant ships, metal-cutting machine tools, presses, press-forging and other equipment for heavy industry, including the oil and electric industries.

The Soviet Procurement Commission's job was to monitor Germany's compliance with its commitments and to check the quality of the finished products. The group I was assigned to worked at a Krupp factory in Essen. Seletsky and I were given the task of monitoring the assembly of the gun turrets for the cruiser *Lutzov*.

At that time I had already asked myself this question: Why had the Germans agreed to supply us their most modern military systems when the Wehrmacht was already planning to attack the Soviet Union? There must have been a number of reasons for this. First of all, in line with his broad disinformation campaign, Hitler wanted to convince Stalin that he had totally rejected the goal of "eliminating Bolshevism," which he had proclaimed in *Mein Kampf,* and that he had shifted Germany's policy toward cooperation with the Soviet Union. Secondly, underestimating Soviet scientific and technological potential, Berlin's strategic planners did not believe that the Soviet Union was capable of mass-producing sophisticated weapons systems even when supplied with blueprints, and that the many items sent to the USSR would in the end make little or no difference. In any case—so they must have reasoned—even if the USSR did manage to get some types of modern armaments into production, the Wehrmacht would have time enough to defeat the Soviet Union before it began turning out those weapons on a massive scale. Thirdly, due to the naval blockade imposed by Great Britain, Germany was desperately short of strategic raw materials, and the Soviet negotiators, particularly the people's commissar for foreign trade, Anastas Mikoyan, demanded the latest technology, including military hardware, in exchange for Soviet supplies. At that juncture, Hitler could not afford any complications in his relations with the Soviet Union, and with the nonaggression pact and the Treaty on Friendship and the Border, he was not only able to avoid a possible war on two fronts but also to circumvent the British blockade.

Documents of the period indicate that the German High Command objected to the delivery of military supplies to the Soviet Union. Grossadmiral Räder was the most outspoken critic of Hitler's decision to supply the USSR. But the Führer ignored the protests of his commanders, considering the Soviet shipments too important to be interrupted. He thought he was justified in his position, particularly since the Soviet side scrupulously complied with its commitments. In a little over a year, from the spring of 1940 to June 1941, while the trade agreement remained in effect, Germany received 1 million tons of wheat, 9,000 tons of oil products, 100,000 tons of cotton, and 500,000 tons of phosphates—adding up to a large amount of strategic materials. We also allowed Germany to ship through Soviet territory 1 million tons of soybeans from Manchuria and large amounts of rubber, tin, and other materials from Southeast Asia. In addition to all that, the Soviet Union agreed to purchase metals and raw materials for Germany in third countries. As was pointed out by Minister Julius Schnurre, head of the German delegation at the trade negotiations with Moscow, "Stalin provided generous assistance in this regard on repeated occasions." Schnurre stressed that the trade agreement meant that "the gates to the East are wide open for us. . . . Thereby the effectiveness of the British blockade is seriously weakened."

Stalin also allowed the Germans to navigate via the northern sea route, as well as to refuel and repair their ships in the ports beyond the arctic circle. The Germans began using these facilities starting in September 1939.

Unfortunately, we were not able to make full use of what we obtained from the Germans. We succeeded, for instance, in installing only two out of four gun turrets on the cruiser *Lutzov* by the time it was towed to Leningrad. In any case, the ship was destroyed in a German air raid in the first days of the war. Nevertheless, Soviet experts were able to study the very weapons we were to confront in June 1941. They used that knowledge to design new types of weapons systems, and this helped them to develop tanks, artillery pieces, and aircraft that by the end of 1942 were superior to what the Germans were using.

A Cup of Tea

THE FIELD ON WHICH Vladimirov, the Red director of the Bolshevik factory, rode his horse has long since been built over. Most of the area has been occupied by the Dovzhenko Movie Studios. High-rise apartment buildings today tower all around. But in the early 1920s, this empty lot was used to test planes manufactured by Remvozdukh, a factory located behind our house. The factory built light biplanes: a wooden frame covered with oilcloth, one small engine, and one propeller made out of pieces of hard wood glued together. Boys from all around the neighborhood looked forward to each occasion when a new aircraft would be rolled out of the Remvozdukh gates. We would mill around it, knowing that our help would soon be needed. Our task was to grab hold of the plane's tail and to hold on to it, keeping the plane steady while the engineer hand-turned the propeller, trying to start up the engine, and then again while the pilot was revving up. At just the right moment, on a cue from the engineer, we were to let go and scatter. The plane would roll over the grass, picking up speed, and would finally soar up into the air to our cheers of joy. After making a few circles over the field, the plane would begin its landing sequence, and we would run across the field again, coming back to crowd around it, staring in awe at the pilot as he climbed out of the cockpit. His clothes were all of leather, and his helmet and goggles made him look like a dragonfly.

Behind Remvozdukh was another interesting place, a sporting-goods factory owned by a NEP mogul named Smirnov. With winter approaching, my father decided to order a so-called Finn sled, which had long, narrow runners and a high-backed seat. When he went to see Smirnov, he took me along. The factory was fairly small, employing only some twenty people, but all of them were past masters of their trades.

The owner of the factory, a tall, athletic-looking man, showed us the production process. We began our tour at the lumberyard, where lumber was kept at a certain temperature for months and even years. This was considered necessary to prevent the wood from warping in the future. Smirnov also manufactured propellers commissioned by

Remvozdukh. The lumberyard abutted on a woodworking shop, with metalworking, finishing, and paint shops following. The finished products looked attractive and were renowned for their excellent quality. This small factory could easily have been developed into a large-scale sporting-goods manufacturer. But in the early 1930s, the Smirnov factory was closed down, the owner was sent to Siberia, its foremen left their jobs, and the smoothly running operation ceased to exist. I have never again seen the kind of products that Smirnov used to manufacture.

The area where the Bolshevik factory was located was not just a working-class neighborhood. A nearby green park was home to the campus of the Kiev Polytechnic Institute. Scattered around it were the houses of the faculty, as well as the students' residence halls. That is why the nearby Pushkin Park, with its open-air movie theater in the summer and a skating rink in winter, attracted a motley crowd. In those days, mostly American-made movies were playing: the thirteen-part series *The Mistress of the World*, the five-part *The Queen of Forests*, the four-part *The Sharks of New York*, as well as *Blood and Sand* with Rudolph Valentino and *The Thief of Baghdad* with Douglas Fairbanks. But European films were also shown, such as *The Nibelungs, Dorothy Vernon, He Who Laughs*. There was quite a crush in Kiev when two American movie stars, Mary Pickford and Douglas Fairbanks, visited there. They came to our country to join with a local moviemaking company, Mezhrabpom Rus Studios, to produce two hilarious comedies, *Mary's Kiss* and *A Cup of Tea*, costarring the famous Russian comedian Igor Ilyinsky. The movies, which were turned out quickly, played to huge audiences in Pushkin Park. The premiere was, of course, held at the gorgeous downtown movie theater in Kreshchatik Street known to Kievites by its old name, the Shantzer, after its pre-Revolutionary owner.

At the time, Kreshchatik was not the wide and coldly imposing street it is today. It had its special charm, especially in the section that stretched from Dumskaya Square (subsequently, the October Revolution Square) to Fundukleyevskaya Street (later to become Lenin Street). This short strip alone had five movie theaters, including the Shantzer, with spacious foyers decorated with marble columns, mirrors in gilt frames, and art nouveau chandeliers. In addition to foreign films, movies produced by the budding Soviet moviemaking industry were also being shown, such as *Father Sergius, Aelita* and *Little Bricks of Clay*. This last had a screenplay loosely based on a popular hit song of the day about the love of a woman brickmaker for a manual laborer called Sim who, after his appointment as a Red director, turned into "Comrade Simeon."

The basement of almost every building in Kreshchatik housed an activity advertised by the odd sign BILLIARDS/BEER. Inside, men would spend their after-office hours shooting pool and sipping frothy beer. Sidewalk vendors sold fragrant waffles with cream, which they made right on the spot in special waffle-makers. Next to them, teenage kids were hustling devil-shaped inflatable balloons that made piercing noises and milk candies packed in little wooden boxes. Coffee shops were all over the place. Signs over still more coffee houses—SEMADENI, MIKADO, VALENTINE—could be seen in the nearby side streets. Many of them were privately owned and their proprietors operated little pastry shops. Usually, such coffee parlors had two rooms. The first one had a counter offering a take-out selection. The other, inner room contained numerous little marble tables and wicker chairs. Patrons would take their time relishing pastries, cakes, or ice cream, enjoying a drink of soda, coffee, tea, or hot chocolate. There were always tables available. In doorways, gateways, and small shop windows private entrepreneurs were offering footwear and ladies' bags and then fashionable leather jackets in any desired color. In general, leather items were in plentiful supply, probably because a large number of horses and cattle had died during the Civil War, and private tanners had accumulated great quantities of hides. As it turned out, even in those very hard circumstances the hides did not deteriorate; someone took care to dress them, and as soon as the New Economic Policy permitted, curriers got busy and within months leather goods were in plentiful supply all around the country.

In those days, Kreshchatik was the place for promenades, meetings, and amorous encounters. There, futurist artists exhibited their works, amateur stand-up comedians sang funny songs accompanying themselves on accordions, and street clowns and jugglers made people laugh. And another event drew people there. Every now and again, a young couple would make an appearance, both completely naked with only a narrow ribbon over their shoulders reading, "Shame on shame!"

In a word, Kreshchatik was then an extravagant place.

Hotel Essener Hof

THE MANAGEMENT OF THE KRUPP COMPANY put us up at their hotel Essener Hof, a somewhat old-fashioned building with luxurious furniture and a beautifully decorated restaurant. The rooms were spacious with high ceilings, but only one bathroom was on each floor. In those days, even expensive hotels did not necessarily have bathrooms in every room.

Bathing at Essener Hof was an elaborate ritual. Two rosy-checked, well-endowed young maids officiated at the ceremony, set by prior appointment for a specific hour. They piled freshly pressed, still warm towels and sheets one on top of the other, unpacked fragrant soaps, laid out little boxes with aromatic creams on the shelves, placed snow-white rugs on the tile floor, filled the bath with hot water adding some pine extract, and finally, would knock on the guest's door and solemnly declare that everything was ready.

We had our meals out on a glassed veranda facing an old park. Our waiters wore uniforms and looked stately and dignified. Unfortunately, we had no time to revel in the luxury: after an early breakfast we would set off for the factory, and when we came back to the hotel on our lunch break, we only had time to down a quick snack before hurrying back to the shop.

After a tour of Germany, People's Commissar Tevosyan, who headed the Procurement Commission, arrived in Essen to check on how our group was doing. Our meeting, attended by a representative of the Krupp company, took place in the lobby of the hotel. A waiter served refreshments and put out boxes with cigarettes and cigars. Tevosyan asked Ustinov to brief him on our work. The main problem was that the experimental assembly of the gun turret for the cruiser *Lutzov* was proceeding too slowly because of a delay in the deliveries of component parts. The Germans were obviously dragging their feet. Granted, a gun turret was a complex piece of equipment: it goes down three floors under the deck and has numerous devices for loading and ejecting shells plus hydraulic units for barrel movement. But still, work could have progressed much faster. In the few weeks that had gone by, not even the first turret had been assembled. Moreover, we had to work in cramped conditions. Our work area was walled off from the rest of the shop by huge tarpaulin curtains, probably so that we couldn't see what else was going on there.

"We have no intention of prying into German secrets," Ustinov said, "and it wouldn't be a bad idea to enlarge the area around the turret."

The representative from Krupp explained that the delay in the assembly was caused by an increased number of orders from the German government. Responding to this, Tevosyan said he couldn't accept such an explanation and added that he would have to discuss all of that with the company's top management. He then began plying the company's representative with detailed questions about the construction of the turret.

At this point the conversation ran into difficulties. The woman who acted as the people's commissar's interpreter wasn't too well versed in the technical terminology and was unable to translate into Russian much of what the engineer had to say.

I volunteered to help.

When the meeting was over and the people began to leave, Tevosyan asked me to stay. He wanted me to tell him more about myself, where I'd studied German, and what education I'd received. He must have been pleased with my answers. He suggested that I take a temporary leave of absence at the Krupp factory and accompany him on a trip through Germany and, later, to Holland where he would soon be going to learn how Soviet orders to build refrigerator ships were being implemented. Two weeks later, he called me to Berlin.

In the meantime, the first gun turret was finally assembled. We began testing its units. A German engineer, Franz Hüsker, was helping us with the tests. We became friends. He had worked for a long time in Indonesia when it was still a Dutch colony. I was a frequent guest at his house, where he had assembled a rich collection of Indonesian art—graceful statuettes, figurines of the shadow theater, rare conch shells, wonderful wickerwork made from bamboo and rice straw. His wife, Kate, and two school-age daughters were also very hospitable to me. I enjoyed my visits with that family. They brought a welcome change into my life there in Essen.

The Hüskers were bicycle enthusiasts. They found a spare bike for me, and when the weather cooperated, we would ride our bikes out into the beautiful countryside nearby. On my days off when the weather was bad, I couldn't think of a better way to spend my free time than to stay in my hotel room and read. I bought a couple of books in a bookstore close to our hotel, including a beautifully illustrated edition of *The Decameron*. One evening when I was looking through the newspapers that had piled up over the week, a woman named Zina who worked as an interpreter for our group stopped by my room.

"Sorry to bother you," she said, "but do you have anything to read?"

I pointed to a stack of books on the side of the table. She began picking them up one by one, and I noticed that *The Decameron* had caught her eye.

"You can take that one with you," I told her.

"But isn't it an obscene book?"

"Nonsense! This is a classic, a must for every educated person."

She was hesitant. She wanted to take it, but felt uncomfortable.

"Bring it over here and sit by my side," I told her. "I will read one story to you."

Zina gave me the book and sat down, somewhat away from me. The book was, of course, in German, but that wasn't a problem for us. I don't remember which story I chose to read, but in any case Zina was shocked and began scolding me for it. She made no move to leave, though. By the standards of the time, especially given our puritan Soviet upbringing, that book was the peak of eroticism for us. I edged closer to Zina, and we began looking at the pictures together, some of them quite suggestive. Then it was Zina who wanted to read another story.

Until that evening, we had been totally indifferent to each other, but on reading *The Decameron* together, we felt we were being drawn closer. We were amused by the book's ambiguous and sometimes totally explicit scenes. Our hands found each other, and unaware how it happened, we were in each other's arms. Suddenly, she grew all tense, dug her sharp elbows into my chest, and pushed me away.

"What is it? What's the matter?" I whispered.

"The Trade Union Organization has taught me to be firm." Zina's voice rose to an unnatural pitch.

"What's the Trade Union Organization got to do with it? What has it got to do with us?" I asked, bewildered.

"Silly, don't you see?" she replied more calmly. She moved farther away from me and explained in a low voice, "The Trade Union is the Party. When abroad, Communists are forbidden to admit they are

Party members, but so that we know who we are, we say we are with the Trade Union. And we must be morally firm. Are you not a Party member?"

No, I was not a Party member. Not only that, I was also a bachelor and unaware of the all-seeing eye of the Trade Union.

For some time after that episode, I was concerned that Zina might squeal on me. It could be one of a Trade Union member's duties to report to appropriate authorities "Comrade So-and-so's inappropriate behavior." But nothing happened.

And we never read together again.

Soon Zina was transferred to the trade mission in Berlin.

During Easter, Valentin Petrovich Seletsky and I decided to take a walk down the Rhine River. Our plan was to take a train to Rüdesheim and then to walk along the river to Bad Godesberg.

The train quickly gathered speed. Cozy little houses whirled past us—tiled roofs, green lawns, miniature faience dwarfs around their flower beds. Suddenly, as if in a movie, the idyllic scene was disrupted by a long train of cars carrying covered guns, tarpaulin-wrapped tanks, and soldiers in steel helmets. The formidable armada was inexorably advancing toward the borders of France, Belgium, and Holland.

A short stop. A young girl entered our compartment. She had chestnut-colored hair, a little turned-up nose, bright blue eyes. Seeing that our compartment was half-empty—I was standing in the passageway by the window and only Seletsky was in there—she bashfully asked if there would be room for her. I hastened to open the glass door for her. The girl hung up a light overcoat, placed a small travel bag on the shelf over the seat, and settled down by the window. A lady selling hot drinks was passing in the corridor. I stopped her and, ordering three coffees, offered one cup to Seletsky and one to our new companion.

"Thank you very much," she said simply, and took the cup.

I introduced myself by my first name.

"Malvina," she responded.

We spoke about the beauty of the Rhine and the early spring. I went back to the window in the passageway. Soon Malvina joined me. She was surprised to learn that we were Russians and that we had come to work at the Krupp factory. Her father also worked there but had been called up in the army. His unit was on the border with France and she was on her way to see him there.

"My friend and I," I explained, "have decided to spend the holiday walking along the Rhine."

"I love this area," Malvina said. "We walked all around the place when I was still at school. How come your German is so good?"

I told her I had been to a German school in the Ukraine.

"Is it possible that there are German schools in Russia?" She sounded surprised.

"There were, when I went to school."

I knew that our school had been closed down, and that its founder and principal, Friedrich Fibich, had been sent to Siberia on charges of espionage, accused of being "an enemy of the people." But I didn't tell her that.

Another train carrying tanks and troops passed by.

"I'm very worried about my father. He is not strong. But who cares! They need more soldiers. We were hoping through winter and spring that the war would be over after Poland and that they would let Father go. But now it's clear that this is going to last a long time. With my training as a nurse, I won't escape the front either."

It was getting dark. The light in the compartment was turned on. Seletsky was making signs, inviting us inside. But something was holding us back in the semilit passageway. We kept on talking about everything and nothing at the same time. We were just enjoying each other's company. A voice over the intercom announced the next stop—Rüdesheim.

"We are getting off there," I said.

All at once it became cold and awkward.

"Pity," Malvina said tersely.

Knowing it was an impossible thing to ask, I blurted out, sort of mechanically, "Why don't you get off there with us?"

She stood silent for a while, then looked at me closely. "Why not indeed? I could continue on my trip tomorrow morning."

I was flabbergasted by her reply. But there was no turning back.

She calmly re-entered the compartment, took her bag and overcoat, and returned to the passageway.

Back in the compartment, as I was reaching for my bag, I whispered to Seletsky, "She is getting off with us."

"Just what we need," he grumbled good-naturedly.

The evening was wonderful. The moon was not up yet but the sky was already silvery with a shimmering light. We were walking along a quiet street looking for a place to stay. Almost every gate had a sign, ROOMS TO LET.

We stopped by a house with two rows of windows in a tall roof. The landlady showed us three rooms in the upper garret that suited us perfectly. She also prepared our meal—scrambled eggs and a bottle of Rhinewein. After we wished each other pleasant dreams, we went to our respective bedrooms. I had not discussed anything with Malvina, but I left my door unlocked. That night, she came into my room. She didn't have the slightest idea about any Trade Union and its rigid rules. . . .

The moon rose up over the river. The ragged contours of medieval castles stood out sharply against the moonlit sky. A quiet night, a night before the storm that could have whirled away into nothingness both Malvina the nurse and her father the soldier.

The next morning, after a quick cup of coffee with fresh rolls, we went to the railway station to see Malvina off.

A brief farewell, the wave of a kerchief from the window—and the train disappeared around the bend.

Seletsky and I set off on our walking trip along the left bank of the Rhine. The day was sunny and warm, and by noon it had become quite hot. Green vines stretched all around as far as the eye could see. At every kilometer there was a cellar where farmers treated travelers to cool homemade wine. Little ships and barges plied up and down the river, and austere old fortresses perched on the hilltops. A fair number of castles were in good shape, some of them turned into private museums. You entered such a museum as if traveling in time back into the Middle Ages. Every item seemed completely unaffected by the passage of centuries. We also went to see the huge steel statue *Germany*—a monstrous, giant Valkyrie brandishing a sword. A fitting monument to triumphant militarism! We had lunch at a little restaurant located on the slope of a hill and, after a short rest, continued on our journey. By nightfall, we had reached Bad Godesberg.

When we planned our itinerary, we had decided to spend the night there and had sent a cable to reserve a room at the Hotel Dresen. The place had caught our fancy because in September 1938, a short time before the Munich deal, Hitler met British prime minister Neville Chamberlain there. The parking lot in front of the hotel was packed with automobiles. A discordant chorus of voices was heard coming from the open windows.

When we entered the hotel lobby, we saw a crowd of SS troopers. We went up to the registration desk and identified ourselves. After checking his big ledger, the clerk politely said that he was expecting us and gave us our guest cards. All of a sudden, a man dressed in a uniform of a senior SS officer emerged behind my back.

"Who are they?" he asked rudely.

The clerk, looking lost, handed him our passports.

"They have no business being here," the SS officer barked out. "Let 'em get the hell out!"

I turned around to face him and said calmly, "You could be a little more polite. You must have forgotten that our two countries enjoy cordial relations."

The trooper's short neck turned red. It looked as if he was ready to jump at me. But he restrained himself and hissed, "You'll soon learn what our relations are. We will show you."

He turned abruptly on his heel and stalked off.

The clerk began apologetically explaining that the SS unit had gathered for a meeting in Bad Godesberg, that the hotel was filled to overcapacity, and that he was sorry about the misunderstanding. He immediately gave us the address of a private house located close by that rented out rooms. That was where we spent the night.

Next morning, after breakfast in a nearby cafe, we set off to walk along the hilly bank of the Rhine. A few times on our way we came across young officers riding well-groomed thoroughbreds, wearing kid gloves, immaculately tailored uniforms, and military hats coquettishly perched on their heads. Their horses prancing about, they were showing off in front of each other, happy and carefree. It was obvious that, forced to do nothing for over six months, they were bursting with pent-up energies. We met more such cheerful young officers at the Hotel Petersberg where we had lunch. They were accompanied by young girls wearing dresses with the bright flower patterns that were in vogue at the time. Their colorful frocks turned the round tables at which they sat into splashy flower beds. None of them seemed to be concerned about the future. They were still captivated by the romanticism of the blitzkrieg campaigns. They seemed to have no inkling that a bloody, five-year war was only just beginning.

From the restaurant terrace we had a beautiful view of the river and of the city of Bonn, shrouded in mist, at that time just another little place with nothing special about it. We were going down a winding path in semidarkness, surrounded on all sides by serene green trees.

Suddenly, loud shouts exploded out of the solemn silence of the forest. A bunch of Wehrmacht soldiers were heading toward us, accompanied by two damsels. All of them were blind drunk. One of the soldiers was drinking out of a bottle as he walked, beer running down his chin and onto his jacket. One of the women was sticking her finger into his chest, making silly giggles. We stepped out of their way.

Seletsky looked at them as they staggered past us and said grimly, "Can it be that this bunch of drunks will someday invade our country?" We didn't know then that "someday" would come very soon.

Villa Hügel

AFTER THE MEETING HELD BY TEVOYSAN, the Krupp factory agreed to make a slight enlargement to our work area. The tarpaulin curtains were moved a little farther back. As for the delay in the deliveries of the parts for the gun turret, this issue was raised when Tevosyan visited the Krupp family mansion, the Villa Hügel.

At the appointed hour, two black Mercedes-Benz automobiles with little flags on their fenders were waiting for us at the entrance to the Hotel Essener Hof. Drivers dressed in black uniforms and wearing hats with lacquered peaks swung open the doors for us with studied politeness. Tevosyan and I climbed into the first car, Ustinov and Seletsky into the second.

After crossing the city line, we soon found ourselves on a narrow road that wound up and down the hills and eventually led us to the house of the company's top man. Servants in gilded livery stood motionless at the entrance to the palatial residence.

We went up marble steps into a spacious lobby where a thin, old man with parchmentlike skin and a hard look on his face came out to greet us. That was Gustav Krupp von Bohlen und Halbach, Germany's cannon king. In the past, he had been opposed to Hitler and, prior to the latter's appointment as Reich chancellor in 1933, had even warned German President Hindenburg not to do "such a silly thing." But later, sensing the kind of profits he could reap from Hitler's program for the rearmament of Germany, Krupp switched and sided with the Nazis, becoming one of the Führer's most ardent supporters. For his part, Hitler, who needed the backing of the industrialists, showered Gustav Krupp with favors and even awarded him the honorary title of Hero of Labor.

After greeting his Soviet guests, Krupp took Tevosyan's arm and led him away into a large, brightly lit hall. We followed them and found ourselves in a luxurious room with old tapestries covering the walls, paintings in gilded frames, tall cabinets holding porcelain and bronze. Quite a number of people were present—the Krupp company managers and some military men, including a few SS generals.

Our host introduced us, explaining to his guests that Minister Tevosyan held a high-ranking position in Moscow's Party hierarchy and, on top of that, was a metallurgist, who had trained in Germany, including at the Krupp company mills. His remarks were met with lukewarm applause.

Waiters brought in trays with glasses of champagne. Gustav Krupp raised a toast to the "cooperation between Germany and Russia," mentioning in passing that the new relations between the two countries were very profitable for his company, too. The toast sent ripples through the audience; a few chuckles could be heard. Then Tevosyan said a few words in response, concluding his speech by raising his glass to Soviet-German cooperation.

After that everyone was invited to proceed to the next room where long tables were set out with all kinds of refreshments and sweet snacks. People became noticeably more animated. It became noisy and hot. Sometime later, I noticed that the host approached Tevosyan. I hastened to join them. Gustav Krupp invited his Soviet guest to a study next door where, he said, it would be nice and quiet.

The room was small, dimly lit, with cozy burgundy leather armchairs. The flames of the fireplace flickered faintly on the oak paneling of the walls. A silver coffee set, a sugar bowl, and a milk pitcher glittered on a low table. A few cut-glass decanters also stood there.

"I hope your colleagues are pleased with the way the cooperation with our company is developing," Gustav Krupp inquired when we settled down around the little table. He was, of course, aware that we were very much unhappy with the way things were going, but had decided to start off on a positive note.

Tevosyan didn't start recounting his grievances right away either: "We value highly the opportunity to work together with a company as renowned as yours. It represents a whole concept—of efficiency, quality, modern technologies. The systems that we purchase from you are also very important to us." Tevosyan sipped his coffee and gave his interlocutor a searching look.

After a brief pause Krupp observed that this cooperation was a new thing, and as with any new undertaking, frictions and difficulties could occur.

"You are quite right," the people's commissar echoed. "Frictions and difficulties are inevitable in such an undertaking. However, there are certain agreements, there is a schedule for the deliveries that both sides must comply with."

"What do you mean?" There was a harsh note in Krupp's voice.

"The cruiser *Lutzov* that we bought from Germany will soon be towed to a Baltic port. But for the time being, it is just a hull with no armaments. We were hoping that in the most immediate future we would get at least one of its four gun turrets. Its experimental assembly began only a few weeks ago. But things are moving very slowly. Your company is violating the schedule for the delivery of the component parts."

A servant walked in. He filled our glasses with liqueur, poured coffee into our cups, and bowed out.

"Still, let us first drink to our cooperation." Krupp sounded conciliatory.

We raised our glasses and took a sip of the sour-sweet drink.

"Commitments must, of course, be kept," Krupp continued. "This is our tradition. But there are forces involved here that are beyond our control. In spite of all the efforts of our beloved Führer—and Mr. Stalin is also supportive of them—all attempts to persuade the British and the French to put an end to the war and to reach a reconciliation are being spurned. London and Paris persist in their belligerent policies. One would think that the problems of Eastern Europe have all been happily resolved. The Polish issue that worried the world has been settled, and both our countries have agreed to maintain peace and order in that part of the continent. What else could the British want? They want to destroy Germany, as well as Russia at the same time. They hate us. The situation in Europe remains tense. New armed conflicts can flare up at any moment. That is why Germany must maintain the Wehrmacht at an appropriate level. The Führer is urging us to spare no effort toward this end. And we are doing our patriotic duty."

"All this is absolutely true," Tevosyan countered, "but you must understand us, too. We keep our commitments by delivering to Germany grain, oil, strategic metals. We are helping you bypass the British blockade. But we also have obligations to our people. We cannot ignore our own national security. We bought a cruiser in exchange for our deliveries. It is an important component of our defense. I would urge you, as president of your company, to take the necessary steps to ensure that the commitments undertaken by your side are carried out in strict compliance with the established schedule."

The servant routine was replayed one more time. Maybe this was done on purpose to give Krupp time to think through his arguments.

"Very well," he said after a short pause. "I will look into it. But you have to bear in mind that at this very point in time we are finishing assembly work on a similar cruiser, the *Prinz Eugen*, intended for the German Navy. After that work has been completed, we will speed up deliveries of the gun turrets for the *Lutzov*."

Tevosyan thanked him and looked at his watch. Krupp caught his glance and said, "It's getting late and I still have things to do today."

We came out into the large hall where Ustinov and Seletsky joined us. After saying goodbye to Gustav Krupp, and after a general farewell to his guests, we went out on the porch in front of which the drivers stood motionless next to their limos.

The moon was shining brightly on the pebble-covered paths. The night was quiet and peaceful. There was no sign to indicate that soon, in early April 1940, fresh blood would be spilled.

Many years later, after the end of the war, I had a chance to visit the Isle of Capri. The Soviet people are drawn there to see Maxim Gorky's Red Villa. I also visited the abode of the "proletarian writer with a Neapolitan tan." But I was no less interested in another property, one that had a bronze plaque on a thick wall that cut off a sizable part of the southern coast of the island. The sign read VILLA KRUPP. After the war, the Krupp family donated that estate to the municipality of Capri. But for a long time, it was out of bounds to anyone except the most trusted friends of the Cannon King. Being homosexual, he had searched for a place offering total seclusion and had decided that nothing would be found more suitable than that isolated rocky slope on the Isle of Capri. The area was surrounded by a high wall that was under twenty-four-hour surveillance. On the south an impregnable rock descended vertically into the sea. Steps were cut into the rock leading to a small man-made pier. Trusted people brought young men there who interested Krupp, and nobody else ever saw them or knew their names. In those days, homosexual-

ity was like a shameful disease, and Krupp carefully protected his secret, even though it was the subject of wide rumors.

To a certain degree, Gustav Krupp kept his word. Work on the gun
assembly accelerated. By the end of 1940, both front turrets were successfully installed on the cruiser. But then everything came to a halt.
The vessel was never fully equipped even by the time Hitler's Germany attacked the Soviet Union. As said earlier, the cruiser *Lutzov*
was sunk by the Luftwaffe in the very first days of the war.

There was some truth to Gustav Krupp's explanation for the delay.
In the first months of 1940, Hitler was indeed preparing for military
operations in the West, planning to invade the British Isles after defeating France. But there were also other considerations. The Führer
was still obsessed with the idea of eliminating Bolshevism. Forced by
circumstances to agree to deliver modern armaments to the Soviet
Union, he used every possible pretext to delay their shipment. In this
context, the last thing he wanted to see was work on the cruiser *Lutzov* completed.

The Way It Was

IN OCTOBER 1923, I began attending classes in the first
grade of the school located near the Bolshevik factory, and two
nights a week I studied German and English with a visiting private
tutor. I resisted those studies, unaware of the important role the
knowledge of foreign languages would play in my life. But my parents kept my nose to the grindstone, convinced that no matter what
became of me, language skills would stand me in good stead. I had
to resign myself to it. But as a reward for good behavior my parents
promised to take me along on their trips to town.

When my mother planned to do a lot of shopping in town, my father allowed us to take the horse-drawn carriage, and Uncle Ivan
would drive us downtown and then wait for us at an agreed place. In
addition to its small private shops, Kreshchatik and the nearby streets
had numerous large stores with beautiful shop windows. The most
fashionable shops belonged to foreign concessions. The stationery

store in Fundukleyevskaya Street was popularly known as the Armand Hammer Store. The shop offered not only excellent pens, pencils, diaries, notebooks, drawing paper and instruments, but many other wonderful things: photo albums, notebooks for writing down poetry, brightly colored ribbon bookmarks that had a flower or an animal embossed on them. The place also stocked glossy paper of every color of the rainbow, funny-shaped erasers, watercolors, oils— in a word, everything. Movie fans were drawn here by high-quality photos of movie stars, mainly from Hollywood. The Austrian store, Altmann, had all kinds of woven and woolen items—pullovers, sweaters, jackets, socks, and also footwear. The pencils offered by the Czech Cokhinor rivaled those supplied by Hammer. And no lines anywhere.

At the same time, a considerable number of people were out of work. There was always a line outside the employment agency, and finding a steady job could take a long time. However, one could always eke out a living by doing odd jobs. It was, of course, painful to see homeless children. But somehow I don't remember ever seeing them crestfallen. Almost all of them sold something, offered to carry your bags for you, but would also clean out your pockets if you weren't careful. After the Civil War the city was being rebuilt. Streets were being paved, sidewalks were being repaired. Huge tanks for melting asphalt were everywhere. Homeless people warmed themselves near them in cold weather and slept next to them at night. That was a common sight. The police left them alone, and in the morning they would go their separate ways.

Quite often after shopping downtown, we would make a stop in Podol. At one time, a ghetto was in this part of town, located on the bank of the Dnieper River. Later, when settlement restrictions were effectively lifted, many Jews, especially the more prosperous ones, moved to the upper part of Kiev. They included the owners of fairly large enterprises and construction companies. Not far away from Kreshchatik, millionaire Ginsburg had built Kiev's first high-rise compound with luxury apartments. Its owner has long been gone, but his building, dominating the city skyline as before, is still called the Ginsburg house. Mering Street is also widely known. The man who gave the street its name built a few blocks of beautiful, profitable houses right before the Revolution. Located next to them is the Passage building constructed by the Russiya Insurance Company. It was packed with shops and cafes. All these buildings made downtown Kiev look beautiful.

With the establishment of the Soviet regime there was no discrimination by ethnic origin whatsoever. On the contrary, the city had Jewish schools, a theater, a synagogue. A newspaper was published in Yiddish. But Podol remained a predominantly Jewish neighborhood. All kinds of craftsmen ran their shops in the area—tailors, shoemakers, jewelers, watchmakers, metalworkers, leatherworkers, etc. They were cordial to their customers and would provide either service on the spot or offer delivery when more time was needed. At busy street corners and in front of large stores, the "crimson hats" were offering their services. These were people of different ages wearing crimson-colored hats. They knew the city like the backs of their hands and were ready to deliver letters, flowers, a cake, or a larger package to any address anywhere. In addition, a pneumatic mail system was functioning in the city. A telegram, an express letter, or a small parcel would be placed into a capsule that would then travel through special tubes under air pressure to any part of the city, and from there it would be hand-delivered to the addressee.

Podol was renowned for its bountiful fish market and the abundance of its fruits and vegetables. In the wee hours of the morning, huge flat-bottomed boats would dock at its piers. Ever since the time of the Zaporozhye Sich when the Cossacks settled in Zaporozhye in the sixteenth century, an area "beyond the cataracts" (*za porozhy*) on the lower Dnieper, these boats have been called *duby* (literally, "the oaks"). Each such boat had eight to ten rowers and a slanting Turkish sail in case of a tailwind. But for most of the way, the boat would be rowed. The cargo was loaded in tiers: the catch of the day would be splashing in vats placed on the boat bottom, fruits and vegetables would be piled all the way up to the gunwales. The fragrance of spotless, red-cheeked apples drowned out all other smells. Huge watermelons from Kherson were heaped high on the barges moored a little distance away. Closer to the building of the Contract Market were rows of booths selling all kinds of food. Plump, rosy-faced Ukrainian women stood behind wooden, hand-painted counters, wearing colorful scarves around their waists, embroidered blouses, and necklaces made out of numerous beads of coral and glass. Young girls invariably had a wreath of fresh flowers in their hair, while older women wore close-fitting caps. They would call out to the passersby, one louder than the other:

"Hey, mister, miss . . . try our bacon, our sausage, our *galushki* (meat dumplings), our *varenniki* (potato dumplings) . . ."

The homemade sausage, *ryazhenka* (broiled milk with brown crust), garlic bacon, *varenniki* with cherries in sour cream, were absolutely irresistible even to a monk.

When the "contract markets" for wholesalers were held in Podol—and they took place every fall—crowds of incredible size would gather there. Wholesale sellers and buyers came from all around the country and from abroad, just as for the Nizhni Novgorod market. Both private and state-owned companies participated. Everything was on sale from grain, meats, and fruits to manufactured products, furniture, and household items. In special places the individual buyer could purchase any item in any quantity, such as a tea set, a carpet, a bicycle, or musical instruments. Weapons were also on sale, both wholesale and retail, including hunting guns, small-caliber rifles, hunting knives, and cartridges. Even though the Civil War had ended only a short time before, no one seemed worried that arms were freely available. Hunting rifles were registered with amateur hunters' organizations, and as for small-caliber guns, no one paid any attention to them at all. My father gave me such a gun as a present. The brand name was Monte Cristo. I used to take it with me to the forest just outside the city limits to shoot birds, which I would then stuff and use to decorate my room.

In 1929, my school buddy Koka Yushkov was going with his mother to a children's resort in Anapa on the Black Sea. They invited me to join them. At first my parents were against the idea, but they eventually gave in to my repeated pleas. I remember well our train ride to the Tikhoretskaya Station from where we continued our journey on a bus. The abundance of food offered by the local people at the train stops was indeed impressive. Vendors stood all along the platform with all kinds of stuff laid out on straw mats covered with linen towels decorated with handwoven roosters: pots with over-cooked milk sealed with a brown crust, homemade sausage, bacon, hot potatoes steaming in pans, plates with famous Ukrainian *grechaniki* (buckwheat pancakes), smoked fish, a variety of berries and fruits. A traveler could always find homemade, fresh-from-the-oven bread, buy cookies and biscuits, and have tea since there was always boiling water available from special boilers right there on the platform. The police didn't drive away those self-proclaimed salesmen, as they did routinely after the beginning of collectivization.

With paper bags full of ripe, delicious cherries in our hands, Koka and I would walk up and down the platform, spitting out stones with relish.

"You know something," I told him, "I haven't been on a train since my parents and I traveled from Petrograd to Kiev during the Civil War. The cars then were crammed with people. They were everywhere: on the floor, on all the benches, and even on the luggage racks all the way up near the ceiling. When the train stopped, no one ventured out for fear of losing his seat or not being able to squeeze back in at all. And then again, there was absolutely nothing to be had at the stations."

"Well, all that is over now. That can't happen again."

I agreed with Koka, unaware that we were both wrong. In less than a year all that abundance would be gone. Crowds of dispossessed farmers, craftsmen, and artisans forbidden to work would again be hanging off trains traveling all around the hungry, devastated country, looking for a roof over their heads and food for their families.

Life in Anapa turned out to be as good as it was in Kiev. Koka's mother rented the wing of a house belonging to a Greek family. It had three rooms and a kitchen. The owners had a well-tended fruit garden and all kinds of household animals that dug and pecked under the house, which was raised up on concrete piles. They would sell us goat's milk, eggs, fruit, and vegetables. And the pears that those hardworking gardeners grew were unmatched. The city's stores offered meats of all sort and fresh fish that was supplied by Turkish fishermen who would put out to sea the night before in their felucca boats. The fish they usually caught was called *barabulka*, a small fish with red scales that was delicious when fried with potatoes and onions. I also saw shrimp for the first time there. At that time the authorities were not concerned that the fishermen who fished at night could run away into Turkey. They always came back home, bringing fresh seafood with them. That was the way it was both in the Crimea and the Caucasus.

Collectivization affected not only those who tilled the land but also those who sailed the sea. The borders were sealed not so much to prevent spies from infiltrating the country as to prevent its own citizens from fleeing the land of the Soviets. At sundown, boats would be locked up in a barbed-wire enclosure. Nets were requisitioned. The Turkish fishermen were left with nothing to do, and soon they, just like the Greeks, Tartars, and many other people, were resettled God knows where. Fresh fish disappeared with them. It hasn't returned to this day. (Today people wonder why fresh fish is nowhere to be found in Leningrad (St. Petersburg) while just next door, in the

port of Helsinki, seafood is all over the place.) Fruit gardens with-
ered away, private plots of land grew barren, trades died out. Anapa
turned into a wasteland.

After a morning at a beautiful sandy beach, Koka, his mother, and
I would go for lunch at the restaurant at the resort community center. It was truly a solemn occasion. The dining area was impressive in
size, as was the open-air veranda with tables under colorful umbrellas. Waiters in off-white lustring suits, piqué vests, and with a towel
thrown over one arm preserved a pre-Revolutionary look. Even
though many people came down for the season, there was no shortage of tables. The menu offered a wide selection and the service was
impeccable. To the right of the entrance was a bar, and we would cast
envious glances at the young men standing there offering drinks to
the stylishly dressed young women.

In the evening there would be a movie or dancing at the community center. Koka and I would also hang out there, admiring graceful
dancers and feeling terribly lonely. Pretty soon, however, we met two
sisters on the beach. One of them, a blonde named Nina, was our
age; the other, Vera, was about sixteen. For some reason, Vera
seemed to prefer me while Koka liked Nina. From a distance, our two
couples must have looked quite funny: Koka was tall for his age and,
because of this, somewhat awkward, while Nina was miniature and
nimble. My girl was not only three years older than I was but also
taller. No matter how much I tried, I could only reach up to her
shoulder. As it turned out, Vera was quite a mature girl and had already had some experience in dealing with boys. She was an excellent swimmer and looked gorgeous in her black swimming suit that
fit her slim body like a glove. Koka and Nina would splash around in
shallow water, while Vera and I would swim far out, feeling close in
the middle of the sea. From time to time, dolphins would play near
us. They were quite tame and would jump out of the water, their
smooth skin shimmering in the sun.

After basking on the hot sand, Vera and I would take a walk along
the shallows stretching for a couple of kilometers toward Bold Mountain. The entire beach was open to the public. There were no hospital solariums. People could lie down anywhere they pleased.

I would recount to Vera the stories told me by my father, who, after
graduating from the Maritime School of Engineers, sailed on a
cruise around Europe, from St. Petersburg to Odessa. I described in
colorful detail Gibraltar and Istanbul's Golden Horn, its Blue

Mosque, and the Byzantine Santa Sophia. Many years later, whenever I visited Istanbul and the Yugoslav isles in the Adriatic Sea, which looked so much like scenes from novels by Russian novelist Aleksandr Green which Vera and I had read, I would recall the childhood dreams we dreamed that blissful summer of 1929 in Anapa.

That abundance and that way of life lasted right up to the beginning of collectivization. On a hot summer day in any village, at least in the Ukraine, you could knock on the door of any house, and the people there would bring you out a jar of cold milk from the cellar, a piece of home-baked brown bread, as well as a slice of bacon or a wedge of comb honey. People gave from the heart and would not take any money. Two years later, forced collectivization in this land of plenty brought about a terrible famine that carried away millions of lives.

Some of our economists, even those who criticized the draconian measures of collectivization, argue that in the late 1920s our country, with its predominantly privately owned farms, was unable to produce enough grain for export to earn the hard currency needed to meet the nation's industrialization targets. Therefore, they concluded, agricultural production had to be nationalized one way or the other. They may have been right, but it was not just a matter of grain. Private farms supplied the country with meat, milk, fruits, and vegetables. Private businessmen worked in the service sector, produced food, worked as artisans, tailors, watchmakers, shoemakers, and bakers. But I am not going to engage in a theoretical argument here. I just wanted to show the way it was, how people were thinking, and what happened as a result of the sweeping collectivization, for example in Kiev, where I saw it all with my own eyes. The entire infrastructure was destroyed. The service sector was disrupted. Artisans, small shop owners, shoemakers, tailors, watchmakers—all were gone. The Contract Market was closed down. Shops in Podol were demolished. The rosy-cheeked girls who treated passersby to their homemade *varenniki* were whirled away to the four corners of the land. The flat-bottomed boats were confiscated—to rot away on the deserted banks of the Dnieper River. The concessionaires had to clear out. There was nothing left in the city. It was as if a hurricane had swept through it.

And another thought keeps gnawing at my mind. Perestroika has been under way in our country for a number of years, and life in this vast and fertile land, so rich in talent and natural resources, is only getting worse. How is it that in the early 1920s, after three years of the bloodbath of the First World War, four years of the fratricidal Civil War, and the ruthless requisitions of War Communism, it took less than two years not only to feed the people, something we've been dreaming of ever since, but to restore a fairly comfortable way of life and to ensure an abundance never seen again?

In the 1920s, we didn't have the openness we enjoy today. The code of conduct was fairly rigid. The controls were firmly in the hands of the central authorities. But somehow most people didn't seem to care. After the long years of the Civil War, with all its hardship and hunger, people wanted to enjoy a life of quiet and, more importantly, of plenty. The New Economic Policy gave them all of that. They had it almost overnight, and people calmed down and got to work. I think it all happened so quickly because the right people were still around. The children of farmers, worn out by the many years of slaughter, refused to stay in the trenches of the World War and came out and fraternized with the enemy, thereby deserting the front. And when, after the Revolution, the Bolsheviks promised them land, they were prepared to suffer through four more years of hardships and horrors in the Civil War, which ensured victory for the Soviet regime. When the NEP was introduced and the farmers got a chance to work freely on their land, they fed the entire country with one harvest. The artisans were also waiting to launch into unrestrained production, just as the people in the service sector were waiting for their opportunities. It was also important that the hardships the people had endured had not warped their minds. Vast masses of people everywhere were hungry for work that would bring satisfaction and prosperity. And the chervonets, the new Soviet ruble, introduced at the right moment with an abundant supply of food and goods, clearly demonstrated that it made sense to work hard and well.

Of course, at that time there was also resistance from the Party apparatchiks. We know that Lenin led a vigorous campaign against them. He won because his authority could not be questioned—and because the apparatchiks had not yet been able to take command. The NEP lasted almost eight years. The forcible and ruthless collectivization campaign that deprived the farmers of the land they had dreamed about for centuries inflicted a terrible wound on the country that has never ceased bleeding to this day.

Why was it not possible to replicate the experience of the early 1920s in today's context? At first, many people believed that the introduction of some elements of the NEP today would quickly improve the situation. Many bold ideas have been advanced since April 1985, and many decisions have been taken, including those at the top level—all to no avail.

In addition to the other generally recognized obstacles to perestroika, two main obstacles stand in its way: the structures of the command-and-administer system that have remained intact at various levels and the mentality of many people in the country deformed by Stalin's regime. Sweeping prohibitions, egalitarian psychology, negative attitudes to those who want to work and make good money, primitive requirements as far as the quality of life is concerned, inertia and indifference—all these factors are exacerbated still further by unrelenting shortages and by the declining purchasing power of the ruble.

How can we expect changes for the better when the farmer has no assurance that his children, grandchildren, and their children will inherit his land to keep and cultivate? When the director of a collective farm can use some pretext to take away a private farm? When bureaucrats can introduce new and confiscatory taxes at any moment? When honest cooperative workers are totally dependent on the arbitrary decisions of the authorities? When the individual entrepreneur, like the farmer, is unable to hire the temporary help he needs? When there are no middlemen who are prepared to take the products from the manufacturers and deliver them to where people need and want them?

All these questions should have been addressed in the very first months of perestroika. But the authorities began taking concrete measures only when perestroika was already into its sixth year, when the standards of living were by then in free fall.

We can only hope and pray that our long-suffering people do not run out of patience and do not rise up in a new and frightening Russian Revolution.

Business in Rotterdam

In EARLY APRIL 1940, Tevosyan, whom I was accompanying, visited a German submarine base in Kiel. I was surprised that the Germans seemed to have no secrets from the Soviet people's commissar. He could see whatever he wanted to see. This game of openness was part of Hitler's disinformation campaign, part of his efforts to convince Stalin that Germany had no intention of going to war with the Soviet Union in any foreseeable future. There is no question that Tevosyan's report on his tour of the German military facilities, filed through the USSR embassy in Berlin, had an influence on Stalin's assessment of Hitler's plans.

Moscow was pleased with the mission to Germany of the people's commissar for the shipbuilding industry. But before he was allowed to return home, Tevosyan got orders to visit Rotterdam.

At that time the USSR did not have diplomatic relations with the Netherlands. In The Hague, there was only the Eksportkhleb, the Soviet grain exporting agency, and a regional office of Morflot, the Soviet maritime shipping company. But we had no problem obtaining our visas at the Dutch embassy in Berlin, and on the evening of April 6, 1940, Tevosyan and I left Berlin by express train for The Hague.

We were traveling first class in a sleeping car that had spacious individual compartments each fitted out with a washbasin. In addition to a bed and a table, there was room for a chair and a small bar stocked with drinks. Tevosyan, like all of Stalin's other bureaucrats, had developed the habit of working at night and going to bed only in the morning. After we had dinner in the restaurant car he invited me to join him in his compartment, and we spent the next couple of hours talking about all kinds of things.

The people's commissar was of the view that the "phony war" with nothing happening at the front couldn't last much longer. Sooner or later, someone's nerves would snap and then shots would be fired. The question was who would fire the first shot and what would happen next. The Maginot Line and the Siegfried Line stood in a static face-off. Many years had been needed to construct and fortify these giant defenses. We knew from the Finnish war how difficult it had been to penetrate the Mannerheim Line, and it stood no comparison to the Maginot Line. A war in the West could last for many years with each side entrenched in its positions. The important thing was for our country to stay out of it for as long as possible. Let the capitalists fight it out among themselves.

"Of course," the people's commissar went on to say, "the Germans can violate the neutrality of Holland and Belgium and bypass the Maginot Line. But I don't think they will do that. If they do not respect the neutrality of small countries, this would create total chaos. I don't think Hitler will do anything like that."

Being a young man with little experience, I found that reasoning quite sound. It clarified for me the position of the Soviet government and, of course, of Stalin himself. I saw clearly now why Soviet materials continued to be shipped into Germany on a regular basis even though the Germans didn't comply with their delivery schedules. The idea was to gain time, to appease Hitler, and at the same to demonstrate to him that it made no sense for Germany to go to war with the Soviet Union since this would effectively cut it off from a rich source of supplies.

I found the night I spent with one of Stalin's people's commissars, particularly one close to the master himself, interesting also because it gave me an opportunity to catch a glimpse of the man behind the mask that party officials usually wore. They all had the same look— severe, unshakable in their resolve, and indifferent to trivial earthly matters—as if service to the Party, their work, and nothing else were all that mattered.

Listening to Tevosyan's intimate account of how he, home on a few hours' break before the beginning of his night vigil, played with his little son, seeing his eyes light up when he spoke about the mountain village in Armenia where he spent his childhood, I saw clearly that he was no stranger to simple human joys.

But he allowed himself to bare his heart like that very rarely. His usual appearance was that of a person totally committed to the goals set by the Party's Central Committee and by Comrade Stalin. All such "iron" people's commissars were slaves to these ideas both by choice and by constraint. In the name of such ideas they could be as hard as rock, ruthless, and even inhuman. Those who were ready to carry out the orders from above deserved praise and rewards. Those who would not or could not do so were doomed to be brushed aside.

They were just as uncompromising about their responsibilities. They worked without sleep, without rest, and only occasionally—because they were doing their duty as they saw it—would they allow themselves the luxury of spending some time with their families. In this sense, they thought they deserved the privileges and perks established by Stalin's code in line with the existing pecking order. If they didn't do their job well or disobeyed their master, they would have to leave and humbly accept the fact that they had been removed.

For his part, the master knew how to take good care of those who served him faithfully. He showered medals, decorations, and titles of heroes upon the workers and farmers who set carefully orchestrated records. He made them deputies and they docilely raised their hands in the Supreme Soviet, flattered to have the honor to be involved in "running the country," which, according to Lenin's formula, was something any cook was capable of doing. Talented designers of military equipment and academicians were presented with villas and large plots of land. Writers and poets who sang the praises of the great Stalin's era were allowed to travel abroad. Composers and performers who wrote or sang the leader's favorite songs received as gifts automobiles, which were way out of reach for the ordinary citizens. It was at that time that special medical centers, sanatoriums, and resorts for the elite appeared. Those who were at the top and enjoying all those luxuries had not the faintest thought for the millions of prisoners, including their former friends and colleagues, who were digging the frozen earth in Vorkuta, Kolyma, Magadan, and other Siberian sites for gold, diamonds, and other treasures that enriched the State Collection, from which the Leader of the Peoples handed out generous gifts to his loyal subjects.

The psychological basis for the command-and-administer system that Stalin had created over the years of his reign was a combination of fawning loyalty, blind enthusiasm—and fear. When the master was no more, when fear disappeared and enthusiasm fizzled out, the system began to backfire and the country ended up on the edge of a precipice. I believe that one of the main reasons for the failures of perestroika is that Stalin's system continues to operate, particularly in remote areas. Considering the fact that the people have totally lost their enthusiasm for the master's way—and have freed themselves from fear—the inertia of the system itself has become the primary obstacle to progress.

We arrived in The Hague early in the morning and were met on the platform by Eksportkhleb's director, Mr. Lvov, a stocky gray-haired man well advanced in years, and by the Morflot representative, my old buddy from my navy years, Kostya Yezhov. I hadn't known he was in The Hague and was glad to see him. Of course, we wanted to talk about so many things, but the people's commissar decided to go to Lvov's office right away to get information about the situation in the country and to discuss the arrangements for the next day's trip to Rotterdam.

Kostya and I were able to meet only late that night. The coffee shop we went to was crowded, but we were able to find a table.

"All places are packed here," Kostya explained. "People argue late into the night. No one believes that The Netherlands will be able to preserve its neutrality. But for the time being, the intelligence agencies of all countries are putting its neutral status to good use. I'm sure there are a fair number of German, British, French, and other secret agents here. The Germans are particularly active. It looks like they are getting ready for something."

Kostya deluged me with questions about the situation in Moscow, asking whether things had eased up a little after the end of the Finnish War.

"The people who have been coming to Berlin recently are saying that things are better," I replied.

"Good," Kostya sighed. "I hope my family in Leningrad are also having a better time."

Upon reaching Rotterdam, Tevosyan and I had stopped by the hotel for only a few minutes and had then headed straight for the shipyard since the company's management was already expecting us. We were led into a room tastefully furnished for business—wooden paneling polished with fragrant wax, comfortable leather chairs and sofas, low tables. The room was permeated with the aroma of expensive cigars and strong coffee. Cigarettes and cigars, as well as everything needed to serve coffee, were laid out on the tables.

Tevosyan asked how the manufacture of the refrigerator ships was coming along. He was not quite satisfied with the response provided.

"We would like to get the vessels as soon as possible," he said. "The current situation is complex. Anything can happen. The earlier the work is completed the better. We are even prepared to pay a premium for the delivery of the refrigerator vessels ahead of schedule."

"This is a very attractive proposal," the president of the company observed, lighting up a cigar. "We will think it over. But precisely because of the tense international situation, we are getting many more orders, and we must fulfill all of them on time. That is why I can't tell you anything about an early delivery of your vessels without first studying the question. As for your concern, well, Holland is a neutral country. I don't think that in our age anyone will dare violate the principle of neutrality. We have received repeated assurances from the warring parties in this regard, including from Germany. And generally speaking, there have been no hostilities anywhere for such a long time that we are beginning to think that maybe this is how this unwanted war is going to end."

Tevosyan expressed his doubts about an early end to the war. He was rather inclined to think that it would spread, given the serious differences and vital interests involved.

After the meeting, we went to the construction site. One of our refrigerator ships was standing on the ways, the other had only recently been lowered into the water. Tevosyan spoke with the workers and foremen and thanked them for the good, high-quality work. Indeed, the workmanship was excellent. I had had some shipbuilding experience at the Kiev shipyard and could appreciate the mastery of the Dutch shipbuilders.

The company management suggested that the next day we could make a boat trip to Amsterdam and Saandam, where we hoped to see the little house of Peter the Great.

After the meeting at the shipyard, we made a brief tour of the city. We sailed on the canals in a motorboat. I was struck by the number of people on bicycles. Biking appeared to be the principal means of city transportation. Flocks of girls dashed down a path along the canal specifically reserved for bikers. Catching my roving eyes, Tevosyan wrinkled his nose in disdain. "Don't be distracted by that silly stuff," he said.

In the evening, there was an official dinner where brief statements were made. Finally we returned to the hotel, all excited about the next day's trip. We agreed to have breakfast in Tevosyan's room.

I woke up in the morning, took a shower, and turned the radio on as I began shaving. What I heard was so unexpected that I cut myself. The newscaster was saying that that night German troops had landed in Norway and Denmark. The "phony war" was indeed over! I quickly finished my ablutions and ran over to Tevosyan's room. He was already sitting at the table. For breakfast, he was not served slices of ham, but a whole ham and a whole cheese. He was helping himself, cutting slices off one and then the other. A basket of fruit, thermos jugs with coffee and tea, and a milk pitcher were placed on the table.

"You are late," the people's commissar grumbled good-humoredly.

"Don't you know what happened?"

"I don't think they have earthquakes here, do they?"

"It's worse than that! The Germans have invaded Norway and Denmark!"

The people's commissar's carefree mood was gone in a second. He got up and began marching up and down the room.

"This should have been expected. I told them yesterday it was going to start soon! And they kept talking about neutrality. Naive people!" Tevosyan spoke, oblivious of the fact that only recently he himself had been telling me that the Germans would respect the principle of neutrality.

"What are we going to do now?" I asked.

"The trip is, of course, out of the question. We must return to Berlin at once."

"Why?"

"You are a strange man indeed! It is almost certain now that the British will come here to Holland. And they will ask, `What is a Soviet people's commissar doing here?' I wouldn't like to meet them here."

Tevosyan became silent, still continuing to pace the room. He walked up to the window and moved the blind aside. In the street everything was quiet.

"This is a deceptive quiet," he said pensively, and after a pause continued in an energetic voice, "Get a car right away and we will take the shortest route to the German border, without going into The Hague. Leave a message with the clerk saying that I have been urgently summoned back to Moscow."

I gulped down my coffee and dashed off to carry out the people's commissar's order. It was not difficult to hire a car. We threw our luggage into the trunk and set off on the road. The bridges and the lock gates were protected by Dutch soldiers. Tanks were parked at some street crossings. The highway was empty. There was no panic anywhere.

By nightfall we had reached a train station on the border, paid the driver, and crossed into Germany. We spent a long time waiting for a train at that miniature, squalid train station. But the next morning we were in Berlin. And the next day Tevosyan left for Moscow.

At that time, I had no idea that the few days I had spent with the people's commissar would make a basic change in my future life.

"Fun Corner"

IN THE SPRING OF 1926, my father got a new job. As an engineer specializing in shipbuilding, he was assigned to work on designing a new shipyard on the Dnieper that was being built using technology developed at the machine-building plant Leninskaya Kuznitsa, where he was made chief engineer. We had to leave the beautiful director's estate of the Bolshevik factory and move to the city center.

With a heavy heart I made a final tour of my realm in the thickets of the garden. I climbed up the spreading branches of the oak where my friends and I had built a hut. I bade farewell to the grotto where the lilies of the valley had only recently shed their petals. I did not forget to run over to the narrow-gauge locomotive that stood motionless outside the estate fence. It had been abandoned there since the Civil War and was a source of much joy to us, the kids in the neighborhood, adding reality to our games of the Red Army armored train that we rode, beating off the assaults of the White Army battalions. I didn't suspect that all that fairy-tale world I was leaving was already doomed.

Soon after that, work to reconstruct the Bolshevik factory got under way. A new boiler shop was to be built on the site of the director's estate. The trees were uprooted and the old house was leveled to the ground. When in the fall of 1930, after completing a seven-year school program, I came to work as an electrician at the Bolshevik factory, not a trace was left of my dear garden. "Why couldn't they have expanded the factory in another direction?" I thought to myself. A field stretched all the way to the horizon in the opposite direction. But in those years who would think that a beautiful fruit garden could still be useful to people, that the huge nut trees that someone must have put in a lot of effort into growing could continue to give nuts? To the sound of the hymn of the workers of the world, "The Internationale," people were enthusiastically "tearing down to the ground" all that was old so that then they could build "our own, new world."

My father was able to join a co-op that had just constructed a two-story, four-family apartment house in Lipki, formerly an aristocratic neighborhood in Kiev. The co-op, which had the somewhat frivolous

Ukrainian name of Vesely Kut, "Fun Corner," was built in a nice spot at the corner of Levashovskaya and Institutskaya streets, one subsequently renamed after a leader of the German Communist party Karl Liebknecht and the other changed into October 25 Street, to commemorate October Revolution Day. The sponsors of the co-op didn't know then that life for the people who moved into the new house would be no fun, as they had hoped it would be when they put the project together.

We got an apartment on the first floor. It had three separate rooms, plus a kitchen with a wood-burning stove and a bathroom with a water heater. Every room also had a tile stove in one corner since central heating was rare in those days. Each family had a storage space in the basement where they kept firewood and coal. There was also a cellar in the basement where barrels with marinated apples, sour cabbage, and pickles were kept during the winter. My mother made preserves the very first fall we moved there. For some reason I always woke up at the crack of dawn, and it was part of my household chores to fetch firewood and coal from the cellar, to light up the tile stoves, and when my parents woke up, light the fire in the kitchen stove and in the water heater in the bathroom. Logs for the whole winter were sawed and chopped by the monks from the Laura Monastery located close to our house. They also gave my father aromatic herbs (*zubrovka*), which he put into vodka to make a *nastoyka*. The Laura bakers baked huge square loaves of fragrant black bread with an embossed cross on top. We bought it regularly at the monastery bakery.

The new place had its own attractions. The yard wasn't large but was big enough for soccer. At the corner across the street from our house was a park that belonged to the trade union of the Soviet sales workers. It had an open-air theater, and when no show was staged, a movie would be playing. Before the Revolution, the residence of Kiev's governor-general had been located there. So that the carriages that rumbled along the cobblestones wouldn't disturb the inhabitants of the house, the entire street in front of it was asphalted, and that must have been the only place in the whole town that had had an asphalt surface. The house burned down during the Civil War, but the asphalt remained and kids rode their bicycles there. A short while after we moved in, my father gave me a bicycle as a present. After repeatedly scratching my knees and elbows bloody, I got the hang of it and pretty soon became quite a pro, dashing about with my hands off the handlebars, making other boys green with envy and sending the girls into raptures. One girl, the black-haired Tamara, the daughter of our neighbor Popondupolo the Greek, who owned a small metalworks shop, put a spell on me. The Greek had to be doing pretty well with his shop. Tamara wore high-priced, fashionable clothes, and a fragrance of expensive perfume trailed behind her. Her father owned a horse and carriage. His beautiful wife would ride at his side dressed up in lace and a veil coming down from the wide brim of her hat as Popondupolo rode up and down Kreshchatik in the evening showing off to the crowd. Slouching carelessly in his seat and puffing away at an aromatic cigar, he was viewed with mixed feelings by the passersby. Some looked at him with awe and envy; others leered at him angrily, as if warning him that one of these days they would take care of this bloodsucking capitalist.

Our other neighbor was Professor Zadorozhny, an expert on Ukrainian history and literature. He sprouted a mustache à la Taras Shevchenko, a Ukrainian classic of the last century, wore embroidered blouses and the traditional Ukrainian wide pants, the *sharovary*, which he tucked into his boots with their tops pleated like accordion bellows. Zadorozhny and my father became friends. He would often stop by at our place and, after a few *zubrovkas*, would give a beautiful rendition of Ukrainian folk songs accompanying himself on the bandore. He awoke my love for the folklore, history, and legends of the Ukraine, which in fact had become my second homeland.

The fourth dweller in our house was the chairman of the co-op, Naum Solomonovich Rothstein. There were no passports in the Soviet Union at that time, and no one suspected that they would soon be introduced, particularly since the older generation remembered well the humiliating czarist passport system.

When we moved in into our apartment, Naum Solomonovich just entered us in the house ledger and that completed the registration procedure. He was a nice old man, always willing to give a piece of advice on different subjects, always ready to help in one way or another. There is no question that largely because he was such a caring and outgoing person, Vesely Kut was a friendly place where people were prepared to help each other and wished each other well. The co-op had plans to build a few more apartment houses, and Rothstein often came to see us to seek my father's advice about the advantages and disadvantages of a particular project.

I liked my new neighborhood for its beautiful parks that stretched along the steep banks of the Dnieper: the Mariinsky, the Czar and Merchant Gardens, the green grove of Vladimir Hill crowned with a bronze figure of Prince Vladimir, the Baptist of Russia, holding a huge cross in his hands. Also located there was a big round building with a tall glass dome on top that housed a panoramic representation of Golgotha. The realistic pictures from the life and crucifixion of Jesus Christ, created by the great masters of an earlier century, left a profound mark on my impressionable young mind. The visions I had from reading the New Testament were depicted there in flesh and blood, as it were, inspiring awe and humility. In the early 1930s, the Golgotha building was torn down and the panoramic canvas disappeared. But maybe it hasn't been destroyed. Maybe one day it will turn up again, and our contemporaries will be able to enjoy that work of art that portrayed the Bible story with such forceful realism.

Lutheran Street

WITH THE FALL APPROACHING, it was time to start thinking about sending me to a new school. My parents wanted me to continue my foreign-language studies. In that area of Kiev there were communities where people of German origin had lived for many years. The street around which the Germans had settled was called Lutheran Street (it was later changed to Engels Street). In a seven-year German school there, all subjects were taught in German, and Russian and Ukrainian were treated as if they were foreign languages. Next to the school, there was a Lutheran church where an old, respectable-looking German, Herr Ulpe, played the organ. He agreed to be my private tutor. Even though I spoke German quite fluently, my knowledge was not enough for the third grade of a specialized language school. For two months before classes began and also during the first term, I regularly visited the Ulpes, each time immersing myself in the peculiar atmosphere of a patriarchal German family. I was greatly impressed by what I saw there. Their large apartment was trim and tidy; the kitchen utensils were sparkling clean; the windows had lace blinds; the oak panels in the master's study were polished with aromatic wax. A sense of contentment and prosperity was everywhere. It turned out that Herr Ulpe was not a professional organist. He had only recently retired, and for a long time before that, starting even before the Revolution, he had taught German history and literature in the German gymnasium that was located near our vocational school. He was strict with me, but was also able to get me interested in learning. He had a large collection of folded posters with scenes from German city life depicting people in various walks of life: artisans, farmers, students, salesmen, etc. Those posters served as visual aids in the study of the language and in building a vocabulary.

My memory has preserved especially well the snapshots of the Rhine with its grape arbors, old castles, picturesque river crossings, and churches with high steeples. I gratefully recall Professor Ulpe's posters, which allowed me to get a feeling for the atmosphere of Germany long before I was able to roam the banks of the Rhine in person.

Besides the language, my tutor, on his own initiative, taught me a number of other sophisticated skills: chasing on copper, making relief maps, and wood carving. Herr Ulpe, always solemnly dressed in a long jacket and snow-white shirt with a stiff starched collar and wearing a wide tie with a golden pin, enjoyed smoking cigars. I used the empty cigar boxes to hone my wood-carving skills. Thin copper plates upon which I embossed different designs with special heated irons, as well as thick cardboard and white papier-mâché pulp for relief maps, were on sale at the Armand Hammer Store in Fundukleyevskaya Street. When the relief was ready, I painted the map surface in oils: white mountaintops, green slopes, yellow deserts. I enjoyed these activities and developed a liking for drawing.

Soon after we moved to Lipki, my parents met a nice old man who became one of their friends. He also liked Father's *zubrovka.* But before he would have one drink too many, every time he came to visit he would volunteer to give me a drawing lesson. Uncle Savely, as everyone called him, was a graduate of the Imperial Academy of Fine Arts in St. Petersburg and was a talented portrait painter who showed much promise. But gradually he developed a drinking habit and lived in poverty in a small leaning log house situated between Mariinsky and the Czar Hills. Before the Revolution, a large floricultural farm and a famous French restaurant, Château des Fleurs, had been there. At the time I am writing about, the restaurant was no more, but the flower farm was still in business, spreading the fragrance of roses and carnations in the neighborhood. Uncle Savely's hut nestled at its southern edge. Uncle Savely was a jack-of-all-trades. Not only did he still have what it takes to paint a great portrait or a country scene, he could also make a reflector photo camera, bring an old watch back to life, or give the voice back to an old master's violin. Uncle Savely taught me the basics of drawing, which was to become my lifelong hobby.

Early in 1930, Uncle Savely suddenly vanished. When he came to see us for the last time, we already knew that the flower farm was closing down, that all the nearby buildings, including Uncle Savely's little house, would be demolished, and that in their place a stadium with a soccer field, volleyball grounds, tennis courts, and other sports facilities would be erected. There were also plans to build a large office building with a restaurant.

That news was the last straw for Uncle Savely. He drank much more than usual that evening, furiously cursed those who had come up with the idea of building the stadium, and finally left, sad and lost. That was the last we ever saw of him.

And the stadium was completed. Its owner turned out to be the Dynamo Sports Club, which represented the athletic organization for the State Security Police. The sports complex was named after the people's commissar for the internal affairs of the Ukraine, Balitsky, who was the brains behind the project to build a sports arena in place of the flower farm. Soon after that, Balitsky was arrested, together with some other Ukrainian leaders, and shot on charges of "espionage and dangerous nationalism."

Could it be that heaven had heard Uncle Savely's curses?

Through Professor Ulpe's and my own efforts I was accepted into the third grade of the German school. It had a full seven-year curriculum of studies, just like other Soviet vocational schools of the time, which provided the country's youth with primary education. But the atmosphere there was different from that in the school located near the Bolshevik factory. Almost half of the kids in my new school were from German families. Others were Ukrainians, Russians, Jews, or Poles. My new school also presented a motley picture in terms of the social origin of its student body. It comprised the children of workers, of salaried employees, scholars, artisans, and private entrepreneurs. We, the third-graders, looked down upon the first- and second-graders and wouldn't have anything to do with them. On the other hand, we envied the fourth-year students and tried to imitate them in every way we could.

CHAPTER THREE

Return to Rotterdam

EVENTS EVOLVED RAPIDLY. On May 10, 1940, without any warning, German armies invaded Holland and Belgium. Hitler justified his new aggression by the need "to enhance the neutrality" of the two states. Of course, nobody believed him. But the blitzkrieg, which had worked so successfully in Poland, worked this time, too. It took the Wehrmacht only a few days to occupy Holland. Belgium's lot was no different. And then the battle for France began.

In mid-May, I was called to Berlin. The USSR deputy trade representative in Germany, Kormilitsyn, was going to Rotterdam to find out what had happened to our refrigerator ships, and since I had already been there, I was to accompany him.

The railway link between Berlin and The Hague was quickly restored, and on the train with its excellent restaurant, the only reminder of the war was a large number of men in uniform. A few railway bridges on Dutch territory had been damaged. As the train approached them, it would slow down to a crawl and move over tracks propped up by the temporary supports erected by the Wehrmacht's engineers, groping its way, as it were.

In The Hague there were no visible signs of hostilities. In some places German guards were posted, but in general law and order was maintained by the Dutch police.

After a brief stop at Eksportkhleb, where Kormilitsyn was briefed by Lvov, still in shock after Germany's lightning invasion of the country, we set off for Rotterdam by car. Only on the highway did we see for the first time clear evidence of the foreign occupation. German armored vehicles and soldiers carrying automatic weapons and wearing helmets could be seen at road crossings, bridges, and river locks. Khaki-painted German staff cars were dashing back and forth. A few times we were stopped by military patrols for a documents check.

As we approached the city, we could see a dark cloud hanging over it. The smell of overroasted coffee and something else burning floated in the air. It was coming from the bombed-out areas of Rotterdam and the port warehouses where colonial goods were stored.

At the shipyard we were met by the company representatives whom I had met on my previous visit. When we were inside that same cozy office in the administration building, they told Kormilitsyn the bad news: the ship that was on the building ways had burned up during a bombing raid; but the good news was that the vessel that was in the water had survived the attack. We went to inspect it. Walking past what used to be the building ways, we saw a pile of scrap metal, bent and twisted by fire. On the surviving ship, the construction of the deck superstructures and finishing work on the ship's hull were in their final stage. The characteristic smell of red lead, lubricating oils, and paint vividly reminded me of the distant, peaceful summer of 1937 when I took part in the sea trials of tugboats in the Kiev shipyard.

The company's management promised to finish the work at a stepped-up pace, and indeed the ship was ready by the fall and sailed to Leningrad.

After taking care of our business in Rotterdam, we drove to Brussels. Because of the hostilities there was no communication between Moscow and its embassy and trade mission in Belgium, and Kormilitsyn was instructed to clarify the situation on the ground. The Dutch countryside looked quite peaceful. The only reminder of the occupation was the German officers next to the Dutch and Belgian guards at the border checkpoint. We had no visas, only some papers we had received from the German Ministry of Foreign Affairs before we had left Berlin. That was all we needed to cross the border. But as we moved deeper into the Belgian territory, we felt the closeness of the war. A few places there must have seen some pretty heavy fighting. Damaged and burned-out military equipment lay on both sides of the highway. Every now and again we came across groups of people lugging their pathetic belongings on bicycles, prams, or carts.

The luckier ones had carriages, which were loaded up with bags, bundles, and some pieces of furniture. The refugees of World War II were starting their long and arduous journey.

We were met at the embassy in Brussels by Ambassador Rubinin, a polished diplomat of the Chicherin school who had miraculously survived the purge of the People's Commissariat for Foreign Affairs in the late 1930s. He informed us that neither the embassy nor the trade mission was damaged, that all staff were safe and sound, and that, generally speaking, so far there had been no major problems.

Rubinin offered us sandwiches with caviar and cheese, coffee with biscuits, and then suggested we take a tour of the city.

I was struck by the atmosphere in Brussels. Everything looked as if there were no war at all. Belgian policemen directed the traffic, elegantly dressed people filled the festive-looking boulevards, and fashionable ladies wearing furs and dignified gentlemen sat under brightly colored umbrellas at marble tables placed on the sidewalks, engaged in easy conversation. The fragrance of coffee, expensive cigars, and delicate perfume wafted through the air. Gorgeous stores abundantly stocked with all kinds of stuff, pyramids of fruits and vegetables, mouthwatering windows of pastry shops. Only the small groups of German officers that we came across every now and again, and the complete absence of people in Belgian military uniform, reminded us that the country was under German occupation.

Then, of course, it all changed. The organized plunder of the territories seized in the West began, even though it was not as sweeping as in the East. But in the first days of the occupation, life in Brussels was still normal.

At the end of the day, Rubinin invited us to a nightclub, which was also crowded. Couples were dancing on a large lit-glass circle stage. Then a bosomy beauty came on that same stage and did a striptease. She was followed by a magician. Then people began dancing again. As was customary in places like that, only champagne and wine were served. There were no snacks, except maybe peanuts. The main box was taken up by a group of German officers with a monocled general among them. With the arrogance of conquerors they were watching the conquered amuse themselves.

In the morning, after spending the night at the trade mission, we set off for Waterloo to see the monument to the historic battle that marked an end to Napoleon's era. The memorial had not been affected by the war that had raged through that area, but the nearby small town of Namur was completely reduced to rubble—the ruins were still smoldering, and the remnants of the walls stared at us gravely through the empty panes of the windows. The air was filled with the sickly smell of decomposing bodies buried under the debris. That entire zone of death was surrounded by German soldiers, but they let us through when we showed them the German Foreign Ministry papers.

The battle in France was drawing to a close. Every day the German High Command reported in its bulletins that more towns had fallen. The Maginot Line didn't fulfill the role it was designed for, to be an impregnable rampart, and was bypassed by the Germans.

I was going back to Berlin with a heavy heart. How could this be happening? The proud and haughty victors of World War I were beating a disorderly retreat, even running in panic under the onslaught of their once defeated enemy. It was the retribution for the unfair diktat of Versailles. Throngs of refugees in Belgium and France, exhausted, hungry, dressed in rags; and the spruce, disciplined, and confident soldiers and officers of the Wehrmacht. What a striking contrast! Was there no force capable of stopping that wave that had already swept vast territories of the European continent? And where would it head next?

To the roll of drums and the shouts of "*Sieg Heil!*" Radio Berlin is broadcasting to the world the news of Germany's glorious victories. Paris has fallen. The newsreel is showing the Arc de Triomphe with the German troops parading under it. Hitler is posing for a picture in front of Napoleon's tomb. The British expeditionary force is surrounded at Dunkirk. Abandoning their weapons and ammunition, the soldiers cross the English Channel during a respite that the Führer generously grants them. France capitulates. The next newsreel shows Hitler in the Forest of Compiègne dancing with joy near the historic railway car in which, on November 11, 1918, the capitulation of the kaiser's Germany was accepted by Marshal Foch. This time, on June 21, 1940, it is Hitler's Germany that is forcing stringent terms of capitulation upon France.

Back in Berlin, the troops returning from the campaign in the West are marching on parade. Hitler himself is reviewing it. I am on a nearby stand, in the Victory Alley, and I see people reach out their hands toward the Führer as he is slowly driving by in an open limo. Finally, Hitler is on the podium, dressed in a modest jacket adorned with the Iron Cross; all around him are field marshals, generals, admirals, SS top brass.

Hitler throws out his hand in a Nazi salute, as if giving a blessing to the troops marching past him in perfect formation. It is an awesome and frightening sight.

The trade mission receives invitations to the diplomatic box at the Krol Opera, the former opera theater where, after the fire in Reichstag, the "parliamentarians," appointed by Hitler, hold their sessions. We arrive early and watch the hall fill up with people. Most of them are in uniform—Army, Navy, SS, or SA. Very few people are in civilian clothes. Seated in the presidium on the stage is Göring, dressed in a silvery Reichsmarshal's uniform designed especially for him. Decorations and medals are all over his chest. Next to him are Hess, Goebbels, Himmler, Ribbentrop, and other Nazi top brass. Still no sign of Hitler. The audience is hushed in expectation. Suddenly, deafening applause and loud shouts split the air. Somewhere below our box, Hitler must have appeared. Slowly, without looking at anyone, he is walking down the aisle toward the stage. His right hand is raised in a Nazi salute, his left is placed on the belt of his jacket. He seems to be oblivious of the frenzied crowd, of the shouts *"Sieg Heil!" "Heil Hitler!" "Heil Führer!"*

As I am watching all that, I am thinking to myself—and the thought scares me—how much there is in common between this and our congresses and conferences when Stalin makes his entry into the hall. The same thunderous, never-ending, standing ovation. Almost the same hysterical shouts of "Glory to Stalin!" "Glory to our leader!"

Hitler gets up on the stage and walks up to Göring. Still up on their feet, the audience sings "Deutschland über Alles." More clapping, more shouts. After a few minutes, Hitler makes a sign with his hand. Silence falls. Göring gives the floor to "the Führer and the Reich chancellor of Great Germany." More applause. Hitler begins his speech and the hall becomes quiet.

After defeating France and giving the British an opportunity to evacuate from Dunkirk an army nearly half a million strong, Hitler believed that London would be ready to talk peace. He mobilizes all his actor's talents to project himself to the world as a man who, in spite of his enormous success, is moderate, even modest, willing to talk and make compromises. Not a single hysterical shriek, not one sharp phrase—graciousness incarnate. True, he vents his sarcasm on Churchill, who recently became the head of the British government. But he is magnanimous with ordinary Englishmen, pointing to a way out of the war that will allow Britain to save face and promising to preserve the Empire intact.

"At this hour," Hitler solemnly proclaims, "I owe it to my conscience to appeal one more time to the reason of Britain. I believe I can do that, since I am not begging for something as a loser, I am appealing to reason as a winner. I see no justification for the continuation of the conflict." But London responds to that appeal with a firm "No!"

A disappointed Hitler signs an order to speed up the preparations for Operation Sea Lion, the invasion of the British Isles.

Heavy bombing raids on British towns begin. Coventry is destroyed. Westminster, the House of Parliament, has been hit. But the British are stiffening their resistance. They shoot down Luftwaffe aircraft. Air alerts are becoming more and more frequent in Berlin. British bombers penetrate the air defenses of the Reich's capital.

In early summer I ordered a suit and an overcoat at a tailor's in Taunzienstrasse. I was promised quick service. But the tailor was called up, and things got kind of stuck. One day I went to the store to inform the people there that I couldn't wait any longer, but quite unexpectedly, I found out that my tailor had been demobilized after an injury and was back on the job. When he came out to give me my clothes, I didn't recognize him. Only recently a plump young man, he was now a mere wreck of his former self. He smiled, but pain and horror were in his eyes. He noticed my surprise and said:

"This is what war does to people. I was duped by the stories of victories and eagerly went to the front. Don't believe those stories. It's hell and death out there. And now my body is alive, but inside I'm dead."

Tears welled up in his eyes. It looked as if he knew something that one who hadn't been there couldn't even begin to imagine. At that time, the people of my generation in my country didn't know what it was either. But soon millions of Soviet people were to come face-to-face with that terrible mystery.

In August, I was called up to Moscow. I was to report immediately to the people's commissar for foreign trade, Anastas Mikoyan.

Natasha

THE DISCIPLINE IN THE GERMAN SCHOOL IN KIEV was strict, but respect for the teachers wasn't its only underpinning. Despite the wide claims that beatings and other forms of physical punishment were unthinkable in a Soviet school and entailed a severe penalty under law, students at the school in Lutheran Street knew otherwise. Those who didn't do their homework or misbehaved were made to kneel on chickpeas in a corner of the classroom for the entire duration of the class, their ears were pulled, and a whack on the head was altogether routine. If anyone complained, he or she could expect even harsher treatment. All classes in the first grade were taught by a tall, young, red-headed Saxon named Paul Radeschtock. The students addressed him as Genosse Paul, "Comrade Paul." He had just arrived from Germany where for some reason or other he had to get out fast. Rumor had it that he had been a hit man of the German Communist Party. After carrying out some important mission for the leadership, he had had to go into hiding. We didn't quite know the meaning of the term *hit man*, but to us it sounded pretty scary, and we were all a little afraid of Paul. He also taught gym to seniors and was ruthless to those who made him angry. His favorite trick was to clinch the offender's head under his mighty arm and rub some soap into his mouth. It was made out of cod-liver oil and tasted awful. The poor kid, in an effort to spit out the disgusting froth, would make bubbles with his mouth and bawl, half-suffocated. This would inflame the torturer even more, and he would continue the execution with relish. The other students stood around silently, trembling with fear. But one day we decided to take revenge.

When I first came to school, I learned that ever since the previous year, the boys in the two upper classes—since the German school opened only recently, it had only four classes—had formed into two gangs. Each had its own leader. One was called Leonid, the other's name was Zunka (who was later to leave for Palestine with his grandfather). I joined the latter's gang right away because Zunka reminded me of my favorite movie star, Douglas Fairbanks. Most of the time the two groups just wrangled with one another, but sometimes it ended up in fights. More often than once, I came home with a bloody nose. Mother would be horrified and demand that Father go to the school and make sure that the outrage be stopped; but Father would try to joke about it, saying that a man must be able to stand up for himself. But when a common enemy appeared on the scene, when, for instance, a gang from another school led by its leader Mazai showed up and began teasing our girls, we would, of course, join forces and forge a united front. During one such truce the plan of revenge took shape.

"How long are we gonna put up with Paul's humiliations?" Zunka asked his rival. "We have to teach him a lesson even if we have to suffer for it."

Leonid began thinking, biting hard on his nails, which he always did when he was concentrating. Finally he replied, "I have an idea. Let's discuss it." And they withdrew into the bathroom.

Soon the plan was elaborated in every detail. Everyone involved got a specific assignment. It was decided to carry it out at the next gym class.

When Paul was demonstrating to us a running technique, Leonid tripped him up. He fell and immediately we were all over him: five boys were pinning down his arms, ten others were holding his legs. Maybe because it was so unexpected or maybe because fear doubled our strength, but the Goliath was nailed down to the floor, and after a few unsuccessful attempts to free himself, he lay still. Zunka placed his knee on his chest and began rubbing Paul's mouth with that same soapy detergent. We went into raptures when our torturer began spitting foam and making bubbles. We knew that in his rage he was capable, if not of killing, at least of seriously maiming anyone he could lay his hands on. That is why we had previously agreed that we would let him loose all at once to give us time to get out of the gym. Paul was bellowing like a raging bull, the soap suds were getting into his eyes. On a cue from Zunka, we let go of our prey and scattered in all directions. Paul didn't have time to catch anyone. We were safe.

We expected that he would complain to the principal, that there would be an investigation, and that maybe we would all be expelled from school. But one, two, and then three days went by, and nothing happened. Maybe, on reflection, Paul decided that it would be humiliating for him to disclose the incident. And then again, maybe he appreciated our reckless courage and our fearless resolve to stand up for ourselves and our friends. At the next gym class he acted as if nothing had happened. And we respected him for it. He also cleaned up his act, no longer subjecting us to the detergent executions, but limiting himself to light raps on the head, something other teachers did, too.

The positive side to the stringent code and the inevitable punishment was that the students got solid knowledge. Much of what I was taught then I remember to this day, and I am able to reproduce by rote entire pages of text. As for the German language, it has in fact become my second mother tongue. That was probably why our parents, who doubtless knew about the "executions," did not protest or take their children out of the school.

I felt bad about not being a senior. I felt closer to those boys in spirit. I also thought that in terms of maturity I was more like them than the third-graders. Even the best friend I made was not in my class but was a fourth-grader named Michel. He was an ethnic German, in fact a Bavarian, even though he had a Russian family name, Voronov. His background was quite unusual. He was born in the picturesque little village of Sonthofen in the Bavarian Alps one year before I was born. His father, Fritz Ubelhor, was killed at the front during World War I, and a Russian prisoner of war named Voronov was sent to work on their farm. At first he just did odd jobs, herded the cows, and worked in the field. But soon he began to live with Michel's mother, and they had a boy named Hans. After the Treaty of Brest was signed, Voronov returned to the Ukraine with his new family, registered his marriage, and settled in Kiev. That is how Michel became a Voronov. But he didn't forget his home country and dreamed about going back to Bavaria. He would tell me about the Alps with great passion and taught me Bavarian songs. We became so close that I asked Michel's parents to let him spend his vacations with me in Svarichyovka, where, from force of habit, my mother and I would head for the summer. Michel's family was poor; his father worked in some shop and made little money. On top of that, he drank. Michel's parents were happy about the invitation as they wouldn't have to feed him for a few months. My parents also welcomed the idea, pleased that I would have a companion to play with and a partner with whom I could practice my German.

But playing was the last thing on my mind that summer. My yearning to join the circle of senior students was intensified by a teenage love that smote me. I fell in love with Natasha, a fourth-grader who was starting fifth grade the next year. I clean forgot Tamara, the daughter of the Greek NEP mogul. Now Natasha was the most beautiful creature in the world for me. I always wanted to be near her. I wrote ardent letters to her, shedding tears of ecstasy over them. But my love was not requited. I convinced myself that she would start paying attention to me only when I caught up with her at school. And I made a desperate decision: during the summer vacation I would complete the program for the fourth grade, and in the fall, I would take an exam for the fifth grade. I don't know where I got the will or what gave me the strength to sacrifice my summer break, to forgo the pleasures of life in the country, to forget the night horse rides and fishing, to give up mushroom-picking and virtually go without swimming.

The Russian novelist Turgenev once said that love was stronger than death, more powerful than fear of death. I experienced similar sentiments at the time. I was happy to sacrifice anything to achieve my goal. I had no doubts nor felt any fear that all my efforts might prove of no avail. Some mysterious force filled me with energy and determination. From the very first day in Svarichyovka, I knuckled down over the books that Michel had brought with him. A true friend, he was trying to help me cope with what seemed an impossible task. But I did it—I passed the exam and was transferred into the fifth grade, and claiming my right of the victor, I sat at the desk next to Natasha.

Today when I look back at that adventure, I can't help thinking that had I not jumped from the third to the fifth grade, my life would have taken a different course. I would have completed the seven-year program one year later, that is to say, not in 1930, but in 1931, when deadly hunger was tightening its grip on the Ukraine. And would have graduated from the Kiev Polytechnic the year World War II began. Everything would have shifted and gotten mixed up. How can one not believe that a man's life is a patchwork of coincidences?

My fifth year at school must have been the happiest time in my teenage years. My unsullied love for Natasha, the opportunity to be near her, turned the time I spent at school into sheer joy and sweetened the pill of studying. There was much fun there, too. Under the direction of our teacher, Aunt Hedwig, who also taught singing, music, and drawing, amateur shows were staged in which all participated. We staged our shows at the Business Club in Kreshchatik, where there was a large hall with a stage. The shows were attended not only by our parents, but by the city folks in general, who were attracted by the colorful flyers that we made ourselves. One of our regulars was the consul general of the Weimar Republic. With his hair cropped short revealing the powerful back of his head, he closely resembled Germany's president, Field Marshal Hindenburg. He had the bearing of a military man and must have been a Reichswehr general. On the outskirts of Kiev, a military unit was stationed where the soldiers and officers were of German origin. They were our school's patrons and we often visited them. Everything there—the posters, slogans, and diagrams—was in German. Orders were also given in German.

The German consul general was a frequent visitor to that unit. At that time, the Red Army General Staff closely cooperated with the Reichwehr's High Command; they conducted joint maneuvers near Kiev in which our patrons, the German soldiers, also participated. In the summertime, we would spend a few weeks in their boot camp at Darnitsa, a Kiev suburb. We looked after their horses and acted as scouts during their exercises. I also remember quite well the parties we used to have at the spacious apartment of our classmate Shura Zetlin. He lived close to school in the Gorodetsky building, which stood out because of its unusual and extravagant architecture. Before the Revolution, Gorodetsky must have been the most fashionable architect of his time. In Kiev he designed the Historical Museum, with its Greek portico, Doric columns, and the two lions at the top of the wide staircase, the bank building in the Mauritian style, and other edifices. But his own building in Bankovskaya Street was the most whimsical. Gorodetsky, a passionate hunter who every year went on a safari in Africa, decorated his huge house with the figures of elephants, tigers, lions, and condors, placing mermaids at the corners of the roof, their tails raised up in the air like grotesque candles. Under the Soviet regime, a number of families moved in there, including Shura's father, a popular gynecologist with a private practice, who ended up with an entire floor to himself. Another reason why we liked visiting there was because the Zetlins had a little monkey, mysteriously the only survivor from the Gorodetsky zoo. Even though the odor it gave off was not altogether pleasant, we forgave it all for the funny faces it made and, in general, for being such an exotic creature.

At such parties, we recited German, Russian, and Ukrainian poetry, staged amateur concerts, played lotto, a game of spillikins, and another sophisticated game called the flirtation of flowers, which had been around since before the Revolution and was still popular among the youngsters from the families of the intelligentsia. In that game every player got a card in which the name of a flower was used to invoke a passage from a classic. By calling out the name of the flower and addressing it to a fellow player of the opposite sex, messages were exchanged without anything being said out loud.

Those were the happy, halcyon days. . . .

But starting the next year, a bad stretch set in. All of a sudden, the fire went out of my love for Natasha; I became lonely and disillusioned while she suffered in secret. Michel's mother divorced Voronov, took her children, and went back to Sonthofen. That was the first blow. I was losing my best friend, losing him forever, because a foreign country seemed to me as far away as a distant planet. We took our last walk on the steep bank of the Dnieper where we had so often played together, bowed our heads at the Askoldov's grave in the hope that the mysterious power of the founders of Kiev would one day bring us together again. Our anguish was so strong that we would have been happy to jump into the river. But we had to resign ourselves to our destiny.

Strange things began happening at school, too. Tante Hedwig was arrested. A rumor went about that she belonged to some subversive organization. Barely a few months went by and the math and physics teacher, Schilling, disappeared. Tante Hedwig had allegedly denounced him as the leader of a "group of saboteurs." We couldn't imagine what they could have done to harm our country, but were still inclined to believe the rumors reaching us. Soon after that, "hit man" Paul was also arrested. He disappeared without a trace. New teachers came to the school. They spoke bad German. A number of subjects began to be taught in Russian. The last person to be taken away was the school's principal, Fibich, whom we all adored. The church in Lutheran Street was closed down. It was a good thing, I thought to myself, that the Ulpes had managed to leave for Germany. Otherwise they would have been accused of espionage, too. It was becoming increasingly clear that before long the German school would be closed down, which indeed soon happened. After us, only one more class managed to graduate.

The Arrest

WHEN I STARTED THE SIXTH GRADE AT THE GERMAN SCHOOL, I began to see my father less often. He was completely immersed in his work, splitting his time between designing the new shipyard and finding a place for it. He would leave home early and come back late, and I had my classes in the afternoon since a Ukrainian seven-year school used our premises in the morning. As far as Sundays were concerned, the situation was totally confusing. Probably in order to make people forget the religious meaning of Sunday and to break their habit of going to church, the authorities introduced a five-day week with every fifth day declared a day off—the fifth, tenth, fifteenth, twentieth, twenty-fifth, and thirtieth of every month. Work at factories was organized in shifts around the clock to ensure nonstop production. As a result, many family members had their days off on different days of the week and had virtually no time to be with each other.

Soon it became clear that because of that work schedule it was impossible to find a worker who was needed at the factory at that particular moment. This would cause confusion and the "continuous production process" had to be discontinued. Finally, the Kremlin experimenters, after inflicting considerable damage both to the family and production, reintroduced the normal seven-day week with the day off falling on Sunday.

That must have been one of the first arbitrary decisions by the Party and the government. A great number of them accumulated over the years of the Soviet regime right up to Gorbachev's campaign to fight alcoholism and heavy drinking in the late 1980s, which totally disrupted our trade. One can only wonder why the leaders, who claimed that their decrees and actions were grounded in science, were unable to think through and predict the consequences of their decisions. It was also interesting that the people were never able to figure out whom they had to thank for another hopeless problem on their hands.

On rare occasions, when he had a chance, Father would take me along on his boat trips on the Dnieper. Together with a government commission from Moscow, he was looking for the most suitable place to build a shipyard. We would travel a long way up the river and then go back downstream. Geologists studied the shallows and bays where factory buildings could be constructed. They all were beautiful, picturesque spots with pristine sandy beaches surrounded by thickets of red willow, with water meadows, backwaters, and copses coming right up to the steep banks. But in those days the country was preoccupied with industrialization. People dreamed of construction scaffolding, smoking factory chimneys, and electric power lines crisscrossing the planet. Few people gave any thought to the fact that the construction of industrial giants, like the projected shipyard, meant the destruction of the environment in that area of the Dnieper River, an end to the free and easy life of both people and animals alike.

Fortunately, and my father influenced that decision, it was decided to build the shipyard in the inlet opposite Podol where shops for repairing ships had existed for many years. The banks of the Dnieper up and down the river remained intact—that is to say, until after the war when a dam for a hydroelectric power plant was constructed near Vyshgorod, most likely because Podgorny and other Ukrainian leaders misunderstood the meaning of the word *prestige*. The dam devastated the area and flooded hundreds of thousands of hectares of fertile lands and pastures.

The construction of the shipyard got under way, and my father's time was totally consumed by it. It was a difficult period for him in general. After the trial of the so-called Industrial Party when Ramzin, a prominent scientist and designer of steam boilers, and other engineers were convicted, arrests spread to technical specialists who had received their training before the Revolution. Not only engineers working with my father but also qualified workers began to disappear. After another of his colleagues would be arrested, Father would come home gloomy and taciturn. He just couldn't understand why those people chose the path of sabotage and why they all confessed to their crimes. He would often say:

"There is some terrible mystery here. It's as if everyone is under a spell. It doesn't make sense for them to engage in sabotage. They hold good jobs, they do interesting work. Why sacrifice all that? It's incredible. And then again, the acts of sabotage they are accused of are not the result of evil designs; they follow from haste and poor workmanship that's typical of any construction project we undertake."

Some longtime Bolsheviks were not spared either. There was this boy at my school named Petya, the son of a talented engineer who had joined the Revolutionary movement when he was still a young man. I often saw his father and mother, a beautiful brunette, at our school's amateur shows at the Business Club. He had a little beard, and his chest was decorated with the then still rare Order of the Red Banner, which he was awarded for some brave operation during the Civil War. How could he be a saboteur?

"He is not a saboteur," Petya was saying, smothering his sobs after his meeting with his father, a short time before he was sent to Siberia. "He believes that by confessing to the acts of sabotage he didn't commit, he is doing one last service to the Party and the cause of socialism. The country is surrounded by enemies; there are internal enemies, too. The people must remain vigilant and continue to believe in a bright future. In his opinion, by making a confession he strengthens the system created by the Revolution and upholds the people's faith in Stalin, whose name has come to be synonymous with socialism."

At that time, many confirmed Communists thought along those lines. They, too, believed that the authorities were infallible. The very thought that a lawless and arbitrary rule gripped the country was frightening and inadmissible. People had to be forced into believing that their rulers were always right. If a man was arrested, he therefore was guilty. Any attempt to justify him would amount to casting a shadow of doubt on the motives guiding the actions of the authorities and, consequently, would mean questioning the fairness of the system. Both the executioners and their victims shared that thinking. That was why if someone was taken away by the security police—NKVD or GPU—he never came back. He disappeared without a trace, as if he had never existed in the first place. Even the names of the most prominent Party leaders were erased from the people's memory.

That was the fate of Secretary of the Central Committee of the Communist Party of the Ukraine Postyshev, Chairman of the Ukrainian Council of People's Commissars Lyubchenko, People's Commissar for Internal Affairs Balitsky, and soon after him, Kosior, first secretary of the CPBU (Communist Party of the Bolsheviks of the Ukraine). Among the people immediately around me, NEPman Popondupolo with his entire family was arrested, and Professor Zadorozhny was declared "a dangerous Ukrainian nationalist" after he was taken away. At the time of their arrest and while their apartments were being searched, Naum Solomonovich, the chairman of our "Fun Corner" cooperative, was present as a witness. At that moment, "Seat of Sorrow" would have been a more appropriate name for our apartment building.

My father knew he hadn't done anything wrong, but it was evident that the wave of repression worried him. He never told me anything, but was probably waiting for a knock on the door in the middle of the night. He would startle whenever he heard the pattering of someone's footsteps in the street or when a car pulled up to our house late at night. All our family lived with an anxiety we hadn't known for a long time. And then the thing we dreaded most happened.

My mother is shaking me nervously. Through my sleep it occurs to me that it must be the dead of night, and I don't understand why she is waking me up. I rub my eyes open and see a sinister sight. My mother is in tears. My father is standing motionless in the middle of the room, a gown thrown over his nightshirt. He is wearing his pants but is barefoot. The bright light from all the bulbs in the lamp bring into sharp relief his usual bags under his eyes, which now appear puffed up. Huddling in the corner against the tile stove are the two witnesses—Naum Solomonovich and Matryona, our yard-keeper's wife. Two soldiers are standing by the door leading into the hall, another is over by the window. Bayonets are fixed to the muzzles of their rifles. A man in the uniform of a senior GPU officer is fumbling in the drawers of my father's desk. A search! the thought flashes through my mind—which still refuses to believe that this is happening to us. Once again something snaps in my chest, but with much greater force than in any previous traumatic experience.

Maybe this is just a search. Maybe after they don't find anything they will go away and leave us alone? Wishful thinking! The man in the GPU uniform raises his head and casts a glance at my father:

"What you waiting for. Get dressed!" And turning to my mother: "Help him pack his things. You can put something warm on, too."

Then this is not just a search; this is an arrest and for a long time. It is late fall now and the air in these parts is mild and wet. Warm clothes are needed only for winter. . . .

The search continues. The drawers are pulled out of the chest, the linen is inspected, then they begin to work on the bookcases. We have more than a few books—there will be a lot of work. There is no time to put everything back into place. After leafing through each volume with a practiced movement of the fingers, the GPU officer throws it on the floor. One is piling up on top of the other. The soldiers help the officer move the kitchen cabinet, then the piano. He looks inside the piano, groping in there with his hand and touching the strings that strike a long and mournful sound. My heart is breaking. I can barely hold back my sobs.

The searchers move to my parents' bedroom. We follow after them. My father is already dressed. I admire his self-control. He is observing everything with such composure as if whatever is going on were no concern of his. The soldiers look under the bed, pointing their flashlights there. They inspect the wardrobe. A thick family photo album is lying on my mother's dressing table. It holds the memories of three generations of the Titovs. Turning the thick pages over, the officer pauses at a picture I had known since I was a child—the photo of Uncle Leonid, my mother's brother, an officer in the czarist army, decorated by the two Crosses of St. George in World War I. The back of the photo has a hasty note in black ink: "Goodbye, my precious ones, tomorrow I will be shot."

After reading the note, the officer turns to my mother: "What is this?"

She explains, "My brother joined the Red Army and was shot by the Whites."

I know she is not telling the truth, and I understand why. Her brother was shot by the Bolsheviks, like many other czarist officers.

The man turns the photo distrustfully in his hands, thinking what to do with it. Then he places it on top of the album and says, "Put it away out of sight, just in case."

Could it be that a human emotion stirred within him?

My mother silently hides the photograph in the pocket of her gown.

The time has come to say our last goodbye. My mother is clinging to my father, not letting him go.

"That's enough, comrade!" the officer snaps out sharply.

Father lifts me up and, giving me a kiss, whispers into my ear, "Remember, I am absolutely innocent."

These words raise a storm of protest in me and I choke with tears. He places me down on the floor, picks up a bundle with his things, and without turning around, steps out into the hall. A guard opens the door and walks out first. Father walks out after him, followed by the officer and two more guards. The witnesses, their heads bent down, leave without saying a word. We don't even close the door after them, stunned by what has happened and still unable to grasp the full extent of the tragedy that has descended upon us. Mother pulls me to the window. A lamppost casts a dim light on an ugly-looking Black Maria, in Russia baptized a "Black Raven." It has no windows— just an iron-barred door in the back. Father is helped through the door, and two guards climb up after him. The officer gets into the seat next to the driver. The engine cranks up and the Black Maria leaves carrying off my dad. . . .

Could it be forever?

Father's arrest marked an end to our previous life. From a normal family we had turned into the family of a subversive. People turned their backs on us. From the experience of my schoolmates in a similar situation I knew that I was in for a hard time at school. No one would say anything out loud, but I could feel the alienation. Some, convinced of the infallibility of the authorities, would look at me as if I were a leper. Others, possibly not believing that the accused parent was guilty, would fear for their lives and try to keep away from me anyway. In those days, the entire family didn't automatically follow its head to prison, but one way or another a shadow of suspicion fell upon all the relatives of the arrested person. One could expect neither help nor sympathy from anyone. In anticipation of all this, I decided not to go to school the next day, and Mother, sharing my sentiments, didn't object.

The following morning, after tidying up the apartment a little and drinking some strong tea, Mother and I set off for Rosa Luxemburg Street where the city's GPU office was located. At the information desk we learned that "the accused" would be transferred to the Lukyanovskaya Prison in a few days, where he would be allowed to receive parcels from outside twice a week.

I will remember that saddening system for the rest of my life. The prison was located on the very edge of Lukyanovka, formerly a prosperous suburb, famous for its beautiful villas and estates owned by Kiev's rich. I knew that neighborhood well. Since before the Revolution an officers' shooting range had been in that area, and my father and I often went there to watch marksmen's contests. We also went there to see my mother's dressmaker, who lived on one of the estates, occupying a little room in an old house. While my mother had her fitting session, I would roam around the garden, its paths already overgrown with grass and its flower beds unkempt, which suited me perfectly because I could run around wherever I wanted. Many imitation antique sculptures were in the garden—beautiful nymphs and scary satyrs—and although many of them had parts of their bodies missing, they turned the garden into a livelier place, adding to it mysterious charm. From those early trips to Lukyanovka, I had kept fond memories of the place. Those remembrances, however, were dimmed by the grim picture of silent people lining up at the little window of the Lukyanovskaya Prison to hand in their packets for the prisoners.

Mother would wake me up at four o'clock in the morning, and after we packed our bundle, we would go to the tram stop to catch the first car for Lukyanovka. The car we boarded was always half-full, but it would fill up with people along the way, all of them like us—mournful figures with bundles and baskets. Taking the window seats opposite one another, Mother and I would doze to the rattle of the windows and the rumble of the wheels, starting out of our sleep from time to time and looking around fearing we had passed the prison. During those rides I would have one and the same dream: We walk up to the window, but it doesn't open. We knock, and suddenly the gates swing open and Father comes out to meet us, cheerful and full of energy, the way he was a long time ago when he met us at the White Pier in Podol. After that bright and joyful vision, the reality of the dark winter morning, the prison wall, and the line at the little window in the iron gate was indeed a rude awakening that broke my heart.

Mother had no money, and we had to rent out one of the rooms in our apartment. It was a painful decision for Mother to make, but there was no other choice. Fortunately, the tenant turned out to be a nice man. He was about forty, tall and thin. A modest person, he did everything not to be a burden. Not only that, he often shared his food ration with us, offering us canned beef, which I found to be an exquisite delicacy. He would often go away somewhere, and when he came back, he would bring some food: vegetables, potatoes, cabbage, and sometimes salted fish and sunflower oil. Gradually, we became friends. He came from a working-class background. A professional revolutionary in the past, he had fought in the Civil War and later worked in some central-government agency in Kharkov, then the capital of the Ukraine, and was sent to the Kiev region to organize collective farms. That was why he was often gone. He was by nature a kind man, and it was obvious his job was a burden to him. When I woke up in the middle of the night, I often heard his deep sighs and, sometimes, even awful moans.

One day Mother asked him about that. He was silent for a while, hesitant about what to say, but then answered after all:

"My work is very hard. It's not easy organizing collective farms. But as a disciplined Party member I must carry out my assignment. You can hardly imagine what it's like to fight the kulaks and to drive people from their native land. It's a terrible human tragedy. Not only the head of a kulak household has to be deported, but their wives, elderly parents, and children—all have to go. If you could only see how they say goodbye to their homes, their cattle, and the land they had fought for during the Civil War on our side! At a sight like that you would not only start crying in the middle of the night, you would want to run away to God knows where."

But he continued to toe the line and, even though he had an advanced case of tuberculosis and a constant bad cough, smoked one cigarette after another. We remained friends even after the capital was moved to Kiev. He got a good apartment in a new building constructed in our district. But his health was rapidly deteriorating. He was wasting away right before our eyes. Shortly before he died he told me:

"You are still young and anything can happen in your life. But no matter where you are, never forget our people. They have endured and will suffer incredible hardships, but they deserve a better life."

It seemed to me that in saying those words he was painfully aware that by carrying out his orders he was making people suffer even more and couldn't forgive himself for it as he was about to die. Indeed, what a terrible summing up for anyone to make.

Return to Moscow

AND SO, AFTER HALF A YEAR ABROAD, I was leaving Berlin to return to Moscow. A Soviet citizen who was suddenly told to go back to his home country usually experienced a feeling of uneasiness. Could it be that someone had denounced him? Was there some problem back home? And even though the cable sent to the trade mission clearly stated that I was to report to the Secretariat of the People's Commissariat for Foreign Trade, some kind of a ploy couldn't be ruled out—maybe the authorities didn't want to alarm the "offender" and thereby provoke him into doing something they didn't want him to do. The officials in charge of personnel working abroad had developed a whole range of ploys to lure a person back home. In my case I wasn't aware of any serious problems on the job; but maybe I had overstepped the line by acting too independently and by making too many friends. A feeling of uneasiness was gnawing away in the back of my mind.

Over the few months I had worked in Germany, I had accumulated some personal effects. Once abroad, a Soviet citizen would buy things a person from a normal country wouldn't even think of getting, since he could purchase everything at home, especially big items. With us, it didn't happen that way. In those days—just as today, half a century later, by the way—people brought home refrigerators, radio-gramophones, radios, cameras, sheer stockings, and fashionable clothes from the West. They didn't buy soap, toothpaste, shaving cream, or razors to take to the Soviet Union since there was always plenty of that stuff. When I returned from Berlin, I brought clothes, a gramophone with a Telefunken radio, one of the best cameras on the market at the time, watches, and a few other trifles.

I was accompanied to the Friedrichstrasse Railway Station by Valentin Petrovich Seletsky. He helped me settle down in the compartment and stayed with me until the train left.

"I envy you—going home," he said. "And I don't know how much longer we will have to stay here. I hope everything is going to be all right there for you. Let me know if anything happens."

He was worried about me after all, concerned that an unexpected surprise was waiting there for me. Too close contact with foreigners could create problems. We learned that lesson well. But still I was yearning to return home. I was eagerly awaiting that moment when I would step down on my native land again. The trip back home took me through Polish territory. The bridge in Frankfurt on the Oder was not yet fully repaired. German engineers were working there. As we moved deeper into the countryside, everything looked peaceful, but in the cities we could see buildings destroyed by the war. The railway station in Poznan lay in ruins, and as for Warsaw, the train traveled around it and we could see the city skyline only from a distance.

Finally, we reached the Soviet-German demarcation line. The train stopped before a bridge. An SS officer accompanied by two soldiers in green steel helmets entered the car. They checked our papers thoroughly, but didn't inspect our luggage. The whistle blew and we moved on. The train rumbled across the bridge and slowly climbed the western bank of the Bug River. And there it was at last: a striped border post marked with a sign USSR. A young soldier wearing a faded field shirt and a wide cap with a red star was standing next to the post. When I saw him, I felt a lump form in my throat. My heart ached with joy, and no matter how hard I tried to control myself, tears welled up in my eyes. My soul soared.

But my joy was to be short-lived. The train stopped at the platform of the border railway station where we were to remain for two hours while the narrow-gauge rolling stock was replaced for the wider tracks of the USSR.

Loudspeakers creaked out an order: "Comrades, everyone should get off the train with their luggage for customs clearance."

A long line of people carrying suitcases, boxes, and bundles stretched from the train to a gray building. Bulky luggage was being unloaded from the baggage car. All that stuff was laid out on elongated squat tables covered with sheet iron. With great gusto customs officers were poking about in clothes, turning out pockets of jackets and pants. It looked more like a search than a customs check. Books, newspapers, magazines, letters, sheets of paper if something was written on them, were handed over to a guard, who stacked them up in a pile and then carried them off somewhere. That was how the slogan "Our borders are sealed" was being put into practice.

Finally, my turn came. After rummaging in my suitcase and finding nothing pernicious, the customs officer demanded, "Open the box."

"It's a radio."

"Please open the box," he repeated sternly.

"It's factory sealed." I hated to have to cut the twine and tear off the masking tape. But at the time I didn't know how dangerous it was to argue with a customs officer. He snapped out sharply, his irritation showing, "I told you to open that box. What do you have in there? Are you trying to conceal something?"

I was itching to tell him that we shouldn't be forgetting our manners, but thought it better not to and began unpacking the box. He looked at the polished top of the radio.

"Take it out!"

At that point I saw my mistake. Now he was going to give me the rough treatment. I had to be patient. He ordered me to take off the back panel of the set and spent a long time fingering the coils, lamps, and condensers, looking up at me from time to time as if playing a children's game: Is it cold? Warmer? Hot? . . . What if he saw my eyes say "Hot!" when he stumbled on a stash with some subversive stuff in it. But he didn't find anything. He straightened up, disgust written all over his face.

"How many watches are you carrying?" he asked suddenly, squinting at me.

"Here!" I pulled up the sleeve of my jacket, showing him my watch.

"And how many do you have in your pockets?"

How did he know, was he clairvoyant or something? Or was it that someone in Berlin had squealed on me after all? But I had nothing to fear. Just two ladies' watches—it was nothing!

"I bought a little watch for my mother . . ."

"What else?"

"One more for my girlfriend . . ."

"Let me see!"

I placed two little boxes on the table.

The officer opened one, then the other. "This is not good. . . . Were you trying to take this contraband in secretly?" my torturer said slowly, relishing the words, his lips pursed in a malicious smile.

"What do you mean, 'contraband'? I presented these things to you for inspection."

"Only on my demand. And in general, only one watch is allowed to be taken into the country. I'll have to write up a report."

At that point I understood that it was pointless to argue. I took my watch off my wrist and placed it on the table next to one of the boxes. I closed the second box and moved it to the side—that one was for Mother.

"I should notify your superiors at your place of work about this. But I won't. I will just give you a receipt for the confiscated items."

You are too kind, I said to myself, cursing, and began repacking the radio. By that time there wasn't a trace left of the blissful state of mind in which I had arrived.

The Belorusskaya Station in Moscow was crowded as usual. The line at the taxi stand looked hopelessly long. I was lucky to talk the driver of a black limo into taking me into town. He drove a ZIS automobile, an official car, similar to the Chaika of today. They were manufactured at the Stalin Automobile Plant, which explains the *S* in the name. The trip wasn't long, only as far as Smolenskaya Square. Having no other choice, I decided to take a chance and stay at the officers' hostel that I knew at the corner of Arbat.

Aunt Nusya, the caretaker, seemed glad to see me. A bed was available in the room where I'd lived before. I said I'd take it and promised to register my stay later at the General Staff of the Navy. I freshened up with cold water, put on a clean shirt, and took out a pack of stockings from my suitcase. On the way out, I stopped by briefly at Aunt Nusya's to give her the stockings, which sent her into raptures, and headed for the People's Commissariat to report that I had arrived.

Meeting Mikoyan

THE USSR PEOPLE'S COMMISSARIAT FOR FOREIGN TRADE was then located at the corner of Kuibyshev Street, opposite the Polytechnic Museum. I called the secretariat from the security office where they issue the grounds passes. I was told that in a few minutes someone would come down to escort me in. It was true then: the people's commissar did call me in. But how could Anastas Ivanovich Mikoyan—one of the top Soviet leaders, a colleague of Stalin himself, and a member of the all-powerful Politburo—how could he even have heard about me? It could only be that Tevosyan spoke favorably about my interpreting skills. So what turn would my life take from here?

"Valentin Mikhailovich?" A hoarse voice interrupted my thoughts. Standing in front of me was a man of medium height wearing an immaculate gray-striped, three-piece suit, a light blue shirt, and a bow tie instead of the customary four-in-hand. I took him for someone who had done a lot of traveling.

"Let's go, the people's commissar is waiting for you."

We took an elevator to the fourth floor and entered the secretariat, where I was introduced to an elderly, elegantly dressed lady, the people's commissar's personal secretary.

"Please take a seat. Anastas Ivanovich will soon be able to see you," she said, motioning toward the chair by the window.

It had already grown dark. The square was lit up by bright streetlights, and ads flashed on the roof of the Polytechnic Museum:

"Here's something up for grabs: our succulent crabs," "I am in love with jam!" "Fresh catch from the Don River: a special gift to give her." As I was to find out later, the ads were Mikoyan's idea—he was also in charge of domestic trade. He commissioned famous poets to write catchy one-liners for advertising, as Mayakovski used to do. And it was not just agitprop. Not only in Moscow, but in other major cities as well, the shop windows displayed pyramids of Chatka crab tins. Inside the stores behind one of the counters there would be wooden barrels with black and red caviar; on thick wooden boards lay salmon, sturgeon, and other fish delicacies as well as cheeses, hams, and sausages. Well-stocked wine and liquor sections that in addition to the usual selection offered new brands—gin with a smiling Dutch sailor on the label—and Soviet whiskey. And no lines anywhere! After things had turned a little worse during the months of the war with Finland, the food situation in the country had noticeably improved.

Three people came out of the office, and immediately a buzzer sounded behind the secretary's back. She disappeared behind the door, and when she came back, carrying a leather folder in her hand, she turned to me and said, "You may go in now."

Behind the first door, there was another. When I opened it, I entered a relatively small room with dark brown wooden paneling. I was struck by the modest size of the office. It was only later that I learned that the sessions of the collegium of the People's Commissariat and other meetings, attended by many people, were held in a large round hall on the fifth floor.

Mikoyan was sitting at his desk by a tall window. The bronze desk set with a spread eagle, the lamp with a green shade, and stacks of paper almost completely hid his miniature figure. He was scrutinizing me with a stern and maybe even unfriendly look. I thought that for some reason he was displeased. Was he going to give me a dressing-down by any chance?

"At your orders, Comrade People's Commissar!" I hastened to salute him.

Mikoyan smiled, revealing under a well-groomed little mustache an uneven row of yellowish teeth, stained by many years of smoking. The stern look was immediately gone. He often hid behind that charming smile during difficult negotiations with foreigners. And the angry look on his face resulted from his hooked nose and the deep wrinkles around his mouth.

"Please sit down," he said in his hoarse voice.

I sank into one of the leather armchairs.

"When did you get back from Germany? Do you have a place to stay?"

I explained that I had put up at a hostel where I had lived before my trip to Germany. Mikoyan pressed a button. The secretary walked in.

"Tell Fyodor to prepare a place for Comrade Berezhkov to stay," he said. Then he added, turning to me, "My administrative assistant will take care of that right away."

I mumbled my thanks, saying that I could stay on at the hostel.

"Modesty becomes a Bolshevik," he declared, "but not to excess. Now tell me, what's happening in Germany. The Germans must be bursting with conceit after their victory over France?"

I told him what I saw during the Victory Parade in Berlin and at the Reichstag session where Hitler made a speech. I tried to convey to him the atmosphere of mass psychosis and exaltation that had gripped Germany. I also described to him the work our group did to check product quality at the Krupp factory.

"Tevosyan told me you accompanied him to Holland and then again traveled to Rotterdam and, if I'm not mistaken, to Brussels. What's the situation like there?"

After carefully listening to my brief report, Mikoyan said that in the immediate future the surviving refrigerator ship would sail from Rotterdam to the Leningrad port.

"Tevosyan was pleased with you," the people's commissar added. There was a pause. Mikoyan took a box of Troika cigarettes from the table. They had only recently appeared in the stores and had immediately become popular. He opened the box and offered me a cigarette. Under the silver foil I could see an untouched row of golden filters. Smoking in the people's commissar's office was perhaps a rude thing to do, I decided. Maybe he was deliberately testing me.

"Thank you. I gave up only recently," I fibbed.

"Very wise," Mikoyan praised me as he took a cigarette from the box and lit up. Honeylike fragrance filled the air.

I was somewhat ill at ease under the scrutinizing gaze of the people's commissar. How much longer was that pause going to continue? And why had he called me in anyway? But then with a vigorous movement he put out the unfinished cigarette in the heavy marble ashtray. He must have made a decision.

"What do you think about transferring to work at the Commissariat for Foreign Trade?" Mikoyan asked. "There will be important talks with the Germans, and I need a good interpreter with work experience in Germany. Tevosyan believes you can handle it."

"It's a great honor for me, and I will certainly try to justify the trust you place in me. But what will my superiors say? I am still doing my military service in the Navy."

"I am aware of that. Admiral Kuznetsov and I will reach an agreement that you will be temporarily reassigned to work in the People's Commissariat for Foreign Trade. By the way, you're not a Party member yet. I'd advise you to take care of that problem. I believe that if you submit an application in the unit where you serve, you'll be accepted as a candidate. Give it some thought. And tomorrow morning, come to my secretariat, to the German desk. Tochilin and Chistov there will explain everything to you. Goodbye."

Outside in the waiting room the commissar's administrative assistant was waiting for me—that same elegantly dressed man.

"Let's go, I have arranged a place for you to stay," he said.

The black Buick that waited for us at the entrance took us down Kuibyshev Street toward Red Square. At that time, it was still a two-way street. When we reached the Lenin Museum, we turned right and stopped in front of the Metropol Hotel. There was no way I could have expected that I would end up staying at such a posh place. I was given a two-room suite on the second floor with a bath, a telephone, and a spacious glassed-in balcony. Later I learned that sometime in the past, Bukharin had lived in that suite and kept stuffed birds and other hunting trophies on the balcony.

"Somehow I don't feel comfortable about moving into such a large space," I said. "Don't you have something more modest?"

"You shouldn't feel that way," my escort countered. "We have a few rooms here. The Commissariat pays for them. It's quite all right for you to stay here until you get an apartment."

"Can I bring my things over? They are in Arbat, near Smolenskaya Square?"

"Of course. I'm going to walk back to the office and the car is at your disposal. This is one of the cars that the Commissariat's secretariat has on call. They can be used for business purposes."

It was as if I were dreaming. The conversation with the people's commissar, his suggestion that I write an application to join the Party, the gorgeous suite, the car I could use when I needed it. Of course, Mikoyan would discuss the question of my becoming a candidate for Party membership with whomever it was necessary to talk to. The political directorate of the Navy also had to be aware of that. But was I prepared to join the Party? And would I succeed working for such a demanding and strict boss as Anastas Mikoyan? Membership in the Party was probably one of the prerequisites for working in the Commissariat. But how was I to bring myself to take that momentous decision? Would I do it just to join the secretariat's staff? In fact, I could already consider myself appointed to the job. But it was also clear that Mikoyan had no doubt that if I submitted an application I would be accepted as a candidate for Party membership. It all boiled down to a question of principle. There was more to it than that, however. Rejection of such a highranking position would entail unpredictable consequences. We all knew only too well the Leninist-Stalinist dictum, "He who is not with us—is against us." I would not just stay a non-party member, I could become an "anti-Party element." I hadn't thought about it in those terms before. During one of the periodic enrollment campaigns, this one conducted in the Ukraine in 1934 to mark the tenth anniversary of Lenin's death, I was included, unbeknownst to me, in the so-called Leninist Komsomol List of candidates. Then the organizers forgot to follow up with some paperwork for our group, nor did we show too much eagerness, and so I remained a nonmember. On the other hand, I had always tried to carry out my responsibilities conscientiously, firmly believing that the Party kept our country on the right track and that Stalin was a follower and legitimate successor to Lenin. So why not become a member of the Party of Lenin and, in the position I was offered, make my own, albeit modest, contribution to the cause of building socialism? At that time, of course, I couldn't even imagine that fifty years later, after the bloody events in Vilnius, Lithuania, in January 1991, I would have to take the decision to leave the CPSU!

All this was going through my mind as I sat on the balcony of my suite in the Metropol Hotel, surrounded by the sounds of Moscow at night. Below I could hear the subdued voices of the people coming out of the Maly Theater after the show and the jingles of the passing streetcars. To my left I could see limos rolling up to the Grand Hotel. In those days, restaurants stayed open until four o'clock in the morning. The food at the Grand Hotel was excellent and the service impeccable: waiters from the old regime still worked there, full of dignity and yet attentive and considerate to the customers.

The next morning, I reported to the People's Commissariat. I introduced myself to Tochilin, a nice, kind, and well-mannered man.

He was in charge of a group of the people's commissar's aides. Tochilin showed me an excerpt from an administrative memo signed by Mikoyan: I was to become an employee of the People's Commissariat for Foreign Trade attached to the Soviet-German Economic Relations desk.

Free Again!

THE WINTER OF 1928–29 was particularly hard for us. The predawn trips to the Lukyanovskaya Prison in a cold, rumbling train, the fear for Father, the virtual vacuum that had formed around our family, the wary treatment I was getting at school—all had a deadening, depressing effect on me. All the more so since the town lived on as if nothing had happened. And why indeed should it be otherwise? It was our private grief, wasn't it?

Meanwhile, the New Economic Policy remained in effect and on the surface life in Kiev appeared to be the same. In Kreshchatik, renamed Vorovsky Street after the Soviet diplomat killed by White Army émigrés in Switzerland in 1923, people in festive clothes sat at cafe tables, fans of Hollywood movies milled about in the movie theaters, and lively shows were playing at the circus. But all of that was not for us. We were indeed having a hard time. With Father's arrest, our family was deprived of its livelihood. We had no savings, and there was no one to help us. Mother earned some money by giving private lessons in English and German.

Soon the relatively carefree life of the Kievites was shaken by events that unfolded at the Kiev Pecherskaya Monastery. The newspapers and radio reported that a monk had lured a girl into the caves under the monastery, raped her, and then cut up her body with an ax. The press carried gruesome pictures of the woman's dismembered body and a photo of the monk, a long-haired, thin man with insane eyes. A widely publicized court hearing was being prepared with appearances by numerous witnesses and victims of the "lascivious" monks. A sinister picture was being painted of the evil things that were allegedly going on under the golden domes of the monastery.

Maybe today it may finally be possible to find out what, in fact, happened then. Were there indeed some shady goings-on transpiring behind the monastery walls, or was an individual case used to mount a virulent campaign to prepare for a new attack on the church? Since time out of mind, the Kiev Pecherskaya Monastery had been venerated not only in the Ukraine but throughout the Russian Empire as a most holy place. Despite the systematic antireligious propaganda and the many years of persecuting the clergy, despite the destruction of churches, the confiscation of church treasures, and the elimination of many other monasteries, the Kiev Pecherskaya Monastery had survived and continued to be greatly revered by the people, a situation unacceptable to the authorities who wanted to discredit it. Attributing the crime to a monk presented an opportunity to do just that. It provided a convenient pretext for mounting a malicious campaign to put the monastery in disgrace. The defendant was tried in open court. The sessions were attended by delegations from factories, groups of students, and farmers from nearby villages. They came to the hearings as if going to see a show. "Demands by the working people" were engineered urging that "this den of iniquity and bloody crimes" be immediately closed down and the monks dispatched to labor camps for reeducation. The authorities managed to set at least some people against the monastery. It was soon transformed into an ethnographic museum.

We at home were eagerly awaiting the rare letters from Father. It was of course impossible to find out from them what was happening to him. But by receiving them from the Lukyanovskaya Prison, we could at least assume that the "incriminating charges" against him were still under investigation. In his letters he tried to cheer us up, assuring us that we would soon see each other again. He asked us not to lose heart and urged me to study hard at school.

In early March, we received a note from him that got us excited. Father told us that the investigation was drawing to a close and that in this connection he was promised a visit from his family. My heart was breaking, torn apart by alternating pangs of joy and pain.

"When and where are we going to see him?" I would ask Mother. "I won't bear it if after a brief meeting we lose him again, maybe forever . . ."

Knowing that I couldn't keep my emotions in check and was prone to bursts of uncontrollable tears, I was even afraid to meet my father.

Would I be strong enough to act like a man or would I break down in my father's presence, making it even harder for him?

Before the meeting Mother gave me a sedative, hoping it would numb my sensitivity.

The meeting was scheduled to take place in the GPU building in Rosa Luxemburg Street, which ran parallel to our street, which was named after Karl Liebknecht. Here the two German revolutionary martyrs were close together, just as they had been at Landwerkcanal in Berlin where in 1919 they met their death. The tragic irony was that in the basement of the building in Rosa Luxemburg Street both Russian revolutionaries and German Communists who had emigrated to the Soviet Union—such as Paul Radeschtock from my school—suffered death, innocent victims of Stalinist repression. Was that what was in store for my father? I was asking myself this question as I approached the sinister building that could well have had cut out on its pediment the phrase *Lasciate ogni speranza, voi ch'entrate*, "All hope abandon, ye who enter here!"

The guard found our names on the list that lay on the table, told us to wait, and reported our arrival to someone over the phone. A few minutes later a man dressed in civilian clothes came out.

"Follow me," he said dryly, and began climbing up some stairs.

After walking down a long corridor with many doors, we turned a corner. Our escort led us into a small room with a window covered by some thin fabric that let the light in from outside. In the middle of the room was a small table with two chairs on each side. Mother and I sat down. The escort walked out and we were left alone. I wanted to say something, but Mother put her finger to her lips, hushing me up. "Here even the walls have ears" was the thought that flashed through my mind.

We waited for quite a while, curbing our impatience. Finally, the door opened and Father walked in. I bit my lip until it bled and drove my fingernails into my palms, hurting myself physically to conceal the pain I felt within my soul.

Father had grown thin and gaunt. His hair had become even grayer, and only his mustache remained black as before. The bags under his eyes sagged even more. His face was ashen from the long stay in the cell. Yet he tried to look cheerful. When the going got tough, he always tried to cheer us up. But when I saw him, it was even harder for me to control myself.

Father was escorted by a short man dressed in a military uniform with a bandolier running over his shoulder. He had the insignia of a senior officer. His hair was red and curly and it looked as if it had been a while since it had been combed.

"Inspector Abram Iosiphovich Fuchs," he introduced himself.

He told Father to sit down at the table opposite Mother and took the chair next to him. Father put his arms across the table and took Mother's hands into his. Then he grasped my hands in a similar manner and squeezed them firmly.

"Well, here we are at last," he began, trying to put on a cheerful smile. "As you can see, everything is quite all right, but, of course, I have missed you terribly. Now tell me—how are you doing?"

"Misha, darling, I was getting desperate, I couldn't wait to have this meeting!" Mother exclaimed, unable to control the surge of her emotions. But she quickly got her feelings under control and, in a calmer voice, began telling him how we had been getting along, embellishing her story to cheer him up.

Father asked me about my school and my grades and praised me for doing well in the sixth grade.

"Now you have to do even better in the seventh, your last grade, and finish school among the top students of your class," he said. "If I get to stay here longer, you'll have to become the breadwinner for the family."

Inspector Fuchs made a strange *hem* sound at these words, and I was badly hurt by them. Could it be that he wouldn't be back a year from now? Was that what he was trying to say?

Mother interpreted Father's remark the same way I did. She began assuring him nervously that we were all right, that he shouldn't worry about us. Then she suddenly said:

"We are confident that our Soviet justice system will get to the bottom of all of this. It will not harm innocent people. Here we are seeing each other after a long separation, and I had already lost hope that this would happen. Everything will be straightened out and you'll come back to us. I'm sure of that."

Did she truly believe that? Or was she just trying to cheer him up and, more importantly, flatter Inspector Fuchs? It was unlikely that her ploy would have any effect. But a few minutes after that, Fuchs said that he was going to leave us alone to say goodbye and left the room. Father picked up where Mother had broken off:

"You're quite right, of course. Innocent people are not convicted in our country. I also believe that I'll be set free."

As he was saying that, he clasped Mother's hands again and I noticed that he slipped a tightly folded piece of paper through his fingers into Mother's palm.

"Take good care of yourself, Misha, dear," Mother said in a loud voice, as if also speaking to the eavesdroppers at the door. "Don't worry about us. It'll work out and we'll be together again."

We spoke a little longer about some trifling matters.

Then Fuchs walked in and said that the meeting was over. We hugged each other, and in my excitement I didn't even notice how Father left. Just that all of a sudden, we were alone.

The same man in civilian clothes reappeared and escorted us to the exit door. The guard there checked us out on his list and we went out into the street.

When we got home, Mother unfolded the note. It contained just a few tightly written lines in Father's beautiful hand, that of a professional draftsman:

"They have not been able to force any false confessions out of me. All charges have crumbled. The 'case' has disintegrated. Now they will either send me to a camp anyway . . . or set me free. Love."

We didn't know whether to feel happy or sad about that piece of news. But we felt that one way or the other our torture of uncertainty would soon be over.

Another month went by filled with the trips to the Lukyanovskaya Prison, standing in lines at the little window to hand in our package and waiting for the fateful news.

We got few phone calls in those days. Sometimes the phone would be silent for weeks. But then, in the middle of April, it rang. I picked up the phone. A person with an unfamiliar voice asked whom he was speaking to. I said who I was.

"Tell your mother," the voice in the receiver said, "that tomorrow at eleven o'clock she has to be at the GPU building on Rosa Luxemburg Street. Do you understand?"

"Yes, I do," I replied, seized with excitement.

When Mother came home in the evening and learned about the phone call, she began bustling about. She sliced up a loaf of bread and began drying the pieces in the oven. She got a few warm things together: a sweater, a few pairs of woolen socks, a thick knit scarf, *valenkis* (felt boots), and a fur hat. She did all that in silence, totally focused on what she was doing. I began to get worried:

"Why are you doing this? Maybe they will set Father free."

"Don't say that!" she cut me off sharply. "It's better to prepare for the worst, or else I won't be able to get over it."

The next morning we got up early and waited impatiently for the hands on the clock to move up to half past ten. The little bag with the warm things, dried bread, and some other foodstuffs had long been packed. Mother picked it up and we headed for the GPU building. We went inside and were escorted to the same room on the second floor as on our earlier visit. We didn't have to wait long. Just as last time, Father was accompanied by Inspector Fuchs. Mother and I stood there not knowing what to do. Father was silent, a faint smile on his lips. Finally, Fuchs spoke to Mother:

"You didn't have to bring the bag. You'll have to take it back."

My heart sank. Could it be possible that Father wouldn't even be allowed to take the warm clothes with him? Or was he in for something even more terrible—was he going to be sent to a place where a man didn't need anything any longer?

In the meantime, Fuchs continued after a pause:

"We have carefully studied the charges brought against Mikhail Pavlovich. He has been falsely accused. He hasn't committed any illicit acts. We express our apologies to him and congratulate him upon his return home and reinstatement in his job. It has been a misunderstanding. Consider that nothing has happened." Fuchs turned to me. "And you, too, should know that your father hasn't even been under investigation and there hasn't been any arrest. I repeat, he has just been invited here to clear up a misunderstanding."

I was dumbfounded. Mother also couldn't believe what we heard. Father was free then! And not only free, it was as if nothing had happened to him. He was even reinstated in his job! Mother put her arms around Father and kissed him. Then she walked up to Fuchs and gave him a kiss on the cheek. I jumped at Father and put my arms around his neck. My heart was thumping against my chest with unexpected happiness. To think that just a short while ago we were preparing for the worst.

Father gave Fuchs a rather cold goodbye. That nettled me since all that time Fuchs was smiling upon us benevolently. It seemed to me he was also glad our ordeal was over. A GPU inspector was also human, wasn't he? I was prepared to forgive him even if he had treated Father badly on occasion.

It was only later that we learned that in order to get Father "to confess," he was severely beaten, made to stand for days in a narrow cell, deprived of sleep, placed in a cell with criminals, and subjected to even more iniquitous forms of torture. But Father had an inexorable will as well as the body of an athlete. That helped him endure everything. A number of times he had passed out, but he never signed the papers the inspectors wanted him to.

Reluctantly and not all at one go, Father told us about what he had been through in prison. He made Mother and me swear that we would never tell anyone about it. And it was not just that he had signed a "nondisclosure" pledge. He understood that knowledge of his secret would put us in jeopardy.

I was shocked by his disclosures. It was hard to believe. Trying to justify what had happened, I told myself that only the most perverted and vicious inspectors abused people in that manner.

It seemed a miracle that Father was let go without any consequences that could complicate his subsequent life. That rarely happened. That extraordinary outcome had an impact on me, too. I came to believe that if a person was truly innocent, no one was going to harm him, and even if he was arrested, he would eventually be set free. Maybe because of that, in later years I felt no fear when I walked into Stalin's office or sat next to him, oblivious of the danger that insatiable monster presented to anyone who came in contact with him.

Assistant to the People's Commissar

TODAY IT WOULD BE INCONCEIVABLE that a young engineer who had spent only a few months working at the Krupp factory in Germany and had been trained only in a narrow field of naval technology could be appointed to a position of great responsibility in the Commissariat for Foreign Trade. The job required experience in international trade and vast knowledge in the areas of commerce, the history of Soviet-German economic relations, and familiarity with precedents, countless legal norms, and existing treaties.

When in August 1940 I sat down at my desk in the secretariat of the people's commissar, I didn't have the slightest idea about any of that. Only the self-confidence of youth can explain the lightheartedness with which I accepted Mikoyan's offer. But how could Mikoyan, a man of experience, choose a novice for his assistant? His need for an interpreter was probably so urgent that he was willing to accept one with only limited work experience in Germany. I more or less fit that bill. But there was a more important reason, too: the People's Commissariat for Foreign Trade, just as other Soviet government agencies, had been purged by Stalin and left with virtually no staff. There was a dire need for new personnel, and under those circumstances, the eligibility criteria were less rigorous.

In fairness, it should be pointed out that Mikoyan managed to keep some old-time specialists. I remember well how at the sessions of the collegium, after a heated discussion of some issue and when opinions diverged, the people's commissar would turn with great respect to his experts, Kelin and Frei, who sat a little distance from the rest, and say, "And now let us ask our wizards what their thinking on this is." And he would carefully listen to their lengthy comments on the question under discussion, their analysis of the pros and cons. Usually both experts came up with similar recommendations. But sometimes Kelin and Frei held opposing views. When this happened, Mikoyan would get irritated. He would demand that they consider the proposals once again while the collegium moved on to the other items on the agenda. The experts would confer in a whisper in their corner or leave the meeting room altogether. If there was no agreement when they returned, the people's commissar would turn the question over to the members of the collegium, who, after some further discussion, would ultimately approve one of the options open to them.

The two experts reminded me of the prophets of the Bible or the oracles of antiquity: Frei, heavy, slovenly dressed, with a shock of gray hair, and Kelin, a tall, lank, balding man in a meticulously pressed suit, a shirt with a starched collar and a bow tie.

I immediately saw how rudimentary my own knowledge was. I had to go through thick files of recent commercial correspondence, minutes of trade negotiations, cables from Soviet trade missions abroad, as well as excerpts from the decisions of the Party's Central Committee and the Soviet of People's Commissars. I also read Soviet-German treaties and agreements going back to the Weimar Republic. I had to study all those materials in addition to my regular work and daily negotiations with the Germans, which I attended as an interpreter. My responsibilities also included writing up Mikoyan's conversations, copies of which were sent to the other members of the Politburo, as well as drafting cables to the Soviet trade mission in Berlin.

In September–October 1940, intense trade negotiations were under way with Germany. In addition to Minister Schnurre, who had already participated on the German side in the preparation of the trade agreements in August 1939 and February 1940, Ambassador Ritter also took part in the talks. He was Germany's ambassador at large, responsible for economic matters and trade agreements with other countries, including the USSR. A stout man with a barrel chest and broad shoulders, he looked more like a wrestler than a diplomat. A true fighter, he was ambitious, aggressive, and full of stamina. I had the impression that Mikoyan, who also had extraordinary qualities as a fighter, thought highly of Ritter. The Germans were demanding an increase in Soviet deliveries. They were particularly interested in oil-producing crops from Bessarabia and in certain strategic materials. At the same time, the deliveries of the equipment that we had purchased from them were being delayed. As is known today, at that very time Hitler had begun to question the advisability of a landing on the British Isles.

On September 7, the Luftwaffe carried out a major air raid on England's cities. The London docks sustained serious damage. Some areas of the capital and some other cities were reduced to ruins. The Führer was so pleased with those results that he decided to postpone the landing, hoping that he would be able to bring Britain to her knees through air attacks alone. The report by Grossadmiral Räder also played a significant role in that decision. Because of the heavy concentration of British naval ships in the English Channel and the deteriorating weather conditions, he warned Hitler of possible negative consequences of an attempted landing. As a result, the final decision concerning the landing, scheduled by the Führer for September 14, was never taken.

On September 19, Hitler issued an order to pull back the landing forces deployed in northern France that had not yet been rendered inoperational by British air attacks. When in October the British Air Force inflicted heavy losses upon Göring's Luftwaffe, the Führer had to put off Operation Sea Lion to the early summer of 1941. The relevant directive indicated that if the question of landing in the British

Isles should arise again, new guidelines would be issued at an appropriate time. That effectively meant that the invasion plans had been abandoned.

What were Berlin's further plans? Hitler returned to the idea of "eliminating Bolshevism," which he had never rejected. As early as July 31, 1940, at a meeting with his generals in Berghof, he declared:

"Britain's only hope is in Russia and America. If the hope for Russia dies, it will die for America, too, because with the elimination of Russia there will be a total reevaluation of the role of Japan in East Asia. As soon as Russia is defeated, Britain will lose its last hope. Then Germany will reign supreme in Europe and in the Balkans. Therefore, in the course of this conflict Russia must be eliminated."

In line with those objectives, the German General Staff gave orders to launch preparations for the deployment of troops in the Eastern regions, and on August 26, on Hitler's orders, one infantry and two tank divisions were moved up to the Soviet border. In early September, on the pretext of making a transit move into Norway, German troops were deployed in Finland. The Wehrmacht began concentrating its forces along the borders of the Soviet Union.

An interesting detail: On August 14, 1940, Hitler requested a schedule of Soviet deliveries covering the period "until the spring of 1941." That was the target time for the attack on the Soviet Union. Ritter and Schnurre, of course, knew about Hitler's request when they urged an increase of Soviet deliveries to Germany. It was difficult for me to judge to what extent Mikoyan was informed about Berlin's plans. In any case, as a member of the Politburo he had access to the reports of the Soviet intelligence in Germany, which, as we now know, was well aware of what was going on. Be that as it may, he firmly stood his ground and demanded that any concessions by the Soviet side be matched by Germany's compliance with its obligations. Sometimes, when Ritter was unable to have his way at the People's Commissariat for Foreign Trade, he, together with Ambassador Schulenburg, would take his case directly to Stalin. Quite often Stalin magnanimously granted their requests. By that move Stalin wanted to indicate that he was the boss and took all the decisions. At the same time, he was signaling Hitler that he, Stalin, could be relied on.

When that happened, I often noticed that Mikoyan became gloomy, and during the dinner with the Germans to mark another "agreement" he would permit himself an extra cognac.

Ambassador Ritter left Moscow at the end of October. Although he had not fully carried out Berlin's instructions, he had reason enough to be pleased. It appeared that Stalin believed the explanations given for the delays in German deliveries, as well as the assurances provided that after the completion of the preparations for the invasion of Britain, everything that hadn't been supplied would be made up for. The "boss" promised that the Soviet Union would fulfill its commitments and would give favorable consideration to Germany's additional requests. Ritter thought that he had managed to outflank that stubborn and shrewd Armenian Mikoyan. And although for the time being Ritter had been given only assurances, Stalin was as good as his word and it was unlikely that Mikoyan would dare challenge his boss.

Both Ritter and Schnurre were in an elated, even playful mood at the farewell reception held by Mikoyan at the Reception House of the People's Commissariat for Foreign Affairs in Spiridonovskaya Street on the eve of the German delegation's departure.

That was how I got inside that beautiful mansion, realizing my longtime dream.

One time in the early 1930s when I spent my vacation in Moscow, I stayed with a former classmate who, when he moved to the capital, got a room opposite the Reception House. In the evenings when we went to the skating rink in the Patriarch's Pond, we often left his house at a time when guests were arriving for a reception at the mansion—diplomats in shining limos with little flags fluttering, people's commissars in Buicks with tinted windows, the Red Army's top commanders—we were able to recognize Tukhachevsky, Blücher, Yegorov. It was a tantalizing, inaccessible, fairy-tale world of wise statesmen, military commanders, and diplomats who had traveled the world. Early in the evening, when the cut-glass chandeliers were already turned on and the off-white blinds not yet drawn, we could catch a quick glimpse of that mysterious world peopled by the rulers of our destinies. Who could have thought in those days that the distinguished marshals, like so many other participants in those receptions, would soon fall victims to the bloody repressions, and that the mansion's hospitable host, People's Commissar for Foreign Affairs Maxim Litvinov, would meet his death in the kind of suspicious automobile accident that happened so often during Stalin's rule.

But at the time, everything inside looked to us to be stable and indestructible.

And there I was walking in after People's Commissar Mikoyan,
climbing a wide marble staircase with exquisitely beautiful handrails.
In terms of its architecture and its interior design the house was a
true work of art. Before the Revolution, it had belonged to a rich textile manufacturer, Savva Morozov, a connoisseur and patron of the
arts. The best art and sculpture of the early twentieth century decorated Morozov's mansion. The stained-glass windows and the hall
staircase, which impressed me by its elegance, were created by
Vrubel. The spacious reception halls, each with its distinct style, were
decorated with works by the best Dutch, Spanish, and Russian masters. All around the house there were cabinets with fine bone china,
statuettes, unique silver plates.

In the Green Hall, located to the right of the lobby, there was already a group of guests. Among them I could see a few employees of
the People's Commissariat for Foreign Trade. My attention was
caught by a short, stocky man with a round, balding head and whitish
goggle eyes, who was standing by himself. He was wearing an excellent tailor-made dark suit, a snow-white shirt, and a black-striped tie.
He looked very sure of himself, even cocky, and when Mikoyan entered the hall, unlike others, who hurried toward him, he walked
over to the commissar slowly, leisurely. Looking relaxed, he shook
Mikoyan's hand and began joking with him about something as if
they were old friends. That didn't look quite normal, and later when
Tochilin and I were standing by ourselves, I asked him who he was.

"Dekanozov," Tochilin whispered to me. "He is Beria's man, recently appointed deputy people's commissar for foreign affairs."

At that point I didn't suspect that I would soon be getting to know
him quite well.

The German delegation arrived. The waiters began serving drinks.
Mikoyan and Ritter were congratulating each other on the successful
conclusion of the negotiations, each for different reasons. Ritter was
pleased with Stalin's assurances while Mikoyan was content with at
least the minor achievement that for the time being we had committed ourselves only to considering the wishes of the German side.

The master of ceremonies invited everyone to proceed to the dining room. We crossed the lobby again and found ourselves in a spacious room painted in light gray with a huge fireplace. Carved, high-
backed chairs were placed around the table. Everyone sat down
where the name cards indicated. I thought that on that solemn occasion, which I attended in my humble capacity as an interpreter, I

would get a seat in the second row between the host and the principal guest. But my place setting, exactly the same as everyone else's, was put to the right of Mikoyan's. The next day, Tass carried a brief report saying that the dinner, hosted by the USSR people's commissar for foreign trade Anastas Mikoyan in honor of Ambassador Ritter, was held in an informal, friendly atmosphere.

I liked my work in the people's commissar's secretariat; I learned many useful things, and whenever there was something I wasn't clear about, I always got help from Tochilin or from Chistov, an expert on Germany more experienced than I was. However, I was not to stay there long.

Sailing to Novorossiysk

I WAS LOOKING FORWARD to the summer vacation of 1929 with special impatience. We were starting the seventh, our last, grade and felt grown-up even though none of us had yet turned fourteen. But at that time, the school's seventh-year graduates went to work almost immediately. Those who wanted to continue their studies attended night school to prepare for exams to enter vocational schools and colleges where one could enroll at sixteen and seventeen respectively. I had one whole year to go before I had to make that decision. Meanwhile, my mind was set on a cruise in the Black Sea subtropics, promised to me by my father.

After spending the first weeks of my vacation with the Yushkovs in Anapa, I was going to sail by small boat to Novorossiysk, where the large ship *Gruziya* was arriving from Odessa, carrying my parents. My little travel bag in hand, I climbed on board and settled down on the deck close to the side of the boat.

"Heave away!" the captain called out from the bridge.

Each time when one stage of your life suddenly comes to an end and you enter upon a new one, you experience a keen sense of loss. This is particularly true when happy, carefree days are over. And every time a new period begins, even if it promises to be better, it is still filled with the unknown. Some people, who learn from long experience that every new turn in their lives makes things worse and not better, feel anxious and nostalgic about bygone days no matter how hard they may have been. This was how most of our people felt about the reforms of the late 1980s and early 1990s.

As we approached Novorossiysk, the sea and landscape noticeably changed. The dolphins who had accompanied us all the way from Anapa fell behind and headed toward the tankers and the dry cargo carriers anchored at the entrance to the harbor.

I came out on the pier and found myself in my father's arms. He looked me over and said, "That's my boy, so tanned, so grown, but thin as a starving Indian."

My parents had called me "a starving Indian" ever since I was a child because I was skinny—which was often the case with the children of the War Communism era. Most of them eventually put on weight. But I remained as thin as a rail.

"But it's all right." Father smiled and took me by the hand. "Now we'll feed you well here."

He still felt guilt for the hardships and hunger we had endured during his arrest.

We walked up to the ladder that ascended to the promenade deck. Mother was waiting for us there. She looked so young, fresh, and cheerful in her light white lace dress and her veiled, off-white, wide-brimmed straw hat. She bent over me and kissed me on the head. The fragrance of her Lorigan perfume enveloped me, carrying me back into a childhood that now seemed so far away.

Night Call to the Kremlin

SOON AFTER THE NOVEMBER HOLIDAYS, very late at night (we regularly worked until five or six o'clock in the morning), Anastas Mikoyan called me into his office. I thought he wanted to talk about some documents that I had just translated. But he had a surprise for me.

"You have to report immediately to the secretariat of the Chairman of the Council of People's Commissars. My car is waiting at the entrance. Take it so as not to waste time getting a pass. The driver will take you through the Spasskaya Tower gate in the Kremlin to the Council's building. They are waiting for you there. Now go!" he said sharply.

I had a feeling he was unhappy about something and was reluctant to send me there. He, of course, already knew something I wasn't yet aware of. I would never have an opportunity to work with him again.

After leaving his office I stopped in at my room to lock the safe and then went down and outside. The driver already knew everything and, without waiting for any explanations, sped down Kuibyshev Street, then across the empty Red Square heading directly toward the Spasskaya Tower gate. The guard at the entrance to the Council's building had also been informed about me and gave only a cursory glance at my ID card.

"Go up to the second floor, turn to your right, and go to the end of the corridor," he instructed me.

Soon I found myself in front of a door with a plate that had the following inscription in gold: RECEPTION ROOM OF THE CHAIRMAN OF THE SOVIET OF PEOPLE'S COMMISSARS OF THE USSR.

For the people of my generation that post had great significance. It synthesized the attributes of the supreme authority, the romanticism of the Revolution, the heroism of the Civil War, and the construction of a new life, of which we were also a part now. More importantly, the position of Chairman of the Council of People's Commissars was closely associated with Lenin, and that was why Molotov, who then filled that post and who since the spring of 1939 had also served as People's Commissar for Foreign Affairs, appeared to me to be Lenin's direct successor.

I was met by Kozyrev, Molotov's first assistant in the People's Commissariat for Foreign Affairs. He told me to take a seat and disappeared behind a door that led into the adjoining room. About five minutes later he returned and said, "Comrade Molotov will see you now."

It is not difficult to imagine the awe I felt when I opened that door. But Molotov was not in the next room—it was the security room, which somewhat allayed my nervousness. I opened the next door with less trepidation. It was a large room with a long table along the wall and rows of chairs, but no one was inside there either. A door was left ajar at the end of that room, and I headed toward it. When I entered that study, I saw Molotov sitting at his desk bent over papers, so familiar from pictures: his large Socratic forehead, twinkling eye-glasses, and a little mustache covering his harelip. For some reason I thought that was what a scholar should look like, maybe even a wizard. Only the most capable disciple of Lenin could run such a huge nation, and at that time we believed that the leadership was taking the country along the right path, guided by the Marxist-Leninist teachings. Only a loyal and staunch comrade-in-arms of Stalin, an erudite scholar, an all-seeing and all-knowing leader of the people, could live up to that challenge. We believed all those things because we were thoroughly brainwashed. At a Party meeting where I was admitted as a candidate for Party membership only a short time before I was called into Molotov's office, I was absolutely sincere when I declared that I considered it a great honor to become a member of the party of Lenin and Stalin and that I wanted to be in the vanguard of the builders of communism.

Finally Molotov lifted up his head, looked at me, squinting his eyes, and invited me to sit in a chair next to his desk.

Then he began asking questions—where and when was I born, what school I went to, where I studied foreign languages, what my parents did for a living, and what my impressions were of Germany. Suddenly, he asked:

"And where is it written that 'our duty as Communists is to master all forms, to learn to supplement one form with another with maximum speed, to replace one with another, to adapt our tactics to any change brought about not by our class nor through our efforts'?"

His question was so unexpected that at first I was at a loss, especially since I understood that my destiny depended on the correct answer. Molotov looked at me searchingly while my mind was feverishly searching through the classic works of Marxism-Leninism that I'd recently read. It was a familiar quote, I had come across it only recently. . . . Suddenly I remembered: "Lenin. 'Left-wing Communism: An Infantile Disorder.' "

"Correct." Molotov nodded approvingly.

I had been lucky. Had Molotov chosen another quotation, something I didn't know, I would have flunked his test. Why had he chosen that particular quote? Maybe it was because of the recent sharp changes in our relations with Germany? Lenin's dictum was intended to justify a change of tactics forced upon our country. As for me, it was just a happy coincidence that I had read it only recently.

At last Molotov, pleased with my "grounding in theory," decided to explain why he had called me in: "Mikoyan spoke to me about you. He believes you are a competent interpreter. Tomorrow our government delegation, which I am entrusted to head, is leaving for Berlin to participate in important negotiations with the government of Germany. You have had some work experience in Germany and interaction with the Germans. Will you join us?"

I couldn't think of anything better to do than stand to attention and declare loudly, "At the service of the Soviet Union!"

Molotov rose from his chair, put out his hand to me, and said with a faint smile, "You may go now."

That was how my first meeting with Molotov went. At the time he was undoubtedly the second man in the country after Stalin.

The next morning I received my diplomatic passport, and in the evening a special train carrying the Soviet government delegation set off from Moscow's Belorusskaya Station for Berlin.

At the talks in the Imperial Chancellery the German side was represented by Hitler and Ribbentrop, along with two interpreters. For the Soviet side there were Molotov and Dekanozov, and also two interpreters—Pavlov and myself. On the first day of the negotiations, after the second talk with Hitler, a reception was held at the Imperial Chancellery. Molotov took Pavlov with him and told me to draft a cable for Moscow. At that time, tape recorders did not exist and stenographers were not invited to the talks at all, and so the interpreter had to take notes during the meeting.

Having made myself comfortable in the office adjoining Molotov's bedroom at the Bellevue Palace, a hotel used by the German government for high-ranking guests, I started my work by deciphering my notes. After spending considerable time doing that, I called in a typist from the Commissariat's secretariat, which had arrived in Berlin with us in somewhat reduced numbers. The typist had barely had time to insert a clean sheet of paper into her typewriter when the door was flung open and Molotov appeared in the doorway. He looked at us in sudden anger:

"What d-d-do you think you're doing? How many pages have y-y-you already transcribed?" He developed a bad stutter whenever he was in a temper.

Without yet knowing the reason for his anger, I hastened to reply, "I was just getting ready to start dictating."

"Stop this minute!" the people's commissar snapped out. Then he came closer, pulled out of the typewriter the page that didn't yet have a single line typed on it, looked at the pile of clean sheets of paper lying there, and went on to say in a calmer voice, "Consider yourself lucky. Can you imagine how many ears might have heard what Hitler and I spoke about one-on-one?"

He looked around at the walls, the ceiling, pausing on the huge Chinese vase filled with freshly cut fragrant roses. And then it dawned upon me. There could be microphones anywhere in the room with the wires running to British or American agents, or maybe even to the Germans who would also be interested to know what Hitler spoke about with Molotov. I broke into a cold sweat.

I was lucky again. But now I understood: I couldn't depend on luck alone, I had to use my head, too.

Noticing my confusion, Molotov switched to a calm, businesslike tone and said, "Take your notes and come with me."

The typist, who had been sitting petrified through all of this, made a beeline for the door, and Molotov and I moved to the bedroom. We sat down side by side near a little table.

"I will start drafting the cable and will hand you the pages to check against your notes. If you have any comments, insert them directly into the text or write me a note. We're going to work in silence. Is that clear?"

"Yes, Vyacheslav Mikhaylovich, and I'm sorry."

"Don't lose time . . ."

Today, knowing much about Molotov that I didn't know at that time, I can wonder how I escaped that incident without any repercussions. Considering that everyone at that time was suspicious, he could have assumed that I deliberately wanted to dictate the cable out loud to pass on the secret information. Fortunately for me, he must have attributed my faux pas to my lack of experience.

On the way back to Moscow, Molotov invited me into his compartment. Dekanozov was with him.

"We have been talking here about you," Molotov began. "We believe that now that you have participated in the important talks with the leadership of the German government, there is no point in your returning to the People's Commissariat for Foreign Trade. What do you think about getting a transfer to work in the People's Commissariat for Foreign Affairs?"

"It is a great honor for me. But will I be able to handle it? I don't have the specialized training."

"That is unimportant. We all have to tackle different things. I will speak to Mikoyan when we return to Moscow. I don't think he will object. There will be much important work with the Germans. Maybe Comrade Stalin will also need you as an interpreter. I will take you to work in my secretariat on the German desk."

That was how I began my diplomatic service.

At that time, in 1939–40, many new people came to work for the People's Commissariat for Foreign Affairs. Those diplomats, launched on their careers by Molotov, became famous after the war. Among them were Gromyko, Sobolyev, Zarubin, Gusev, Vinogradov, Semyonov, Malik, Novikov, Kiselyov, Chernyshov, Smirnov—mostly people with engineering, economics, and even liberal arts training, who had never dreamed of a diplomatic career. They joined the Commissariat on the recommendation of some district or city Party organization or perhaps just by chance, as was the case with me, and often wondered why fate had chosen them for the diplomatic service. In his memoirs, Andrey Gromyko asked himself how he, an economist by training, should have ended up in the People's Commissariat for Foreign Affairs. He saw a possible answer in that, from time to time, he gave lectures on international topics. But the real reason lay elsewhere: In the late 1930s, the People's Commissariat for Foreign Affairs was purged no less ruthlessly than the other Soviet government agencies. Stalin's orders were carried out by a special commission composed of Molotov, Malenkov, Beria, and Dekanozov. That same group of four selected and confirmed newly appointed diplomats, including Gromyko, even though in his memoirs Gromyko mentioned only Molotov and Malenkov.

When I joined Foreign Affairs in 1940, only a handful of people were left who had worked with Chicherin and Litvinov. We filled the still warm seats of the diplomats of the Lenin school, who had only recently been purged. I was inducted into the Commissariat by only two members of the commission, Molotov and Dekanozov. Malenkov was probably not paying any attention, but Beria remembered me. Maybe that was why later I began to have problems that I could trace back to him.

I didn't work in Molotov's secretariat for long. In late December, I was appointed first secretary of the USSR embassy in Germany, where I replaced Pavlov, who was recalled to Moscow to work in the People's Commissariat for Foreign Affairs.

After Germany attacked the USSR, I returned to the Commissariat and was soon made Molotov's aide assigned to work on Soviet-American relations. That was when my knowledge of English came in handy. During that period Stalin did use my services as an interpreter, but not at the negotiations with the Germans, as Molotov had thought he would, but at the talks with the Americans and the British.

CHAPTER FOUR

Famine in the Ukraine

IN THE PAST, the word combination that is the title of this chapter would have been taken as a contradiction in terms. A fabulously rich country with fertile lands, vast natural resources, and a hardworking people; a country that even during the Civil War and War Communism was able to feed itself, albeit frugally; a country that needed only one harvest to feed its people when the NEP was introduced; and suddenly—famine! In time of peace, too!

When in the fall of 1929 we returned to Kiev from our trip to the south, no one could even imagine that something like that could possibly happen. Abundance was still in evidence all around. Carts with fruits and vegetables on every corner, stores, both private and state-owned, filled with foodstuffs and goods. Spruced-up couples strolled up and down Kreshchatik; in the evenings, fun-seekers packed movie theaters, restaurants, cafes, and billiard halls. True, from time to time "bag people" could be seen in the streets—farmers fleeing from the villages where collectivization had been especially "successful." But they were believed to be the dispossessed village rich who had been punished for resisting the authorities. And Stalin's newspaper article "Dizzy With Success" created an impression that the excesses that were rumored to be occurring in the countryside were the work of overzealous bureaucrats. Now that the general secretary himself had taken them to task for it, they would cool their enthusiasm and everything should work out fine. The city lived its normal life without even suspecting that soon it—as, indeed, the entire country—would be afflicted with a terrible calamity.

A few new students joined our seventh grade. Their families had moved to the Soviet Union from Germany, where there was a growing danger of power being seized by the Nazis. In December, an all-Ukrainian Pioneers' meet was convened in Kharkov, and our school was also invited to participate. Genosse Paul, our Pioneer leader, decided to pass our group off as German Pioneers. Or maybe he acted on instructions from the Kiev Komsomol Committee. Such deceptions were often practiced then. For example, "envoys from the Canton Commune" would speak at every major conference. They would be presented as having just arrived from China although they had lived in Russia for a long time. In those days, the Canton Commune was on everybody's lips, and every presidium wanted to have a Chinese on it. As far as we were concerned, Paul's idea reflected reality to some extent. The newcomers were indeed German Pioneers. They had arrived only recently and had even brought their own banner. And then again, Paul was a genuine Saxon. And although we were not Germans, we could very well pass for them. Paul gave us a stern warning that throughout the trip we were to pretend that we didn't understand Russian and speak only German among ourselves.

Advance word was sent along our itinerary that a delegation of German Pioneers was heading for Kharkov, then the capital of the Ukraine. We traveled by train, occupying an entire car. Local Pioneers and Komsomol members met us at the stations along the way with music, banners, and flowers. Brief meetings were held right on the platform with short speeches in German. Then, as was customary in such situations, "friendly discussions followed" during which, in response to all questions addressed to us, we just raised our clenched fists and called out, "*Rot Front, Genossen!*"

At first I felt uncomfortable having to play that comedy. But gradually I grew to like it, and at a mass rally in Kharkov I even made a fiery anti-Nazi speech, reaping thunderous applause.

We were put up with the families of Kharkov Pioneers, two to an apartment, and in the evenings, when everybody sat down around a samovar to have tea, the most difficult test would begin. The neighbors' children came to see the "foreign Pioneers." Because they didn't know German, when they spoke, they used their hands a lot trying to explain what they were talking about. For our part, although we understood them perfectly, we had to pretend we didn't understand a word. We were barely able to hold back the Russian words that were at the tips of our tongues. It was a good thing my friend Zunka and I shared a separate bedroom because we feared we might talk in our sleep. For us it was just a game, and when we were by ourselves, we laughed our heads off thinking how smart we were, fooling everyone around us.

But later, on reflection, I came to the conclusion that Genosse Paul and our other mentors did us a great disservice: they essentially gave us a lesson in lying, cheating, and hypocrisy. And it was anything but funny. On the other hand, that experience may have prepared us all for the future life in our country where people would have to say one thing and mean another.

Father often went to Kharkov on business and brought back presents, such as new clothes or beautifully illustrated books. Since I had some free time on the morning before our departure, I also decided to buy a souvenir to take back home with me. I went into one store, then another, then a third one. Everywhere the shelves were empty. I couldn't understand what was going on. In Kiev the shops were packed with all sorts of stuff. And here, in the capital of the Ukraine, there was nothing. I decided to go to a restaurant to eat, but there, too, all items on the menu were crossed out—except for scrambled eggs.

We returned to Kiev by an overnight train. Back at home I told Mother about the situation in Kharkov, and she said in reply, "While you were gone, everything has disappeared here, too. I just don't understand where everything has gone to."

We didn't yet know that the "great breakthrough" was occurring and that an era of sweeping collectivization had begun. The brief breather of the NEP period was cut short, as if by a knife. The policy to liquidate the kulaks as a class, and, essentially, to eliminate all individual farms, agitated the population. Panic buying began as people snatched up anything they could lay their hands on. The authorities, for their part, blocked new supplies. As a result, in a matter of a few days the market was depleted. The situation was further exacerbated by the mass closure of private enterprises, craftsmen's shops, bakeries, cafes, and everything else.

In order to "stabilize" the situation, Stalin began to crack down harder. An internal passport system was introduced; food was given only upon presentation of food ration cards, and clothes could be obtained only with special coupons. Father, as the factory's engineer, received a worker's card, while Mother and I got those for dependents. But the food we could get with those cards meant half-starved living. Soon the so-called Torgsin stores (*Torgsin* is a Russian abbreviation for *torgoviya sinostrantsami,* "trade with foreigners") opened up around the city. That was essentially an attempt to get the last valuables that the people had managed to preserve. The people had to choose either to go hungry or to give to the state all they had managed to keep through the Civil War or purchase during the NEP in exchange for butter, condensed milk, and white bread. Mother took to a Torgsin store the last keepsakes from our grandmother and grandfather, and along with those items a few ten-ruble czarist gold coins that Father had bought for chervontsi to make tooth crowns. Once again, as during the Civil War, the country was on the verge of famine.

As I am writing this, I am thinking to myself: More than sixty years have gone by since the grand plan for the construction of socialism and communism was proclaimed. And what has happened? Never did I expect to see my country go back to using food ration cards again. With over seven decades of Soviet rule behind them, the Soviet people still line up for hours to buy shoddy goods and the most basic things. The huge administrative apparatus never managed to resolve the problem of soap shortages. When that problem arose under War Communism, it took my father a week to learn how to make his own soap, and he solved the problem for the village where we found shelter. Moscow held out longer than other cities, but in the spring of 1990, after six years of perestroika, it also had to introduce what amounted to a system of rationing. That was the sad outcome of over seventy years of arduous work, incredible hardships, and the loss of millions of lives of the people of our country!

At the end of May, our class took its final exams, and in September 1930, I began working at the Bolshevik factory. During the time I spent at the factory shops pursuing my youthful interests, I learned some skills that come in handy now. I was made a junior electrician with a salary of forty rubles a month and a worker's food ration card.

The workers at Bolshevik treated me well. Many of them knew my father, and even today, some remember his son, the boy, who spent days in the pattern and foundry shops. In those days, the factory was undergoing reconstruction. Transmissions, drive belts, and pulleys were being replaced by electric motors. The newly installed American equipment that had CINCINNATI written on it had built-in motors. But at the same time, the factory was using its own resources to modernize old units. A special shop was set up where generators and engines were made. The coils were made primarily by women, while men assembled and installed the engines. My job was to make collector brushes. I used a hacksaw to cut cubes of a given size out of a large piece of pressed graphite. Then through a galvanization procedure I put a layer of copper on one end and attached wire terminals. I liked my work. The only problem was that by the end of the day I was covered all over with graphite powder, looking as black as an African. No matter how hard I tried to scrub it off, the graphite ate into my eyebrows and eyelashes, earning me the nickname of "chimney sweep" at home.

In order to get to the factory by seven, I had to wake up at four in the morning. When the five-year plan got under way, public transport, like all other municipal services, became unreliable. The trams didn't run on schedule and it was not always possible to squeeze into a car. People hung off the tram steps and rode the rear bumpers. In a word, taking a tram to get to work was chancy. On most days, I walked the seven kilometers from our house to the factory.

It wasn't so bad in the summer when the sun rose early. But in winter, it was oh so hard to trudge in the dark along snow-covered streets. I have especially bad memories of the winter of 1931–32. The bony hand of hunger was already holding the people by their throats. More and more refugees were fleeing into Kiev. From time to time they would be taken away somewhere, but soon groups of emaciated farmers—men, women, children and the elderly—reappeared again. Wrapped in rags, they had already traveled all over the Ukraine and now came to find their last refuge in the once rich and hospitable city. But there was no longer anyone there to help them. Taking a shortcut, I would go down a steep hill following the path that led from the once lively but now gloomy Lutheran Street, by that time renamed Engels, directly to the Bessarabia Market. The market was boarded up because no one brought any food to sell there anymore. But vagabonds always hung around the place. I will never forget how I had to step over the corpses of those poor wretches, frozen solid and slightly covered up by snow. By morning, they would be picked up by the militia. But in the early hours when I was on my way to the factory, the sight of those mournful mounds of rags and frozen human flesh was indeed eerie.

While continuing to work at Bolshevik, I enrolled in evening language classes to study English and German. My knowledge of these languages was fairly good, but I wanted to perfect it. More importantly, I wanted to get a diploma that would qualify me to work as an interpreter. The program was designed to span three years, and I graduated after studying for less than two. I was in a hurry because I was preparing to enter Kiev Polytechnic. I had a dream of becoming an engineer like my father, but I had to study at the night school. I couldn't leave the factory because of the ration card I got there and the difficult situation my family was in. By that time I was making one hundred rubles. And that was already something.

Life was hard though. There was nothing left to take to a Torgsin store. And no matter how much money one had, it didn't help. There was just no food to be had anywhere. Father and Mother grew thin, and I turned into a skeleton altogether. I was already in my second year at college when I happened to meet a former schoolmate. He told me that Intourist had recently opened an office in Kiev and was looking for young men and women who knew foreign languages to train as tour guides and interpreters. The terms were quite attractive: a salary of 150 rubles, but more importantly, free meals with tourist groups, plus a sizable food ration. I jumped at the offer. It was 1934 and the third year of the terrible famine in the Ukraine. Life didn't offer anything to look forward to. It was, of course, impossible to combine work at the factory, night school, and the Intourist program. After some deliberation and a family council, I decided to take a chance and handed in my resignation at the factory.

But the risk I was taking wasn't all that high. With a diploma as an interpreter and knowledge of two foreign languages, I had no doubt I would be accepted. That was indeed what happened after a brief conversation in the admissions office. The training program was designed to last three months. We learned about the history of Kiev, its sights and outlying areas, studied the fundamentals of Soviet labor law and the legal system, and, of course, the theory of Marxism-Leninism. Professional guides shared their experience with us. I got a lot out of the program in terms of my general education by learning about the ancient architectural landmarks and the paintings and culture of Kievan Rus. These studies and two years of work at Intourist also helped me overcome my innate shyness and awkwardness. At special political indoctrination sessions we were taught the ploys to use to create a favorable impression on foreign guests about the Soviet way of life. This training was also useful. In fairness, I have to admit that some things I learned there came in handy later during the discussions I participated in, including the "scholarly debates" in which we all specialized in passing off black as white.

By spring, when the first foreign tourists were due to arrive, we were well armed for our first encounters.

In 1934, for the first time since the October Revolution, the Soviet Union opened up its borders to foreign tourists. Life was still very hard, especially in the Ukraine. As a result, the authorities worked even harder to attract foreigners. And it has to be admitted that a huge amount of work was accomplished. The guide-training program was only a small, albeit an important, part of it. The best hotels and restaurants that had survived since the time of the czar were completely overhauled. Quality tableware, table linens, napkins, and bed linens were purchased; kitchens were renovated, refrigerators installed. Passenger cars and buses were bought in the United States and Italy. The buses had a tarpaulin top to be used in case of rain. Attractively appointed hotel shops were well stocked with imported goods. Good-looking girls were hired to sell them—nothing was overlooked! Customer service departments in the hotels were furnished with foreign-made office furniture and were decorated with paintings, colorful panels, and advertising posters. Expensive carpets were laid out in hotel corridors decorated with antique furniture.

And all that was done in the year of the famine! We were typical Stalin Potemkin villagers. Stalin enjoyed impressing foreigners and he knew how to do it. It was no coincidence that he was able to fascinate world-famous writers and thinkers, people with discerning, sharp minds. Henri Barbusse, for instance, was known to have said that "Stalin is the Lenin of today." The leader of the people could be quite charming, using every means at his disposal when he wanted to win somebody over to his side. In general, the popular opinion of Stalin at that time was that he was a good boss, intolerant of waste, and demanding strict financial discipline from one and all. Hoping for a better future, the people believed that he was making the country richer for their benefit. But Stalin had a peculiar idea of the national prosperity. In his understanding it had nothing to do with the way the people lived. The people could go poor so long as the state was getting richer. Foreign tourists, carefully chaperoned by their guides, saw only the prosperous state, which was all they were supposed to see. As a result, they left the country with no idea whatsoever about the real conditions of life in the Soviet Union.

Intourist had a gorgeous hotel in Kiev, the Kontinental, located in Nikolayevskaya Street, right next to Kreshchatik (during the war the hotel burned down, and a conservatory was later built in its place). The hotel hired the best chefs, waiters, and doormen—all trained before the Revolution. The doormen were dressed in custom-tailored uniforms with jackets laced with gold and pants striped with gold. Special athletic-cut uniforms were also made for the drivers of the shining Lincolns and Fiats. A snow-white yacht with a well-stocked bar was waiting for tourists on the Dnieper River. And on top of it all, a trip to the Soviet Union at that time was inexpensive. A hundred dollars bought a weeklong trip to Kiev, Moscow, and Leningrad, including board, bed, and service. Of course, a dollar in those days could purchase more. But be that as it may, many tourists left the Soviet Union firmly convinced that it was the most inexpensive country in the world. It was at that time that our foreign trade bureaucrats came to believe that the ruble was worthless and that it was "advantageous" to waste our human and natural resources to earn hard currency.

A Model Kolkhoz

WHEN I RECALL THAT PERIOD, I can't help being amazed at the cynicism with which the country's devastated agriculture was portrayed to foreign tourists as a prosperous industry. Let me describe my first encounter with a model kolkhoz.

A rich American couple came to Kiev. They purchased a first-class tour and were entitled to a private car and a guide. We especially liked such well-to-do tourists. They were much less trouble than a large group; in addition, an interpreter had the same food as his clients, and when they traveled around the country, he got a place in an international-class sleeper car and a room in the best hotels. I had just been hired by Intourist and was given as my mentor an interpreter named Klara, a woman with some professional experience. And so the two of us were assigned to the American couple.

I liked Klara. She wasn't tall, but was graceful and looked like a porcelain statuette. She seemed quite young even though she was about three years my senior. At first, conscious of her role as my guru, she was quite strict with me.

On their very first day, the Americans asked to visit a kolkhoz. Klara instructed me to get in touch with Fainberg, the head of the service department, who found out which farm we could go to. On his list he had only three kolkhozes that were open to foreigners. To be on the safe side, we had to notify the kolkhoz chairman, which, because of the poor telephone service, sometimes took a full day. By the evening, everything had been arranged. I also informed my friend Stepan, the driver of the Lincoln that the two of us used, about the upcoming trip.

While I was taking the interpreter-guide classes, I worked for a while in the Intourist garage doing all kinds of odd jobs. I washed cars, changed oil, flushed radiators, and checked the cars leaving the garage for gas, etc. In those days, there were no gas stations in Kiev. Once a week Stepan, who was the youngest driver in the garage, and I took a truck and drove to an oil terminal located near the city's freight-train station. We filled up a few cans with gas, loaded them on the truck, and returned to the garage where the fuel was stored in a fenced-off area. The cans were placed on a platform so that when an automobile pulled up to it, gas could be poured into its tank. When a car came to fuel up, I had to twist the lid off the can, put a hose in it, and suck the air out at the other end of the hose before putting it into the car's trunk. Everything else happened automatically according to the principles of physics. Sometimes gas got into my mouth and then a lot of spitting needed to be done.

Stepan and I became friends. He was about twenty-five while I was eighteen, but he treated me as his equal. He taught me to drive, and when we were on our own, he would let me take the wheel of the Lincoln. On our nights off, we would invite girls to go for a ride out of town.

In the morning we took our couple to tour the Pechersk monastery and, in the afternoon, set off for the kolkhoz. The foreign guests turned out to be quite knowledgeable about agriculture. A member of the board of a U.S. bank, Bill (he suggested right away that we call him that—and his wife, Susie, using their first names) owned a large dairy farm not far from New York City. He had read stories about the horrors of collectivization and expected to see tangible proof of the advantages of private ownership.

But he was in for a surprise. The farm we were taking him to was called a model kolkhoz for a reason. After a tour of the farmstead, a chat with the chairman in his spacious office, and a visit to two farmers' houses, quite good by prevailing standards, we headed for a cattle-breeding farm located a few kilometers away. Not without difficulties, because he had to step on the brakes all the time driving his Lincoln along a narrow, bumpy road, Stepan got us to our destination. There, too, everything was in order. In the cowshed, swept clean for the occasion, pedigreed bull calves were lined up along the troughs, filled with fodder, into which they dipped their heads from time to time. They didn't look as if they had been starving. Then we went to see a pigsty. There we saw huge, clumsy sows surrounded by their frolicsome sucklings.

Bill, clearly impressed by what he saw, asked many pertinent questions. What breed the cattle were. How much milk the cows yielded. How strong the bloodstock of the bulls was, etc., etc. Answering him was good practice for my English. Even though I was familiar with the way things were on ordinary, not model, farms, the state of that kolkhoz seemed to suggest that a kolkhoz could be run as a profitable venture.

On a daily basis, the press carried reports about our "marvelous Michurin apples," the "wonder wheat" produced by Soviet selectionists, fantastic yields of milk by "record-setting cows," etc. And we believed that after the first five-year plan, maybe a second, our country would become the richest country in the world and its citizens the happiest people on earth. In the meantime, it was best not to show foreign tourists the present sorry state of our country, but to give them a peek at its bright future. I felt no qualms about deceiving that nice couple. We still do it today. A housewife, cursing, spends hours on line to get the basic necessities. Whenever she is lucky to get some delicacy, especially caviar or Chatka crabs, she puts it away, out of reach of her family members. But when she happens to entertain a foreign guest, all of that is laid out on the table. And the guest, enjoying the delicacies, is thinking to himself: These Russians, they seem to be doing pretty well, and the reports about their hardships are clearly exaggerated.

As Bill was saying goodbye to the manager of the cattle-breeding farm, he said excitedly, "I never expected to see this here! The stories we read in our newspapers are lies. Now I do believe that collective labor is as good, and maybe even better, than individual labor. We will have things to learn from you. I wish you every success!"

Then, after a pause, he asked, "But tell me, your farm is not an exception, is it? Other kolkhozes are run as wisely, aren't they?" Bill may have been getting suspicious. Were we making a fool of him?

"But of course!" the farm's manager assured him, even though he knew only too well that in most other kolkhozes the cows were too weak to stand on their feet because of the lack of fodder, and they had to be held up by ropes.

"This is a remarkable achievement!" the gullible Bill declared, all his suspicions gone.

While we were visiting the kolkhoz, which took longer than we expected, it suddenly became very cold. It was early spring, and the weather was changeable. The wind rose and it began to drizzle. Klara hurried the Americans but they didn't want to leave. Finally, we set off on the way back only to find out that the dirt road, dug up by tractor tracks, had become impassable. The ruts were full of water, and the heavy car was skidding from side to side. Stepan decided to leave the road and to drive right across the field to the highway. That was a bad decision. After a few kilometers, the car got stuck in the soft, sodden earth. Any attempt to get the Lincoln going only drove its wheels deeper into the black slush.

Bill got out of the car and, after evaluating the situation, said calmly, "It's hopeless. We are stuck here. Our only hope is the Russian frost," and he smiled at his joke, revealing an even row of teeth.

Of course, we didn't think it was funny. Frosts weren't due until the fall, and we couldn't possibly count on them. The three of us—Stepan, Klara, and I—became seriously worried. But the Americans were completely unperturbed.

"The answer," Bill said, "is to build good roads with a hard surface. This is what we do in America. This is probably the only thing that you need."

Of course, good roads were by no means the only thing we needed then—and still need. But Bill, fascinated by the cattle-breeding farm, didn't suspect that.

We began conferring with one another about what to do. No rocks or twigs were around to put under the wheels. It was growing dark. The gusty wind from the north was getting stronger. Perhaps the most reasonable thing to do would be to spend the night in the car. But there would be a terrible commotion in Kiev. An American couple missing! The American couple had to be taken to their hotel. Moreover, the women were lightly dressed. At a minimum, they had to get to an inhabited place and, if they were lucky, hitch a ride into town.

Finally, we decided that Klara and the Americans would go ahead on foot, while Stepan and I would stay in the car overnight, thinking that tomorrow would be another day.

The three figures moved away toward the horizon and finally disappeared in the dark. Stepan and I took another walk around the Lincoln, which stood there useless in the middle of a waterlogged field. Stepan started the engine and tried to move the car one more time. It wouldn't budge. There was no point in burning any more gas. We had to reconcile ourselves to the fact that we were stuck and would have to wait here until dawn. We got inside the front seat and lit up cigarettes. The time seemed to drag. Questions were gnawing at the back of my mind: Had Klara and the Americans made it to the highway? Did they find a car going their way?

No sooner did I doze off than there was a rap on the window. I rolled down the glass and saw Bill. Could something have gone wrong?

"What happened?"

Bill laughed. "Don't worry, everything's okay! I put them in a car going toward Kiev. And I decided to come back to you two to see how you would manage to get out of here."

I made an effort to control my irritation at his levity. "You shouldn't have done that. You should have gone to town. How could you have left the women alone?"

"What's wrong with that? In America, women are totally independent and they can take care of themselves. Are yours different? The guys in the car were nice. They promised to take Susie and Klara right to the hotel."

"Our women are of course also independent. But anything may happen. Well, there's nothing we can do now. You'd better get inside."

I was still worried. Stories about dispossessed kulaks hiding in the woods were still fresh in my memory. Hungry and desperate, they sometimes attacked lonely travelers at night and even stopped cars to rob people of their money and food. Tragedies sometimes happened.

Recently, however, there had been less trouble. Almost all "brethren of the forest," as they were called, had been caught. But maybe some hadn't? Local people, too, could sometimes be up to mischief. Even in Kiev people got robbed. Smack in the center of the city, right there at the corner of Vladimirskaya and Fundukleyevskaya streets where for a long time there remained the ruins of a building that had occupied the entire block and had burned down during the Civil War. (It was subsequently restored and given over to the Ukrainian Academy of Sciences.)

One late fall night, my parents and I were returning from a party and were walking down Fundukleyevskaya Street past those ruins. There wasn't a soul around. Suddenly, two gunslinging shadows jumped from behind a heap of broken bricks.

"Hands up!" a hoarse voice ordered.

We froze, obeying the command. One of the robbers stood a few steps away, pointing his gun at us. The other one came up to Mother.

"Show me your hands!" he told her.

She put out her hands with her rings on her fingers. One was her wedding ring, another one had a large ruby, and still a third had a golden leaf covered with small diamonds.

"Take 'em off!"

The bandit pointed the muzzle of his gun at her golden chain, then at her earrings. Mother obediently took them off and placed them in the robber's hand. Having pocketed the jewelry, he turned toward Father, who was still holding his hands up. That was what saved him his fine Moroccan-leather wallet with his papers and money. His unbuttoned jacket under the coat pulled back, and when the bandit frisked his chest, he didn't find it. He only found a few banknotes in the coat pocket, which seemed to satisfy him. Still pointing their guns at us, they began backing off toward the ruins. At that point Mother regained her innate self-control and suddenly exclaimed:

"Comrade, please, give me only two rings back. The wedding ring and the one with the ruby. This is a keepsake from my grandmother. It's very dear to me."

And she headed right toward the muzzles. Before Father and I had time to call her back, an incredible thing happened. The bandit who took the jewelry lowered his gun. He put his hand in his pocket and pulled out a handful of rings, chains, and bracelets and put out an open hand toward her.

"Here's for your courage, madam. Which are yours?"

Mother walked right up to him and with her two fingers fished the rings out of the heap of golden trinkets.

"Thank you," she said calmly and walked back to us.

I couldn't believe my eyes. A robber, and all of a sudden a noble one.

"Now don't budge for ten minutes," that same hoarse voice ordered, and the bandits disappeared in the ruins.

Father scolded Mother for her folly, but she was caressing the rings she had reclaimed so miraculously and didn't pay any attention to him.

I always recalled that episode whenever I found myself in similar situations. And there were a few. In some cases, I was held up by bandits at gunpoint. The last incident happened in the early 1980s. And it didn't happen in some dark alley or in some old ruins, but in downtown Washington, D.C., right opposite the White House in the lobby of the fashionable Hotel Hay-Adams on Sixteenth Street.

At that time I worked in the Soviet embassy in the United States, representing the USA and Canada Institute of the USSR Academy of Sciences. The director of our Institute, Academician Arbatov, usually stayed at the Hay-Adams whenever he came to Washington. On this occasion, we had spent the evening out of town, visiting with Congressman Stephen Solarz. We returned around midnight. Normally I accompanied the guest I was taking care of to the hotel's entrance and, after saying goodbye, would head for home. But on that occasion Arbatov invited me up to his room.

"I don't feel sleepy at all," he said. "I have a bottle of Armenian cognac. We'll have a drink and talk, if you are not too tired. . . ."

I was happy to agree.

An hour later we wished each other good-night. I walked out into an empty corridor and pressed the elevator button. When the elevator stopped on the first floor and its door opened, I witnessed a strange scene. Four black youths in fairly shabby clothes that struck a discordant note with the rich interior of the lobby stood frozen in its four corners. The night porter was bent somewhat unnaturally over the counter. At first I thought that something had broken down and a repair crew had been called in. But why were they so tense and looking at me so strangely?

"Hi, guys, what's going on here?" I asked all four of them, heading for the door.

There was no answer, but one of the youths jumped up to me. Then I saw the gun in his hand. A tiny little thing. Its barrel barely noticeable. A recent report in the press about such toys flashed through my mind: dealers brought them in from Germany as assembly sets for kids, and in the States they were put together and sold at a bargain price. A lethal weapon. A favorite in the American slums: it costs nothing and is easy to dispose of.

The black guy, the gun in his left hand, began patting me over. He wanted to make sure I wasn't armed. It is well-known that many Americans never part with their weapons. I, of course, didn't have one. But a wallet was in the back pocket of my pants. The robber pulled it out and began retreating slowly, keeping his gun pointed at me.

"Take the money," I said to him, "but give me back the wallet. I have my papers there."

I didn't want to lose my driver's license, gas credit card, and the State Department diplomatic ID. Losing them is like losing a limb. And I was thinking of the time it would take tomorrow to obtain duplicates.

The thought that there might not be a tomorrow for me somehow didn't even cross my mind. I demanded loudly that my papers be returned to me. But the man seemed not to hear me. The others also stood around in silence. Maybe they are drugged, I thought to myself: they seem to be slow to react. Without thinking of the consequences, I walked up to the robber and snatched my wallet from his hand. He was astounded. He hadn't expected such a rash move from me. But the next moment he swung his arm out and hit me on the head with the butt of the gun. I still had time to open the wallet and show him the greenbacks—just a little over two hundred dollars.

"Take the money." I held out the open wallet.

He grabbed the entire bankroll, and I, pleased with the success of my move, returned the wallet to my pocket.

The man ordered, "Lie facedown on the floor!"

Stepping aside, I saw two men in the hotel uniform lying facedown on the carpet between the sofa and the chair. I thought it an unseemly posture. I just kneeled down and placed my head on the arm of the chair. Only at that point did I feel the blood that was dripping down my cheek. A blood vessel must have been cut. The bleeding was getting worse. Red spots appeared on my shirt and on the chair.

Glancing toward the counter, I saw that two robbers were trying to force a safe. The blood was getting into my eye, and I wanted to wipe it off with a handkerchief. The man who was standing near me reacted nervously to my move. He walked over to me and then noticed

the watch on my wrist. Holding the gun to my temple, he began un-
fastening the metal band. Luckily, the clasp was tight and he could-
n't open it. At that moment, the safe door came screeching off its
hinges. The man jumped away from me and ran toward the counter,
and I took the watch off and put it in my pocket. It had some sentimental value for me and I didn't want to lose it. The guy came back
and found me in the same position only without the watch. He made
an angry grimace. I thought he was going to hit me again. But he
slapped himself on the pocket of his jacket where something jingled
and walked off. He must have concluded that he had taken the watch
off and put it in his pocket.

What was going to happen next? I was wondering. I had heard of
cases where bandits, before getting away, shot potential witnesses.
That was why they ordered us to lie facedown. It was easier to shoot
into the back of the head. If that was what they were going to do with
us, it was pointless to worry about the future. But what if not? At that
point I began playing out in my mind different scenarios of how
things could unfold. Undoubtedly, the newspapers would carry reports about a holdup at a fancy establishment like the Hay-Adams.
They would describe it in every detail and provide pictures. In my
imagination I could already see my bloodied face on a newspaper
page with the caption "Soviet Diplomat Wounded!" That was the last
thing I wanted. Our relations with the United States were already
fairly poor, and here was this—an attack on a diplomat. The reporters might even insinuate a "failed assassination attempt" on Academician Arbatov, member of the CPSU Central Committee, a
deputy, a public figure, close to you know who . . . etc., etc. God for-
bid it should turn into something like the shot fired in Sarajevo.

I hadn't the slightest doubt that what had happened was a pure coincidence. The robbers were after the money in the hotel's safe, and
to my misfortune I happened to step out of the elevator when the
robbery was in full progress. A shout rang out:

"Stay put for fifteen minutes. Nobody moves or we shoot. We'll be
watching you."

Having taken the contents of the safe with them, the four bandits,
their backs to the door, guns pointing at us, left the hotel one by one.
We all breathed a sigh of relief. We were lucky. The robbers had decided not to make too much noise. After all, the White House was
close by. Five minutes went by, then ten. Everything was quiet. I
asked, "Isn't it time to call the police?"

"Forget it!" I heard a whisper. "Don't move. It's not time yet."

We waited a little longer and got to our feet. The porter dialed a number. A few minutes later we heard the siren of a police car and the screeching of tires. A camera flashed outside the windows. A crime photographer was in a hurry to take a shot of the hotel entrance. While the night porter and the doormen bustled to the door, I walked over to the elevator, unobserved, and pressed the button. The door opened and closed noiselessly behind me. In a moment I got off at the fifth floor. I walked over to Arbatov's room and pressed the bell.

"Who is it?"

"It's me, Yuri. Please open up, I have a little problem."

The door opened a crack, held in position by two chains. Arbatov peeped through but didn't recognize me. It wasn't surprising—my face was smeared with coagulated blood, my shirt and light jacket covered with dark red spots.

"It's me all right."

"Good Lord! What happened?"

"Let me tell you what happened."

In a few words I described the incident to him and said that I had decided to avoid an encounter with the police in the sorry state I was in. Then I went into the bathroom, cleaned up my face, washed my shirt, and scrubbed the spots off my jacket. We hung up the laundered things to dry on the lamps. Arbatov just couldn't understand how something like that could happen right in the center of the U.S. capital. Some forty minutes later, I looked out the window and saw the police leave the hotel. Only one patrol car was left on the opposite side of the street. The bleeding had stopped. My clothes had dried. We agreed on the program for the next day and said goodnight to each other. I went down to the lobby and walked out into the street as if nothing had happened. The porter, who was talking to a reporter, didn't pay any attention to me. My car was parked nearby, and twenty minutes later I was home.

Even though I had tidied myself up, Lera, my wife, knew right away there had been some trouble. I had to tell her the story. Used to the fact that I got into some kind of trouble on a regular basis, she calmed down, washed the wound, and put a Band-Aid on it.

At eight o'clock the next morning I was already at the hotel, and Arbatov and I set off for a working breakfast at the Capitol. The TV news and the *Washington Post* briefly reported the Hotel Hay-Adams robbery, saying that "no one had been hurt."

But let us return to now-remote 1934.

We decided not to explain to Bill the reason why we were so concerned for the women he had so lightly sent off in a strange car. We could do nothing about it anyway. We began settling down for the night. We lowered the blinds and covered the windshield and the back window with the floor mats. Bill and I settled in the backseat, Stepan perched in front.

I had no idea how long I slept. I pulled the blind aside—it was pitch dark all around. The rain had stopped and it had become quite nippy. I touched Stepan on the shoulder: "I think we should start the engine and turn the heater on."

Even before he could do it, we heard some voices. I bent over toward Stepan: "Somebody's coming this way. Let's sit still. Let them think there's no one inside."

Bill moved. I warned him, "Please be quiet."

He squeezed my hand understandingly. We lay down on the seats. The voices—of two people—came nearer. Suddenly, everything became still, and then we heard, "Look what's here!"

"Where did this come from?"

"Must've gotten stuck."

Cautious steps could be heard on both sides. We heard heavy breathing. We held our breath, trying not to stir. Suddenly, the car rocked from a blow. Was it an iron bar or maybe a sawed-off shotgun? If the latter, maybe we were in for big trouble. Somebody began pulling at the handle of the front door. At that point Stepan understood that we couldn't pretend any longer not to be there.

"Get back or I'll shoot!" Stepan bawled at the top of his lungs.

The strangers didn't expect that and fled.

Maybe they meant no harm, but we couldn't take any chances. Of course, Stepan had no gun, but from a psychological point of view, he had made the right move. We didn't go back to sleep after that. I told Bill that those people could have been some drunken bums.

"We have plenty of those in America. We are better off staying away from them," he agreed good-naturedly.

At dawn, we got out of the car. The blow had landed on the rear bumper, but the damage was minimal: only a small dent. We locked up the Lincoln and set off to look for the nearest dwelling.

The village we came upon stretched along a road that ran between two rows of pussy willows. The first two houses had boarded-up windows and no sign of life. They must have been abandoned by dispos-

Lyudmila Titova, Berezhkov's mother, a student at the Smolny Institute in St. Petersburg.

Berezhkov's father (at right), a student at St. Petersburg's Polytechnic Institute, earned his living by private tutoring.

V. Berezhkov, 1938.

Stalin receiving Ribbentrop in the Kremlin on August 23, 1939, before the signing of the Soviet-German Non-Aggression Pact and the Secret Protocol.

A friendly handshake between Stalin and Ribbentrop after the signing of the Soviet-German Treaty on Friendship and the Border. Moscow, Kremlin, September 28, 1939. Chief of the Red Army General Staff Marshal Shaposhnikov is at center.

Molotov greeted at the Anhalter Station in Berlin on November 12, 1940. In front row, left to right, Field Marshal Keitel, Reich Minister Ribbentrop, People's Commissar for Foreign Affairs Molotov. Second row: Soviet Ambassador in Germany Shkvartsev (between Ribbentrop and Molotov), and Councellor of the German Embassy in Moscow Hilger (right of Molotov). Berezhkov is in the party accompanying the principals.

Ribbentrop greeting People's Commissar Molotov arriving in Berlin on November 12, 1940. Councellor of the German Embassy in Moscow Hilger is at center.

Molotov and Hitler in the Imperial Chancellery.

Molotov and Hitler during their talks at the Imperial Chancellery, Berlin, November 1940. Councellor of the German Embassy in Moscow Hilger is at center, acting as the interpreter for the German side.

Molotov and Hitler relaxing on a coffee break during their Berlin talks in November 1940. Seated around the table, left to right: Hitler's personal interpreter Schmidt, Councellor of the German Embassy in Moscow Hilger, People's Commissar Molotov, Deputy People's Commissar for Foreign Affairs Dekanozov (back to camera), Hitler, Ribbentrop, Berezhkov, and Keitel.

Molotov paying a visit to Reich-marshal Hermann Göring.

Molotov meeting the Führer's deputy in the Nazi Party, Rudolf Hess.

Beria's man Vladimir Dekanozov, Soviet Ambassador in Germany before Hitler's invasion of the Soviet Union in 1941.

Ambassador Dekanozov leaving the Imperial Chancellery after submitting his credentials to Hitler. Berlin, December 1940.

Hitler receiving Soviet Ambassador Dekanozov in his office in the Imperial Chancellery, December 1940. Seated from left to right: V. Berezhkov, V. Dekanozov, Adolf Hitler, and Head of the Imperial Chancellery Otto Meissner (at right).

Nazi Foreign Minister Ribbentrop gives a warm smile to Ambassador and Mme. Dekanozov at a reception in the Soviet Embassy in Berlin to mark the Red Army Day, February 23, 1941. V. Berezhkov is at left of Ribbentrop.

Hauptsturmführer Heinemann leaning on the window of a train car carrying Soviet diplomats through Austria, Yugoslavia, and Bulgaria to the Turkish border to be exchanged with the German diplomats being evacuated from Moscow through Armenia to eastern Turkey, July 1941.

Hitler with the leader of the SA storm troopers Ernst Röhm not long before the Night of the Long Knives when Hitler brutally slaughtered Rohm and his followers. After the bloodbath Stalin commented to his colleagues in the Politburo, "Hitler is great! He showed us how we should treat our political opponents."

A lighter moment in the Kremlin after a stormy confrontation of the two leaders, Stalin and Churchill, during the British prime minister's visit to Moscow in August 1942 when he informed his host that despite the earlier promises given by Washington and London, the second front would not be opened in France that year.

Celebration of Churchill's birthday in Teheran, November 1943. Roosevelt, Churchill, and Stalin over the birthday cake.

Presentation of the Royal Sword to Stalingrad, Teheran, November 1943. The men behind the two officers in the foreground are, from left to right: Churchill, Eden, Voroshilov, and Stalin. Berezhkov is at far right, behind the Soviet officer.

At the ceremony, presenting the Royal Sword to the city of Stalingrad for the valor and courage of its people and defenders. Stalin is kissing the sword's blade. Left to right in the foreground: Churchill (his back to camera), Stalin, Molotov, and Berezhkov. Teheran, November 1943.

A walk in the park of the Soviet Embassy in Teheran, November 1943. From left to right: G. Marshall, Stalin's bodyguard, British Ambassador in Moscow Archibald Clark Curr, Harry Hopkins, Berezhkov, Anthony Eden, Stalin, and Voroshilov.

The Big Three in Teheran. Berezhkov is in front of the column. November 1943.

sessed kulaks. The third house had smoke coming out of its chimney. We knocked on the door. It was opened by an elderly woman wearing a black cap and a scarf full of holes thrown over her shoulders. We greeted her. I apologized for disturbing her so early and asked if we could come inside.

"Come in," she said after a pause.

Two men were sitting at a table, probably her husband and son. A chunk of black bread lay on a plate. A pot with potatoes could be seen in the Russian oven. I explained who we were and added that we had an American tourist with us.

"Sit down at the table," the older man said in Ukrainian, not a bit surprised.

We were quite hungry and didn't have to be asked twice. The woman placed the pot on the corner of the table, put some boiled potatoes onto our plates, and poured sunflower oil over them. She poured carrot tea into aluminum mugs. It occurred to me that for Bill, a tourist traveling first-class, this was a pretty meager breakfast. And after he had had that unscheduled meal he would have less than a high opinion of the food the people on the kolkhoz ate. I knew that Fainberg would let me have it for that! And the fact that we allowed the American to spend a night like that also meant trouble. But Bill didn't complain; not only that, he even said that the food was "tasty and nourishing."

It became clear from the conversation with the man of the house that we were not in the kolkhoz we had visited the day before. This was by no means a model farm. Another blunder for me! But at least we got help. After we had had a bite, we went to the kolkhoz office, where we got two oxen to pull us out.

"Will they be able to pull that monster of a car out?" Stepan asked doubtfully.

"Oh, yes, they will. They are hardy."

Huge, with sand-colored hides with black spots, curving horns, and rings in their noses, the oxen were staring curiously at the outlandish monster that was also colored in tones of sand and black. Ropes were attached to their harness. Stepan and I tied them to the front springs of the car. Bill sat behind the wheel and started up the engine. We pushed the car from behind. At the sound of "Giddap!" the oxen pulled, the car shifted, slowly climbed out of the rut the wheels had dug the night before, and began moving over the field. I found that sight highly symbolic. Ukrainian oxen were bringing back to life a wonder of American technology!

Bill opened the door of the car and called out, "This car by itself is a heap of metal. It's useless without highways and other infrastructure. I told you, you should hurry up and build hard-surface roads!"

Whenever our television shows villages outside Moscow where inclement weather makes the roads impassable and even tractors get stuck in the sticky mud, I always recall that scene. Half a century has gone by since then, and there are still no hard-surface roads around our villages and fields.

The Red Kapelle

ON THE FATEFUL MORNING of June 22, 1941, the Reich minister's Mercedes was waiting for us—Dekanozov and me—at the entrance to Ribbentrop's residence to take us back to the embassy. As we turned a corner from Wilhelmsstrasse into Unter den Linden, we saw a line of SS troopers in front of our embassy. We were effectively cut off from the outside world. The phones were dead. We were not allowed to go into town. There was nothing left to do but wait for further developments.

Around two o'clock in the afternoon a phone rang in the embassy office. An officer of the Protocol Department of the German Foreign Ministry, Erich Sommer, was calling to inform us that until it was made clear what country would take it upon itself to represent the Soviet Union's interests, the embassy would have to appoint a diplomat to effect liaison with Wilhelmsstrasse. Ambassador Dekanozov entrusted me with that mission, and I so informed the Protocol Department when they called back again.

"I have to advise you," a voice on the other end of the line explained, "that on his trip to the Ministry for Foreign Affairs, the embassy representative will be accompanied by the officer in charge of the guards posted around the embassy, SS Hauptsturmführer Heineman. Through him you can get in touch with the Protocol Department, if need be."

Thus, I was granted permission to travel only to the Wilhelmsstrasse and only accompanied by Heineman. Yet it was important that we inform Moscow about the situation at the embassy—and about the proposals by the German side concerning the evacuation of the Soviet personnel. Essentially, their idea was to exchange an equal number of staff, a proposal that we found totally unacceptable. The Reich government, which over recent months had recalled from the USSR most of its employees and their family members, had a little over a hundred of its citizens left in Moscow. We had about a thousand of our people in Germany. Stalin, concerned about making Hitler suspicious, had forbade us from reducing the number of our employees in Germany. More than that, new officials with their families had kept arriving at the embassy right up to the very last day. Now, in accordance with the German scenario, only one hundred of our people could be exchanged, while almost nine hundred Soviet citizens would have to remain in Germany. It was important to advise Moscow to retain the German embassy staff there until the exchange issue was satisfactorily resolved. Our attempt to dispatch a cable failed. And in those days diplomatic representations didn't use radio telecommunication.

Ambassador Dekanozov, concerned over the situation, decided to discuss a possible course of action. On June 24, he called to his office the military attaché, General Tupikov; the embassy attaché, Korotkov, at that moment substituting for the KGB resident, Kobulov, who was away in Moscow; and myself, the only diplomat who sortied into town on a regular basis and conducted negotiations with the German Foreign Ministry.

"Let us see once again," the ambassador began, "if it is possible for someone to leave the embassy grounds unobserved. If it is, then we could establish contact with our friends working in the underground and through them get information over to Moscow."

"My people have carefully studied that option," Tupikov reported. "The entire block is surrounded. At night, the area is patrolled by guards with dogs."

"Maybe Berezhkov could try to get away from Heineman?"

"Heineman doesn't let me out of his sight," I observed.

"What kind of a man is he, this Heineman?"

"Generally speaking, my relations with him are quite good. He is a man advanced in years, well-balanced, not like those young SS fanatics."

"Is it possible to feel him out, to find a way to approach him?"

I suggested that a lunch or dinner be arranged for Heineman and me at the embassy. The idea met with approval.

"There is a little problem though," Korotkov joined in. "I am the only one who has been staying in touch with our friends. They will not agree to contact anyone else, especially at a time like this. And on top of that, as you know, their radio transmitter has broken down. We have just received a new one from Moscow. But how can we get it to them? This is our top priority."

"Therefore," Dekanozov summed up, "under any scenario our goal is to set up a meeting between Korotkov and our friends. There will be no excuse for us if we fail to do that."

I want to emphasize that he was not referring to some paid collaborationists. Our friends, who maintained contact with the experienced Soviet agent Aleksandr Mikhailovich Korotkov, were confirmed fighters against fascism. For many years some two hundred people in their underground organization had considered it their patriotic duty to supply valuable secret information to the Soviet Union, which they regarded as a force capable of thwarting Hitler's plans to enslave the peoples of the world. The leaders of that organization, Harro Schultze-Boysen and Arvid Harnack, had access to the most closely guarded government secrets.

Luftwaffe senior lieutenant Schultze-Boysen came from the family of a Prussian officer and was closely related to Grossadmiral Tirpitz. Schultze-Boysen enjoyed the complete trust of the German High Command. However, when a student he had been involved with left-wing groups and German Communists. In the early 1930s, he edited an antifascist youth magazine, *Der Gegner*. After Hitler came to power, his storm troopers raided the magazine's editorial office and Schultze-Boysen found himself behind bars. His high-placed relatives interceded on his behalf and got him out of prison, and his involvement in the antifascist movement was written off as "the mistakes of youth."

But when he got out of prison, Schultze-Boysen didn't stop his struggle against fascism. He understood that now his methods had to be changed. During the Civil War in Spain, he contacted the Soviet embassy in Berlin and maintained a discreet connection. At the same time, he made friends with Reichsmarshal Hermann Göring, who was pleased to know a young officer from an aristocratic family. Göring even agreed to be Schultze-Boysen's best man at his wedding, which put the latter's reputation beyond any possible suspicion. His amicable relations with one of the top leaders of the Third Reich made it possible for Schultze-Boysen to enter the Ministry of Aviation, where he became head of the Intelligence Department. But his brilliant career rise didn't go to his head nor distract him from his main purpose—to topple the Nazi regime. The organization that Schultze-Boysen led continued to operate deep underground.

Another convinced opponent of Nazism was Arvid Harnack. Holding a doctor's degree in philosophy and law, he organized a network of seminars to study scientific socialism even before Hitler seized power. In his lectures and at the seminars he advocated friendship with the Soviet Union and warned the German people about the impending threat of fascism. When the Nazis came to power, the group he headed went underground. As a ploy to cover up his activities, Harnack joined the National Socialist Party and took a job at the Ministry of the Economy, where he soon became director of one of its departments. He made contact with Schultze-Boysen and they decided to merge their two groups into one organization.

Having access to secret military and economic information, Schultze-Boysen and Harnack concluded that an early attack by Hitler's Germany against the Soviet Union was inevitable. They informed Moscow of the imminent attack (which Stalin didn't want to believe in) and took special care to preserve their contacts even after hostilities broke out. That was why they were eagerly awaiting a replacement for their broken-down transmitter.

Senior Lieutenant SS Hauptsturmführer Heineman turned out to be a talkative man. On the second day after we met, I already knew that he had a sick wife, that his brother served as a guard in the Imperial Chancellery, and that his son, Erich, was soon to graduate from officers' training school after which he would be sent to the front. I was surprised when Heineman confessed to me that he had asked his brother to find a place for Erich in the rear. Such a confession coming from an SS officer to a Soviet diplomat was somewhat disquieting, especially when his country was at war with the USSR and he was the commander of a unit posted to guard the Bolsheviks. Was he trying to provoke me into speaking to him confidentially? Maybe deep down in his heart, he didn't harbor any hostile feelings toward us and was even prepared to help. In any case, it was worth our while to take a closer look at him. After the meeting with Dekanozov I decided to make an attempt to establish "friendly relations" with Heineman.

One evening after he had inspected his guards, Heineman stepped inside the embassy to find out whether we had anything we wanted to transmit to the Wilhelmsstrasse. I invited him to come in, have a drink, and relax a little. We sat down in the deep armchairs in the living room in front of a low glass table.

"Would you like to have a bite of something to eat?" I asked my guest after we had a few vodkas. "You must be tired after the day's work, and then again it's been a while since you had lunch."

At first Heineman refused, saying that he wasn't allowed to do that while on duty. But finally he relented.

That night we had a fairly frank conversation. After a few drinks Heineman began telling me that, according to his brother's information, the Imperial Chancellery was very much concerned about the unexpected resistance the German troops had run into in the Soviet Union. In many areas, the Soviet soldiers were holding out till their last bullet, and when their ammunition ran out, they were engaging in hand-to-hand combat. Nowhere else since the beginning of the war had the German troops met with such resistance or suffered such casualties.

"Some people in the Imperial Chancellery," Heineman said, "even wonder whether Germany should have started the war against the Soviet Union in the first place."

That statement already sounded like an expression of opposition, but I couldn't possibly expect that from an SS officer.

Still uncertain as to what to make of Heineman, I listened in silence. Only when he began talking about his son again did I observe that the war didn't have to happen at all, and that then not only would his Erich be safe, but the lives of many Germans and Russians would be spared.

"You're absolutely right!" Heineman exclaimed. "Who needs this war?"

The next day I invited Heineman for breakfast. He agreed right away, without standing on ceremony. The important thing for me was to find out how useful he could be to us. I should broach that subject cautiously, I was saying to myself, so that if his reaction was negative, I could turn everything into a joke. The first question I asked myself was, why would he want to help us? If despite the fact that he was an SS trooper and an officer he was not a confirmed Nazi and was serving Hitler for expediency, I could play on his negative attitude to the war and his fears for his son. For instance, I could promise that should Erich be captured, he would be treated with special care. If, on the other hand, Heineman was just a cynic who wanted to make some money for his services, then there was no problem. But what if he tried to trap us into "buying" an SS officer and then turned us over to the Gestapo? But why would he want to do that? He might, of course, be tempted to make the decision on the basis of who would pay him the most. Well, if that was the case, I didn't think that Dekanozov would haggle.

Heineman showed up at the appointed hour for breakfast. After a few remarks about the reports from the front, he again touched upon the subject that was painful for him—his son.

"In the next few days," he went on to say, "Erich will be graduating from officers' training, and in accordance with the German tradition I will have to pay for his dress uniform and buy him his personal weapon. And then on top of that, my wife is sick. I have had to spend almost all my savings on her."

I didn't know whether there really was a custom that a new officer had to purchase a dress uniform and personal arms, but the fact that Heineman had begun talking about money looked like a promising development and I decided to follow up on it.

"I would be happy to help you," I observed casually. "I've been working in Germany for quite a long while and have been saving up for a major purchase. But now it doesn't make sense anymore and the money will be lost anyway. We are not allowed to take anything out of the country except a small suitcase with personal belongings and a small amount of pocket money. I don't feel very comfortable making this offer, but if you want it, I could give you a thousand marks."

In those days that was a considerable amount. For instance, in 1940, when I returned from Essen to the trade mission in Berlin, I rented a spacious room in a boardinghouse, but with a common bathroom, for only five marks a night.

Heineman became pensive. He looked at me closely and was silent for a long time. He was clearly wondering whether it wasn't too risky to take the next step. I went on nonchalantly sipping my coffee from my cup. Finally, Heineman spoke:

"I am very grateful to you for the offer. But how can I take such a large sum just like that? It's impossible."

"Well, you decide. I told you that the money is as good as lost to me anyway. I won't be allowed to take it out. Your government will con-fiscate it together with the other funds that we have here at the em-bassy. A thousand marks is nothing for the Third Reich and it may come in handy for you. But again, you decide; it doesn't make any difference to me who gets this money."

I poured more coffee into his cup and filled up his glass with cognac. Heineman lit up, sat back in his chair, and drew deeply on his cigarette a few times. I felt a struggle was going on within him.

"Well, I think I'll agree," he said finally. "But you, of course, understand that not a soul is to know about this!"

"Don't worry about it. These are my personal savings. Nobody even knows I have them. I'm giving them to you and that's the end of the story."

I took out my wallet, counted one thousand marks, and put them on the table. Heineman slowly reached out to collect the money. He pulled out a large wallet from the back pocket of his trousers and, after carefully smoothing out the bills, put them away into one of its sections. He put the wallet back in his pocket and sighed heavily.

We were off to a start of some kind.

Heineman said, "I want to thank you one more time for this. I'd be glad if I could be of service to you."

I could have taken him up on his offer right away, but on reflection, I decided it was enough for one day. It was best to leave everything at that for the time being.

"I don't need anything," I replied. "I just happen to like you and am glad to be able to help you. It doesn't cost me anything. I can't use this money anyway."

We stayed there a little longer. When Heineman began saying goodbye, I invited him to come in during the day so that we could have lunch together.

The embassy cook, Lakomov, on personal instructions from Dekanozov, prepared an exquisite lunch for us. Caviar and salmon from the government-provided stocks, consommé, cutlets à la Kiev, ice cream, coffee, and, of course, vodka, Georgian wine, Armenian cognac, and liqueurs. Lakomov would also serve us, dressed in a jacket and a bow tie.

By the time Heineman arrived, everything was ready: I could treat him to a good lunch and make an appropriate proposal. We had previously discussed the situation with the ambassador and with Korotkov and had outlined a plan.

When, over dessert, Heineman returned to the morning's conversation and again expressed his desire to be of service to me, I replied, "Well, you see, Herr Heineman, as I told you, I personally don't need anything. But one of the embassy staffers, a friend of mine, asked if I could do something for him. It's a purely personal matter, and I didn't even tell him I would talk to you. And, of course, he doesn't know anything about our relationship," I added to calm Heineman down.

"And what is this about? Maybe we can think together how to help your friend?"

"You see, he met this German girl here and they became friends, but then the war broke out so suddenly he didn't even have a chance to say goodbye to her. He wants so much to get out of the embassy for at least an hour to see her one last time. They may never see each other again. And so he asked me to help him. But we are under strict orders not to leave the embassy. I will probably have to disappoint him."

"Let me see. I think it may not be so hopeless after all."

Lakomov brought in boxes with cigars. After Heineman lit one up, he became pensive. He remained silent for a long time. Then he said, as if thinking out loud, "My boys posted around the embassy know I accompany you when we have to go to the Wilhelmsstrasse. They have gotten used to seeing us leave together. It's gotten to be a routine matter for them. I don't think they will pay any attention if we put your friend in the backseat, go into town, and set him down somewhere. We will pick him up at an agreed place in one hour and return to the embassy. I think this could probably work, don't you?"

Out of caution, at first I began assuring Heineman that he shouldn't be exposing himself to such a risk over an affair of the heart involving people he didn't even know, and that my friend would eventually somehow survive without saying goodbye to his girl. But Heineman was energetically defending his plan. Finally, after playing hard to persuade for a while, I accepted his proposal, and we began discussing its details.

"If we take care of every detail," he was telling me, "everything will go smoothly."

Of course, I couldn't be completely sure that the SS officer wouldn't let me down or that he had really agreed to help us. When we were saying goodbye, I told him that I still had my doubts about taking him up on his offer. But I invited him to stop by later that night just in case.

When Heineman left, we got together to discuss the situation. We agreed we had to take the chance. But no matter how important it was to get the transmitter over to our friends, we decided against taking it on the first trip. We had to make sure Heineman could be trusted. Finally we decided that Sasha Korotkov would go empty-handed, and if he was detained, he could tell his captors the story of his girlfriend. In the worst-case scenario, the German Protocol Department would lodge a protest with us. We also had to make sure that Sasha was not tailed. Another consideration to bear in mind was that we hadn't received any information from our friends since the beginning of the war. We first had to find out that they were all right. Of course, there was a risk that there would be no second trip. But still we decided to keep the transmitter out of it for the time being.

Heineman was on time, as usual. Korotkov and I were there to meet him.

"Please meet Sasha, the Sasha I told you about."

They shook hands and Heineman said, "So you are the one who has been charmed by our girl. Well, I will try to help you."

We sat down at the table. Heineman was in great spirits. He joked a lot, told us about his son, whom he had taken to the Bavarian Alps in the summer before the war, where they had a good time. Every now and again he would poke fun at Sasha, recalling how he himself, at the end of World War I, a prisoner in France, had fallen in love with a Frenchwoman whom he eventually had to leave.

"Even though I am no longer young," Heineman said, "I understand very well what it means to you to be able to see this girl one more time."

We agreed to carry out our plan the next morning at eleven A.M., after Heineman had inspected his guards.

"A word of advice," the SS officer volunteered. "Don't take your huge Soviet automobile. We would be better off taking a small-size German car. We will be less conspicuous."

It was a good piece of advice. Indeed, the Embassy ZIS-101 always attracted the attention of the public. I decided to take the Opel that was parked in the embassy garage. Nobody in the streets of Berlin would pay any attention to us in that car. Heineman said he was going to get in touch with the Ministry of Foreign Affairs to find out whether I would be asked to come to the Wilhelmsstrasse the next morning. It all looked as if we were planning a picnic. Maybe Heineman did believe the story about Sasha's girlfriend? If not, he was pretending very well, trying to arrange a date for the lovers.

Anxiety was gnawing away at our hearts. It was rather late when Heineman left, and we still didn't know for sure how he was going to act the next day—nor even what tomorrow would bring.

The next morning, Heineman didn't show up at the agreed time. We became worried. What if he had betrayed us and the Gestapo was already aware of our plans? For three long hours our nerves were on edge.

At two o'clock in the afternoon the bell at the gate rang. It was Heineman. He apologized for being late. His wife's condition had taken a sudden turn for the worse. He had had to call in a doctor and stay longer at the house. On the other hand, he had made arrangements with the Foreign Ministry, and on account of his family problems there would be no meetings scheduled at the Wilhelmsstrasse. Therefore, we could carry out our plan in peace.

We walked into the reception room. While Sasha was treating Heineman to ice-cold vodka, I took the sand-color Opel Olympia out of the garage and drove it up to the inner entrance. Heineman climbed into the front seat with difficulty. The long broadsword in its silver scabbard at his side was getting in his way. Finally, he unclasped the buckle and threw the sword into the backseat where Sasha was already sitting. The gate swung open, Heineman saluted the SS soldiers, and we drove out into Unter-den-Linden. I looked into the rearview mirror to make sure there was no tail.

On all previous days we had driven only to the Foreign Ministry. So as not to arouse any suspicions, I turned left as usual in front of the Brandenburg Gate and drove down Wilhelmsstrasse for a few blocks. The streets of Berlin looked strange. It was overcast, yet warm and dry. The glass sparkled in the shop windows, passersby went slowly about their business, flowers were on sale at street corners, old ladies were walking their dogs—nothing seemed to have changed. At the same time, the knowledge that the war had already been raging for a few days left a special imprint on the seemingly peaceful scenes of Berlin.

We had previously agreed to set Sasha down at a large supermarket, Kaufhaus des Westens, in Taunzienstrasse. It was a perfect place to blend in with the crowd. The subway stop was also right there. Two hours later we were to meet at the Nollendorfplatz subway station.

When the car stopped, our passenger got out quickly and immediately disappeared in the crowd. We drove on and for a long time circled aimlessly around the streets. Then we took the Charlottenburg Bridge toward the famous Fünkturm, the tall, openwork radio tower. During the day, that place, popular among Berliners for night promenades, was usually empty, and we decided to go there to kill time.

First we took a stroll in the park around the radio tower. Then we sat down at a table at a summer cafe. Heineman said that now he wanted to stand me a drink and ordered two Berliner Kindl beers. Back in the car, he had been silent most of the time: he must have been nervous, too. Here at the table he regained his usual eloquence and kept telling me one funny episode after another from his school days. I listened to him absentmindedly, thinking about Sasha and whether everything was working out for him.

Then it was time to go to the agreed meeting place. As we approached Nollendorfplatz, I saw Sasha from a long way off. He was standing in front of a shop window and seemed to be contemplating the goods displayed there. But he was looking for us out of the corner of his eye. When I pulled over, Sasha walked over to the curb, waved to us casually, and after a few words of greeting slowly got inside. To an outside observer it looked like a chance meeting of friends. As he was settling down in the backseat, Sasha firmly squeezed my shoulder. My heart jumped with joy—his mission must have been a success.

"How's the girl?" Heineman asked.

"Everything is fine, thank you very much. She was so glad to see me."

Heineman began making some suggestive jokes, but we didn't listen to him attentively. After circling the streets a little longer, I drove up to the embassy and honked. The gate opened. Once inside the inner yard, we sighed with relief.

A dinner for three was waiting for us. We wanted to get rid of Heineman as quickly as possible, but we had to spend more than an hour with him, listening to his never-ending stories. After the nerve-racking tension of the day we were overcome with apathy.

When Heineman was gone, we discussed the results of the operation with those who knew about it. Sasha reported that our friends were fine. He informed them that we had received a radio transmitter and would try to deliver it to them in the near future. Then it would be possible to transmit our information to Moscow.

And so part of the mission was accomplished. Now we had to carry out the main task—getting the transmitter to our friends.

The next day Sasha and I had breakfast with Heineman. He was telling us the latest news from the front that he had received from his brother. It was different from the victorious reports carried by the German newspapers. The Soviet units were putting up fierce resis-

tance. German losses were much higher than the preliminary esti-
mates of the German command. All this, in Heineman's words, was
causing serious concern at Hitler's headquarters. Then we began
talking about yesterday's sortie. Heineman asked Sasha jokingly
whether he wanted to see his girlfriend one more time. That was the
opening we were waiting for.

"Of course, I do," Sasha said. "But I hate to trouble you again."

Heineman observed that although there was some risk, we could
probably do it one more time.

"Since you're kind enough to agree," Sasha said, turning to him,
"I would like to have a little more time this time, three or four hours.
And I would like to take some souvenirs to her."

"I can see that you acquire an appetite in the course of the meal,
as the French say," Heineman joked. "But I understand you. Tomorrow is Sunday, the Foreign Ministry will be closed. We won't be called
in there, and we'll have the whole day at our disposal. Let's leave at
around ten and return by lunchtime."

I was struck by Heineman's carelessness. A question could arise: If
the Foreign Ministry was closed, why were we leaving the embassy?
But he probably thought that his soldiers were not used to thinking
and would conclude that if their boss was going somewhere, then
something needed to be done. I decided against alerting him to that
eventuality, thinking that if we put off the trip, we might not have a
second chance.

The next morning at the appointed hour, the Opel was already
parked inside the gate. Heineman arrived ten minutes early. As we
were saying hello to each other, I noticed that this time he was not
carrying his broadsword. Instead he had a holster, the handle of a
Walther glistening dimly from it, attached to a broad belt fastened
tightly over his jacket. I became worried. Former misgivings came
back to haunt me. Heineman must have carried a gun before—
maybe he kept it in his pants pocket—but I had never noticed it. Now
it was clearly visible and within easy reach. What if he had decided to
catch us red-handed, as it were? As soon as we were out of the gate,
would he put his Walther to my temple and order me to go to
Gestapo headquarters? And we with our radio transmitter there in a
suitcase in the backseat.

I gave Sasha a quick look. He probably had his doubts, too. What
were we to do? Give up the trip? We had to feel Heineman out.
Maybe he would somehow give himself away.

"I see you are not carrying your broadsword today, and it is so becoming to you," I observed, forcing a carefree smile to my lips.

Heineman replied quite naturally, "You see, the broadsword gets in the way in the little Opel. And since I knew we would be going in the same car, I decided to leave it at home. But according to regulations, if you are not carrying a broadsword, you have to have a gun on your belt."

That explanation sounded quite credible and it calmed us down a little. But what about the suitcase? The radio transmitter was tucked away in a secret compartment with "souvenirs" thrown on top to cover it up—hand-embroidered Ukrainian shirts, towels, lace, and Matryoshka dolls. Sasha threw the suitcase on the backseat and said, trying to sound casual, "Souvenirs for my girlfriend, little trifles."

Heineman looked closely at the suitcase but said nothing.

Now, I was thinking to myself, he's going to say, "Show me what you got for your friend there." Or worse still, he would poke his hand inside the suitcase and hit the partition covering up the transmitter, which was close to the surface. A chill ran down my spine. This was the make-or-break moment.

I walked around the car, my legs stiff with tension, opened the door, and invited Heineman to take his usual seat. He paused for a few seconds and then got inside.

"Well, well, well," he said, making himself comfortable, "a suitcase full of gifts. Your girlfriend is going to be very happy."

We made it! But the bitter taste stayed in my mouth for much longer.

When we drove out of the gate, we headed for the subway station in Uhlandstrasse. That place was also always crowded. We agreed to meet three and a half hours later at the Wittenbergplatz subway station. I pulled over. Sasha whisked the heavy suitcase into the air, as if it were a feather, and disappeared into the subway entrance.

We had plenty of time and decided to take the belt parkway. We made a stop in the forest. The weather was beautiful. The clouds were slowly floating across the sky, and the beauty of that peaceful, serene scene caused an involuntary protest in my mind. Over in the East, bloody battles were being fought, villages were burning, and our people were dying, and here I was, taking a stroll alongside an SS *Hauptsturmführer* in a sun-drenched forest filled with herbal fragrances!

We drove back into town. Heineman suggested we go somewhere and have a snack. We parked the car near a restaurant at the corner of Kurfürstendamm, opposite Gedächtniskirche, walked through a glass revolving door into a spacious hall, and began looking for a suitable table.

Suddenly, somebody called out, "Hey, Heineman! Come over here."

Six SS officers were seated at a large round table. Beer mugs were all over it. There was no question that the company knew Heineman well. The SS troopers were waving at him, inviting him to join them at their table. What were we to do? Leaving was already out of the question. But there would be a scandal if it became known that an interned Soviet diplomat was walking around Berlin.

At that moment I heard Heineman's hurried whisper: "I will introduce you as my wife's relative from Munich. You work at a military plant and that is why you don't talk much. Your name is Kurt Hüsker. Be careful."

We came up to the table where the SS officers—some on their feet and others only half getting up from their chairs—greeted us by barking out, *"Heil Hitler!"* Heineman responded in a resonant voice and I mumbled the same words of greeting under my nose.

After Heineman introduced me to them, we sat down and ordered a round of beer. The conversation naturally drifted to the hostilities on the Soviet-German front and the night raids on Berlin, recently resumed by the British Air Force. I had no doubt that my knowledge of the language, which I had perfected during the time I had worked in Germany, wouldn't let me down, but still I was grateful to Heineman for his idea about my work at a military plant in Munich. That allowed me to sit there in silence most of the time. In any case, no one at the table suspected that I was not whom I was claiming to be.

Heineman looked at his watch. It was time for us to leave. But his friends didn't want to let us go. When we finally left, we were running half an hour late and I had to push our little Opel to the limit to get to our meeting place as quickly as possible.

Sasha was already waiting for us, and, of course, he was nervous. When he was in the car, he squeezed my shoulder again, as he did the last time, and I was glad to know that everything had gone all right. We got back to the embassy without any problems.

Later, Heineman, with his SS unit, accompanied us when the Soviet embassy staff were evacuated in two trains from Germany to the Turkish-Bulgarian border. But the last time I saw him was on July 2, 1941, when we were leaving Berlin. Over breakfast he presented his photo to me, one that had an inscription on the back.

"It may so happen," he said as we were saying goodbye, "that I will
have to mention the service I rendered to the Soviet embassy. I hope
it will not be forgotten."

He had obviously known that Sasha's girlfriend was not what she
seemed to be and that something much more serious was going on.

In the first years of the war, the underground antifascist organization led by Schultze-Boysen and Harnack transmitted a large amount
of valuable information to Moscow. It related both to the situation in
the German rear and to Germany's military plans. Encoded radi-
ograms contained intelligence about the reserves of strategic materials, the production of aircraft, and new weapons systems. By trans-
mitting vital information about the losses sustained by the Nazi army,
the planned Wehrmacht offensive operations, and the sending of
saboteurs behind the Soviet front line, the German antifascists were
doing their patriotic duty to the German people who were also
crushed under the Nazi boot. It was a different matter to what extent
the Soviet command used that priceless information. But one thing
is certain: the transmitter we delivered helped save many lives of our
people at the front and in the rear. The Abwehr and the Nazi security service had a hard time uncovering that organization, which they
baptized the Red Kapelle. In late August, early September 1942,
some members of the organization were hanged in the Pletzensee
Prison in Berlin. They were brave on the scaffold. When the execu-
tioner threw a rope around Harnack's neck, he called out that he
had no regrets about what he had been doing. Schultze-Boysen wrote
in the last letter before he died that his actions were always prompted
by his reason, his heart, and his convictions.

Recalling those staunch, selfless people with their clear consciences,
I can't help thinking about the postwar history. So many people like
them sacrificed their lives for the sake of the noble ideals they fervently
believed in. When fascism was at last defeated, it seemed that those sacrifices had not been in vain. A "workers' state" appeared on German soil
that proclaimed its plans to build "a happy socialist society." The people
of my generation believed that this goal could be achieved throughout
the socialist community, and especially in the German Democratic Republic. But the model that was forced upon all of us proved to be un-
sustainable. Attempts to impose it by force resulted in numerous losses
and cataclysms that shook Eastern Europe to its foundations. And the
German Democratic Republic, at one time the pride of the "world Communist and workers' movement," ceased to exist altogether.

After his return to Moscow, Sasha, or rather Aleksandr Mikhailovich Korotkov, climbed high up the career ladder. We rarely met. But our paths crossed again in 1943 in Teheran where he was with the people who were providing security for the Big Three. Then I saw him again in 1954 at the Geneva Conference on Indochina. For a number of years, Korotkov held ranking positions working in the GDR. In the late 1950s, he died suddenly on a tennis court in Moscow.

From Ankara to Moscow

THE TWIN-ENGINE DOUGLAS was parked on a concrete pad in front of the squat building at the Ankara airport. The USSR ambassador to Turkey, Vinogradov, and a representative of the Protocol Department of the Turkish Foreign Ministry, were seeing us off. Despite the early hour, the sun was already hot. The bright blue dome of the cloudless sky arched over the flat plain covered with yellow grass. The still air promised a sultry, windless day. The captain of the aircraft, dressed in a military pilot's uniform, stood motionless at the bottom of a ladder.

Our group, for whom this farewell ceremony was being held, comprised primarily the top people of the Soviet embassy to Germany who had remained in Berlin right up to the time of the attack by Hitler against the Soviet Union. At that time only a few people in the Soviet colony in Berlin had diplomatic status: two counselors, one first secretary, two second secretaries, one third secretary, four attachés, one consul, military and naval attachés and their first deputies. The trade representative and his deputy also had diplomatic passports. The support staff at the mission wasn't too numerous either. By the beginning of the war, roughly half of the diplomatic staff were away on leave. Naval Attaché Vorontsov and Counselor Kabulov had left for Moscow with their families as early as May. Sensing that the Nazi invasion was inevitable, they had decided to quit Berlin well in advance. Ambassador Dekanozov had also sent his family back home.

Counselor Amayak Kobulov, a brother of Bogdan Kobulov, Beria's first deputy, was the resident of the Soviet Committee on State Security in Germany. In appearance, he was the exact opposite of Bogdan, a repulsive, short, fat, and creepy character. Amayak—a tall, slender, and handsome Caucasian, sprouting a well-trimmed little mustache and a shock of black hair, urbane, even charming—was the life of any party and would play the role of a *tamada*, the Georgian toastmaster, so disarmingly that few people suspected what his real responsibilities were. In those days, nobody could have imagined how the career of this bon vivant would end. Yet in December 1953, after Stalin died, Amayak Kobulov was executed by gunfire—together with his brother Bogdan and along with Dekanozov and others convicted in connection with the Beria case.

After we had crossed the Bulgarian-Turkish border at Svilengrad—while the German diplomats who had left Moscow also crossed the border from Armenia into Turkey—there was no need for the ambassador to take care of the Soviet personnel anymore. That responsibility devolved on the USSR consulate general in Istanbul, where a short time after our arrival a Soviet ship, the *Svanetia*, docked, took most of the Soviet colony on board, and set off for Georgian Batumi along the coastline of neutral Turkey. For the rest of us, that is to say, our small group of diplomats, which included, in addition to the ambassador, Embassy Counselor Semyonov, the military attaché, General Tupikov, Attaché Korotkov, and myself together with my wife, Galina, we took the overnight express for Ankara. There at the Ankara airport, a chartered plane sent from Moscow to pick up our group was already waiting for us. But since we wouldn't leave until the next morning, we had a whole day to spend in Turkey's capital.

Dekanozov, who remained deputy people's commissar for foreign affairs, together with the USSR ambassador in Turkey, Vinogradov, and Semyonov with them, left to pay a visit to Turkey's Ministry for Foreign Affairs. Galya and I, joined by Attaché Korotkov and General Tupikov, decided to take a walk in town.

Ankara looked like a large village, especially when compared with the splendor of Istanbul where everything reminded one of the wealth and grandeur of the Ottoman Empire. The streets here were dusty and dirty. Stunted trees lined the capital's main thoroughfare, Atatürk Boulevard. We went into a coffeehouse and were served fragrant Turkish coffee, *rahat lakoum*, and nuts halva. A glass of ice-cold water was placed next to each cup of coffee.

We didn't see any special sights in that city, which came into prominence after Turkey's revolution at the wish of its leader, Kemal Atatürk, with the exception of some colorful and exotic little shops of artisans selling their handicrafts. Since the Germans had required us to leave everything we owned behind in Berlin, permitting us to depart with only one small suitcase each, we decided to buy a few things to meet our basic needs. Out of the stuff I bought in Ankara, some thermal underwear and heavy shirts turned out to be particularly useful to me during the years of the war to come.

On the following day, after saying goodbye to the people who came to see us off, we boarded the plane and took off for home. We made only one stop on the way, in Leninakan, already on Soviet territory. The runway there was a metal grid placed on top of green turf.

When we got out of the plane, we saw a small lodge a short distance away from which a few people were hurrying toward us. They were the local bosses. They had been advised of the arrival of a member of the Communist Party's Central Committee, Deputy Foreign Minister Dekanozov, and they had tried to organize a fitting welcome. They were lugging along baskets filled with all sorts of food: a whole spit-roasted lamb, lavash bread, a battery of bottles of Armenian dry wine, fruits, vegetables, and oriental sweets. A cloth was spread out right there on the grass next to the plane and the feast began, interspersed with the inevitable and unavoidable toasts.

There wasn't even a mention of the war. Less than a month had gone by after the invasion, and here, away from the front, the people didn't seem to be particularly worried. They were probably unshaken in their belief in the promise made by their leader that we would beat the aggressor on his own territory. Without information about the actual developments at the front, they expected that the Red Army would roll back the enemy hordes and enter German territory, where the German workers and farmers would turn their arms against the Nazis and the war would end with our total victory.

Georgia's capital also rolled out the red carpet for us. Dekanozov, who had kept his apartment there after he moved to Moscow, went home, while we stayed at the Hotel Tbilisi. Our suites, with their carpets, mirrors, and large terraces, reminded us of Tiflis's pre-Revolutionary wealth when French financiers held strong positions and did much to develop and make more beautiful the city's main street, which was then named after Shota Rustavelli, a classic of Georgian literature. It was noisy and crowded. In the hotel's restaurant, with its high glass ceiling, music was playing. After dinner we sat out on the terrace observing the well-dressed throngs of people, mostly men, who were slowly strolling up and down the brightly lit boulevard, lined with tall, branchy plane trees. Here, too, the war had not yet left its sinister mark on the carefree atmosphere of that southern town.

Early next morning we left for Moscow. Now we had more passengers on board. We had been joined by Dekanozov's family: his wife, Nora Tigranovna, and their two teenage children, Nana and Redjik. After a brief stop in Rostov, we flew on along the Volga, finally turning west near the city of Kuibyshev. We had made a circuitous detour to avoid the German Air Force, which was active in the southern Ukraine. In the afternoon, after circling a few times over the roofs of the buildings in Moscow, we landed at the Central Airport in Leningradsky Prospekt.

It was warm and sunny in the capital. When the engines cut off and we descended to the green grass at the edge of the runway, it was hard to control our emotions. The silence all around us seemed deceptive. All this time I was thinking about the fierce struggle that our country was engaged in against a strong and treacherous enemy. Yet here, in the very center of Moscow, it was surprisingly quiet, the fragrance of warm clover filled the air, and larks were peacefully fluttering in the sky. But already in Leningradsky Street we could observe the ominous signs of the war. A huge poster fixed to the side of one of the buildings caught our eyes—a Russian woman with a stern face was holding up a piece of paper with the text of the military oath in her hand and a caption below that read: "Mother Russia is calling!" Our car passed a volunteer militia unit marching in uneven formation. The facades of the buildings were painted with strange patterns of green and brown, and the glass panes in the windows were pasted over with strips of paper.

Thus, from the very first minutes of our arrival, Moscow presented an austere military look.

After we arrived, everyone dispersed to his or her apartment. But I again had a problem. Since I no longer worked in the Commissariat of Foreign Trade, I couldn't count on a room at the Metropol. Dekanozov suggested that we go to Kuznetsky Most and wait there for the head of the Foreign Ministry's administrative department, Alakhverdov, who would be given instructions to find a temporary place for us to stay.

Our fears about the situation we found ourselves in proved unfounded, and the question resolved itself rather quickly. After the Germans seized Norway, Denmark, Holland, and Belgium, Stalin, probably in a move to appease Hitler, broke off diplomatic relations with those countries, and the mansions that had been occupied by their missions stood empty. One of them, the former mission of Norway, located in Ostrovski Street, was turned into a housing unit for the staff of the People's Commissariat for Foreign Affairs. The diplomats who came back home after the beginning of the war and were retained to work at the Foreign Ministry's headquarters were housed there on a temporary basis. Alakhverdov took us there.

Our room was completely empty, but by night two folding beds, bed linen, a fairly beat-up desk, and two chairs were delivered. There was only one bathroom on our floor, on which a few other people were staying in similar rooms, and in the morning we had to stand on line to get in. Still, Galina and I, who had no place at all to stay in Moscow, thought that our room at the mansion in Ostrovski Street was a fortunate solution to our housing problem. We stayed there until October 16, 1941, when, after the Germans advanced to the Moscow suburb of Khimki, the People's Commissariat for Foreign Affairs was urgently evacuated to Kuibyshev.

The very first night we were awakened by an air alert. The women and children went down to the basement. The men climbed up on the roof to put out incendiary bombs. Our antiaircraft guns couldn't repel all enemy aircraft. Some bombers penetrated the defenses and reached downtown Moscow. They were clearly visible in the searchlight beams. A heavy demolition bomb exploded in the area of the Nikitsky Gates. A house in Hertzen Street was almost totally destroyed and the Timiryazev monument was split in half by the explosion. Incendiary bombs came pouring down upon us. Two of them fell on the roof near me. I put them out in a bucket filled with sand.

The next morning, Dekanozov called me to his office and informed me that I had been appointed his assistant. He asked me what I thought about it.

"For me, an assistant to the deputy foreign minister is a ranking position. I will try to fulfill my responsibilities to the best of my abilities," I replied.

"Well said. In fact, you had already been my assistant in Berlin. Here of course it's going to be more difficult, but I am sure you will cope. I wish you every success."

I thanked him and asked what specifically I would be required to do.

"First of all, you will have to read the files on the countries and top-ics that have already been put together by the manager of my secre-tariat, Markelova, and her three assistant secretaries. Then every day, by the time I come in, you will have to have carefully read the Tass in-formation bulletin and selected the important items for my atten-tion. You will also read other materials and cryptograms addressed to me, and if they require any follow-up from relevant departments of the Commissariat, you will instruct them on it and will compile their reports by their subject matter."

Dekanozov went on to explain that he was responsible for Iran, Turkey, Afghanistan, Mongolia, China, and Sinkiang, as well as for the countries allied with Germany. In addition, he was in charge of the Commissariat's finances, including its foreign-currency account, and also directed personnel and consular affairs. In short, there would be no shortage of problems.

Room in the Kremlin

NOT LONG BEFORE HITLER'S INVASION, Stalin assumed the re-sponsibilities of chairman of the Council of People's Commissars, making Molotov his first deputy and allowing him to keep his post of people's commissar for foreign affairs. But Molotov's office remained where it had been before—in the Kremlin, on the second floor of the building of the Council of People's Commissars. Close by, around the corner and down the corridor, I shared an office with Pavlov, who by that time had been appointed assistant to the people's commissar re-sponsible for Soviet-British relations. When in late July 1941, Harry Hopkins, President Roosevelt's special representative, came to Moscow, I was among the welcoming party at Moscow's Central Air-port in Leningradsky Prospekt. However, Litvinov interpreted at his talks with Stalin. I was entrusted with that work only two months later when a British-American delegation, headed by Lord Beaverbrook and Averell Harriman, came to Moscow in late September 1941. Soon after that I was appointed Assistant to the People's Commissar for Soviet-U.S. Relations and moved into the Kremlin.

Harriman had a joke about how I made my first appearance in Stalin's study. When his talks with Stalin began, someone else was interpreting for the Soviet side. The interpreter for the Americans was Charles Bohlen, third secretary of the United States embassy in Moscow.

During the talks Stalin's interpreter appeared to be having some difficulties with what Harriman had to say, and Bohlen began helping him. Stalin didn't like that. He turned to Molotov:

"Why is this American correcting my interpreter? That is no good. Where is that young man who interpreted at your talks with Hitler, Vyacheslav? Let him come and help us."

"But he was interpreting into German."

"Never mind. I will tell him and he will interpret into English."

That was how I was brought before the boss to become his personal interpreter.

By telling that story, Harriman was laughing about the omnipotence of the Great Leader. Just by ordering an interpreter, he could make him translate in any language.

The first time I ever saw Stalin was in late September 1941 at a late-night dinner held in the Kremlin in honor of the Beaverbrook-Harriman mission. The guests assembled in the room adjacent to the Catherine's Hall a short time before eight P.M. Everyone was waiting for Stalin to appear. Finally, a high door swung open—but it wasn't Stalin. Two of his bodyguards walked in. One stopped by the door, the other took up his position in the opposite corner. Several more minutes went by. All this was probably done on purpose. The boss was deliberately delaying his arrival, thereby raising his guests' expectations to a higher level.

The door opened again, and this time Stalin walked in. When I took a look at him, I felt a shock. He was completely unlike the image of Stalin I had formed in my mind. He was short and haggard, his tired face, covered with smallpox scars, was the color of the earth. His military-cut uniform hung loosely on his lean frame. One of his arms was shorter than the other and almost totally hidden in the sleeve. Could this be Stalin? It was as if they had substituted someone else for him.

From our childhood we had been taught to regard Stalin as a great and wise leader, endowed with an awesome power of foresight. We saw his portraits, his bronze and marble monuments; he was on posters carried during festive demonstrations and parades; we had gotten used to seeing him tower above the rest. Our youthful imagi-

nation completed the picture by turning him into a tall, slender, almost mythical being. And there he was, plain and simple. Yet everyone seemed to hush up in his presence. Walking slowly on a carpet
in his Caucasian boots, he greeted everyone present. His hand was
quite small, his handshake limp.

Those were the hardest days of the war. Hitler's troops had penetrated deep inside the Soviet territory. They had reached Leningrad
and Kiev and were rapidly advancing toward Moscow. The Soviet
units, forced to retreat farther and farther, sometimes didn't even
have enough czarist rifles to go around. I was witness to Molotov's
conversation with a commander of one of the units that was defending the capital. The officer was complaining that he had only one
rifle for every five soldiers and was begging Molotov for help. But
Molotov, who knew the real situation, replied bluntly:

"If they have no rifles, let them fight with bottles."

It was at that time that the famous Molotov cocktails—bottles filled
with a flammable mixture—came into being. A soldier of a volunteer
unit would hide in a dugout waiting for a tank, and when it would
rumble over his head, he would get up and throw the bottle into the
tank's exhaust pipe. When he scored a hit, the tank would burst into
flames, but the next tank would shoot the brave soldier at point-
blank range. Tens of thousands of volunteers died like that near
Moscow. A good number of my friends were among them.

Terrible misfortunes, the loss of vast territories, the death and
capture of millions of people, could not have left Stalin unaffected,
even considering his total lack of respect for human life. But something else depressed him most: his misjudgment of the situation before the war. He had ignored all warnings, firmly believing that
Hitler would not start a war in the middle of summer. Hitler's admirer only recently, he now could not forgive him for putting him,
the wise leader of the people, to shame before the whole world.
The infallible Comrade Stalin, like a child, had been taken for a
ride by an Austrian lance corporal. Stalin had not forgotten the humiliation and the fear he had experienced and became even more
suspicious than before—about everything. Even inside the building
of the Council of People's Commissars he was always accompanied
by two bodyguards. They escorted Stalin even when he went to see
Molotov.

It often happened that when leaving the people's commissar's secretariat and turning the corner to go to my office, I would see a guard

I knew emerge from behind the opposite corner. Each time that happened I would be overcome by confusion. No, it wasn't fear. I was convinced that such an encounter wasn't dangerous for me personally. But I would get an irresistible, subconscious desire to hide. Stalin was to appear in a few seconds. Thoughts would be racing through my mind: What was I to do? Go back inside the secretariat or make a dash for my office and hide behind the door there? Maybe I should hide behind one of the drapes that covered the tall windows facing the inner yard? But what if Stalin saw that someone was hiding there and concluded that I had evil intentions toward him or had something on my conscience? Whenever an interlocutor failed to look him in the eye, Stalin was quick to suspect sedition: "Why are your eyes so shifty?"—and that question could seal a poor fellow's fate.

After considering all the options—and well aware that I had little time left—I would press my back against the wall and wait. Stalin's party would slowly go past me. I would call out in a cheerful voice:

"Good afternoon, Comrade Stalin!"

He would remain silent, make a slight gesture with his hand in response to my greeting, and turn the corner. Now I could breathe a sigh of relief. Nothing had happened, right? Then why was it that the next time I found myself in a situation like that I would be transfixed again?

I would also become nervous whenever the boss's first aide, Poskrebyshev, or one of his deputies, would tell me well in advance that there would be a meeting with the Americans and that I was to be the interpreter. However, in such cases I could rationalize my fear—I was going to climb Olympus. And then there would also be some nervous concentration, the desire to do the job as best I could so that He would be pleased.

In those days the Kremlin was closed to the public. But I had a pass to all areas, except to the corridor leading to Stalin's wing of the building. A special pass was made out for each trip there.

The atmosphere in Stalin's offices was calm and businesslike. In the little room next to his secretariat where I had to wait for the word that our guests had passed through the Spassky Gate, glasses and bottles with mineral water were set out on black trays painted with bright flowers, and a row of simple chairs was lined up against the wall. Some authors now write that all visitors, even Molotov, were searched before entering the leader's study, and that electronic devices were kept under the chairs to detect hidden weapons. There was nothing of the kind. Firstly, at that time there were no such electronic systems, and secondly, over the period of almost four years that I reported to Stalin's office, I wasn't searched once, and speaking more generally, I wasn't subjected to any special clearance procedures. At the same time, in the last and most difficult months of 1941, amidst the fears that German agents had infiltrated the capital, each one of us had received a gun. I, for instance, had a small Walther that I could easily hide in my pocket. Around six o'clock in the morning when we had completed our workday, I would take it from the safe and head for the building of the People's Commissariat for Foreign Affairs in Kuznetsky Most where I could get some rest in the basement, undisturbed by frequent air alerts. In the fall and winter months, the sun rose late and the streets were dark. Quite often I would come across a military patrol that would check my papers. But I might also bump into a German saboteur. It was for such eventualities that we were issued our handguns. When we reported for work in the Kremlin, we were to put our guns away in a safe. But nobody ever checked whether I had done that or was still carrying a gun when I was going to see Stalin.

My opportunities to observe Stalin were limited by my specific functions as an interpreter. I always saw him in the company of foreign visitors, to whom he played the role of a hospitable host. When the officer on duty informed me that the guests had passed through the Spassky Gate and that only minutes remained before they would show up, I would head for Stalin's office, past the secretariat, Poskryobyshev's office, and the security room. Here there were always a few people—both in uniform and in civilian clothes—and in a chair right by the door the boss's chief bodyguard, General Vlasik, would usually be dozing. He used every chance to take a nap since he had to be with his boss twenty-four hours a day. I would enter the office unannounced and would always find someone there: Politburo members, top military leaders or ministers. They would be sitting at a long table, notebooks in front of them, while Stalin would be pacing up and down the carpet. He would either be listening to one of those present or talking. My appearance served as a sort of a signal that it was time to conclude the meeting. Glancing at me, Stalin would usually say:

"The Americans will be here any minute now. Let's take a break."

Everyone would quickly gather their papers, get up from the table, and leave the room. Only Molotov would stay. He was present at all

Stalin's talks with foreigners, although he rarely said anything. Sometimes Stalin would turn to him with some question, calling him "Vyacheslav." For his part, Molotov, when in the company of foreign guests, invariably stuck to the official "Comrade Stalin."

It should be admitted that despite all his repulsive personal traits, Stalin was capable of charming his interlocutors. He was unquestionably a great actor and could play the role of an affable, modest, even a common man. In the first weeks of the war, when it seemed that the Soviet Union was about to collapse, all visiting foreign dignitaries, starting with Harry Hopkins, were pessimistic. However, they left Moscow fully confident that the Soviet people would fight on and ultimately win. But the situation was indeed desperate. The enemy was relentlessly pushing eastward. Almost every night people had to go down into bomb shelters. So what was it that made Hopkins, Harriman, Beaverbrook, and other experienced and skeptical politicians change their minds? Nothing else but their conversations with Stalin. Despite the seemingly hopeless situation, he was able to create an easy and calm atmosphere.

Sometimes Stalin would reinforce his charm with a drinking binge. He himself never drank much in the presence of foreigners but with the help of his "Georgian hospitality" he got his guests very drunk. Thus, in early spring Japanese Foreign Minister Matsuoka came to Moscow to sign the Neutrality Treaty. Stalin and Molotov made him so tipsy he had to be carried out of the Kremlin and into his railroad car.

The chimes of the Spasskaya Tower clock barely penetrated the office where silence always reigned. The boss was radiating benevolence as he unhurriedly conversed. Nothing dramatic seemed to be occurring outside the walls of that room, nothing seemed to worry him. And that was reassuring. His interlocutors didn't know that at that very moment steps were being taken to evacuate people from Moscow, bridges and government buildings were being mined; an underground city administration had been set up and its future officials had received passports with false names. His visitors didn't suspect that their host in the Kremlin office, who looked so carefree, was considering different options for an urgent transfer of the government to a safer place. After the war, in a candid moment, Stalin confessed that the situation had been critical. But then he was cleverly hiding that knowledge behind a nice smile and a composed manner. Speaking about the needs of the Red Army and of industry, Stalin

mentioned not only antiaircraft and antitank guns and aluminum
for the production of aircraft, but also equipment for business enterprises and entire factories. At first his guests were puzzled: it
would take many months, if not years, to deliver and install the
equipment and to start the production process. Yet Western military
experts were claiming that Soviet resistance would be broken within
the next four to five weeks. What construction of new factories was
he then talking about? It was even risky to send weapons to the Russians—they could end up in enemy hands. But if Stalin was putting
in requests for factories, he had to know something that neither the
experts nor the politicians in the Western democracies knew. And
what were they to make of Stalin's calm demeanor and the assurances he gave to Hopkins that if the Americans supplied aluminum,
the Soviet Union could go on fighting even for four more years? It
was obvious that Stalin had a better understanding of the situation!
And so Hopkins, Beaverbrook, and Harriman began assuring
Roosevelt and Churchill that the Soviet Union would hold out and
that it made sense to start making arrangements to deliver military
supplies to their staunch Soviet ally. Of course, Stalin was bluffing;
but fortunately he was able to bluff it out. That was also the case in
the second half of December 1941, when British foreign minister
Anthony Eden visited the front line near Moscow, and when Stalin
observed:

"The Russians have been in Berlin twice. And will be there a third
time."

Stalin's faithful supporters may invoke such statements as proof of
the leader's foresight. But I think here, too, he was playing the role
of an optimist. Among the inner circle of people around him in
those days, he often confessed that "everything that had been
achieved by Lenin had been lost," that a catastrophe was unavoidable. With his affected cheerfulness he concealed his lack of faith in
the people, whom he called "fools" and "imbeciles" even as they were
adulating him. Yet those same people, whom he didn't like and who
scared him, sacrificed millions of their sons and daughters to make
his prophecies become reality.

Stalin always treated me in the same even, indifferent manner.
Sometimes it seemed to me that he was looking right through me, as
if he were unaware even of my presence. But as I soon found out, for
each occasion he personally selected one of the two interpreters he
had available. Sometimes, when there was going to be a meeting with

the Americans, Pavlov would be called in, and when the British were arriving for talks, I would be summoned, even though the United States was my area and Britain was Pavlov's domain. Sometimes it happened that for a few weeks at a time only one of us would be invited to interpret, regardless of whom the talks were with. On such occasions, the person left out would feel ill at ease and nervous, wondering what could have upset the boss, what could have caused his displeasure. But then everything would go back to normal. We didn't hear any critical comments and, of course, didn't dare pursue the matter further. Maybe it was all just a little game he played with us to keep us on our toes and to maintain "a healthy competition" between us.

Stalin had a peculiar sense of humor. One story has it that once the head of the political directorate of the Red Army, Mekhlis, complained to the supreme commander that one of the marshals at the front had a new wife every week. "What are we going to do about him?" asked Mekhlis. Stalin continued to look grim and didn't answer. Mekhlis thought he was thinking of some severe punishment and already regretted he had made his report. But suddenly Stalin looked at him with a naughty smile and said: "We are going to envy him."

In another story, over a number of wartime years, every now and again Stalin teased another marshal with a question: Why hadn't he been arrested in 1937? Before the marshal had time to open his mouth to say anything, Stalin would sternly order him to go. That went on right up to the end of the war. After each such episode, the marshal's wife packed a bundle for him with warm clothes and some food, expecting that her husband would be sent to Siberia any day. Then Victory Day came. Stalin, surrounded by his commanders, was making a speech.

"We knew both hard times and the joy of victories, but we were always able to joke. Right, Marshal?" and he called out the name of the poor butt of his jokes.

But sometimes Stalin's "jokes" were not funny. At one time he was vacationing in Abkhazia at a place called Cold River. One night he was kept awake by the barking of a dog. He got out of bed and summoned his guard.

"Find that dog and kill it," he ordered.

Soon everything was quiet. In the morning Stalin asked: "Did you find that dog?"

"Yes, Comrade Stalin," replied General Vlasik, his chief body-guard.

"Did you kill it?" Stalin continued.

"No, we did not," Vlasik answered. "It was the guide dog of a blind man. But we shipped them far away."

"Bring that dog back!" Stalin barked out. When his order was carried out, Stalin took a gun and personally shot the dog.

"Next time you disobey, this is going to happen to you" he warned his bodyguard.

Sometimes I had difficulties writing telegrams to our ambassadors in London and Washington. A draft telegram had to be prepared right after the conversation while Stalin was still in his office.

Out of force of an old habit he had developed while working in the underground, Stalin worked the whole night through, and he usually received diplomats very late, sometimes even at the crack of dawn. The conversation often went on for two or three hours, but the telegram had to be no more than two pages long. Having finished dictating, I would go back to Stalin's office. He would look through the text, make some amendments, and sign it. But on occasion he didn't like my version. That irritated him. He was never rude, though; he would just reproach me:

"You were sitting there interpreting, you heard it all, and you didn't understand a thing. Is this important what you wrote here?"

However, he understood that I was doing my best, it was just that my best wasn't good enough for him. And there was no point in sending me back with a simple instruction to "do it over again." He would then say:

"Take out your notebook and write this down." And he would dictate the points that he considered important.

After that it wasn't difficult to draft a new telegram. But each time that happened a bad feeling stayed with me for a long time afterward.

To Find the Culprit

ON NUMEROUS OCCASIONS I observed that Molotov would get nervous whenever a proposal he had advanced didn't meet with Stalin's approval. For a few days he would be grim and irritable, and it was best to stay out of his way.

The widespread opinion in the West that Molotov didn't take any initiative and acted strictly on Stalin's instructions appears unfounded, just as is the view that Litvinov pursued an "independent" policy that was discontinued when he was removed from office. Of course, there were nuances and special considerations. But when I was looking through the files of the past years in the secretariat of the People's Commissariat for Foreign Affairs, I found out that Litvinov, even with respect to the smallest issue, sought authorization from the Communist Party's Central Committee, that is to say from Molotov, who was responsible overall for foreign policy. In his capacity as people's commissar for foreign policy, Molotov enjoyed considerable independence, maybe also because he was in constant contact with Stalin and, consequently, was able to discuss different issues with him in passing, as it were, and come to an agreement.

Normally, important proposals were drafted by the staff of the People's Commissariat. A draft report would be initialed by a deputy people's commissar who was in charge of that problem or that country, and after that it was submitted to the people's commissar. In most cases, Molotov took the final decision. It was, of course, possible that he would secure his boss's prior agreement either over the phone or at his dacha on the preceding day. Be that as it may, according to my observations, in many cases Molotov took full responsibility for the decisions.

The documents formulated on key policy issues were, of course, submitted to Stalin for approval. Usually, they would soon return to the secretariat of the people's commissar with the large letters *J.S.* scribbled across them with a thick blue pencil. On Stalin's desk, next to a massive writing set, was a bronze cup that always had numerous large blue and red octangular pencils sticking out of it. He would place them in his palm and sort them with his fingers, as if exercising his half-paralyzed hand. His initials invariably galvanized the entire administrative staff into action.

Today I often wonder why it is that over recent years numerous government decisions and presidential decrees have simply been ignored by the administrative apparatus. Such a situation was absolutely unthinkable in Stalin's time. The administrative system Stalin created—in addition to faith in it and some enthusiasm for it—was firmly based on three pillars: discipline, fear, and reward. True, by the 1940s, the enthusiasm had somewhat diminished. But the fear had grown stronger, reinforcing strict discipline. At the same time, the system of rewards had become much more elaborate. It was at that time that the system of perks for the top *nomenklatura* evolved that has survived to this day. The prospect of losing the benefits of a good life was, of course, an important incentive to carry out the leader's instructions. But knowing that disobeying the will of the boss could cost one one's life had an even more powerful impact on people, from a worker who produced a defective part, to a farmer who left an ear of wheat in the kolkhoz field, to a minister and even a Politburo member. And the system functioned.

Now the enthusiasm has vanished and the fear has disappeared. On top of that, not a single minister has been deprived of his privileges because of poor performance on the job. At worst, he would be retired with a large state pension that ensured him a relatively high standard of living for the rest of his life. In these conditions, the administrative and management system that has remained in place even after the six years of perestroika has come to a grinding halt. We saw the government and the top party leadership try to resuscitate it with a stream of decisions, decrees, instructions, and appeals. But the situation was only getting worse—and society was edging closer to a day when it could explode with unpredictable consequences. The system may start functioning again—if fear is reintroduced into people's minds. Yet this will not resolve the fundamental problems and can only dash all hopes for a better future. The only way out is to dismantle Stalin's system as quickly as possible and to move to a market economy.

It took half a century for the idea of perestroika to emerge. But fifty years ago the leader's initials sufficed to inspire terror and ensure obedience. Sometimes a report would come back to Molotov's secretariat without the initials; its first page would be crisscrossed, but this time not in blue, but in red pencil: Stalin had not approved the submitted document. That would be an emergency and Molotov would be profoundly shaken. Such foul-ups really upset him. I don't think he feared possible consequences for himself because, at the time, Molotov was perhaps the man closest to the boss.

But then again he probably also understood that if that happened too often, Stalin could get angry and begin to suspect that even the people's commissar, who had to see eye to eye with him on all issues, was deliberately undermining him. I think that Molotov felt so upset about it only because he had drawn conclusions that differed from his boss's views even though he had the same facts at his disposal. Of course, it didn't even occur to him that he could be right and Stalin be wrong. By that time, all the people around the leader were prepared to accept Stalin's judgments unquestioningly, sometimes even without understanding the essence of the matter. Maybe they genuinely believed that Stalin was always right. But most likely they remembered what happened to those who had dared to express a doubt.

Molotov maintained even relations with his immediate subordinates; he was coldly polite, almost never raised his voice or used bad language, which was common practice among the leaders of the day. But he was also capable of giving such a dressing-down to a young diplomat who couldn't give a good account of the situation in the country where he was stationed that the poor fellow would pass out. When that happened, Molotov would sprinkle some cold water on him from a carafe and call his guards to take him out into the secretariat office where we would all try to bring him around. Usually, the matter was not pursued any further, and the culprit, after spending a few anxious days in Moscow, would return to his post and subsequently even be advanced up the career ladder. I believe Molotov showed some tolerance in such situations because they often involved inexperienced diplomats whom he himself had cleared for recruitment and thus probably felt partly responsible for. If they were fired after being only recently hired, Stalin could interpret that as a major shortcoming in the personnel work of the People's Commissariat.

Sometimes, however, Molotov concluded that strict, harsh measures were called for. After the signing of the nonaggression pact with Germany in August 1939, a new ambassador, Shkvartsev, was appointed to Berlin. He had been director of a textile institute and was recommended for work in the People's Commissariat for Foreign Affairs by the regional party organization. In November 1940, when

Molotov arrived in Berlin for talks with Hitler, he first of all called on Shkvartsev to get an update on the political situation there. But the ambassador was so helpless in making his report that after listening to him for ten minutes the people's commissar told him to pack his bags and get back home. Soon after that, Dekanozov was appointed the USSR ambassador to Germany, while also keeping his post as deputy people's commissar for foreign affairs. Later, when the war started, Shkvartsev, having tasted the pleasures of a life abroad and being fed up with the tedium of textile production, bombarded Molotov with letters, offering his "diplomatic experience at a difficult time for the Motherland." Those letters, of course, ended up in the wastebasket.

If something in the administrative mechanism malfunctioned or wasn't done right and Stalin demanded that "the culprit be found and punished," the victim had to be found immediately, without any prolonged investigations. Anyone arousing the leader's slightest displeasure would be ruthlessly disciplined.

The following episode comes to my mind. At one time Stalin sent a cable to Roosevelt and was expecting an early response. However, one day went by, then another, then a third, but nothing came back from the Americans. Molotov instructed me to find out whether the telegram had been delayed in transit. The person responsible for government correspondence was head of the coding section of the Commissariat. I contacted him to find out what had happened. He made some inquiries and reported back that the telegram had proceeded without any problems to the last point along the route for which the Soviet side was responsible. From that point on, the Americans took over, and since no word had come from them, he assumed that everything was in order. Nevertheless, I suggested that we contact the Americans. It turned out that they had experienced some difficulty on their side that delayed the arrival of the telegram in Washington by two days. Considering the fact that a war was going on and that anything could happen, I concluded that there was no case of negligence. I reported to Molotov accordingly.

"So who is to blame?" Molotov asked sternly.

"I don't think anyone is, at least not on our side."

"What do you mean, no one is? What will I say to Comrade Stalin? He is very displeased and has ordered me to find the culprits and punish them. And you are telling me that no one is to blame! You're one of those rotten intellectuals!"

I stood there, my head hung low, not knowing what to say in response.

"Well, why are you standing there like a statue?" Molotov called out irritably. "Go and call Vyshinsky!"

I shot out of the office.

At that time Vyshinsky was first deputy people's commissar for foreign affairs, but we all remembered him as the procurator-general who had acquired a sinister reputation during the political trials of the 1930s. This man will surely find a culprit, I was thinking to myself as I dialed his number on a Kremlin telephone.

Andrey Yanuaryevich didn't keep us waiting for long: twenty minutes later he walked into our secretariat. Vyshinsky was known for his rudeness toward his subordinates and his ability to arouse fear in the people around him. But with his superiors he was subservient and eager to please. After entering the people's commissar's reception room he was modesty incarnate. Probably because he had been a Menshevik in the past, he was especially afraid of Beria and Dekanozov. Dekanozov even referred to him in public by no other name than "that Menshevik." Even though Dekanozov was second deputy people's commissar, and Vyshinsky, as first deputy, was responsible for relations with the United States and Britain, I could often observe that Dekanozov was the first to react to requests for instructions from our ambassadors in Washington and London. He would give orders to prepare an answer for them and would sign the telegram with specific instructions while Vyshinsky would only get a copy after it was already on its way. And Vyshinsky didn't pluck up his courage to protest even once.

Vyshinsky seemed to experience his greatest fear in the presence of Stalin and Molotov. When they called him in, he would go into their office hunched over, walking somehow sideways, with a fawning smirk on his face that made his little yellowish mustache stand out on end.

That was how he looked this time. I followed him into the office. Molotov told me to brief him on the results of what he called my "pathetic investigation." That signaled to Vyshinsky what was expected of him. When I concluded by saying again that I couldn't find the culprit, Molotov turned to Vyshinsky:

"Comrade Stalin demands an investigation and a strict punishment for the culprits. I entrust you with this matter."

"Understood, Vyacheslav Mikhailovich. May I go now?"

Molotov nodded. I handed my report to Vyshinsky and he noise-lessly sneaked out of the office.

When he was gone, Molotov turned to me and explained, already in a quiet voice, "Whenever something goes wrong, there is always someone to blame for it. So what if they have always monitored the telegram only on our territory? Who instituted that procedure? The entire route should be checked. Who then instituted that defective procedure? And you're telling me no one is to blame."

Soon we learned that the head of the encoding section had been expelled from the Party and fired from his job. We never saw him again. Comrade Stalin's instructions—to find and punish the cul-prit—had been scrupulously carried out.

Molotov remembered that episode for a long time. When he would walk on business into the room I shared with Pavlov—and that happened quite often—and would see the door of my safe ajar, he would say jokingly:

"I see the rotten intellectual is baring his soul again, his safe wide open, documents are all over his desk—walk right in and take a good look at them. Oh, these Russian intellectuals!"

Belaya Tserkov

BY THE FALL OF 1934, the flow of tourists had considerably diminished. The foreigners, who traveled on business and who were also serviced by Intourist, were mainly businesspeople invited by the Soviet authorities to participate in the construction projects of the five-year plan. Among them were a fair number of Americans who helped in the construction of the Dneproges, the first dam on the Dnieper River and a huge hydroelectric power station. I was assigned to accompany one such group.

We left by train in the afternoon and the next morning arrived in Zaporozhye. Since we couldn't expect to get good food on the road—the train restaurant served only weak tea with a piece of sugar and pearl-barley porridge—the Intourist catering service had packed a good meal for the trip. Usually it included caviar, Chatka crabs, ham, cheese, butter, white bread, boiled eggs, jam in attractive little jars, tea bags, and sugar. Things like that hadn't been in the stores for a long time, although the food industry continued to produce them. It couldn't be, I was thinking to myself, that they produced quantities only sufficient for foreigners. Of course, the country's top leadership was also getting those goodies. But there had to be much more food produced than that. So where was it all going? For the time being that remained a mystery to me.

In the fall and winter months, the guides at Kiev's Intourist had plenty of free time, and each of them put it to different use. Some took refresher courses, others began studying another foreign language. Yet others would take leave without pay to do written translations. At that time I was appointed acting manager of the Intourist office in Shepetovka, a city on the Soviet-Polish border, then a place bustling with activity. Three times a week a Trans-Iranian Express left Shepetovka for Baku carrying Western businessmen, Afghan Astrakhan fur traders, Iranian oil producers, carpet dealers, and caviar distributors. Diplomats, company representatives, or just plain adventure lovers made a transit stop there when crossing the border in either direction. Many foreign tourists began their tours of the Soviet Union there and returned to the city before leaving for home. A Polish train would bring that motley crowd to the Soviet border. It would pull up at one side of the Shepetovka station platform. In a large hall the passengers got their immigration and customs clearance and then headed to a platform on the opposite side where a Trans-Iranian Express was waiting for them.

The Polish train was quite shabby, the seats caved in, the windows dirty, the paint peeling off the cars. By contrast, the service personnel were quite impressive in their colorful uniforms of the Polish gentry: blue military-cut jackets, bright red belts and shoulder straps, caps with a white eagle badge and a glossy visor—they looked quite imposing.

Our Trans-Iranian Express was up to the most exacting world standards. Almost all the cars in the train were sleepers that had been manufactured in Belgium before the Revolution. On the outside they looked as if they had been paneled with mahogany; they had brightly polished copper handrails and an inscription, SLEEPING CAR, in English. In the first years after the war, such cars could still be seen on our domestic lines. They provided the ultimate in comfort with their spacious compartments, each with two wide beds, one on top of the other. In the daytime, the upper bunk would be lowered to form the back of the sofa. A blue cover with a long fringe would be placed over the entire seat. The compartment had a fold-up table and an easy chair upholstered in red velvet. The brass handles, hooks, and shelves made it look rich and fancy. A bathroom between each two compartments had a glass door with an art nouveau design. It had a washbasin and a shower behind a curtain. Toilets were located at both ends of the car, and earthenware chamber pots painted in bright flower patterns were placed beneath the washbasins in the bathrooms.

The conductors of the "direct link sleeping cars," as the train was known, were each dignified men, displaying pre-Revolutionary training. They combined attention and care for the passengers with an air of self-respect. They wore brown uniforms decorated with gold lace and caps to match. They brewed exquisite, fragrant tea, which they served with long, foil-wrapped crackers. Each morning of the three-day trip to Baku the conductors made up the beds, brushed off dust, and polished copper items. The express also had a restaurant complete with good food, a well-stocked bar, and polite waiters. Everywhere on the train one had a sense of good order, properness, and high discipline. One could only wonder whether that was the result of the training that had endured since czarist times or the effects of the iron-hand management by Stalin's people's commissar for transportation, Kaganovich.

I had to meet every train arriving from Poland, render all kinds of assistance to foreign tourists and transit passengers, issue hard-currency tickets when required, and act as a currency exchange office—in a word, provide services in accordance with the Intourist regulations. During the time I worked at the border, in addition to tourists and businesspeople, more and more refugees from Germany began arriving—Communists and Social Democrats, among them many Jews. They used different crossing points on the German-Polish border and came to the Soviet Union as a place of safe haven. I was instructed to help them, to loan them rubles, put them up for the night at Shepetovka if they arrived on the days when the Trans-Iranian Express did not run. My office had a number of rooms that would be turned into hotel rooms for those occasions. Sometimes entire families with children and the elderly showed up, but more often they were just individuals or married couples. In the evening I would invite them over or visit them, and we would talk for hours about the events in Europe and Germany. Even though they had had to abandon everything and had come to our country with no means at all, they were glad to find their second homeland in the Soviet Union. How could they know what was waiting for them there? I couldn't imagine it either. But most of them eventually ended up in concentration camps or prisons on charges of espionage and acts of sabotage perpetrated on orders from the Gestapo.

At the end of December, a new manager for the Shepetovka Intourist office arrived from Moscow, and I went back to Kiev. I began studying Spanish because we expected the arrival of tourists from Spain next season. There were still food shortages in the city, and the food we got from the kitchen of the Kontinental Hotel, although poor in the absence of tourists, was still a big help for our families as well. With the food ration cards we had at home, a worker's for father, a dependent's for mother, and an employee's for me, we could get only the most basic things and in limited quantities. On the other hand, the things we were entitled to were always available at the store.

New Year's Day was drawing closer, and once again the people were unable to celebrate properly. However, my friend from the Polytechnic Institute and I managed quite well. His father was the director of a large bakery in Belaya Tserkov, a small, old town located close to Kiev, and because of his position their home wanted for nothing.

Modest—that was the name of the baker's son—invited me and our mutual friend Georgi, my school chum and a student at the Kiev Medical Institute, to ring in 1935 at his house. Each of us naturally came with a girlfriend. Modest's girlfriend, Lena, was a student at the Belaya Tserkov Vocational School, and she was waiting for us there. Georgi invited Nina, a girl he knew from his school, and I asked Klara to join us. Over the months we had worked together at Intourist, Klara and I had become good friends, and quite often, together with Stepan and his girlfriend, we would take the Lincoln for a ride out of town or see a show at the theater or when the frosts set in, go to the skating rink at the Dynamo stadium.

At midday on December 30, 1934, our gang descended to the platform at Belaya Tserkov's red-brick station. It was cold but clear and sunny. A three-horse sleigh from the bakery was waiting for us. We threw our things on the straw and settled along the sides of the Rozvalni sleigh. Modest's house, located near the bakery at the edge of town, was a fairly long distance away, and we thoroughly enjoyed our troika ride there. The house was surrounded by tall, hoarfrosted lindens. The garden stretched down toward the river, and one of its pathways formed an excellent slope for sledding. We spent the remainder of the day on that slope. Modest's family was large. In addition to his father, mother, and grandfather, he had two sisters and a kid brother. There was space enough in the house to offer the guests two separate rooms. Georgi and I took one, and the girls moved into the other.

New Year's Eve was spent in preparations for the festive dinner. The girls were helping in the kitchen, and Georgi and I sawed wood for the stove and the fireplace, cut ice in the river, and whipped homemade ice cream. Then we assembled a long table and placed chairs around it. The fir tree had been decorated before our arrival. We only had to clamp on candlesticks and put candles in them. Finally we were told to carry food from the kitchen and place it on the table. I could never have imagined that the job of a director of a bakery could produce such abundance, unseen in those years: fried and jellied piglets, ham, all kinds of fish dishes, caviar, salmon, smoked eels, large baskets with fruits, cakes, and pastries. There was no question that all that had been illegally traded for flour, bread, or pastries. As for drinks, I just lost count of the kinds of drinks that were offered. So they do produce all of this after all, I thought to myself again. Then why is it kept under wraps?

During the two days there we neither read newspapers nor listened to the radio. And that was why it came as a surprise to us when Modest's father came home from work and told us that, as of January 1, 1935, food and other types of cards would be abolished. Everything would be traded freely. Everything would be in plenty. The lean years were over. I just couldn't believe that was possible. The people had been exhausted by standing on endless lines to get the most basic necessities. How much more would it take to feed them well? It was hard to imagine that one could just walk into a store and buy everything that one's heart desired.

The New Year's party at Modest's house turned out to be a great success. We congratulated each other, kissed, and hugged. Although it was difficult to believe that better days were coming, glasses were raised to a "new bright period" in our life, and, of course, we drank to Comrade Stalin, who had kept his promise to lead us on the road to prosperity. We were trained to thank Stalin for everything that the people in a normal country enjoyed by right. Then we went out into the garden to ride down the slope, burn Bengal lights, and set off firecrackers. After that—back to the table for more champagne and then dancing.

We never got around to going to bed, especially since January 1 was then a workday, and Klara and I had to return to Kiev. When we arrived at the railway station a short time before six in the morning, there was a line in front of the bread store there. When I saw that I wondered: Wasn't it just a bad joke about the food ration cards being abolished?

In Kiev the stores were already open, and people were milling around them, too. Riding a train around the city, I noticed that the windows of many stores that had been boarded up during the hungry years and were covered with scaffolding in recent months were lit up and had all sorts of foodstuffs on display. The curious thing was that the lines remained for about a week. Shoppers were allowed to buy any amount of food they wanted. At first people bought up sausage, cheese, ham, and bread by the kilo. But then they saw that the supplies in the stores weren't drying up. More food was brought in from warehouses. And when the people became convinced that the stores would remain well stocked, the crowds disappeared. Now the people had to eat up what they had hoarded up at home in panic buying.

After that the situation, at least in big cities, normalized and stayed like that right until 1940. The same thing happened after the war when a monetary reform was introduced in 1947 and the wartime ration card system was abolished. When those measures were introduced, there were lines only during the first few weeks. Then, thanks to a constant supply of foodstuffs, panic buying ceased and trade stabilized. The farmers were again allowed to keep cattle at home and were given larger plots of land.

In one of my conversations with Mikoyan I asked him how it was possible to achieve such results in 1935 and in 1947. At that time, he was in charge not only of foreign trade but also domestic trade and knew well how it was done.

"First of all," he explained, "through strict economy and a concurrent increase in production it became possible to build up large stocks of foodstuffs and consumer goods. Stalin personally followed the developments and severely punished bad factory managers. A major logistics operation was mounted to deliver all that to the proper destinations, to set up warehouses and refrigerator facilities, to provide transportation to get the goods to the stores, particularly during the critical initial period when the people still didn't believe in the stability of the market. The stores were renovated and decorated in advance. The sales force received special training. The people working in the trade were sternly warned: any abuse, withholding of goods, or profiteering would cost them their heads. Some offenders had to be shot. But the important thing was not to conserve the supplies, not to mete them out piecemeal, but to deliver them all in one day to all the industrial centers. Only that could produce the desired effect."

Today, some of our writers claim that during that period only Moscow and two or three other big cities were well supplied. This is not true. In the summer of 1935, I took groups of foreign tourists to many places. I deliberately walked into stores to see what was on sale. Everywhere the shops offered a wide variety of foodstuffs and goods. But more importantly, there were no lines anywhere and no one was traveling to the big cities to buy food.

Of course, circumstances were different in those days. The people had fear, and those who broke the trade regulations were mercilessly punished. Most likely, measures were also in place to limit access to the cities for out-of-towners. But in parallel with that, the situation in the country was improving, too. The farmers were allowed to raise cattle on their homesteads and were encouraged to work on their private plots of land. It was also true that the farmers working in the kolkhozes, subjected to iron discipline, had no other choice but to do better than before on the collective fields.

If I were to enumerate the foodstuffs, drinks, and goods that appeared in the stores in 1935 and 1947, my Soviet contemporaries probably wouldn't believe me. There was black and red caviar in wooden barrels at quite affordable prices. Huge whole salmon, lox, all kinds of meat, ham, piglets, sausages the names of which have long been forgotten, cheeses, fruits, and berries—all of which could be purchased in any amount and without standing in line. Even at subway stations stands offered sausage, ham, cheese, sandwiches, and snacks. Chops and steaks were laid out on large dripping pans. And when you traveled in the country, you could enter any house on a hot day, and its owners, just as during the NEP, would offer you a glass of milk or cold *ryazhenka* and wouldn't take money for it.

Some people may be tempted to say: You see, the administrative system did work after all! But it was driven by coercion and fear. We should also remember that millions of prisoners lived like animals and worked like slaves to create the country's material wealth, which was then administered through a tough regulatory system.

When farmers were allowed to keep a specified number of cattle, poultry, pigs, and other small farm animals at home, it made a big difference. With the hardships of the hungry wartime years of 1941–45 behind them, they made the best of the opportunity that presented itself, and although the government cleaned out everything that the state farms produced, they had food for their families and could even bring something to sell in the markets in town. That ensured a fairly good supply of farm produce to large cities right until the late 1950s and early 1960s, when Khrushchev, in a flight of fantasy, conceived the idea of bridging the gap between the city and the village.

Claiming that the kolkhozes and state-owned farms were capable of feeding the population of the entire country, Khrushchev first and foremost downsized the farmers' private plots of land and demanded that the number of cattle they had be drastically reduced. Then he came up with the crazy idea of building multistory houses in the villages, like those in the cities, and began moving the farmers from their individual houses into apartments. As a result, members of many families who had tilled the land for centuries were uprooted from their land and were unable to keep any cattle or poultry at all.

That arbitrary measure produced immediate results. Already by 1960, agricultural production began to decline sharply. In spite of what the bosses anticipated, the farmers who had lost their private farms did not work better in kolkhozes and on state-owned fields.

As a result, kolkhozes and state-owned farms couldn't supply the needed foodstuffs for the people in the cities, and the production on private plots of land plummeted. The farmers' children, growing up in city-type apartments, lost touch with the land and didn't acquire the skills necessary for raising farm animals. When they grew up, they did everything to leave for the cities. The population in the country grew older and many villages had few people left.

It is not surprising therefore that today the village folks blame the ruin of the country not so much on Stalin (there are virtually no people left who were old enough to remember the horrors of forced collectivization), but on Khrushchev, who took their last cow away and plunged the villages into misery and devastation.

Since the time Khrushchev proclaimed to the whole world that collectivized agriculture would allow the Soviet Union to catch up and outstrip the United States within a short period of time and would ensure prosperity for Soviet citizens, who, he assured, would already in the 1980s live under communism, tens of billions of rubles were sunk into kolkhozes and state farms. Hundreds of thousands of tractors and combine harvesters were given to state-owned agriculture. Huge amounts of money were spent to cultivate the so-called virgin lands in Kazakhstan. And what are the results that we reap today? Today, we continue to pay hard dollars to buy grain and other foodstuffs abroad, and under Gorbachev the country had to go back to the food ration cards again.

Molotov Enraged

IN ADDITION to its offices in the Kremlin, Molotov's secretariat also occupied an entire floor in the building of the Commissariat for Foreign Affairs in Kuznetsky Most. The people's commissar's office was also located there, comprising three rooms. The first was a meeting room that contained a long table with rows of chairs. The second was the room where the people's commissar actually worked at his desk and that had another smaller conference table for a relatively limited number of participants. The third was the "relaxation room," which had a small bathroom. The furniture in the relaxation room included a sofa for taking a nap and a round table. On the round table there always stood a vase with flowers, fruits from the south, and a plate with shelled walnuts, Molotov's favorite snack. Fresh fruits were flown in by chartered plane from the Caucasus and Central Asia a couple of times a week, and not only in time of peace, but during the war as well.

When the hardships were at their worst, when there was barely enough food to feed the army and millions of Soviet people were going around half-starved and living on their meager food rations, foreign guests coming to Moscow were invariably struck by the incredible abundance of the Kremlin banquets and receptions. Laden with all kinds of food and drinks, the tables were literally caving in. Red and black caviar, salmon and lox, trout and sterlet, fried piglets, lamb and goat, stuffed turkey, heaps of vegetables and fruits, rows of hard drinks and all sorts of wine, ice cream cakes—all of that, as Stalin saw it, was to convince his Western guests that we weren't doing too badly.

The windows of the aides' office in the Commissariat building in Kuznetsky Most faced the inner yard. The room was located next to the quarters of the service staff. Every morning, waiters carried large thermoses and baskets with food for the people's commissar past our office and down the corridor in case the commissar happened to be in at lunchtime. The same routine was followed in Molotov's office in the Kremlin. The food for the top leadership was grown and processed at special farms and food factories under the watchful eye of the people from the Special Department of State Security. The person in charge of this highly sensitive and what was considered to be crucial service was the boss's main chef, a very tall man from the NKVD named Ignatashvili. Stalin, who was paranoid about being poisoned, went out of his way to please him and awarded him the rank of general.

The building in Kuznetsky Most also housed the Commissariat's tailor, where the top officials of the ministry could have suits made for them upon the presentation of special vouchers. In 1942, when I was already working as Molotov's assistant, I received two such vouchers and ordered two suits—one dark brown and the other light gray with a stripe. Soon my new suits were ready, and one spring day I came to work wearing the gray suit. Having put together some papers to present to the commissar, I walked into his office and saw that Molotov was dressed in exactly the same gray suit with a stripe. I felt uncomfortable and saw right away that the coincidence was totally inappropriate. Molotov also looked at me with disapproval and said:

"How did you manage to end up with a suit exactly like mine? What are we going to do about it now? We will be receiving foreigners and they will think we are wearing uniforms."

"I am very sorry it happened. The tailor didn't have any other light fabric, and I decided on this one. I really don't know what I can do now."

"Well, this isn't really your fault. It's that stupid tailor Zhuravski. He should have thought twice before offering the people's commissar a fabric he is giving to everyone else."

During a break I changed into my dark brown suit and never wore the gray again. Molotov also put on his striped gray suit very rarely.

Maybe it was at that time that the idea emerged of making a special uniform for the employees of the Commissariat.

During all the years I worked with Molotov, I think I saw him extremely agitated only once. It was in 1944, when a Swedish mission arrived in Moscow to take part in the talks with the Soviet government on an armistice with Finland. I was not directly involved in those talks, but I knew that the negotiations were difficult. In the opinion of the Soviet side, the trips the Swedes were making back and forth to Stockholm were not producing the desired results, and the Finns were stubbornly refusing to accept Soviet proposals.

At that time the Soviet leadership appeared to be genuinely interested in finding a settlement to the conflict with Finland. A major offensive was planned in Poland, and it was important to disengage the Red Army units tied up in the north and to use them to reinforce the central group of forces before mounting an attack on the German fortifications on the Oder and in East Prussia. At the same time, intelligence reports reaching Moscow indicated that Ribbentrop had recently visited Helsinki and was trying to talk the Finns out of concluding a truce with the Soviet Union, promising them additional military support. It was also reported that new shipments of modern German weapons and additional military units had arrived in Finland. All that could prolong the war with Finland, something that Moscow thought undesirable. The Soviet Union was prepared to give up its demand for Finland's unconditional capitulation, but it continued to insist that the Soviet-Finnish border be moved and that the Soviet Union be granted permission to establish military bases there, which in general was in line with the provisions of the peace settlement of March 1940. Under the circumstances, the Finnish intransigence was inopportune.

I don't recall precisely what the occasion was for the big reception held in the Reception House in Spiridonovskaya Street. Among the guests were accredited diplomats, ranking Soviet officials, top Red Army commanders, as well as the members of the Swedish mission. In the beginning everything was correct and proper. The guests thronged around the long tables laden with all kinds of food and drink. Others stood around, glasses of wine in hand, talking to one another.

I saw Molotov walk with the Turkish ambassador to the Red Hall. They were accompanied by Molotov's assistant Podtserob, a second-ranking official after Kozyrev in the Commissariat. Podtserob spoke

French and interpreted at the talks with those diplomats who didn't know English. Therefore I had a few minutes to get something to eat.

Suddenly, an unusual noise reached us from the Red Hall. We heard loud exclamations with Molotov's voice raised above the rest. He had dropped into a bad stutter, which meant he was very upset about something.

I hurried over to join him, and when I entered the room, I saw the ambassadors of the United States, Britain, Japan, China, and other countries, as well as the entire Swedish mission, gathered around the people's commissar. Waving his hands in the air, something he rarely did, Molotov was yelling out:

"We aren't going to tolerate the Finns' stubbornness any longer. And if these assholes persist, we will make mincemeat out of them! We will stop at nothing! They'd better not think we are simpletons! We won't be f-f-fooled! If they want more war, they'll g-g-get it. There's no force on earth that can stop the Red Army."

His assistants and security men were trying to calm the raging commissar down. Someone pleaded with him, "Vyacheslav Mikhailovich, it is already late, it is time for you to return to the Kremlin."

The security men gently took him under his arms and were leading him toward the door. But he broke away from them.

"Leave m-m-me alone, I know what I'm doing. These stubborn mules will be sorry they were stubborn! We will t-t-teach them."

The guests, who had probably never been present at such a scene before, were looking with consternation at Molotov, who always looked like a man devoid of any emotions. At first I also thought that he had had one drink too many and lost control of himself. It was all so strange. Finally, we managed to drag him away from the crowd, take him into the corridor, and walk him toward the door. On the way out he went on calling the Finns bad names, and even when we had him seated in the car, he struggled to get out of it.

Finally he left in his car accompanied by two security vehicles. The ambassadors also left immediately. They were obviously in a hurry to file reports to their governments about the sensational episode and Molotov's threats to destroy Finland.

The next morning, Molotov called me into his office. He was in a good mood and was smiling mischievously.

"You were at the reception yesterday, weren't you?" he asked, and without waiting for my answer, went on to say, "Describe to me in detail what happened there."

I began describing to him in general terms what I was a witness to.

"No," he interrupted me. "Tell it exactly as it happened, without leaving anything out. What I said. How the people reacted."

I felt uncomfortable reproducing his bad language, but I had to repeat everything almost word for word.

"I think the guests were shocked, even scared," I concluded.

Molotov was obviously pleased. He let me go, saying, "Very good! Excellent!"

And then I understood that he had staged yesterday's scene on purpose; most likely it had even been agreed to by Stalin, or maybe even conceived by the boss himself. And Molotov was pleased he had carried out the leader's orders well. He did scare the Swedes and, through them, the Finns. The Americans and the British also got worried. Now they were going to put pressure on Helsinki, too. There could be no doubt left in anyone's mind now that the Soviet forces were capable of scoring a quick victory over the Finns and even occupying their entire country. And if his outburst of yesterday was taken for what it was meant to be, so much the better. Now the Finns would be more cooperative.

And sure enough, the Swedes soon informed us that Helsinki was prepared to engage in serious negotiations, and sometime later a Finnish delegation arrived in Moscow. At long last an armistice was signed.

Such political ploys, quite numerous in the history of diplomacy, may appear adventuristic and even immoral by today's standards. Admittedly, if Molotov had made good on his threats, the Soviet Union's relations with the United States and Britain could have been seriously compromised. After the bloody experience of the winter campaign, Stalin, of course, knew that even he would probably find it difficult to keep the Finns in subjugation. This consideration may partly explain why Stalin, after securing Hitler's consent to place Finland in the Soviet sphere of influence, didn't impose upon that country the fate of the Baltic states.

After he had retired from office, Molotov had this to say by way of an explanation:

"Finland was spared. . . . We were smart not to attach it to us. It would be a festering wound. The people there are very stubborn. . . . Even a minority there could be very dangerous. And now we can gradually improve our relations. We couldn't make it democratic, just as we couldn't do this with Austria."

In That Moment Before the War

IN THE FIRST MONTHS OF 1935, life noticeably improved, and by the summer it was looking quite normal. Although it was not possible to regain the NEP level of abundance, the people began to breathe more easily. They were getting better food and Stalin's claim that "life's become better, life's become more fun to live" seemed to be getting some justification. The second part of that formula also seemed to be coming true: ". . . and when life is more fun to live, work gets done faster." Private initiative was still not encouraged, unlike in the 1920s, but the government trade and service sectors began functioning more efficiently, making life better.

The capital of the Ukraine was moved from Kharkov to Kiev. That was viewed not only as a tribute to the glory of the historic center of the ancient Slav state, but also as proof of the increased security of the Soviet Union, which was no longer fearful of the close proximity of bourgeois Poland. Many of us began to feel that the terrible sacrifices of the early 1930s had not been in vain, and that in the final analysis Stalin was right when he radically changed the country's system, putting it on the track of industrialization and collectivization.

One sunny summer morning, there was a great commotion in the Intourist hotel Kontinental. Strange young men in civilian clothes but with a military bearing were placing around the hall huge Chinese vases, borrowed from the city Museum of Fine Arts, holding freshly cut, bright red roses. The doormen were rolling out carpets and waxing oak staircase handrails. The saleswoman in the kiosk was practicing her most enticing smile. That kind of treatment wasn't extended even to the richest foreign tourists. Never before did we have to present our IDs as we were required to do now.

Sneaking quietly through the hall, I went into the service department and asked Fainberg what was going on.

"We're preparing a suite for a very important guest from Kharkov," he responded, lowering his voice.

"Who is it?"

"Postyshev will be staying here temporarily. His permanent residence is not ready for him yet. But not a word to anyone. If foreigners begin asking questions, tell them you don't know."

Even then everything that had anything to do with our top leaders was getting shrouded in mystery. For his part, Pavel Petrovich Postyshev, secretary of the Central Committee of the Bolshevik Communist Party of the Ukraine, didn't act like a big boss. In the course of the few weeks that he stayed at the Kontinental, I ran into him a couple of times in the hall or on the staircase. He always greeted me amiably and sometimes even paused to ask me about the tourists who had arrived, to learn what interested them and whether they liked Kiev.

The other leaders of the Republic—Kossior, Lyubchenko, Chubar, and Petrovsky—moved directly into the residences that had been prepared for them. The renovation of Postyshev's villa, on the other hand, had not been completed. Before the Revolution, that building, located in Lipki opposite Mariinsky Park and very near to our house, had belonged to a big sugar producer, Zaitsev. Built in the baroque style, elegant, light, and airy, I thought it was too posh for a proletarian leader. But the villas of the other leaders of the Ukraine were equally luxurious. For instance, Petrovsky, chairman of the Ukrainian Central Executive Committee, a post equivalent to the president of a republic, occupied a palace. The former revolutionary, who had spent many years in czarist prisons and had lived on bread and water while in detention, had no qualms about moving into a building that looked like a Scottish castle—it was made out of gray granite and had tall lancet windows, turrets, and marble columns at the entrance. The Ukrainian leadership drove around in Buicks and Lincolns. With what was essentially a decadent "bourgeois" lifestyle, Stalin deliberately corrupted old-time Bolsheviks. Maybe at first some of them found that life in the lap of luxury was a far cry from what the lifestyle of a servant of the people should be, that it was burdensome and out of place, but they soon learned that if they gave it up, their boss in the Kremlin would only get angry and make sarcastic remarks about their "cheap populism," calling them "show-off democrats." The most important thing about Stalin's perk system was that all those palaces with their numerous servants didn't belong to the "Red barons." They could use them only so long as they remained in good standing with the boss. But at any moment he could take all that away for disobedience, real or perceived insurgence. Usually, he took their lives at the same time.

Although Postyshev, who was also secretary of the city Party Committee, soon moved into a private residence, he continued his simple lifestyle. Often he would walk by himself around his villa. He didn't use foreign automobiles, but rode in a Soviet-made car with a tarpaulin top. Vehicles like that were made at a car plant constructed with the assistance of Henry Ford, in the city of Nizhny Novgorod. Through Postyshev's efforts, Kiev was decorated with bright flower beds. Cobblestoned streets were asphalted. A concert stand was built in Mariinsky Park, and every summer night free open-air concerts were held there. Food stands were set up in the streets of the city. In the Passage department store, near the Kontinental Hotel, and in other parts of the city, children's ice cream parlors opened up serving a variety of flavors—strawberry, pistachio, chocolate, and vanilla.

Postyshev was a frequent visitor at factories. He knew many workers by name and helped them resolve their problems. I think people sincerely liked him. They even devised a work rating system using his name, giving "three *P*s" to the top-quality performance, standing for Pavel Petrovich Postyshev. It was probably that popularity that put Stalin on guard. He didn't like it when others became too popular, since in his view that created dangerous competition. It was also possible that Postyshev's colleagues among the Ukrainian leadership squealed to the leader of the people about the unorthodox management style of the Ukraine's Party secretary. More importantly, at the 1934 Party congress, which Stalin baptized the "Congress of Victors," Postyshev, together with Chubar and Kossior, was among those who called for Stalin's removal from the post of general secretary and his replacement by Kirov, a member of the Politburo and secretary of the Leningrad Party organization. When the election for the Central Committee was held, Kirov received an overwhelming majority of votes. Most of the members of the Central Committee also preferred Kirov to Stalin. But Kirov turned down the proposal to become general secretary. More than that, he told Stalin about everything.

"I appreciate it," the leader of the people thanked him. "I will never forget what you have done."

And he didn't. In early December, Kirov was murdered. The ballot papers with Stalin's name crossed out were destroyed. And soon the secret police began arresting the delegates to the "Congress of Victors" and those members of the Central Committee whom Stalin suspected of disloyalty. The Ukrainian leaders were also purged.

Postyshev, a Civil War hero, a commander who had led his forces to victory in the war against the Japanese and other invaders in the Far East, was the first to disappear. Later we learned how such acts of disappearance were arranged. A Party leader would be urgently called to come to Moscow. Without any suspicion, he would board an international-class sleeper car of an overnight express train in Kiev (or in the capital of some other republic). The train would make only one stop along the way. In the middle of the night, at the Khutor Mikhailovsky Station, a few armed men dressed in the NKVD uniform would enter the car. The senior officer would order the conductor to knock on the door of a certain compartment. The door would open and the leader traveling to Moscow would find himself facing the barrels of guns. While the other passengers slept on peacefully, the captive would be transferred under armed escort to a special railroad car that had drawn blinds and barred windows and was attached to the rear of the train. When the train arrived in Moscow, the doomed person would be taken directly from the Kiev Railway Station to the basement of the Lubyanka prison. After Postyshev, Chubar followed him there. Lyubchenko, chairman of the Council of People's Commissars of the Ukraine, understanding what was going to happen to him, said goodbye to his beautiful young wife, locked himself up in the study of his gorgeous villa, and shot himself. A short time after that, First Secretary of the Ukrainian Communist Party Kossior was arrested and shot. That happened soon after Stalin sent his new man to the Ukraine—Nikita Khrushchev. Petrovsky was lucky: he got off with only a prison sentence. When Stalin died, he was set free and immediately got the job of director of the Museum of the Revolution.

All that happened a little later, but in the summer months of 1935 we felt happy and hopeful. The hungry years were gone. Life held out a promise of many interesting things to come. Father and I chipped in and bought a small sailboat that could carry six people. On my days off, when the wind was favorable, I would take a bunch of my friends, both boys and girls, way up the Dnieper River, past Mezhigorie and Vyshgorod, where many years ago, high up on a hill, stood the palace of Prince Vladimir, the future saint and Baptist of Russia, a man with three hundred wives in his harem. At the place where the Desna, the Dnieper's tributary, flows into that river, we would build a fire and barbecue shashliks and bake a few potatoes. The twigs we fed into the fire gave off a fragrant smoke redolent of ripe apples. In the evening, under the branchy lindens of Mariinsky Park, we listened to classical music performed by the Kiev Philharmonic Orchestra.

The last summer of my work at Intourist was especially interesting. There were even more tourists that year than in 1934, and I had to travel a lot around the country, accompanying them. The railway stations were once again bustling with activity: babushkas from nearby villages were offering berries, fruits, *ryazhenka* in pots with a baked-milk crust on top, boiled corn, and smoked fish. A sense was in the air that the country was gradually coming back to life after the shock of collectivization. In Moscow, Leningrad, Kharkov, Odessa—all cities I visited—life had also returned to normal. It seemed that at long last the country was entering a favorable streak. When the arrests of the Ukrainian leaders began, those who came to replace them soon disappeared in their turn, and as a result the people could no longer remember the names of their new leaders, which, at least as far as I can remember, didn't cast any gloom over our daily lives.

Probably the only arrest I felt doubtful about was when the commander of the Ukrainian Military District, a hero of the Civil War, Yakir, was purged and thus shared the fate of Tukhachevsky and other talented Red Army commanders. I felt sorry for Yakir, a tall, handsome man who was still quite young at the time. He also had a big villa in Lipki, and I often saw him drive past our windows in an open Buick convertible, accompanied by a beautiful redhead. I couldn't believe that dauntless and daring military commander, who did so much to ensure the victory of the Soviet regime in the Ukraine, was a spy, a saboteur, and an enemy of the people.

My work at Intourist took up all of my time and energy. We worked from dawn till dusk, as it were, with virtually no days off, and on our trips around the country, we stayed with our tourists around the clock. But the anticipation of encounters with people from different countries—Britain, the United States, Austria, Germany, Italy, Greece, Japan, India—the chance to talk to them, to learn something new each time, and in turn to tell them something about our country, gave us a profound sense of inner satisfaction. Each one of them had his or her interests, his or her profession. Sometimes, we had to spend the whole day at a court hearing or in a fire department, to interpret at a trade union organization or at meetings with writers, artists, educators, or students. Quite often we went on pleasure trips on the Dnieper. Farmers and agricultural specialists—and

there were a good number of them among the foreign guests—were
taken to the Goloseyevsky Forest where the new Ukrainian Agricultural Institute was located. The road there wound through some
beautiful countryside, up and down hillsides, past lakes and bushy
thickets of sweetbrier. Not only the tourists but the guides, too, invariably enjoyed the trips to the ancient monasteries and churches,
many of them then still pristine in their beauty.

The Church of St. Cyril in Kurenyovka, a Kiev suburb, left an in-
delible impression on everyone who came to see it. Built in the thirteenth century, it was thoroughly renovated at the beginning of our
century. As far as was possible, century-old dust and soot were removed from the Byzantine frescoes and mosaics, and the unpainted
walls and arches were decorated with the works of the best artists of
the time. Vrubel's masterpiece *The Descent of the Holy Spirit,* painted in
the gallery, was profoundly moving. A mental hospital was outside
the church fence, and Vrubel, who suffered from bouts of depression, spent some time there. That made it possible for him to select
his models from the patients at the hospital. As a result, the psychological effect of the line of portraits was very powerful. The Twelve
Apostles looked upon the visitors from the vaulted ceilings; their eyes
and the expressions on their faces revealed the turmoil in their souls.
Each portrait presented an individual interpretation of the impending tragedy—the crucifixion of their teacher, Jesus Christ.

It was like a holiday for the guides when we were sent to Odessa to
work with the tourists who were brought there by an Italian liner, the
Julius Caesar. The tourists came from all around Europe to take a
cruise on the Mediterranean and the Black Sea. Their itinerary included a stop in Kiev. For that occasion, interpreters fluent in English, German, French, Spanish, and Italian were required. Since the
resources of the Kiev Intourist were limited, a few colleagues from
Leningrad and Moscow joined us. They were all young people.

The trip to Odessa was a lot of fun. We enjoyed the luxury of the
Italian liner, the exotic Italian cuisine, the trip on the express train
that had only first-class sleeping cars, two days of sightseeing in the
city, and a return to the Italian ship. That was probably the first time
I saw so clearly how different life in our country was from that in the
West. But I didn't think about it in terms of the advantage of the capitalist system over the socialist way of life. We believed that only rich
people could afford these cruises while the working people in Western countries lived in poverty. At that time, that was true to some ex-

tent. For our part, we were convinced that in the Soviet Union we were building a system that would be fair for all. We didn't think we had to lead the kind of lavish lifestyle that the capitalists indulged in.

As the flow of tourists increased, so did the number of guides. Polyglot Zyazya Lipman joined our staff. He spoke five languages and was cheerful and funny. He was five years my senior but the age difference didn't prevent us from becoming friends. We spent all our free time together. Zyazya soon introduced me to his noisy bohemian crowd of talented young friends. Some of them later became well-known artists, musicians, or writers. Standing out among the rest was a lovely girl named Valya Kulakova. She sang beautifully, played the piano, and could paint. Suitors were hovering around her all the time. Zyazya boasted that he had had an affair with her, but I didn't believe him. She was too unapproachable and treated everyone in the same equal manner. Her father was a renowned cardiologist who treated all of the Ukraine's top leadership and lived in high style. He had a gorgeous apartment in the building at the corner of Levashovskaya and Lutheran streets and spent the summers at his dacha in Mezhigorie. Valya would stay alone in their city apartment, and the cheerful crowd of Zyazya's friends often gathered there. Treating one and all with equal indifference, Valya enjoyed teasing her suitors. For instance, she would meet her guests sitting on suitcases, assuring them that she was leaving for Moscow. Her grief-stricken admirers pleaded with her not to leave them. But Valya remained adamant. A farewell scene would be played out, someone would even shed a few tears, but finally she would declare that it was just a joke, and everybody, relieved, could sit down to a cheerful dinner. One time she announced that she was getting married and invited everyone to a party to mark the occasion—and this, too, turned out to be a practical joke. One day the grapevine brought terrible news: Valya Kulakova had died suddenly of a heart attack. We were invited to come to say goodbye. At the appointed hour, a mournful crowd gathered at the entrance to her apartment building. Zyazya, a crepe band on his arm, appeared in the doorway and asked us to go stand under the balcony of Valya's bedroom.

"That was the last wish of the deceased," he said, barely able to hold back his sobs.

We obediently huddled on the sidewalk, craning our necks to look up. Suddenly, the door of the bedroom swung open, and Valya stepped out onto the balcony: she was completely naked, except for her shoes and a black hat with a veil.

Laughing and cursing, we ran up to the second floor and crowded into her living room. A few minutes later, Valya walked in wearing a long black dress covering her up to her neck and began pouring tea, as if nothing had happened.

When young people today read about the hardships, horrors, and bloody purges of the 1930s, they get the impression that life in the Soviet Union at that time was bleak and hopeless, full of fears, grief, and tears. That is both true and false. The people, who were spared the brutal terror, lived as people anywhere else would, with their share of problems and joys. As they saw the situation improve, they began hoping for further progress and believed that the worst was behind them. Most of the young people were again infected with enthusiasm; they worked, studied, fooled around, fell in love—in other words, they lived their lives in full.

But the young people of my generation also remembered that the Soviet Union was the only country in the world that was building socialism and that it was surrounded by enemies on all sides. We believed we had to be ready for any eventuality, and that was why some practiced parachute jumping, while others joined volunteer groups to study to become pilots. Together with a few of my friends, I enrolled in a training program to become a signal communications expert. I already had some idea about that subject since over a number of years I had tinkered away making radio sets, and on top of that, I had been trained as an electrician. We attended classes wearing paramilitary khaki uniforms, with belts and shoulder straps. That uniform looked very much like the outfit worn by German Communists, and that was why it was called *jung Sturm*. We had a signal communications unit as our sponsor, and we spent a few weeks of summer with them in a boot camp, taking part in field exercises.

In September 1935, we fourth-year students resumed our studies at the Polytechnic Institute's night school. It was time for me to start looking for a job for which I was being trained. I had to say goodbye to Intourist and got a job as a technician at the design office of the Leninskaya Kuznitsa (Lenin's Forge) Plant. The shipyard that my father had helped design had already been built in the backwater near Podol, and the production of passenger ships and tugs had gotten under way. Those vessels had paddle wheels on both sides. I was given the task of making a draft drawing of the mechanism that activated the wooden paddles. When I finished the design on a drawing paper, it was transferred to a tracing paper. One woman who did that, a charming, cheerful girl named Galya, took my fancy. We became friends, and in December 1940, after many adventures and tribulations, when I was appointed first secretary of our embassy in Germany, she and I were married.

Work and studies filled up my entire day. Time went by quickly. Only on Sundays, the only day off in that era, was it possible to relax and have some fun. In the summertime we enjoyed sailing, and in winter we went skiing, skating, or sledding down the hills.

In those years, a new wave of repressions swept the country. After the arrest of Marshal Tukhachevsky and other of the Red Army's top commanders, many engineers, scholars, writers, and performers began to disappear. But only a few of the families I knew lost someone in that mincing machine. That was why I continued to believe that there was some sense in that new upsurge of terror since so many were spared. Maybe those who were taken away were guilty of something after all.

In the spring of 1938, I successfully completed the Institute's program and graduated with a degree of engineer-technologist. I was sent to work at Kiev's Arsenal, renowned for its revolutionary traditions, which was registered under number 393 in the register of defense-industry enterprises. The plant manufactured artillery guns. I was going to become a gunsmith.

But fate would have it otherwise.

CHAPTER FIVE

Stalin and Roosevelt

AMONG THE FOREIGN POLITICAL LEADERS whom I had a chance to observe up close, I was impressed the most by Franklin Delano Roosevelt. In our country he is rightly considered to be a realistic, far-sighted politician. One of the main boulevards in Yalta is named after him. President Roosevelt became a dominant figure in recent U.S. history and in the annals of World War II. I remember him as a charming man with quick reactions and a quick sense of humor. Even in Yalta, when his health had noticeably deteriorated, everyone pointed out that the president's mind remained clear and sharp, capable of quick responses.

For me it was a great honor to have been assigned to interpret at Stalin's talks with Roosevelt during their first meeting. This was in Teheran in 1943. All that happened at that time has been deeply ingrained in my memory.

The Soviet delegation, comprising Stalin, Molotov, and Voroshilov, had left for the Iranian capital one day before my return to Moscow from Kiev, where I had searched in vain for my parents. I had to catch up. Late at night I left for Baku and arrived there the following evening. Early the next morning I took a plane for Teheran. I managed to reach the Soviet embassy by about noon—to find that I was to interpret at the first meeting of the two world leaders. Had my plane arrived only one hour later, I would have been late for that meeting and would have angered Stalin, who personally selected his interpreters for each meeting.

When I entered the room adjacent to the plenary hall, Stalin was already there, dressed in his marshal's uniform. He looked at me intently, and I hastened to proffer my apologies for being a little late, explaining that I had rushed in straight from the airport. Stalin nodded his head slightly, paced slowly up and down the room, reached into a side pocket of his jacket for a box with the name Herzegovina Flor emblazoned on it, took out a cigarette, and lit up. He squinted his eyes, looked at me sternly, and asked:

"Tired after the trip? Ready to interpret? It will be an important meeting."

"I am ready, Comrade Stalin. I rested well overnight in Baku. I am feeling quite well."

Stalin went up to the table and casually dropped the box of Herzegovina Flors on it. He lit another match and puffed again on the cigarette that had gone out. Then he slowly put out the match and, pointing with it at the sofa, said:

"I am going to sit here, to one side. Roosevelt will be brought in in his wheelchair. Let him position himself to the left of the chair where you will be seated."

"Understood, Comrade Stalin," I replied.

I had interpreted for Stalin on previous occasions, but never before did I see him pay attention to such details. It occurred to me he might be nervous before his meeting with Roosevelt.

Stalin, of course, had no doubts about the president's attitude toward the system that had triumphed in the Soviet Union mainly through his efforts. He knew it was very negative. Roosevelt could not be unaware of the bloody crimes, repressions, and arrests in Stalin's empire, of the elimination of private farms and the forced collectivization, which had resulted in famine and the deaths of millions, of the persecution of highly qualified specialists, scholars, writers, all denounced as "saboteurs," of the trials and executions of talented military commanders. The frightening consequences of Stalin's policies had created a very negative image of the Soviet Union in the West.

How will his relations with Roosevelt shape up? Will an insurmountable wall rise between them? Will they succeed in overcoming their mutual distrust? Stalin must have been asking himself these questions.

I believe that in the circumstances of war and alliance, Roosevelt also understood how important it was to find a common language

with the Kremlin dictator. And as it turned out, he succeeded in finding an approach to Stalin that seemed to have convinced the suspicious oriental despot that democratic society was ready to take him
into its arms. At that very first meeting with the Soviet leader, Roosevelt managed to create an atmosphere of confidentiality. There
were no tensions, suspicions, no awkward long pauses.

But then Stalin had also decided to use his charm, and he was
great at that. Before the war, our "helmsman" rarely received foreign statesmen, and because of that he lacked experience. However,
he learned quickly and showed what he was capable of already at the
first meeting with Ribbentrop in August 1939. After Hitler's invasion
of the Soviet Union, Stalin personally participated in the subsequent negotiations. His conversations with Harry Hopkins, Averell
Harriman, Cordell Hull—and his intense correspondence with
Roosevelt—enabled him to get a better understanding of the Americans and to develop his own special way of dealing with them. However, it was still noticeable that before that first meeting with the
president of the United States in the fall of 1943, Stalin did not feel
fully at ease.

Could this be why he was concerned about the seating arrangements? Perhaps he did not want too much light on his face, marked
as it was with smallpox. His marshal's jacket and his trousers with the
red stripes had been meticulously pressed. His soft Caucasian
boots—he usually tucked his trousers into them—were shining. The
special supports under his heels built into the soles of the boots
made him look taller than he was. Stalin tried to create a favorable
impression even by the way he looked. And he began his conversation with Roosevelt with customary Georgian niceties. Was the president comfortable in his residence? Did he have everything he
wanted? Could he, Stalin, be of service? Roosevelt joined the game
and offered Stalin a cigarette. Stalin replied by saying that he had
grown used to smoking his own brand. The president also asked
about Stalin's famous pipe.

"The doctors don't allow it." The omnipotent "helmsman" made a
helpless gesture with his hands.

"Doctors should be obeyed," Roosevelt said in a mentor's tone of
voice.

They asked about each other's health, spoke about the harm of
smoking and the benefits of fresh air. It was beginning to look like a
meeting of two old pals.

At the president's request, Stalin launched into a description of how things were going at the front. Stalin did not conceal the difficulties that had developed in the Ukraine after the Germans seized Zhitomir, a major railroad junction. As a result of this, the Ukrainian capital, Kiev, was again in jeopardy. Roosevelt in his turn also spoke frankly. After describing the fierce battles in the Pacific against Japan, he broached the question of the future of the colonial empires.

"I am speaking about this in the absence of our comrade-in-arms Churchill," the president said, "since he does not like discussing this subject. The United States and the Soviet Union are not colonial powers, and it is easier for us to discuss these matters. I do not think the colonial empires will last long after the end of the war."

Roosevelt said that in the future he intended to talk in greater detail about the postwar status of the colonies. "However," he went on, "it is better to do it without Churchill's participation, since he has no plans even with regard to India."

Stalin was clearly careful not to discuss such a delicate subject. He confined himself to observing that after the war the problem of the colonial empires might indeed become urgent and agreed that it was easier for the Soviet Union and the United States to discuss it than for the countries that possessed colonies. I was struck by Roosevelt's initiative in raising that issue because not long before—at the talks in Berlin in November 1940—I had heard Hitler propose to Molotov that the Soviet Union, together with Germany, Italy, and Japan, should divide up the British colonial heritage. Clearly, those territories attracted many.

In general I had the impression that Stalin and Roosevelt were pleased with their first contact. This, however, could not change them on positions of principle.

The Roosevelt administration was guided by the formula contained in the statement made by the U.S. State Department on June 22, 1941, the first day of the attack by Hitler's Germany against the Soviet Union: "It must be our consistent position that the fact the Soviet Union is waging war against Germany by no means signifies that it is defending, fighting for, or supporting the principles of international relations that we are guided by."

During the war, Roosevelt made a number of friendly comments about the Soviet Union, and about Stalin personally. I believe, however, that he was only paying tribute to the Allied relations in the framework of the anti-Hitler coalition, and to the heroism of the Red Army, which withstood the devastating blows of Hitler's war machine. At the same time, the president was drawing appropriate conclusions from the way the battles on the Soviet-German front were going. Roosevelt believed that the Soviet people, by continuing to resist aggression, were proving the strength of the system. If it survived and continued after the war, there would be no point in again trying to destroy it. It would be better to develop a mechanism that would enable the capitalist countries to coexist with the Soviet Union. This, however, did not mean that Roosevelt approved in the slightest of the Soviet reality.

Stalin also had his reasons for mistrust. Roosevelt's establishment of diplomatic relations with the Soviet Union after sixteen years of nonrecognition, his stated intention to support the struggle of the Soviet people against the Nazi aggression, his readiness to arrange shipments of military materials to the Soviet Union—all this was positive on the balance sheet of the Roosevelt administration. However, a number of factors in the way the anti-Hitler coalition operated increased Stalin's suspicions of the United States. More generally, his deeply ingrained animosity toward the capitalist system constantly nourished his doubts.

I heard Stalin say to Molotov on different occasions, "Roosevelt is talking about Congress again. He thinks I will believe that he is truly afraid of Congress, and that is why he is unable to make concessions to us. He just does not want to do it, and he is using Congress as an excuse. It is all nonsense! He is their military leader and commander in chief. Who would dare object to him? It is just convenient for him to hide behind Congress. But he won't take me in."

Nor did Stalin believe it when, responding to his complaints about unfriendly articles about the Soviet Union in the U.S. and British press, Roosevelt and Churchill explained that they could not control newspapers and magazines, and that they themselves sometimes got rough treatment from the press. Stalin considered all this to be a bourgeois ploy and a double game. However, he saw that the Soviet side was at a disadvantage. When our press published fairly tepid critical comments about the policies of the Western allies (delay in opening the second front, missing deadlines for military shipments, rumors about separate talks with the Germans, etc.), Roosevelt and Churchill protested and complained to Stalin since those were articles published in the official Soviet press.

In 1943, to balance the situation, Stalin decided to launch a new magazine to be called *War and the Working Class*, presenting it as a publication of Soviet trade unions. In reality, Molotov was editor in chief of this biweekly, even though the title page had the name of a fictitious trade union activist as editor. Molotov entrusted me with the technical side of the preparations for meetings of the magazine's editorial board, and I could observe how carefully not only he, but sometimes also Stalin, meted out critical articles. However, now complaints by the leaders in the United States and Britain could be addressed by saying that the Soviet government was not responsible for these materials, and that all grievances should be directed to the trade union organization. Stalin was certain that Roosevelt and Churchill manipulated the press in exactly the same way.

Stalin tried to establish contact with Roosevelt as early as the midthirties. Anastas Mikoyan told me about one such attempt made in the summer of 1935. Not long before Mikoyan's departure for the United States to purchase equipment, a U.S. citizen named Cohn, who was a relative of Molotov's wife, was staying at Molotov's dacha. Before long Stalin made his appearance. After dinner, he took Mikoyan out into the garden and said:

"This man Cohn is a capitalist. When you are in America, meet with him. He will help us establish political dialogue with Roosevelt."

Upon his arrival in Washington, Mikoyan found out that "capitalist" Cohn owned six gas stations and, of course, had no access to the White House. Using Cohn as an intermediary was out of the question. In the meantime, Henry Ford, on his own initiative, offered to introduce Mikoyan to Roosevelt. The then Soviet ambassador to the United States, A. Troyanovsky, immediately reported this to Moscow. However, there was no response, and Mikoyan did not meet Roosevelt. I was puzzled why he had failed to do so, since Stalin was seeking to establish dialogue with Roosevelt.

"You do not know Stalin very well," Mikoyan said to me. "His instructions were to act through Cohn. If I had used Ford's offices without Stalin's authorization, he would have said, 'Mikoyan wants to outsmart us all, he is getting involved in big-time politics.' He would never forgive me for that. He would certainly remember it one day and use it against me."

This episode spoke volumes about the mores among the top Soviet leadership at the time. It also illustrated the ingenuity of the clever Armenian and proved what people in Moscow said about him in jest:

> From Ilyich to Ilyich,
> he survived without a hitch.

And it was true. Mikoyan survived the turbulent years—from Vladimir Ilyich Lenin to Leonid Ilyich Brezhnev. However, what was most remarkable here was how simplistic Stalin's ideas were about life in the United States. He believed that since Cohn was a capitalist, he therefore had to have easy access to the president.

These peculiar ideas about the United States also explain the proposal Stalin made to Hopkins, and subsequently to Harriman, even before the United States entered the war, to send U.S. troops to the Ukraine to conduct military operations on the Soviet-German front. He was naturally refused, but what was surprising was that he was profoundly slighted by the refusal.

However, Roosevelt's initiative, which followed after that, was no less strange. On January 12, 1942, that is to say already after Pearl Harbor, in his talk with the new Soviet ambassador, Maxim Litvinov, who had just arrived in Washington, Roosevelt suggested that U.S. troops could replace Soviet units deployed in Iran, in the Transcaucasus, and in the area of the polar port Murmansk. Soviet soldiers could be relocated to engage in operations in the active parts of the front. The president supplemented his proposal with a kind of a lure:

"The U.S. side," he informed the Soviet ambassador, "will not object if the Soviet Union acquired a port in the north open for navigation all year round, somewhere in Norway, similar to Narvik."

To establish a link to this port, Roosevelt clarified, a corridor could be established through Norwegian and Finnish territories.

From the point of view of contemporary morality, such a proposal, made, moreover, without notifying the Norwegians and the Finns, appeared cynical, to say the least. Furthermore, at that time, Narvik, like Norway as a whole, was under German occupation.

The Soviet government turned down the U.S. proposal. On January 18, Molotov dispatched a cable to the Soviet ambassador instructing him to respond to Roosevelt by saying that the Soviet Union "does not now and has never had any territorial or any other claims to Norway and that is why it cannot accept the proposal concerning the occupation of Narvik by Soviet forces." As for the replacement of the Soviet units by U.S. contingents in the Caucasus and in Murmansk, this "at present does not have practical significance, since there are no hostilities there." The cable went on to say: "We would

The Big Three at the Teheran Conference of the leaders of the anti-Hitler coalition.

The Soviet delegation arriving in Washington, D.C., reviewing the honor guards, July 1944.

Arrival of the Soviet delegation in Washington, D.C., in July 1944. In the foreground from left to right: A. Gromyko with his wife, Deputy Secretary of State E. Stettinius, British Permanent Deputy Foreign Secretary A. Cadogan. Berezhkov is in the background.

The Soviet delegation in
Dumbarton-Oaks, August 1944.
From left to right: Yunin, Slavin,
Krylov, Subolyev, Dolbin,
Gromyko, Berezhkov, Tsarapkin,
Golunsky, Radionov.

The Dumbarton-Oaks Estate in
Georgetown, Washington, D.C.

The Dumbarton-Oaks Estate
where the three allies in the anti-
Hitler coalition—the United
States, the Soviet Union and
Britain—met to draft the charter
of the United Nations.

The Soviet delegation at the Dumbarton-Oaks conference held to draft the Charter of the United Nations. From left to right: Dolbin, admiral Rodionov, general Slavin, Berezhkov, Gromyko, Sobolyev, Tsarapkin, Golunsky, Krylov.

A plenary meeting of the conference at Dumbarton-Oaks held in July-October 1944.

Soviet-British talks in Moscow. From left to right, seated—V. Molotov, A. Harriman, W. Churchill, J. Stalin, A. Eden; standing—V. Berezhkov, A. Curr, V. Pavlov, A. Birse, F. Gusev. October 1944.

President Roosevelt's arrival at Saki airport in the Crimea. From right to left: Roosevelt (in jeep), Churchill, Molotov, First Deputy Foreign Minister Vyshinsky. February, 1945.

The Big Three in the Italian yard of the Livadia Palace during the Yalta conference, February 1945.

Stalin and Churchill at the Vorontsov Palace, Churchill's residence during the Yalta conference, February 1945.

Churchill, Truman, and Stalin in the park of the Zezilienhof Palace during the Potsdam conference, July 1945.

The Big Three at Potsdam, July 1945.

During a break of a plenary meeting at the Potsdam Conference. Left to right: Stalin, Bohlen, Pavlov, Truman, Gromyko, presidential press secretary Charles Ross, Secretary of State Byrnes, and Molotov. July 1945.

Stalin visiting Truman at his villa in Babelsberg during the Potsdam Conference, July 1945. From left to right: U.S. Secretary of State Byrnes, Gromyko, Truman, Stalin, and Molotov.

V. Berezhkov with his wife, Valeria (at left), meeting his mother, Lyudmila Nikolayevna, in 1969, after thirty years of separation.

V. Berezhkov with his wife, Valeria (at right), and his sister, Musa. The last time he had seen his sister was a half-century ago. Los Angeles, 1992.

accept with satisfaction Roosevelt's help in the form of U.S. troops who would fight side by side with our troops against the forces of Hitler and his allies."

However, the United States did not find troops for this.

This episode left a bad impression in Moscow and made Stalin suspicious again. He viewed Roosevelt's proposal as an encroachment on the territorial integrity of the Soviet Union. Still fresh in his mind was the intervention against Soviet Russia after the Revolution, when American troops occupied a number of places in our country. At the same time, one could understand Washington's desire to preserve its forces at the expense of the blood of the Soviet people and to weaken both antagonists in the conflict, Germany and the Soviet Union.

I would like to dwell on a number of key problems that in one way or another influenced relations between Stalin and Roosevelt.

Even though our Western allies did not respond to Moscow's repeated calls to land in France and open a Western front, Washington began studying the feasibility of such an operation as early as the fall of 1941. By the spring of the following year, a version of a plan for U.S. intervention in northern France was ready. Reporting on it to President Roosevelt, General Marshall stated that a landing in France would provide maximum support to the Russian front. The operation, however, was subject to two conditions:

1. If the situation on the Russian front became desperate, i.e., if the success of the German war machine created the possibility of the collapse of the Russian resistance. In this case an attack in the West would have to be considered a sacrifice for the common good.

2. If the situation of the Germans became critical.

This document shed light on the American concept of the second front: while Russia and Germany remained able to continue the war effort, Washington preferred to keep out and avoid sacrificing its own stock of human lives.

By the beginning of 1942, the Germans had mobilized vast forces for a new and powerful offensive deep inside the Soviet Union. Yet our Western allies still did not take any steps to alleviate the situation on the Soviet-German front. On January 31, 1942, observing their inaction, Ambassador Litvinov sent the following message to the People's Commissariat for Foreign Affairs: "Hitler's probable spring offensive, for which he has been building up massive forces, is less than two months away, and by that time we want to secure assistance from England and the United States, and we must make this known right now. We must either demand a landing on the continent or declare that we need the amount of aircraft and tanks corresponding to the enemy's superiority over us in the one and the other."

On February 4, Litvinov received the following answer from Moscow: "We would welcome the opening of the second front in Europe by our allies. However, you know that our proposal to open the second front has already been refused three times, and we do not want to risk a fourth refusal. That is why you are not to raise the issue of the second front with Roosevelt. Let us wait for the moment when perhaps our allies will raise that issue with us themselves." The not altogether diplomatic language of this message reveals its author's irritation. Stalin was displeased and he let his displeasure show.

Did this have any effect on Roosevelt? Maybe to some extent it did. In any case, soon after that there seemed to be a shift in the American position. On April 12, 1942, President Roosevelt informed Stalin that he thought it advisable to exchange views with a ranking Soviet representative on a number of important issues relating to the conduct of the war against the common enemy. He inquired whether the Soviet government was prepared to send Molotov to Washington to engage in such negotiations. The Soviet side immediately agreed. For reasons of secrecy, this visit was code-named Mr. Brown's Mission.

After stopping first in London, where he signed the Soviet-British treaty of alliance in the war against Hitler's Germany and its allies in Europe, and on cooperation and mutual assistance after the war, Molotov headed for Washington. In his talks with Roosevelt, Molotov discussed the plans for the landing of the Western allies in France and the situation on the Soviet-German front.

Molotov said, "If the Allied forces in 1942 pulled back at least forty enemy divisions from our front, the balance of forces would radically shift in our favor and Hitler's fate would be sealed."

After listening to Molotov's statement, made with uncharacteristic feeling, Roosevelt turned to General Marshall with a question: "Are we advanced enough with our preparations to be able to report to Mr. Stalin that we are ready to open the second front?"

The general nodded his head. And after that the president solemnly declared, "Please report to your government that it may expect the opening of the second front this year."

Thus, the president, who was joined in this by Churchill, officially committed himself to carry out the landing. Moreover, a concrete deadline was specified. The joint communiqué stated, "Full understanding was reached with regard to the urgent task of creating a second front in Europe in 1942."

Were Washington and London actually planning a landing in Western Europe at this stage? Was this decision a miscalculation or just a light-headed decision of a kind that would be inadmissible for mature politicians? At that moment it was unlikely that the Western allies thought the Soviet ability to resist was running out and that it was time for the final "sacrifice." And even if they did, they soon came to the conclusion that there was no need to precipitate any "sacrifice."

Sometime later, when Roosevelt and Churchill went back on the promise they had made to Stalin, the president was especially uncomfortable because in his Washington conversation with Molotov he had said a radical reduction of the military shipments so badly needed in Russia was a result of the requirements for the landing in France. When Molotov asked if the shipments might be reduced and the second front still not be opened, Roosevelt assured the people's commissar one more time that the landing in France would take place in 1942. It may be assumed that the president of the United States breathed a sigh of relief when Churchill volunteered to carry out the unpleasant mission to Moscow—to inform Stalin that the landing would not take place.

In this connection, it would be appropriate to recall a passage in the book *As He Saw It* by the president's son Elliot. It offers a good illustration of how Roosevelt understood the role of the United States in the war:

> Just figure it's a football game. Say we're the reserves sitting on the bench. At the moment, the Russians are the first team, together with the Chinese and, to a lesser extent, the British. Before the game is so far advanced that our blockers are tired, we've got to be able to get in there for the touchdown. . . . I think our timing will be right.

Roosevelt shared his innermost thoughts with his son.

In this context, the decisions adopted at the Teheran Conference are usually qualified in our literature as a major victory for Soviet diplomacy. Indeed, at long last, the Western allies indicated a specific date for the landing and, on the whole, kept it. Real help came to the Red Army, which for three long years had been battling virtually alone against Hitler's military machine. The question was, however, was it true that the United States and Britain, by agreeing to open the second front in France, acceded to the insistent demands of Stalin, who even threatened to leave Teheran if no definitive date was given for the invasion of Europe? Or were they primarily guided by their own interests? Could it not be that they had concluded that the situation was developing as envisaged under the second option of the American plan, the imminent collapse of Germany?

By the time of the Teheran Conference, Washington had already come to a decision. While sailing on a cruiser across the Atlantic on his way to the Iranian capital, President Roosevelt called his closest aides to his cabin and shared with them his ideas concerning the second front: "The Soviet forces are only sixty miles away from the Polish border and forty miles away from Bessarabia. If they cross the Dniester River, which may happen within the next two weeks, the Red Army will be in Romania's backyard."

The President concluded from this situation that it was time to act. "The Americans and the British must occupy a maximum part of Europe," he explained. "The British will handle France, Belgium, Luxembourg, and also the southern part of Germany. The United States must move its ships and take U.S. troops to the ports of Bremen and Hamburg, as well as to Norway and Denmark. We must reach Berlin. Then let the Soviets occupy the territory east of the city. But Berlin must be taken by the United States."

In the Far East

THE CLOUDS OF A NEW WORLD CONFLICT were gathering menacingly on the horizon, but we tried not to think about it. Kiev's lively cultural life put the people in a peaceful frame of mind. Quite often the city played host to touring performers from abroad. Soviet musicians, singers, and chess players were winning laurels at international competitions, and there was a growing sense that we were part of a larger world outside the confines of our impenetrable borders. My friends and I didn't miss one concert by the great performers. Musicians such as Sobinov, Oistrakh, Gilels, Kozlovsky, the Polish singer

Eva Bandrovska-Turska, Tsigler's Czech jazz band, and the public's favorite jazzman, Utyosov, usually gave their concerts in the Hall of Columns of the former Merchants Assembly at the corner of Kreshchatik and Aleksandrovskaya streets. Before the Revolution, a monument to Alexander II had stood here. It was blown up in the first months of the Soviet regime, and all that remained was its marble base with its relief depicting the peoples of the Russian Empire and an inscription: "To the Czar, the Liberator, from Grateful Russia."

It has become a tradition in Russia that the initiators of its reforms, intended for the benefit of its people, always die a violent death at the hands of self-proclaimed "friends" of the people. Alexander II, who abolished serfdom in 1861, was assassinated in St. Petersburg in a bomb attack carried out by a member of the Norodnaya Volya (People's Freedom) organization. Stolypin, prime minister of the Russian Empire, who was conducting an agrarian reform that promised land to the farmers and prosperity to the villages, was shot by a fanatical revolutionary. The shot that killed Russia's outstanding political figure rang out at the Kiev Opera House, opposite the box where sat the last Russian czar, Nicholas II. Stolypin's assassination not only put a stop to a promising reform but also brought on a harsh crackdown that eventually led to the Revolution of 1917.

Now, a growing number of ominous developments disturbed the flow of day-to-day life: the defeat of the Republican government in Spain and the rise of dictator Franco in Madrid, brought to power by the German and Italian bayonets; the Anschluss that tied Austria to Germany—with the triumphant arrival of Hitler in Vienna—the Nazi blackmail of Czechoslovakia and the subsequent Munich deal. . . .

At the time the Czechoslovakian situation was sharply deteriorating, I was working at the Arsenal in Kiev. In the design department, where I was given a seat behind a large drafting board, I was part of a group headed by engineer Timofeyev. He was especially attentive to me, helping me master the tricks of the trade. But I didn't get to work with him for long. Mobilization was declared in the Ukraine. All reserve officers, including Timofeyev, were called up into the Red Army. A few times he stopped in at the office, already wearing a military uniform, looking prim and grim. He told us he had received orders to report to the forces deployed along the border with Poland. Under the terms of the agreement between the Soviet Union and France, the two countries were to join forces in assisting Czechoslovakia in case of aggression against it. Press reports about Hitler's threats to Prague and the provocations by the Nazis in the Sudetenland suggested that Berlin was preparing such an act of aggression. Moscow declared mobilization in the Ukrainian military district, thereby reaffirming its intention to live up to its commitments. We were closely following the Munich talks, confident that if Hitler didn't retreat, the Soviet Union and France would provide Czechoslovakia the support they had promised. I believe that, psychologically, our people were ready for this. We were further hoping that our actions would topple the fascist dictatorship in Germany. But Hitler staged yet another hysterical show in Munich, which led to Czechoslovakia's betrayal by the West. France backed out of its commitment to help. Poland refused to allow the Red Army to pass through its territory. The mobilization in the Ukraine was called off, and engineer Timofeyev took off his military uniform and returned to the design office at the Arsenal.

Every morning on my way to the office as I walked through the Mariinsky Park, I looked at the left bank of the Dnieper, stretching below, at the sandbanks, the water meadows, and the specks of villages on the horizon with their churches and belfries. Would there come a time when a German soldier would be standing on that steep bank there, and our army would be rolled back across those fields far beyond the horizon, leaving behind rivers of blood, thousands of people maimed or captured, and the charred skeletons of long-suffering Ukrainian villages?

Having just read a book by a mysterious writer named Ernst Henry entitled *Hitler Against the USSR*, which had come out only recently and created a sensation by predicting that German forces would seize, albeit temporarily, vast areas of Soviet territory, and observing the phenomenal successes that Hitler was scoring, which, not without the help of Western politicians, led to the emergence of the Great German Reich, I no longer excluded the possibility we would have to sustain heavy losses in the event of a war with Germany. I had a personal reason to be preoccupied with all these thoughts. There was no ROTC program at the Kiev Polytechnic's night school. We were all granted an exemption from the draft for the duration of our studies, but afterward we would have to report for active military service. College graduates, however, enjoyed a benefit: they served one year instead of two in the army, and two instead of four in the navy. Would we have enough time to complete our military training before the war broke out?

In early November, I got my call-up papers from the military registration and enlistment center. My orders were to take a medical examination and then to report at a recruiting station. The doctors gave me a clean bill of health. The interview that followed was peremptory, with only a few questions asked about my background. After a short wait in a corridor, I again found myself facing my interviewers, who informed me that I was assigned to serve in the Pacific Fleet and was to leave that same month for Vladivostok. Even though I had always been attracted by the romance of the sea, I was not happy about this. Almost all my friends had been drafted into the ground forces of the Ukrainian Military District. They served nearby, came home on furlough, and in violation of the regulations, wore their civilian clothes and had a great time in familiar surroundings. I wouldn't be so lucky in Vladivostok. For one thing, I would have to serve two years, and not one, like them. Then I would be away from Galya for so long. And on top of that, I was upset by the order to report to the assembly center with my hair cropped to the skin.

I spent my last days before the departure bustling about: I had to fill out all kinds of forms, get my travel documents, and obtain various certificates. My parting with Galya was sweetly painful. I hadn't been away from my parents for any long time either, and it hurt to leave them. All through those days I felt miserable. But I also had this vague, disturbing feeling that something unknown was about to happen, something that was to change my whole life around. Envious of my friends who were staying in the Ukraine, I didn't, of course, know that almost all of them would be killed in the first days of the war, and that most likely I would have shared their fate had I stayed with them.

At the assembly center, quite unexpectedly, I met two conscripts who had graduated from college with me: Arkady Erlikhman and Igor Belyayev. I hadn't seen them in all those months and was glad to learn that they were also going to Vladivostok to serve in the Pacific Fleet. Together we would have more fun and peace of mind. We received our instructions, were told where to report upon our arrival at our destination, and were allowed to go home one last time. The next day we left by train for Moscow, and from there took the trans-Siberian express for the Far East.

As new recruits we had only ourselves to rely on and only our meager pay to spend. Still we decided to stay in the capital for two days. We had a long journey ahead of us, and it didn't make any difference to us whether we got there in ten days or twelve.

We arrived in Moscow in the morning. The weather was gloomy and damp, befitting my mood. People were milling about the square in front of the railway station; it was beginning to drizzle. I felt lost. We had no place to stay and we couldn't count on a hotel. Our passports were taken away at the Kiev recruiting station, and as recruits, we were to proceed immediately to our destination.

"Maybe we should leave today after all?" Igor said hesitantly, as if ready to pass up the pleasures of Moscow.

"Come on, guys, don't give up!" Arkady, the most enterprising of us, protested. "First we have to take care of organizational matters. We have to get to the Yaroslavsky Railway Station, punch our travel authorization papers, check in our luggage, and then we'll see."

We didn't have too many things with us. Each of us had two changes of underwear, warm socks, a hat for cold weather, and some food for the road packed by our thoughtful parents. The trains for the Far East departed from the Yaroslavsky Station, and of course, first things first, we had to get our tickets. And then it made sense to move around town light. In short, we accepted Arkady's idea.

We had a pretty good time during our two days in Moscow. We went to the Tretyakov Art Gallery, the Museum of History, and the Pushkin Museum. We dined at the restaurant in the Moskva Hotel, without pinching pennies, on a sumptuous feast and a bottle of Pertsovka vodka. People looked at our closely cropped heads with suspicion, maybe thinking we were convicts on the run. But filled with a few drinks and swelling with pride because we were joining the ranks of the defenders of the naval borders of our homeland, we looked down at them superciliously. The kindhearted administrator of the Bolshoi Theater looked at our travel papers and, taking compassion on the poor fellows going only God knew where, gave us three passes to the gallery. The day was concluded by the grand finale of Borodin's opera *Prince Igor*. We spent the night on the floor of the Yaroslavsky Station, using newspapers for sheets.

The next morning the weather had improved, and after performing our ablutions in the station's bathroom, we set out on a walk around town since the train for Vladivostok was not leaving until the afternoon. We had lunch at a shish-kebab place near the Khudozhestvenny Theater and soon returned to the station.

The trip from Moscow to Vladivostok took nine days and was quite an odyssey. We were not traveling in the comfort of the international sleeping cars I had gotten used to as a travel guide. Our car had no individual compartments and its seats were hard. A thin mattress would be rolled out over them, which didn't make them a much softer place to sleep. In our cubicle with two double bunks opposite each other across the aisle was another conscript into the Pacific Fleet. Older than we were, he was already thirty when he graduated from the night school of the Leningrad Shipbuilding Institute where he had been granted a delay from service, just as we had. Pyotr, our new friend, was easy to get along with. He treated us to the home-made sausage he had received for the trip from his native village where his parents worked in the kolkhoz.

By the third day of the journey everybody already knew everybody else. During the stops, sometimes quite prolonged, the passengers dashed to get boiled water for tea or some food, which was sold at the stations' buffets or at the stands a little off to the side. Then they walked up and down the platform, waiting for the train's whistle. Farther along the way, already in Siberia, there was only one track, and sometimes we had to wait a long time at the double-track junctions for the oncoming train to pass.

The morning we arrived in Vladivostok it was foggy and warm. My first impression was that the city was very much like a provincial town in the heartland of Russia. But when I got to know it better, I also learned what set it apart. At that time large Chinese and Korean communities still lived there. Some areas looked exactly like the Chinatowns of New York or San Francisco. There was a Chinese opera. Throngs of street vendors offered all sorts of things for the home to the passersby—paper lanterns, fans, or exotic figurines made of ivory. But the main contribution the able and industrious Chinese and Korean farmers made to the city was a wide variety of vegetables. Many were varieties that I saw here for the first time in my life.

I was still there when the deportation of those people began. Soon virtually none were left, which dealt an irreparable blow to the economy of the Maritime Territories. The crafts fell into a decline, the Chinese opera closed down, and the vegetables vanished from the markets. Since that time and to this day, vegetables are brought to Vladivostok mainly from the distant Urals or from the even more distant Ukraine. That was the result of the upsurge of spy mania that followed the 1937 purges of the Red Army's top command. But I was lucky to have seen Vladivostok's better days.

We decided not to hurry to report to the headquarters of the Pacific Fleet. We left our things at a luggage room and set off on a tour

of the city. Since we were in our civvies, the army and navy patrols—
and we met them at every step of our way—didn't pay any attention
to us. We had lunch at the city's best restaurant, had a drink to celebrate our arrival in the place where we were going to serve, and
watched an antifascist movie, *The Oppenheim Family*, that had just
been released based on a novel by Leon Feuchtwanger. In the afternoon we showed up at headquarters.

The officer on duty reprimanded us for not reporting in directly
upon our arrival. Somehow we had overlooked the fact that only one
train arrived daily from Moscow, and it wasn't hard to guess that we
had spent the day loitering around town. He advised us not to violate
the regulations again. Then he gave us a quick briefing and went
over our papers.

We were all assigned to the Engineering Department of the Pacific
Fleet Headquarters. While we were being briefed, a petty officer
named Mishchenko was called in to take the four of us to the navy hostel in Lenin Street, known as an orlop, to use the navy terminology.

The large room on the first floor was filled with rows of beds covered with gray service-issue blankets. Arkady and I had our beds next
to each other, separated by two night tables intended for personal
things. The next morning, we received our uniforms as members of
the Red Navy: one made out of thick tarpaulin for everyday work and
wear and the other—a full-dress uniform for more festive occasions.
The orlop was to become our home for two whole years. All in all we
were about four score young men with engineering degrees. Every
morning, Mishchenko walked us in formation to our workplace
where, still wearing our naval uniforms, we became engineers for
eight hours, and after our workday was over, we went back to being
ordinary seamen, marching back with an uplifting song that our
petty officer led off.

Mishchenko saw to it that we got what we were supposed to get—
and got it on schedule. Twice a week we went to the baths. Once a
month we visited the barber. He allowed us to let our hair grow out,
which put us in a somewhat better mood. At the same time, he was
demanding of the recruits with college degrees, believing that he
had to be especially strict with them.

Gradually we got used to the established order of things with its
duty details, punishments for the slightest transgressions, infrequent
furloughs, and nightly alerts, which our petty officer enjoyed staging.
We began eagerly looking forward to our days off. We couldn't wait

to show off our new uniforms, to walk up and down Lenin Street, the city's main thoroughfare, to enjoy the view of the Golden Horn Bay and the fanciful contours of the hills that provided a backdrop for the city skyline and stood out sharply against the incredibly clear winter night's sky in the Far East, looking as if they had been clipped out of cardboard.

We began our preparations for such days on the town well in advance. We carefully spread our trousers under the mattress to get a perfect overnight crease, burnished the bronze buttons of our sailor's jackets, and shined our shoes until they sparkled. It took special dexterity to fit a wire loop to the rim of the seaman's beakless cap, which made it sit flat on the head, like a pancake. We carefully smoothed out the hatbands that had PACIFIC FLEET proudly written on them. The main decorative detail was on the jacket: its wide, blue sailor's collar with white stripes, called a Jack. In order to look like an old sea wolf, you had to make sure that your Jack was faded, as if bleached by the ocean spray and scorched by the tropical sun. As soon as we were issued our uniforms, we dunked our Jacks in a bucket of salt water and kept them there until they were properly aged.

Every now and again a dance party with refreshments would be held at the club of the Pacific Fleet Headquarters. We made it a point not to miss any of them. These parties were also attended by the civilian staff working in different sections of the Headquarters, including our Engineering Department. A fair number of girls would be among them: typists, secretaries, and drafting artists. In short, there was ample opportunity for amorous adventures. Pyotr, the man who had traveled with us, didn't waste any time and pretty soon had a sweetheart. Not wanting a relationship, I limited myself to a platonic friendship with a lovely, rosy-cheeked typist named Masha, who became my steady partner at dances and promenades. We also held a party at the club for New Year's Eve 1939. A tree was put up and decorated; we chipped in for a dinner, then danced and drew for a lottery. Then we continued to celebrate in our orlop since our petty officer was away spending the night at home. Somebody got a bottle of 100-proof alcohol from somewhere. The more experienced second-year seamen taught us, the greenhorns, the art of imbibing that fiery beverage: down a glass without breathing in, drink some water, then have some food. While we were partying, the serviceman on duty was on the lookout for any unexpected visitors. We were completely off our guard, chatting, cracking jokes, and telling funny stories when suddenly we heard a yell:

"Look out!"

The duty seaman was warning us of approaching danger. But the alcohol had dulled our reflexes. We ran toward our beds to hide under the blankets, pretending we were asleep, but we weren't quick enough, and worse, we had left the incriminating evidence at the "scene of the crime": glasses scattered around and the unfinished bottle of alcohol.

The seaman on duty was standing in the doorway, trying to block the petty officer's view, rattling off his report in a cheerful voice:

"Comrade Petty Officer, everything in the orlop is in order. All seamen are present and accounted for."

But Mishchenko's sharp eye had already spotted what we had been up to.

"Get up!" he ordered in a resounding voice. "Fall in on the first deck!"

That was what the petty officer called the aisle between the beds closest to the entrance door. We had to throw off our blankets and fall in. Admittedly, we looked pretty stupid: some were in their underwear, others were wearing their seamen's striped vests and work pants.

"Call the roll!" the petty officer shouted.

Then he let us have it. There wasn't a bad name he didn't call us. He said he would report all of us, throw us into the brig, order us "off the ship," as if our orlop were a deck on a ship. After he had let off steam, he began working on our consciences, upbraiding us for conduct unworthy of people with college degrees. He was laying a special emphasis on that. Finally, he declared that the next day, which was the New Year's Day, nobody would get a furlough and that everyone would be given a special detail. Some were to wash the floor in the orlop, others were to clean the latrine, still others to sweep the yard.

In the morning, I changed into my work clothes and, arming myself with a swab and a bucket with hot, sudsy water, began scrubbing the floorboards, cursing all the time. It was the first time I had ever started a New Year like that! I didn't, of course, know then that the new year would bring remarkable changes in my life.

January was drawing to a close when our petty officer called me in one day and said that I was to report to the Pacific Fleet Headquarters at twenty hundred hours. This was so unexpected that I couldn't hold back a question: Who would want to see me there and why? Mishchenko advised me to stop asking questions and to prepare my dress uniform on the double.

That was what I began doing, constantly wondering what this summons meant. I didn't recall doing anything in the two months of my service that could have drawn the attention of any ranking officers. I was lost in speculation, but as it turned out, even my wildest guesses were way off the mark. The real reason was simple.

As I said earlier, I had joined the Pacific Fleet in 1938, that is to say soon after Stalin had begun purging the army and the navy. After the top commanders of the Soviet armed forces were convicted and executed, the wave of repression swept through all military districts and fleets. It reached the Far East, too, where all the top commanding officers were replaced. When the new commander in chief of the Pacific Fleet, Admiral Kuznetsov, his chief of staff, Captain Third Rank Bogdenko, and the head of the Engineering Department, Captain-Engineer Second Rank Vorontsov, assumed their duties, they found that their job descriptions prescribed, among other things, that they study English. It was a reasonable requirement. At that time, Japan was our potential enemy while the United States was potentially an ally, which turned out to be the case. Cooperation with the U.S. Navy could develop, so it was desirable for the top staff officers to know at least the basics of English. The admirals and officers who had disappeared either knew the language or had studied it with tutors of the pre-Revolutionary intelligentsia. These teachers were mainly women of the beau monde who had fled Petrograd during the Civil War but for some reason had been unable to reach Shanghai and had got stuck in Vladivostok. After 1937, they, of course, also ended up behind bars as "spies for Japan." Since not everyone could be allowed inside the navy headquarters, the new commanders began looking among the servicemen for someone with a knowledge of English. The head of the personnel department was instructed to go over the files to find a suitable candidate, and he stumbled upon my profile. Thus some people's bad luck brings good luck to others.

Of course, I wasn't aware of any of that when, at the appointed hour, freshly pressed and cleaned, I arrived at the Pacific Fleet Headquarters, located in a building built in the time of the czars. I was impressed by the dark oak wall paneling, the thick carpeting in corridors, the bearing and manners of the officers on guard, and the spacious office of the Fleet's chief of staff, its walls covered with maps. I felt excited, that I was entering on a fascinating and mysterious path.

A somewhat heavy but still young captain third rank rose from the table. He was the chief of staff of the Pacific Fleet, Bogdenko. Another man, Captain-Engineer Second Rank Vorontsov, remained seated in a chair near the table.

"Comrade Chief of Staff, Red Navy Seaman Berezhkov reporting on your orders!" I shouted out cheerfully, putting my hand to my beakless cap in a naval salute.

Dropping a perfunctory "At ease!" Bogdenko invited me to take a seat in an empty chair. Then he took a yellow folder from the desk and began leafing through it.

"It says here that you have a perfect command of English," he began. "Is that correct?"

"Yes, sir!"

"When did you study it? What school did you graduate from?"

I supplied him my background.

Bogdenko again began leafing through the papers in the folder. He took out a carefully folded, perfumed kerchief from the pocket of his jacket and touched his upper lip with it. Then he asked, "Do you think you could teach English?"

I thought for a minute before answering. "I've never done it before. I am an engineer-technologist by training."

"We know that. But you do remember how you were taught, don't you?"

"Yes, sir, I do."

"Well, then, you can probably teach others in the same way."

"I've never had a chance to teach, but I will try if you so order."

"Now you're talking. There is a directive out that requires that the commander, the chief of staff, and the head of the Engineering Department learn English—since the United States is on the other side of the Pacific. You understand, don't you?"

"Yes, Comrade Captain Third Rank."

"We want you to teach us English."

"Yes, sir."

"Let's discuss the details," Vorontsov said.

I was informed that each session should last two academic hours of forty-five minutes each, and that there would be two sessions a week. I would be paid twenty-five rubles for every academic hour. My immediate superiors would be instructed to give me time to work in the city library if I found it necessary to do some preparatory work for the classes.

When I left the headquarters building, I felt as if I had been given wings. An incredible thing has happened in my life, I was thinking on my way back. From now on I will no longer be at the beck and call of my petty officer, and on top of that, I will be able to make some money—four hundred rubles a month in addition to the twelve rubles I was getting as my regular navy pay. Not bad at all!

I began preparing for the classes in earnest. Of course, my good knowledge of the language as well as the fact that I hadn't forgotten how I had been taught stood me in good stead. Furthermore, my students turned out to be diligent. Things were coming along nicely. Soon I was able to buy a FED camera manufactured by the prisoners in the Dzerzhinsky labor camp under a license from the German company Leica. The camera was in fact named after Feliks Edmundovitch Dzerzhinsky, who had been chief of Lenin's secret police. That acquisition immediately turned me into a most sought-after man. "Life is wonderful!" I kept repeating to myself. "It doesn't get any better than this!" But, alas, nothing is eternal under the moon!

Admiral Kuznetsov was appointed people's commissar of the navy and ordered back to Moscow. He was soon followed there by Bogdenko and Vorontsov. The new commanding officers probably had other things on their minds than studying a foreign language. In any case, I didn't hear from them on the subject.

Once again my petty officer had total control over me, and of course, he began exercising it again with a vengeance, assigning me one special detail after another. Life got back into the old rut, and the only thing that made my days different were the infrequent trips I made to a nearby island. This was official business since we were installing naval artillery there. The place bewitched me with the beauty of nature. Sometimes on my days off, I traveled nineteen kilometers out of town to Peter the Great Bay. People began swimming in the ocean there with the advent of warm weather.

The international situation was rapidly deteriorating. In the Far East, one Japanese provocation followed another. The USSR Supreme Soviet published a decree establishing new terms for compulsory military service. It abolished the benefits enjoyed by the college graduates. On top of that it extended the length of service in the navy, meaning we were to remain Red Navy seamen for five years. I became deeply depressed. Belyayev and Erlikhman requested to be transferred to work in personnel. In that case, they would immediately be made commissioned officers and get more money. But something was holding me back. I was waiting for something to happen.

At the very end of August, a telegram came. I was ordered to go to Moscow without delay and report to Naval Command Headquarters.

Recommendations to the Poles

THE POLISH PROBLEM featured prominently in the discussions among Stalin, Roosevelt, and Churchill.

The position of the Soviet Union, as it was then interpreted by Moscow, looked perfectly reasonable. Stalin declared that he wanted to see Poland reborn as a strong, independent, democratic state that would maintain friendly relations with the Soviet Union. At the same time, he insisted on the recognition of the new Soviet-Polish border of 1939 that ran roughly along the Curzon Line, as proposed by the Entente in 1919. On those terms, Moscow was prepared to agree to restore relations with the Polish government that was in exile in London. Churchill came up with a similar proposal in Teheran. He submitted the following formula to Stalin and Roosevelt for consideration: "In principle it has been accepted that the home of the Polish state and nation must be located between the so-called Curzon Line and the line of the Oder River, with East Prussia and Pomerania (Oppeln) incorporated into the territory of Poland."

The Soviet side came out in support of Churchill's proposal. As for Roosevelt, he agreed to that line in principle, even though he warned that until the 1944 presidential elections he would abstain from any public statements in that regard because of a possible negative reaction from the Polish electorate. The two Western leaders also showed understanding for the desire of the Soviet government to have a friendly Poland as its neighbor.

There were no further developments on this issue in the period that followed due to the negative position of the Polish government in exile. But by the summer of 1944, the possibility of an agreement emerged. During one of his conversations with U.S. ambassador Harriman, Molotov put forward new compromise proposals that paved the way for an acceptable solution. The suggestion was to form a government from the Poles who lived in England, the United States, and the Soviet Union, these being people untainted by fascism (and indeed there were people like that in the exiled cabinet in London) and friendly toward the USSR. Among the potential members proposed for such a reorganized government were Oscar Lange, an economist at Chicago University, and trade union leader Krzhitsy, head of the American Slav Congress. Mikolajczyk could remain the premier of that government. Sometime later, the U.S. government issued Oscar Lange a passport to travel to the Soviet Union, where he was to participate in discussions on the Polish problem that were held to coincide with the arrival in Moscow of Churchill and Mikolajczyk.

But before coming to the Soviet Union, Mikolajczyk decided to pay a visit to Washington. He met with Roosevelt and asked him whether the Poles should accept the Soviet proposal. And then something strange happened. The U.S. president, who only shortly before, in Teheran, had agreed to Churchill's formula concerning the border along the Curzon Line, recommended that Mikolajczyk "postpone any settlement of the border issue." After that U.S. secretary of state Edward Stettinius explained to the Poles that, although the Americans were unable to adopt a firm position against the USSR, "Washington's policy would change in the not-too-distant future and would return to its fundamental moral principles, and Washington would be able to provide Poland strong and effective support."

This rapid turnaround in U.S. policy turned out to be of poor service to Poland. The advice given by Washington raised the hopes of the London émigrés. Mikolajczyk refused even to listen to Oscar Lange's arguments in favor of the agreement. He decided not to accept any settlement. The situation was further complicated by the failed Warsaw uprising, organized by the émigré leaders without the knowledge of the Soviet government.

To this day it remains unclear to me why the White House decided to recommend to Mikolajczyk that he turn down the proposed agreement. It appears that election concerns did play a role in that decision, because after the elections Washington clearly lost much of its interest in the Polish issue. Already in the course of the negotiations that took place in Moscow in October 1944, Mikolajczyk sent Roosevelt a telegram requesting his support for the position of the émigré government. He received no reply until November 17, that is to say, well after the presidential elections, nor was it the kind of reply he was expecting. The president curtly informed him that he would support any agreement the Polish government in exile could reach with the Soviet Union. The reply didn't even touch on the question of the border. Earlier, however, the administration's hard-line position on the Polish issue had been leaked to the press, and the Polish Americans had voted for Roosevelt.

Of course, nobody can say with absolute certainty how events would have developed if the 1944 talks in Moscow had reached a successful conclusion. It is quite conceivable that if all the interested parties had reached an agreement, then after the Soviet forces liberated Warsaw, a reorganized government in exile, headed by Mikolajczyk, could have moved there from London, and the Polish people would have been spared many hardships and sacrifices, and relations between the Allies might have taken a less confrontational turn.

The Japanese Card

ALTHOUGH ROOSEVELT HAD DECLINED STALIN'S PROPOSAL to send American forces to the Soviet-German front, even before the United States entered the war, he had shown interest in possible cooperation with the Soviet Union directed against Japan. In the fall of 1941 a letter arrived from Washington in which the president wrote that, according to information received by the U.S. government from a reliable source, Japan was planning to attack the Soviet Maritime Territories. In this connection, Roosevelt proposed to Stalin that he consider permitting the establishment of a U.S. air base in the Soviet Far East. The president wanted to know what the reaction of the Soviet leadership would be if a special U.S. mission arrived in Moscow to exchange views on this matter. At the same time, Roosevelt proposed organizing the deliveries of U.S. aircraft for the Red Army through Alaska and Chukotski.

It was quite possible that the information the United States had about Japan's plans to attack the Soviet Union was reliable. All the more so since Berlin was putting strong pressure on Tokyo to get the Japanese to join the war against the Soviet Union. Stalin was also troubled by that question. But the president's proposal made him suspicious; the intelligence reports that were reaching the Soviet government through its own channels, including those filed by Richard Sorge, provided a different interpretation of the situation. Sorge was a Soviet agent accredited in Tokyo as a German journalist, who was then able to develop close relations with the German ambassador in Japan, General Ott. Sorge's reports were sent to Molotov, and of course, I read them before presenting my brief to the people's commissar. The information suggested that Tokyo's leadership was seriously split over the question of where their main attack should be directed. One group advocated engaging the Soviet Union in the Far East. Another favored an attack on the U.S. Pacific bases and a subsequent shift of operations to Southeast Asia. In his latest reports Sorge had indicated that the balance had tipped in favor of an attack in the southern direction. In the very near future—he wrote in his cryptograms, signed by his code name "Ramzai"—an attack on the United States should be expected, and consequently Moscow didn't have to fear a Japanese offensive, at least in the immediate future. On the basis of that information Stalin redeployed some forces from the Far East to the Moscow area, and in December 1941 they fought in the battle for Moscow, in which the Germans suffered their first major defeat.

In one of his telegrams Ramzai supplied additional details about Japan's plans. He indicated that the most likely target for Japanese attack was the U.S. naval base in Hawaii. That information reached Stalin along with President Roosevelt's insistent warning about Japan's imminent attack on the Soviet Maritime Territories. But Stalin didn't forward Richard Sorge's dispatch to Roosevelt. One wonders why. Maybe he thought Roosevelt would interpret such a move on his part as an attempt to provoke Washington into getting involved in the war, just as he construed Roosevelt's warning as a démarche by the White House to engage the Kremlin in a war against Japan. But I believe it most likely that Stalin was guided by other considerations. He believed that a perfidious and devastating surprise attack by Japan would precipitate the Americans into a fierce fight against the countries of the fascist axis.

The Kremlin's decision to redeploy its forces to the Soviet-German front did not come easy. It involved considerable risk. In that situation Roosevelt's warning and his proposal about concerted action against Japan required careful study. Did he really mean to warn Moscow of imminent danger in the Maritime Territories? Or did Roosevelt, learning of Tokyo's decision to strike the U.S., want to use an agreement on joint Soviet-U.S. military actions in the Far East to get Japan to review its plans in favor of the northern option? Stalin's suspiciousness led him to conclude that, just as in the case of the war with Germany, Roosevelt was hoping to deflect a blow away from his country and redirect it against the Soviet Union. Maybe he wasn't fair in ascribing such motives to the U.S. president, but that was the conclusion he made. As a result he declined Roosevelt's proposal to set up bases for U.S. bombers in the Primorye (Maritime) Territories. And while he agreed to host a special U.S. mission in Moscow, he limited the issues to be discussed to the deliveries of the fighter planes from Alaska that the Soviet Union needed for the Soviet-German front.

After the Japanese attacked Pearl Harbor, Stalin concluded that he was right in his interpretation of the purport of the president's letter. Curiously enough, even after Pearl Harbor, Roosevelt continued to warn Stalin that Japan was preparing to attack the Soviet Union. Thus, on June 17, 1942, the new U.S. ambassador, Admiral Standley, handed Stalin a letter from the president stating that the situation in the North Pacific and in Alaska did not exclude possible Japanese operations against the Soviet Maritime Territories. The letter went to say that "if such an attack is carried out, the United States stands ready to provide air support to the Soviet Union if the Soviet Union provides appropriate landing sites for U.S. aircraft in Siberia. In order to expedite this operation, the Soviet Union and the United States must, of course, closely coordinate their efforts. . . . I regard this issue to be so urgent as to warrant authorizing Soviet and U.S. representatives to proceed with the elaboration of specific plans."

That letter also put Stalin on his guard. He declined Roosevelt's proposal while explaining to the U.S. ambassador that as long as heavy fighting was raging on the Soviet-German front and German divisions continued to advance toward the Volga and the Caucasus Mountains, the Soviet government was not going to take any action that could increase the risk of an armed conflict with Japan.

When Roosevelt was briefed on that exchange of views, he probably understood that he would not be able to provoke Moscow into moves that could indeed complicate the situation in the Soviet Far East. In any case, as early as August 5, a letter arrived in which the president wrote: "I have received information, which I consider to be very reliable, that the Japanese Government has decided against launching any military operations against the Soviet Union at present. As I see it, that means that any attack on Siberia will be delayed until the spring of next year."

Nevertheless, during the months that followed, the U.S. kept on asking the Soviet side when it would be ready to join the U.S. war effort against Japan and, in a more general sense, when Moscow would make a determination in principle regarding its participation in that war.

For a long time, Stalin didn't give any answer to those questions. But when the U.S. secretary of state, Cordell Hull, came to Moscow on a visit, he decided that the time had come to clarify the situation.

On the evening of October 30, 1943, in Catherine's Hall in the Kremlin, Stalin was hosting a dinner to mark the conclusion of the Moscow conference of the Big Three foreign ministers—of the USSR, the U.S., and Great Britain. The longest table was set up along the wall that had windows facing the Moscow River. Stalin sat in the middle of it with Hull to his right and the U.S. ambassador to the USSR, Averell Harriman, to his left. My seat as interpreter was to the right of Hull.

The dinner began with numerous toasts, most of them made by Stalin. Between the speeches Stalin and Hull mainly spoke about the situation at the fronts and the results of the conference that had just ended. From time to time, there were fairly long periods of silence when I had a chance to sneak a few quick bites.

Suddenly, I saw Stalin lean over toward me behind Hull's back and beckon me with his finger. I bent over closer toward him, and he said in a barely audible whisper:

"Listen to me very carefully. Translate this to Hull word for word: The Soviet government has studied the situation in the Far East and has decided that immediately after the end of the war in Europe, when the Allies have defeated Hitler's Germany, it will come out against Japan. Let Hull transmit this to President Roosevelt as our official position. But for the time being, we want to keep this a secret. So you, too, speak in a low voice so that no one overhears you. Understood?"

"Yes, Comrade Stalin!" I whispered back.

Hull became excited when he heard that information. The Americans had been waiting for Moscow's decision for a long time. Now the U.S. government had received an authoritative statement on an issue of vital importance to Washington. The White House hoped that Soviet participation in the war against Japan would help save the lives of millions of U.S. servicemen. In 1945, President Truman had the same concern on his mind in Potsdam. After receiving Stalin's confirmation that the Soviet Union was joining the war against Japan, he wrote in a letter to his wife that the main objective he was pursuing at the conference had thus been achieved and that he was thinking about those young Americans whose lives would now be saved.

Why did Stalin inform the Americans of that decision in October 1943? I believe there were at least two reasons for that. First of all, it happened after the victory at Stalingrad and the defeat of the Germans at the Kursk Bulge. The Red Army was advancing rapidly westward. That was why even if the Japanese learned about the Soviet decision, the risk of their taking preemptive action in the Maritime Territories was minimal. Secondly, by linking Soviet participation in the war against Japan with the defeat of Germany, Stalin was thereby giving Washington a clear signal that the sooner the Allied forces landed in France, which would hasten final victory over the Third Reich, the sooner the Soviet Union would join the war against Japan. And it is indeed quite possible that his move did speed the decision of the Western allies to land their forces in Normandy.

The Bomb Factor

ALTHOUGH THE ATOMIC BOMB became a key element of U.S. policy only under President Truman, nevertheless, while that weapon was still on the drawing board and hadn't even been tested, it was already having an impact on Roosevelt's position and indirectly influencing the formulation of the U.S. postwar policies, especially with regard to the Soviet Union. The special nature of this weapon of mass destruction became a concern first and foremost for the scientists involved in its development. They warned that the emergence of the atom bomb would trigger dangerous consequences. But top U.S. and British political leaders probably thought initially that they were dealing with just a new type of weapon of great destructive power. They ignored the warnings of the bomb developers in exactly the same way as Khrushchev and Brezhnev later dismissed the advice of Academician Sakharov. Roosevelt and Churchill were especially exasperated by the scientists' insistent demands that the secrets of the bomb's production be revealed to the Soviet Union.

Of course there was no historical precedent for one country's sharing with another its knowledge about a new weapon. On the contrary, all such discoveries were closely guarded. But in this case a special situation had developed. First of all, work on the bomb was proceeding at a time of war against a common enemy when the allies were engaged in extensive exchanges of intelligence and information about the latest types of weapons. Radar, sophisticated communications systems, rocket technology, the latest types of tanks and aircraft—all that and much more became a shared technological domain, as it were. Why was the A-bomb made an exception? Secondly, both the United States and Britain, that is to say, two of the three principal coalition partners, knew about the work to develop the bomb. Concealing that from a third partner looked rather sinister. Thirdly, a totally new type of weapon was emerging, a fact of which scientists were acutely aware. Its development required unconventional approaches, a totally new philosophy in fact. But was it realistic to expect that such a new conceptual framework could emerge under wartime circumstances? The answer is—probably not. It took almost half a century for new thinking in foreign policy to sprout forth.

Although the politicians in Washington and London felt uncomfortable about keeping the bomb a secret from Moscow, they decided not to give in to the cajoling of the "naive" scientists. To what extent was Roosevelt and Churchill's position affected by considerations of their postwar attitude toward the Soviet Union? A no less important question is this: What was Washington guided by in deciding to use the bomb in the war against Japan? All these questions arise not only in the context of U.S. diplomacy during the war, but also of the subsequent period and of the factors that led to the outbreak of the Cold War.

In my opinion, the U.S. and British leaders acted on their conviction that a monopoly on the A-bomb would give them a dominant position in the world after the war and make it possible for them to get concessions from other countries, including the Soviet Union.

Such thinking was reflected in the attitude of the person in charge of the Manhattan Project, Gen. Leslie Groves, who had this to say about how he understood his mission:

"From about two weeks from the time I took charge of this Project, there was never any illusion on my part but that Russia was our enemy, and the Project was conducted on that basis. I didn't go along with the attitude of the country as a whole that Russia was a gallant ally. . . . Of course, that was so reported to the president."

And what was the reaction? The commander in chief didn't disavow his subordinate.

In an agreement that Roosevelt and Churchill signed at the Quebec Conference in the summer of 1943, the two leaders stated that the A-bomb would be a decisive factor in the postwar world and would give absolute control to those who possessed its secret. The president and the prime minister pledged not to provide any information to any third party "without mutual agreement."

Let us recall that the Quebec summit took place when preparations were under way for the Moscow conference of the Soviet, U.S., and British foreign ministers and the first meeting of the Big Three in Teheran. In Moscow, the U.S. secretary of state, Cordell Hull, spoke at length about the importance of postwar cooperation between the United States and the Soviet Union and the responsibility of the great powers for the maintenance of peace. In Teheran, in his conversations with Stalin, Roosevelt emphasized on repeated occasions that Soviet-U.S. cooperation after their victory over fascism would be a decisive factor in maintaining peace and ensuring international security. Even as they were making all those statements, work on the Manhattan Project was going full speed ahead. When Roosevelt spoke about the "four policemen"—the United States, the Soviet Union, Great Britain, and China—who would bear the responsibility for ensuring world peace, he didn't mention the fact that only two out of the four policemen would possess the atomic weapon.

Already at that stage, Washington and London were taking steps to block access to fissionable materials for other countries. On June 13, 1944, Roosevelt and Churchill signed an Agreement and Declaration of Trust pledging cooperation between the United States and Britain in establishing control over stockpiles of uranium and thorium both during and after the war. They further stated their governments' intention "to control to the fullest extent practicable the supplies of uranium and thorium ores within the boundaries of such areas as come under their respective jurisdictions, and in certain areas outside the control of the two governments and the two Governments of the Dominions of India and Burma."

In June 1944, Danish physicist Niels Bohr, one of the theorists behind the atom bomb, made one last attempt to convince Roosevelt of the need to inform Moscow of the work on the new weapon. The president promised to take the matter under advisement. However, when he met with Churchill at his country estate in Hyde Park in mid-September, the U.S. president and the British prime minister reaffirmed their pledge to secrecy. Further, the two leaders came to the conclusion that Bohr "was not to be trusted." The last paragraph of the document they signed on September 19, 1944, stated: "It is necessary to investigate Professor Bohr's activities and to take steps to prevent any leaks of information through him, especially to the Russians." As for Bohr's proposal itself, the first paragraph provided a clear answer to it: "The proposal to inform the world community [meaning essentially the Soviet Union] about the 'alloy' [the code name for the nuclear explosive] with a view to elaborating an international agreement to control and use it is unacceptable. The project should continue to be classified as top secret."

In February 1945, in Yalta's Livadia Palace, during the Crimean conference of the Big Three, Roosevelt asked Churchill whether Stalin should be informed of the Manhattan Project. Churchill voiced his categorical opposition, saying he was shocked by such a proposal. Roosevelt did not insist. That was how the last opportunity was missed to create a more favorable atmosphere for postwar cooperation with the Soviet Union.

From the earliest stages of the Manhattan Project, the Soviet leadership was getting intelligence reports from its agents about it. Perhaps Stalin should have informed Roosevelt that the Manhattan Project was no secret to him. That move might have embarrassed our coalition partners. And maybe it would have induced them to discuss establishing joint control both over the bomb and nuclear energy.

The Americans, engaged in heavy fighting in the Pacific, were vitally interested in seeing the Soviet Union join the war against Japan. Suddenly, the Allied forces in Western Europe found themselves in a difficult situation, in the so-called Battle of the Bulge. On the eve of the Yalta meeting they even urged Stalin to start a new Soviet offensive earlier than planned and Stalin accommodated their request. Under those circumstances, confrontation with the Soviet Union was not in the interests of the Western states. Many people in the United States and Britain wanted to preserve relations of friendship and cooperation with the Soviet Union, and Roosevelt could have utilized those sentiments to resist pressures from the extreme right.

Stalin perceived the silence of his Western allies on the A-bomb as a threat. He assigned Beria the task of developing a Soviet nuclear weapon, and that kicked off the nuclear arms race. At the same time Stalin became even more suspicious and skeptical about possible postwar cooperation.

At the Naval Command Headquarters

THE SOVIET PEOPLE had mixed feelings about the nonaggression pact signed with Hitler's Germany on August 23, 1939. On the one hand, any agreement with the Nazis would come as a shock. After many years of intensive antifascist rhetoric, we couldn't grasp the rapid switch from hostility to cooperation.

On the other hand, paradoxical as it may sound, we also felt relieved at the normalization, albeit temporary, of our relations with the Germans. Against the imminent possibility of war, the cold shoulder from the Western democracies, the hostility of the Germans, and the provocations of the Japanese military, we Russians felt lonely, threatened, and isolated—and worried about new sacrifices, sufferings, and hardships.

With the disappearance of the immediate threat of an attack from Germany, many of us began hoping that our country could stay out of the war, at least temporarily. Now that Hitler had turned his covetous eyes the other way, it looked as if the peaceful respite would continue. We believed that if Germany opened a war in the West, it could last many months, maybe even years, while we would be on the sidelines. Of course, at the time nobody could foresee that France would fall in a matter of weeks, and that by the summer of 1940, almost the whole of Western Europe would be under the German heel.

Furthermore, the nonaggression pact could be very advantageous to our country, at that time still the only country to have proclaimed the construction of socialism as its national goal. The Soviet-German trade agreement, concluded a few days before the signing of the nonaggression pact, provided for deliveries of modern equipment and the latest technology to the Soviet Union. Among others, our navy was very much interested in getting new equipment and technology. That circumstance played a crucial role in my life, setting off a sequence of incredible events that led me, a mere seaman of the Pacific Fleet, to the very top of Stalin's administrative pyramid.

What happened was that the navy needed people who knew German. One of my former Vladivostok students mentioned my name at Headquarters, and I was summoned back to Moscow.

The Yaroslavsky Railway Station, where the train from Vladivostok arrived late at night, was packed with passengers in transit. Families with many children were cramming the benches. Single travelers were lying on the floor, their belongings under their heads. I had a hard time finding an unoccupied spot in one of the halls where I could settle down for the night, using newspapers as a sheet and my rucksack as a pillow. By that time, I had already grown used to situations like that.

Sleeping on the stone floor wasn't, of course, very comfortable. On top of that, I had other worries on my mind. What if I went to sleep and somebody filched my seaman's cap with PACIFIC FLEET proudly written across it or pilfered my service boots? My other gnawing worry was about what was in store for me here in the capital and why I had been summoned back.

In the morning, after shaking off the dust of travel and giving myself a quick shave in the station's bathroom, I set off for the People's Commissariat of the Navy, located on Gogol Boulevard. From a pay phone I called a number I had been given and then waited outside the Commissariat in the room where passes were issued. Ten minutes later a door that led into the building swung open and a solidly built, middle-aged man in the uniform of a captain second rank appeared in the doorway.

I jumped up and saluted him. "Reporting at your orders, sir—" I started to say.

"At ease!" He cut me off, speaking in a pleasant, low voice. I continued to stand there motionless, feeling that something important was about to happen to me.

"Please sit down. Let's talk."

His manner and his pleasant tone of voice eased my inner tension. We settled down on a seat by a small table.

Later I learned that this was Yelizar Aleksandrovich Zaitsev, a veteran of the war in Spain where he was awarded the rare Order of Red Banner for distinguished service. During World War II, Captain Second Rank Zaitsev was head of the Foreign Relations Department of the People's Commissariat of the Navy and, ex officio, maintained close contacts with the U.S. and British military representatives. Later he was denounced by Beria as a British spy and sent to prison, from where he came out, only after the 20th Party Congress, a sick and broken man.

In his pleasing manner Zaitsev asked me where I was serving in the Pacific Fleet, what schools I had attended, and where I studied foreign languages. When he learned how I had spent the night, he told me that a bed had been arranged for me at the dormitory of the navy guard, located near the Paveletsky Railway Station. He said that the question of my new duties would be resolved in the next few days and advised me to make the best of my free time to get to know Moscow better. He issued me a temporary ID, which also served as a pass to the dormitory and to the Commissariat building, where I could eat at the Navy Commissariat cafeteria.

A short time after that meeting, Zaitsev called me in again. He received me in his office, which had models of different combat ships all over the room. I learned that I had been assigned to work at the Naval Command Headquarters.

Zaitsev went on to tell me that he had been given an important assignment and that he had decided to get me involved in it. At our second meeting Zaitsev was dressed in a civilian suit. He explained to me that quite often wearing a military uniform was inappropriate for the tasks he was assigned to carry out. For our next assignment, both of us had to wear civilian clothes.

"You don't have any suitable clothes, do you?" he asked with a smile.

"No, I don't, Comrade Captain Second Rank!"

"You don't have to sound so official! You should start getting used to your role as a civilian. You can start by calling me by my first name and patronymic."

"Yes, Comrade Yelizar Aleksandrovich."

"That's much better, and you'll do even better if you drop your 'yes, Comrade' stuff. Now let's talk about your clothes."

Zaitsev called a car and we drove to a warehouse where special-purpose clothes were stored.

Zaitsev selected for me a dark blue striped suit, half a dozen white and blue shirts, a couple of sets of underwear, handkerchiefs, socks, black shoes, and a small leather briefcase. Everything had been made abroad.

"Tomorrow night," Zaitsev said, "we're taking the Red Arrow Express to Leningrad. You are to wear a suit, feel comfortable in it, and report to the Commissariat at twenty-two hundred hours, and don't forget the briefcase."

The Bremen *in Murmansk*

ON THE TRAIN we shared a compartment for two in an international sleeping car. I thought that over tea Zaitsev would enlighten me on our assignment. But he just told me a story about Paris and then gave me a few do's and don'ts about being with foreigners. I thanked him for his advice and added that I had had some experience in that regard during my work as an Intourist guide in Kiev in 1934 and 1935.

"I know," Zaitsev said. "That's why I'm taking you with me."

I could draw only one conclusion from all of this: we were going to have meetings with foreigners.

At the Baltic Navy Headquarters in Leningrad we were met by Captain Third Rank Naum Solomonovich Frumkin. He briefed us in general terms about the situation in the Baltic region after Germany invaded Poland and the measures undertaken by the command of the Baltic Fleet to secure the maritime borders of the Soviet Union. The conversation that followed between Frumkin and Zaitsev gave me some idea about the purpose of our trip. An ocean liner of the German passenger fleet, the *Bremen*, which plied between Hamburg and America and happened to be in New York the day the war began, was about to arrive in Murmansk.

The *Bremen*, like its sister ship, the *Europa*, was a state-of-the-art luxury liner competing successfully with the great British and French passenger ships. At that time, ships were still the principal means of transportation between Europe and America.

After Britain and France declared war on Germany, the British authorities asked the Americans to impound the *Bremen* to compensate for some German debts. The port authorities informed the captain of the *Bremen*, Arens, that his vessel had been impounded and left the matter at that. Captain Arens took advantage of the carelessness of the Americans. At night, the *Bremen* cast off without being observed, sailed out of the Hudson, and disappeared into the Atlantic. The British sent a ship in hot pursuit of the *Bremen*, but it was all in vain. Later it became known that the *Bremen* had veered sharply around to the north, steered safely past the icebergs in a thick fog, and carefully navigated above the arctic circle to reach Soviet territorial waters. When the ship was approaching Murmansk, Captain Arens broke radio silence and contacted Berlin. Berlin, in turn, communicated with Moscow and was instantly granted permission for the German liner to put in at the Soviet port.

By the time the *Bremen* appeared on the horizon, Zaitsev and I, together with the chief administrator of the port of Murmansk and a representative of the local authorities, were already standing on the pier. The huge vessel of 34,000 tons displacement came to a halt in the roads, seeming to fill up the entire bay.

Together with a representative of the German embassy in Moscow, Frau Herwart, we reached the ship by boat. A ladder was lowered and we climbed up on the main deck.

Captain Arens expressed his thanks to us for granting him a safe haven in Murmansk. He treated us to frothy Munich keg beer and frankfurters with sauerkraut. Then we were taken on a tour of the ship. We saw excellent restaurants, music salons, smoking rooms, a swimming pool, open-air and closed promenade decks with rows of reclining chairs, sports areas, and finally, tastefully furnished cabins with all the modern comforts. Each detail spoke of the utmost care taken to make the passengers' stay aboard the ship enjoyable. But no people were on board, except for the crew, which was almost a thousand strong. The crew members remained on board while preparations were made and paperwork completed for their evacuation. In the evenings, the *Bremen* sailors took the boat to the shore where they could relax at the Murmansk International Club. Such clubs for foreign seafarers operated in almost all Soviet ports.

We also went to the Murmansk Club a few times. The atmosphere there was quite interesting. The club regulars were Norwegian, Swedish, Danish, and Dutch sailors from the ships that called at Murmansk. Even though the club had a small reading room where issues of the English editions of the weekly *Moscow News*, the *USSR Construction* magazine, and Intourist promotional materials were laid out on the tables, drinking and dancing were its frequenters' idea of fun. Local belles graced the place with their presence while disgracing it with some aspects of their behavior. Sometimes fights broke out and then a navy patrol permanently posted near the Club stepped in to break it up politely but firmly.

At the club we got to know the sailors better, chatting with them over mugs of beer. Speaking both German and English, I had no problem striking up a conversation since the sailors all knew one or the other of those languages. I also helped Zaitsev, who didn't know any foreign languages, in his conversations at the club. He wanted to get a sense of what the neutral countries were thinking about the war and was trying to glean any information they might have about British and French preparations for active warfare against Germany. At night, when we came back to the hotel, he would carefully write everything down in a thick notebook that he always carried with him.

Finally, the day came when two trains with second-class cars arrived. By that time the lists of the German sailors had been checked and their travel documents were ready. All the sailors left the *Bremen* except for Captain Arens, his two chief mates, and a small group of engineers and sailors who were needed to maintain the ship. The departing sailors boarded the cars, and the two trains, with a short interval between them, set off on their way. Zaitsev instructed me to accompany the Germans to the border, and he left for Moscow. I was traveling in the second train, helping the conductor communicate with the Germans and playing the good host myself. I moved from one compartment to the next, asking people how they were doing, helping clear up little problems in the restaurant car, and making many friends as we journeyed along. It was also good practice for my German.

The *Bremen* remained in Murmansk until the middle of December, and then, under the darkness of the polar night, it sailed along the coastline of neutral Norway into German territorial waters, finally re-

turning to its home port of Hamburg. There the vessel was transformed into a floating hospital, but it was soon sunk by the Royal Air
Force.

When the Soviet Union granted safe haven to the *Bremen* in the
port of Murmansk it was one of the first major breaks Germany got
after the signing of the nonaggression pact. In general, Hitler derived quite considerable benefits from improved relations with the
Soviet Union.

The Yalta Experience

THE SECOND MEETING OF THE BIG THREE, taking place in the
Crimea on February 4–11, 1945, marked a crucial point in the history
of the anti-Hitler coalition. It also brought a new warmth to the personal relations between Stalin and Roosevelt. As the president rode
in his car from the airport at Saki, near Simferopol, to Yalta, he could
see with his own eyes the scale of destruction on Soviet territories
that had been occupied by the Germans. I believe he was quite sincere when he told Stalin that he had become more "bloodthirsty" toward the Nazis after that. The president also stressed that after victory the United States should provide economic assistance to the
war-wracked countries, above all to the Soviet Union. If Roosevelt's
plan had been realized, if U.S. equipment had been supplied to us
and the U.S. experts had taught us to use it, relations between our
two countries could have been very different. When the president
was elaborating his plans for the future in his one-on-one talks with
Stalin in Livadia Palace, he appeared to be confident that Soviet-U.S.
cooperation would be possible in the postwar world. Stalin also welcomed such prospects.

The overall atmosphere at the Yalta conference was favorable and
beneficial to the agreements reached on the issues on the agenda.

At the same time—and with the war drawing to an end—the contradictions within the coalition were becoming more and more evident. On numerous occasions during his talks with Stalin, Roosevelt
emphasized that with the advent of peace the forces speaking out

against cooperation between the U.S. and the Soviet Union would become more vociferous. That was why the president advocated his idea of a postwar order and wanted to speed up the elaboration of the basic principles for the functioning of a new international security organization.

At that time, the three leaders agreed that it was crucial to preserve the unity of the great powers and to create a mechanism that would enable them to act together to maintain a durable peace.

Did they truly believe this? Was it a realistic proposition? Or was it that their publicly stated objectives didn't quite match their real intentions?

Stalin met with suspicion the formula advanced by the British and initially supported by the Americans for the voting procedure in the Security Council of the new international organization. He insisted that the right of veto should be preserved, and when a short time after the Yalta conference an acceptable procedure was agreed upon, he viewed that as a sign of Washington's readiness to shape its postwar relations with Moscow on the basis of equality.

Much has been written about the Yalta conference. The problems discussed there and the decisions made are well-known. But the myth that Europe was divided up in the Crimea lives on. But that is totally inaccurate. The only thing that was discussed in this connection was the partitioning of Germany. Furthermore, while both Roosevelt and Churchill came out strongly at the Teheran conference in favor of dismembering Germany into the small states from which the First Reich had been formed, in Yalta they offered only token support for this plan.

The Soviet side expressed its doubts that dismemberment was realistic. As a result, it was decided in Yalta to refer that question to the European Consultative Commission for consideration. Later, it was taken off the agenda altogether. As for the other Eastern European states, with the exception of the above-mentioned Polish issue, they were not discussed at all in terms of dividing up spheres of influence.

The only territorial issue decided concerned the transfer of Königsberg and the nearest areas of East Prussia to the Soviet Union. Agreement was also reached on the modalities of the Soviet participation in the war against Japan (including the transfer of southern Sakhalin and the Kuril Islands).

Afterward, both Stalin and Roosevelt spoke highly of the Yalta conference. Both cited it as an example of a relation of equality. President Roosevelt described it as a "turning point" in the history of the United States and the whole world. He stated that the conference marked an end of the old system, characterized by unilateral action, closed blocs, and spheres of influence, in favor of a world organization where all peace-loving states could participate.

I believe that the Yalta experience and the degree of trust that Stalin and Roosevelt appeared to have developed there could have led to significant improvements in the international situation and in the relations between the Soviet Union and the United States. At least that was the mood in Moscow. But it didn't last long.

The Dnieper Flotilla

THE REPORT ON OUR TRIP TO MURMANSK that Zaitsev and I filed together was approved at the Naval Command, and I was immediately given a new assignment: I was to travel to Kiev where I would be under the orders of the Dnieper River Navy.

I was happy to have the opportunity to visit Kiev. I had been away for over a year, and now I had a chance to see my parents and catch up with my friends again.

But my joy was short-lived. My orders were to report directly to the headquarters of the Dnieper Flotilla without seeing anyone. There I would receive detailed instructions. I was further advised that the operation was classified top secret and that I had to act accordingly. I was to travel in a naval uniform, but as a senior lieutenant, not a private seaman, which was my true navy rank. Those were the instructions I read in the papers I got together with my uniform. However, I was also informed that I would be an officer only for this one trip.

Early in the morning, the train arrived in Kiev. The square near the railway station was empty. I looked at the familiar façade of the station built in the mid-1930s in the modernized Ukrainian baroque style. It was drizzly and chilly. How many times had I come here to meet or see off foreign tourists! I knew every nook and cranny here, every pass leading to the platforms. A scene flashed through my memory—of a sunny summer day, a bright yellow open bus full of cheerful young men and women, dressed in brightly colored foreign clothes. They had just arrived in the capital of the Soviet Ukraine.

I was brought back to reality by a dirty green car with a tarpaulin top spotted with rain that pulled up beside me, shattering the vision of the blissful summer of 1935. I climbed into the backseat, raised the collar of my coat, and pulled my hat over my eyes to avoid being recognized if we happened to pass somebody I knew.

The people at the Flotilla Headquarters in Podol knew I was coming. There I was informed about the reason for my trip. The Dnieper Flotilla had sailed up the river the night before and had then navigated along its tributary, the Pripyat, in the direction of the Polish border. For our part, we—that is to say, a small group of navy sailors, I among them—were to set off by a fast speedboat in a few hours along the same route.

On September 17, together with other units of the Red Army, we were to cross the Soviet-Polish border and head for Pinsk to recapture that city.

The classified report, which was read to us, stated that the Red Army, on orders from the Soviet government, was to take under its protection our Ukrainian and Byelorussian brothers who lived in the eastern parts of bourgeois Poland. It further stated that although the Red Army and Navy units were entering the territory of former Poland as liberators, they were to crush decisively any resistance that might be put up by the White Poles. In conclusion the report stated that, at the positions indicated in relevant field maps, advance Soviet units would meet German forces. They would come together as comrades, in the spirit of the new relations with Germany.

I was completely taken by surprise with that information. I didn't have the slightest idea that our country would be involved in military operations that Hitler's Germany conducted against Poland. But at least I now knew why they needed my services. A meeting with German "comrades" was to take place at previously agreed positions, and my knowledge of German was again required. It also became clear why my trip to Kiev had been shrouded in such secrecy.

On September 17, before dawn, the monitors and boats of the Dnieper Flotilla sailed up the Pripyat River and crossed the border. The Polish border units were caught off guard. They opened fire but were quickly suppressed by the ships' guns. Then the Polish forces retreating to the east from the advancing Wehrmacht units engaged in a few skirmishes. But their resistance was weak and disorganized.

Their morale was further shaken by our leaflets promising peace, good treatment, and an early return to their families to those who laid down their arms. In reality, most Polish prisoners of war ended up not in their homes but in labor camps, and many of them were shot by Beria's agents.

We reached Pinsk with no losses and only a few people slightly wounded. Upstream from the city the river becomes shallow, and only small boats could continue on. But by then we were only a few kilometers away from where we were to meet up with the Germans.

And we met them—as if we were comrades-in-arms. The German commanders and our officers congratulated each other and drank to the health of their respective leaders. After the operations at Pinsk, Brest, and other places were over, the German and Soviet troops marched together in parades, reviewed by Wehrmacht and the Red Army officers standing side by side on makeshift reviewing stands. It was clear to all of us that nothing of the kind could have happened without Stalin's personal instructions. We also had no doubts that the governments of the Soviet Union and Germany had reached a prior agreement about a demarcation line on the territory of the former Poland. Most likely that agreement had been worked out when the German foreign minister, Ribbentrop, had visited Moscow.

Recently, especially in connection with the fiftieth anniversary of the outbreak of World War II, heated debates have erupted over the events that took place half a century ago and how they should be evaluated. Some writers have condemned the "division of Poland" between Hitler and Stalin, the "occupation" of the Baltic states, and the "immoral collusion" of the two dictators. But the situation was more complicated. As a witness to the events that unfolded in the fall of 1939, I cannot forget the atmosphere in western Byelorussia and western Ukraine in those days. The people there met us with flowers, they held bread-breaking ceremonies to welcome us, gave us fruit and milk. Owners of small cafes offered free meals to Soviet officers. Those were genuine feelings. The people believed that the Red Army would protect them from Hitler's terror. Similar things were happening in the Baltic countries. As the Wehrmacht units marched nearer, many people fled to the east, looking for safety in the territory controlled by the Red Army.

Mrs. Pipes's Confession

SOMETIME IN THE EARLY 1980s, I was invited to speak at an international symposium at Wellesley College near Boston. My opponent in the debate was a well-known U.S. historian, Prof. Richard Pipes, who later became an adviser to President Reagan.

The invitation to address a forum on Soviet-U.S. relations was extended to me by Prof. Nina Toumarkin, who taught Russian medieval history, specializing in the epoch of Ivan the Terrible. Nina, as she later told me, came from the family of St. Petersburg's largest spaghetti makers. The family owned factories and was especially proud to be among the "purveyors to His Majesty's court." But they derived their main income from supplying spaghetti and other flour-based products to the Russian army. After the Revolution the Toumarkins emigrated and Nina was born in the United States.

"In the 1950s I went to the Soviet Union for the first time," Nina recalled. "I was to study at Leningrad University. Immediately, however, I went to the address I had brought with me to see what had happened to our old family factory. Comparing it with the pictures I knew so well, I found that, on the outside at least, the factory looked pretty much the same, the only difference being that the front of the main building, which hadn't been well maintained, had a new sign reading 'Krasny Makaronshchik' ["Red Spaghetti-Maker"]. My parents told me that our products were once very famous. By the way, the macaroni I had in the students' cafeteria at Leningrad University was really quite good."

Nina had invited Richard Pipes to the debate because in the past she had attended his lectures on the period of Ivan the Terrible.

At dinner after the debate I found myself sitting at the table with my opponent's wife. At first, Mrs. Pipes and I just engaged in polite conversation. Then we began talking about the symposium, and at that point she said something I didn't expect to hear from her. She said she was sorry about the sharp remarks her husband had made with regard to the Soviet Union. I observed that, being familiar with Professor Pipes's views, I hadn't expected anything else.

"But I always feel ill at ease in situations like these," Mrs. Pipes complained.

"Is that so?" I was indeed surprised by that confession.

Mrs. Pipes explained, "I will be always grateful to the Red Army, which saved my life and the lives of my relatives in 1939. I was just a little girl then. We lived in Warsaw, and when Germany attacked Poland, we fled to the east. We found ourselves in the area of Pinsk controlled by the Red Army units that had entered western Byelorussia. I will never forget how well the officers and soldiers treated us and other refugees. They gave us food and shelter. Then the Soviet authorities helped us get to Vilnius—at that time Lithuania was still a bourgeois republic. My parents wrote to our relatives in the United States. That was how we ended up here. Were it not for the Red Army, we would have perished. All our relatives who stayed in the Warsaw ghetto were killed by the Nazis. Richard also got out of Poland via the Baltic countries, but he doesn't like to recall that."

At that time, in Pinsk and in other places, we indeed helped many people fleeing from the Nazis. Because of my knowledge of foreign languages, I was kept in the western Ukraine to work with refugees. A great number of them had assembled in Lvov. For instance, we helped the well-known American trumpet player Eddie Rosner, who was touring Poland with his jazz band when Germany invaded that country. He decided to move to the Soviet Union, where he was a great success initially. We also assisted the world-famous singer Eva Bandrovska-Turska to settle down in Lvov. We tried to ease the lot of many other refugees. But of course I had no idea that among the people we helped in Pinsk were family members of a future adviser to the president of the United States.

Different destinies awaited those refugees. Professor Pipes and his wife became U.S. citizens and reached the upper strata of the U.S. middle class. Eddie Rosner and some of his colleagues soon learned firsthand the joys of a life in a labor camp in Magadan, the capital of the Kolyma region in Siberia. There he was given an opportunity to delight the camp administration with his virtuoso trumpet playing.

My encounter with Eva Bandrovska-Turska was a special occasion for me. In the spring of 1937, she arrived in Kiev on a tour, giving a few concerts in the former Merchants' Assembly Hall. Together with her other young admirers, I went backstage with a bunch of red roses and was allowed to kiss her hand. Strange as it may seem, she recalled that fleeting episode and was glad when she saw me in Lvov. I invited her to attend a show by Red Army amateurs and was able to get tickets for us in the first row. But as it turned out, I wasn't so lucky after all because when we reached our seats, we saw that sitting next to us was the chief of Lvov's NKVD, Serov. He rose slightly from his seat, greeting the singer with an impudent smile. She barely nodded back and, when the lights went out, whispered into my ear, "I have been introduced to him. . . . He gives me the creeps."

During the intermission, together with the others in the audience, we walked around the room adjacent to the concert hall. Before we were able to circle it even a few times, we were approached by a young officer wearing a uniform of the interior ministry troops.

"Excuse me," he said, speaking to me. "General Serov would like to speak to you a minute."

I apologized to Bandrovska-Turska and followed the officer. After we crossed a semidark corridor, we came into a small room. In the middle of the room was a table with snacks and refreshments and a few NKVD officers clustered around it helping themselves. General Serov was standing a little to the side. I walked over to him: "Yes, Comrade General?"

"What is your relationship with Eva Turska?"

I explained that I had met her during her tour in Kiev two years ago and that now I had met her again by chance among other refugees.

"Now, this relationship of yours has to stop immediately!" he said sternly.

"But why?"

"None of your business, and in general you shouldn't be asking me questions, not in your rank."

If he had only known that he was talking not to a senior lieutenant but to a private seaman of the Red Navy, he would certainly have sent me to the brig. But I wouldn't give up.

"I don't understand what's wrong with renewing an old friendship at a difficult time for the friend."

"If you don't understand I will explain. We intend to work with her and nobody should get in the way. Do you understand now?"

"I do, Comrade General," I replied, sensing that I could get myself in trouble.

After the concert I walked the singer to her hotel and promised to call her the following day or the day after. But I never did.

General Serov didn't limit himself to a talk with me. The next day I received a coded telegram from my superiors in Moscow. It simply read: Cease all contacts with Eva Bandrovska-Turska.

I have no idea how General Serov carried out his intention "to work" with Eva Bandrovska-Turska. She was soon sent to Kiev and I lost track of her. But later I remember seeing playbills with her name on them somewhere.

After western Byelorussia and western Ukraine joined the Byelorussian SSR and the Ukrainian SSR respectively, the situation there began to deteriorate after Stalin decided to step up the sovietization of the new territories. Well-to-do farmers were deprived of their possessions, collectivization was imposed, private enterprises and artisans' shops were closed down. But what hurt people the most was the establishment of a one-to-one exchange rate between the ruble and the Polish zloty while in reality the zloty had a higher market value. Prices on many goods in the Soviet Union were much higher than in Poland. For example, a certain watch cost three hundred to four hundred rubles in Moscow, while its price in Lvov was thirty zlotys. The prices on other items showed similar discrepancies. As a result, within a matter of a few weeks the store shelves became empty. Our army officers, as well as officials of various Soviet agencies, flooded the liberated areas and bought up everything that was in short supply in Moscow. Small stores and craftsmen went broke. The prices on everything, including food, shot through the roof, while the wages paid to the local people remained the same and were paid in zlotys.

Naturally, all that gave rise to protests. Students began to demonstrate, people were out into the streets. The local security police, led by Beria's satrap General Serov, called those protests "counterrevolutionary, anti-Soviet riots." Arrests began. Demonstrators were severely punished. People were deported. All of which only aggravated the situation.

A number of times I had to visit Serov's department in connection with different cases involving refugees. In the liberated areas the Soviet secret police usually moved into the buildings formerly occupied by the gendarmerie there, a fact that many Ukrainians and Byelorussians, who hated the secret service of bourgeois Poland, found particularly sinister. It was probably convenient to use the premises because they had prison cells in their basements. From a political point of view, however, it was unacceptable because it was an insult to the feelings of the local people. But who was thinking about such niceties at that time?

Inside Serov's building I saw young men who had been badly roughed up. They had blood on their faces and their student uniforms were torn. They were lying on the floor half-conscious. There probably wasn't enough room in the basement cells and the victims of Serov's terror were dragged out of the interrogation rooms and dumped in the corridors.

In September 1939, the Soviet soldiers were met as liberators, with flowers, bread, and salt. And in June 1941, in western Ukraine and western Byelorussia, that was how the Germans were initially greeted. The misguided, repressive policies of the Soviet authorities there in late 1939 and 1940 were also responsible for the protracted postwar fighting with the Bendera bands in the area of the Carpathian Mountains.

Despite the stepped-up sovietization, Lvov in late 1939 still had some remnants of its former glory. In the restaurant of the Hotel George, where I was staying, a big jazz band was playing and the waiters, providing impeccable service, offered a selection from Polish and French menus. Every night, people crowded the Golebnik ("Pigeon House") Cafe, located in the attic of a large supermarket. Those who had a penchant for the exotic could sit over a glass of champagne in the semidarkness of the Bagatelle nightclub, where the walls and the seats were draped with burgundy velvet, and where scantily clad dancers alternated at entertaining the club's patrons with singers, who offered French romantic songs. The store shelves, on the other hand, were already bare, while in the glassed-in area of the supermarket, profiteers were doing a brisk business pushing the latest in fashion at black market prices, which were still lower than the prices in Moscow.

At that time, Lvov could still boast an active cultural life. Small art galleries with modern paintings and a variety of shows and exhibitions all drew big crowds. Well-known Polish performers, fleeing from the Nazis, had moved east and were now settled in Lvov. It was no coincidence that the Polish song "Only in Lvov" was a favorite there.

A good number of theater companies were also there—from Switzerland, Norway, and Denmark. They had been touring Poland when the war began. We helped many of them return home via the Soviet Union.

I didn't stay long in that unique fantasy world. I was summoned back to Moscow. Intense negotiations with the Germans were under way there to elaborate a new trade agreement. Representatives of the People's Commissariat of the Navy also participated. They needed me as their interpreter.

Parental Home

ON THE WAY TO MOSCOW I stopped over in Kiev for a few days and rang in the New Year, 1940, with my parents and friends.

Kiev greeted me with a sunny, frosty morning. The names I had known since childhood were flashing by outside the train window—Irpen, Pusha-Voditsa, Post-Volynski. And then the Kiev station. My heart missed a beat when I saw my father on the platform. He had written in his letters that he hadn't been feeling well recently, but he still came out to meet me. Father had grown much older, and his previously raven locks were now almost completely gray. He had on a worn overcoat and a pre-Revolutionary-style hat with the badge of a certified engineer on it. I felt a little uncomfortable. I had spruced myself up in Lvov and got out of the international sleeping car dressed like a dandy in a fashionable coat with a fur lining and an English felt hat, giving off the fragrance of a Japanese perfume for men. After the hugs and kisses, Father looked me over a couple of times disapprovingly. He found my appearance offensive and incongruous amidst the gray mass of the people crowding the station. But at home he quickly softened, and we spent a few wonderful days together.

Nothing is more joyful than coming home after a long separation. Mother prepared a New Year's dinner Ukrainian style with *kutya*, *vzvar* (traditional Christmas food), homemade sausage, ham baked in pastry, stuffed pike, and finally her specialties: *khvorost* (sweet pastry) and a Napoleon cake with fragrant cream between thin, crunchy layers of puff pastry. In those days, good food was still available in Kiev's stores, although the proverbial "food shortages" had already begun again.

My old chums came to the New Year's party. The smell of a freshly cut pine tree filled the air. The candles were crackling. Father's usual herbal *zubrovka* vodka was glistening in the carafe. The traditional trio was also present: father playing the violin, my school buddy Georg Fibikh on the cello, and me at the piano. Back in the mid-1930s, which seemed so far away now, on warm summer nights passersby stopped on the sidewalk by our window under the blossoming lindens to listen to our amateur home concerts.

And here we were together again, our souls warm, our minds at peace. We remembered the Christmas carol that we had learned way back in the German school: "Stille Nacht, Heilige Nacht," "Silent Night, Holy Night."

I had never been close to my father. He spent all his waking hours at the office, and at night he bent over the drafting board to make some extra money for the family. He was a virtuoso draftsman and a talented engineer of the old St. Petersburg school. As for me, I worked at the factory in the daytime while attending classes at the Polytechnic Institute's night school and then went to work for Intourist. Each of us spent his days in his own way. But the last days of 1939 we were being drawn together by some irresistible force. And our farewell on the first day of 1940 was hard, as if both of us felt that we would never see each other again.

While I had been away, life in Moscow had become much harder. The city looked untidy. There were lines in front of some stores. Because of our failures in the war with Finland, the mood in the capital was gloomy. Stalin's vainglorious plan to bring the unruly Finns to heel in one big push had resulted in a bloodbath and a humiliating stalemate. New forces had to be mobilized to penetrate the enemy's defenses. The transports were packed with military cargoes and that immediately affected the supply situation in the cities.

I was provided with a place to sleep at an officers' dorm at the corner of Arbat and Vesnina streets. Four of us were in a small room. But it was tidy, warm, and quiet, thanks to Aunt Nusya, who took care of the place. A boiler was in the corridor and, on the small table next to it, everything needed to make tea.

My roommates turned out to be guys I knew. They immediately brought me up to date on the hard life in Moscow.

At the Commissariat for Foreign Trade the talks with the Germans on a new trade agreement were drawing to a close. Our group of officials from the Commissariat for the Navy also attended. We were driving a hard bargain with the German delegation, headed by Envoy Schnurre. At the same time, the members of the Soviet Procurement Commission were being selected. They were to go to Germany to monitor the implementation of the agreement and check the quality of the German supplies. I was included on the commission, probably because by that time I had already had some experience from working in the Engineering Department of the Pacific Fleet, but more importantly, because of my knowledge of German.

On February 11, 1940, the new trade agreement was finally signed, and soon after that we set off for Berlin. The Procurement Commission was headed by a member of the Party's Central Committee, People's Commissar for the Shipbuilding Industry I. Tevosyan, a man close to the people's commissar for foreign trade, Politburo member Anastas Mikoyan, and even, it was rumored, to Stalin himself.

Roosevelt's Last Telegram

IN THE LAST WEEKS OF ROOSEVELT'S LIFE, his relations with Stalin were marred by the talks that were going on in Berne between the British and American representatives and SS general Karl Wolf (the Gestapo head stationed in Italy). The participation in the talks of the chief U.S. intelligence officer in Switzerland, Allen Dulles, made them special. The U.S. ambassador in Moscow, Harriman, informed Molotov about those contacts only on March 12, 1945, even though the talks in Berne had started in mid-February.

Stalin reacted strongly to those negotiations. He believed that the Western allies were in fact trying to conclude a separate deal with the Germans behind the back of the Soviet Union. When the Soviet government asked that representatives of the Soviet military command participate in the talks, its request was turned down.

Since the affair was becoming something of a scandal, Roosevelt got involved. On March 25, a personal letter from the U.S. president arrived in the Kremlin. Roosevelt, making reference to an exchange of letters that had passed between Harriman and Molotov, wrote to inform Stalin that "as a result of a misunderstanding the facts pertaining to this matter have been presented to you erroneously." Roosevelt concluded his letter on a conciliatory note: "I hope you will explain to the relevant Soviet officials that we should and must take early and effective actions without any delay to ensure the capitulation of all enemy forces opposing the U.S. troops in the battlefield."

On March 29, Stalin informed the U.S. president that he was very much in favor of ensuring the capitulation of the German armies anywhere on the front. "But," Stalin continued, "I will agree to talk with the enemy about that only if such talks do not permit the enemy to improve his situation, only if the Germans have no chance to maneuver or use these talks to redeploy their forces to other areas of the front, especially to the Soviet front."

Stalin was getting intelligence reports that under cover of the Berne talks Hitler's generals had begun redeploying their forces from Italy to the Soviet-German front. The situation was turning serious. Roosevelt's response to Moscow's sharp reaction came on April 1, 1945. His letter stated that "a regrettable atmosphere of fears and mistrust had developed" around the talks with the Germans on the capitulation of their armed forces in Italy.

It cannot be ruled out that President Roosevelt was unaware of all the details of the Berne talks and that vital information was concealed from him. Numerous facts have come to light about different covert operations by the U.S. secret services. Thus, in October 1943, a U.S. agent, Theodore A. Morde, who was passing himself off as a journalist, met in Turkey with the German ambassador von Papen and handed him a document that was to form the basis of a political agreement between the United States, Britain, and Germany. In particular, the draft agreement stated that the United States and Britain were prepared to recognize Germany's predominant position in continental Europe, including Poland, the Baltics, and the Ukraine.

The drafters of the document were proposing to dismember the Soviet Union and to hand over some of its territories to Germany. In exchange for that, the Germans promised the Americans and the British to open the front in the West.

When Roosevelt learned about these goings-on, he banned any further contacts and ordered that Morde's passport be revoked. However, even after that, secret contacts between U.S. intelligence and enemy emissaries did not stop.

Roosevelt's last message to Stalin regarding the Berne talks reached Moscow on April 13, 1945, that is to say one day after his death. The telegram noted that "the whole story had faded away without producing any benefits. . . . Be that as it may, there should not be mutual mistrust, and slight misunderstandings of that sort should not be permitted to arise in the future. I am confident that when our armies make contact in Germany and join their forces in a fully coordinated offensive, the Nazi armies will disintegrate."

With that message, which turned out to be his last, Roosevelt stressed the importance of trustful relations, the elements of which, in spite of all difficulties, could be seen in the relation between Roosevelt and Stalin.

Had Roosevelt lived longer, relations in the postwar period might have taken a more favorable turn. Conceivably, given a certain degree of trust between Roosevelt and Stalin, the excesses and dangerous confrontations of the Cold War could have been avoided. But Roosevelt's premature death and Truman's arrival at the White House radically changed the situation, provoking a counterreaction from the Soviet side.

CHAPTER SIX

Stalin and Churchill

STALIN AND CHURCHILL met for the first time under inauspicious circumstances. The British prime minister arrived in Moscow to inform the head of the Soviet government that the Western allies were not going to keep the promise they had made only a few months earlier to open a second front in France in 1942. That commitment was formulated in an official communiqué during Molotov's visits to London and Washington in May–June 1942. The published document stated that: "Full understanding was reached with regard to the urgent task of creating a second front in Europe in 1942."

At that time the Soviet Union was going through a hard period. Although the blitzkrieg had failed, and the defeat of the Germans at Moscow in December 1941 demonstrated that the Red Army was capable of dealing heavy blows to the invaders, Nazi Germany remained a formidable adversary. The absence of the second front made it possible for the Wehrmacht command to concentrate huge forces on the Soviet front by the spring of 1942. In the south, all summer long, the German troops had been rapidly advancing toward the Volga and the Caucasus. Despite their massive resistance, the Soviet units were forced to surrender more and more territory to the enemy. There were fears in Moscow that the Germans would again attempt to break through the lines defending the capital.

When Molotov went to London, he asked Churchill how Britain would react if the Red Army did not hold out through 1942. The prime minister had replied that eventually the combined power of Great Britain and the United States would prevail, adding that "the British nation and its army were eager to engage the enemy as soon as possible and thereby help the Soviet army and its people in their glorious struggle." That statement could be interpreted as readiness on the part of the British government to take on some of the German divisions. In addition, the treaty between the USSR and Great Britain that Molotov and Eden had signed during that visit—on the alliance and war against Hitler's Germany and its collaborators in Europe and on cooperation and mutual assistance after the war—appeared to be an important commitment by the two sides to undertake joint action against their common enemy.

Molotov had been even more encouraged by his conversations with Roosevelt in Washington, and by the president's firm promise to open the second front in 1942. The hope that a second front would at last be opened cheered our soldiers at the front as well as the people in their rear. Faith in victory returned, giving new strength to a people discouraged by an endless series of defeats and retreats. But now they were to suffer a new blow to their morale. Churchill couldn't help thinking about all that as he was heading for Moscow.

In the afternoon of August 12, 1942, a group of Soviet ranking officials, headed by Molotov, gathered at the Central Airport in Leningradsky Prospekt, as was usual in such cases. Also present among the welcoming party was the Red Army chief of staff Marshal Shaposhnikov. It was a sultry, windless day. The reception party crowded together under the canopy of the small airport building. The smell of hot wormwood filled the air, bees were humming, and birds were chirping. But that peaceful scene didn't put the people gathered there in a placid mood. For the second year in a row, the Soviet people found themselves fighting a ferocious war virtually alone against a powerful and ruthless enemy, almost single-handed. The people who gathered at the airport, both civilian and military, were directly involved in organizing the resistance to the German invaders. They knew better than anyone else how desperate the situation was, and that was why they were looking so wistfully at the sky, waiting for the distinguished guest from Britain to arrive. Why was he coming on such short notice? What was he carrying in his briefcase?

A black dot appeared in the blue sky. Moving in a wide semicircle, it grew rapidly larger and soon took shape as a plane. Gliding in over the rooftops, it touched down on the concrete runway and, slowing down, rolled off onto the turf. Swinging its wings slightly, the plane taxied across the green field and came to a halt a little distance away from us.

The aircraft looked unusually heavy, its fuselage almost touching the ground. I thought that a door would open in the side of the plane, but instead a ladder was lowered to the grass from a hatch in its belly, and without a pause some legs in heavy boots and crumpled pants began coming down the steps. The legs bent at the knees, allowing a bulky body to emerge from the hatch. And finally Churchill's head appeared. Holding on to his hat, he looked around cautiously, sizing up the situation, as it were. He was obviously not amused. It was his first trip to the land of the Bolsheviks, which, after the October Revolution, he tried "to strangle in its cradle," organizing the intervention by the Entente states. Nor was the present mission altogether a pleasure trip either.

At his very first meeting with Stalin he would have to explain why the promised landing in France would not take place. He wasn't worried about what Stalin was going to think of him. Offspring of an old and proud stock, the Marlborough family, he had little regard for the opinion of the son of a poor shoemaker, that half-educated, bloodsucking dictator. The Soviet press did not carry the full text of Churchill's radio address on the day Germany attacked the Soviet Union. The people of Russia learned only that Britain was ready to support them in their struggle against Hitler's invaders. But Stalin, of course, read the whole text, including that part where it stated that "the Nazi regime is indistinguishable from the worst features of Communism" and that over the past twenty-five years no one had been as consistently anticommunist as he, Churchill, had been. He still stood by his every word.

Stalin paid no heed to that. Moreover, in his very first speech after Hitler's invasion, made on July 3, 1941, he described Churchill's address as "historic" and declared that Britain's readiness to provide assistance could "only stir up feelings of gratitude in the hearts of the people of the Soviet Union." For his part, Churchill also believed, and he said so to his colleagues on a number of occasions, that now was not the time to think about the Soviet system and the Comintern. It was a time to extend the hand of friendship to a country in need.

Stalin had been able to hold out in the war for more than a year. The Red Army, although sustaining heavy losses, was still battering Germany's war machine. It was important not to discourage the Russians too much. Their resistance was vital for Britain and the United States. It allowed them to marshal more forces for a showdown with Hitler at a later moment.

By the time Churchill had climbed out from under the plane's belly, Molotov was already there to meet him. They greeted each other as old friends. The people's commissar introduced Marshal Shaposhnikov to him. Churchill said that, unfortunately, he was not able to introduce the marshal to his own military advisers because the plane carrying them in from Teheran had developed a mechanical problem and had had to turn back. Neither they nor Deputy Foreign Minister Cadogan would arrive until the following day. Churchill was accompanied by Averell Harriman, acting as President Roosevelt's personal representative. The people in the receiving line knew him from his last visit to Moscow. The British prime minister stepped up to the microphone and made a few remarks. He praised the Soviet people for putting up a heroic resistance to Hitler's invaders, promised them support, and expressed confidence that the Allies, through their combined efforts, would put Germany to rout.

A band played Britain's national anthem, followed by the Soviet anthem, "The Internationale." Churchill and Molotov inspected the guard of honor. The soldiers, wearing steel helmets and full uniforms, stood motionless, following the prime minister with their eyes only, while he looked into their faces intently, as if seeking confirmation that they were indeed men of mettle.

From the airport Churchill was taken to a villa that had been reserved for him at Kuntsevo. Harriman was put up at a private residence in Ostrovsky Street. The other members of the delegation were quartered at the National Hotel. Churchill was impressed by the comforts of his villa, something he didn't expect to find in a besieged city. A hot bath was drawn for him without delay, and he took his time luxuriating in it after the long and exhausting trip. An elaborate lunch was served in the dining room. Polished waiters, a large selection of hors d'oeuvres, red and black caviar, cold suckling pig, Georgian, Russian, and French dishes, wines, hard drinks, expensive tableware—the Tory leader hadn't expected to see such things in the land of the Bolsheviks. To be on the safe side, he had even brought some sandwiches along with him from London against the possibility that the inhabitants of the Kremlin were half-starving. Later, he confessed to Stalin that he hadn't expected to get such a sumptuous meal and had had a few sandwiches during the flight, spoiling his appetite. Commenting on that later, Stalin said to his followers:

"Churchill is such a hypocrite! He wants me to believe that he got that paunch of his eating nothing but sandwiches in London."

Molotov recalled that when he was in the British capital in the spring of 1942 and Churchill hosted a lunch for him, only oatmeal and a barley-based coffee substitute were served.

"That was nothing but a cheap show of democracy, Vyacheslav. He was just pulling your leg," Stalin said with conviction. He found it hard to believe that there could be a place where the leaders shared the hardships of their people.

Churchill didn't get much time to delight in the comforts of his residence. That same night he had his first meeting with Stalin.

"Don't Be Afraid of the Germans"

A SHORT TIME AFTER SEVEN P.M., Churchill's limousine crossed Red Square, entered the Kremlin through the Spassky Gate, and stopped in front of the building of the Council of People's Commissars under the fanciful awning over the entrance that Stalin normally used to enter his private quarters. The prime minister was accompanied by Mr. Harriman, British ambassador to the USSR Clark Kerr, and their interpreter, Major Dunlop. Pavlov, as the official interpreter for the Soviet side, met the entire group at the entrance, walked them to the second floor, and then escorted them along the corridor to the office of the head of the Soviet government. I was also called in just before the arrival of the guests to take notes on the conversation. My appearance served as a sort of signal that the foreigners would arrive any moment. Stalin and Molotov broke off the conversation they were having about the visit of the British PM. I only heard Stalin's last phrase:

"There's nothing to be thrilled about."

He looked grim and absorbed. He was wearing his usual semimilitary jacket, and his trousers, tucked as usual into his Georgian boots, hadn't been pressed in a while.

The door opened and Churchill's bulky figure emerged in the doorway. He paused for a moment to look around. His eyes roved over the portraits of the distinguished Russian commanders that were hanging on the wall—Alexander Nevsky, Kutuzov, Suvorov, the blown-up picture of Lenin. Finally his gaze rested on Stalin, who was standing by his desk and carefully examining his foreign guest. What could be passing through Stalin's mind at that clearly historic moment? Was he pleased to have as his guest in the Kremlin the leader of the British Tories, a man who had never concealed his dislike for the system he, Stalin, had created?

Churchill, of course, had come to Moscow only because of the extraordinary circumstances. Before Germany attacked the Soviet Union, Britain had been in dire straits. Churchill himself admitted that the Nazis could overrun the British Isles, promising in such an event to continue the struggle from Canada.

Germany's attack on the Soviet Union had radically changed the situation. London could breathe a sigh of relief. The longer that struggle continued the less was the likelihood that Britain would be invaded and the greater the chance of final victory. But Churchill could not delude himself: the Russians would not ensure his success for nothing. He would have to offer them, too, his blood, sweat, and tears. If he intended to haggle about the second front, he would have to be given to understand that the failure to open it was dangerous for Britain, too.

His face still grim, Stalin began walking slowly across the carpet toward Churchill. He held out a limp hand. Churchill shook it energetically.

"Welcome to Moscow, Mr. Prime Minister," Stalin said in a hoarse voice.

Churchill, a broad smile on his face, assured him that he was glad to have the opportunity to visit Russia and to meet the country's leadership. I found the PM's smile forced, a poor attempt to conceal his nervousness. Foreign visitors often had that reaction when they met Stalin for the first time. Most of them had probably denounced his brutal and inhuman regime, declaring him a ruthless and bloodthirsty tyrant. Yet many of them couldn't help but feel a little awed in his presence. Maybe his absolute power over his subjects created an aura around the Great Leader that made the people who came in contact with him obsequious toward him against their will. Or maybe it was a manifestation of their subconscious fear in front of a monster. But I think it was Stalin's ability to play the role of a gracious host and charming conversationalist that made his guests want to find a common language with him.

Stalin invited everyone to take a seat at the long table covered with a green tablecloth. He sat at the head of the table, offering Churchill a seat to his right and Harriman a seat to his left. The others took the chairs farther down on both sides of the table. After a few polite questions about how Churchill was feeling, about the flight and whether he found his residence to his liking, Stalin came to the point. He proceeded to paint a grim picture of the situation at the front, the expression on his face matching his account:

"The news we are getting from the army units at the front is not encouraging. The Germans are making a push toward Baku and Stalingrad. There is no guarantee that the Russians will beat off their new assault. In the south the Red Army has not been able to halt the German offensive."

Probably in an effort to cheer his host, Churchill pointed out that the Germans were unlikely to mount a new offensive at Voronezh or in the area to the north of the city since they didn't have sufficient air power.

"That is not correct," Stalin objected. "Because the front line stretches over such a long distance, Hitler can concentrate twenty divisions at any given point and collect enough punch for an offensive. Twenty divisions and two or three armored divisions are all that is needed. Given what Hitler has at his disposal now, it is not difficult for him to concentrate such forces. I didn't expect the Germans would be able to amass so many troops and tanks just from Europe alone."

That was already a distinct allusion to the absence of a second front in Europe. Churchill could no longer hold off making the statement he came to Moscow to deliver.

"I believe you would like me to address the question of the second front?" the British prime minister asked.

"As the prime minister wishes," Stalin answered evasively.

"I have come here to speak very frankly about real issues. Let's talk to each other as friends. I hope you'll agree to that and will be as frank in telling me what you consider to be the right course of action at this point in time."

"I am ready for that."

Recalling that during Molotov's recent trips to London and Washington the opening of the second front was discussed, Churchill said that a lack of troops and the means of landing them forced the Americans and the British to conclude that they would be unable to carry out the operation in September, the last month of favorable weather for a landing. Then he went on to provide detailed information intended to support the decision taken by the Western allies.

Listening to Churchill's exposition, Stalin was getting more and more gloomy and finally broke in with a question: "Do I understand you correctly that there will be no second front this year?"

"And what do you understand the second front to mean?" Churchill asked, obviously trying to delay an unpleasant explanation.

"I understand the second front to mean a large invasion of forces into Europe this year," Stalin replied, a tinge of irritation in his voice.

"Britain is unable to open the second front in Europe this year. But we believe that a second front can be formed in another region. An operation on the French coast this year would do more harm than good and would negatively impact the preparations for a large-scale operation in 1943. I am afraid you won't like what you're about to hear, but I have to say it anyway. If this year's operation could help our Russian allies, we would carry it out to divert the enemy forces from the Russian front, undaunted by possible heavy losses. However, if that move failed to divert any forces, it would undermine the prospects for the next year's operation and would therefore be a mistake."

Churchill invited Harriman to express his views on the issue. He was quick to make the PM's position his own. This made it clear that President Roosevelt was also retreating on the promise to open the second front in 1942. Speaking slowly, with a heavier than usual Georgian accent, Stalin said:

"I look at the war differently: no risks taken, no victories gained. The British shouldn't be afraid of the Germans. They are by no means superhuman. Why are you so afraid of them? In order to become real, the soldiers have to go out on the battlefield and be under fire. Until they have been tested in battle, no one can say what they are worth. Opening the second front now would provide you with an opportunity to test your troops in battle. This is what I would do in your place. Just don't be afraid of the Germans."

Churchill found those remarks offensive. Puffing at his cigar, he hotly contended that in 1940 Britain stood all alone facing the threat of Hitler's invasion. That was a clear reference to the friendly relations that Moscow had with Germany at the time. However, the British PM went on, Britain did not flinch, and Hitler didn't have the guts to carry out a landing in view of the successful operations of the British Air Force.

But Churchill's protestation left Stalin unimpressed. He recalled that although Britain did indeed confront Germany alone, it did not act. It did not help Poland. It did not react in any way to Hitler's invasion of Norway and Denmark. It stayed looking on when the German and Italian fascists carried out their Balkan invasion in 1941. Only the British Air Force remained active. But that was not enough.

When Churchill detailed the plans for a landing of U.S. and British forces in North Africa, the atmosphere eased a little. Stalin even saw some positive aspects to that operation. But the sour taste left by the refusal to carry out a landing in France affected the mood in the Kremlin until almost the very end of Churchill's visit. Nor did the mood improve even after the banquet Stalin hosted in honor of his guest in Catherine's Hall. Churchill said he was tired and refused to stay to watch a traditional after-dinner movie, which was interpreted as a sign of strain in the relations between the Allies. Maybe that was what prompted Stalin to make a sharp turnaround. He understood that he couldn't change anything, that he was unable to force Britain and the United States to keep their promise regarding a second front in France and that a further deterioration of relations could only have negative consequences. Furthermore, information about a split in the Allied ranks could leak out and be used by Goebbels's propaganda machine. Since there was nothing to be done about it, they had to make peace with each other, Stalin concluded. They would have to demonstrate to the whole world the unity of the three great powers and their determination to act in concert against the common enemy. And then again, a landing in North Africa, if it did take place, would certainly make things more difficult for the Germans and maybe even force them to pull back some units from the Russian front. In short, it didn't make sense to go on quarreling with Churchill. It wouldn't help the situation.

In Stalin's Apartment

AT THEIR LAST MEETING ON AUGUST 15, on the eve of
Churchill's departure from Moscow, the two leaders were behaving
as if they were old friends. Stalin was so gracious and courteous that
at first Churchill was stunned. But pretty soon he joined his Kremlin
host in the game of "friendship." They covered a lot of ground in
their conversation. Stalin again stressed the importance of an Allied
landing in North Africa—giving Churchill to understand, as it were,
that he had resigned himself to the inevitable—and concluded that
part of the conversation with the words:

"May God help you."

"God, of course, is on our side," Churchill agreed.

"And the devil is, naturally, on mine, and through our combined
efforts we shall defeat the enemy," Stalin said, chuckling, alluding to
a remark Churchill had made on a previous occasion stating his
readiness to forge an alliance with the devil, if need be, provided he
would fight against Hitler.

Then Churchill recalled that through his ambassador, Cripps, he
had been warning Moscow about Germany's preparations for an attack on Russia. Stalin didn't offer any reaction to that statement, saying only that he had always expected an attack, but had hoped to
delay it until the spring of 1942. He couldn't possibly admit that he
wrote the following comment on the memorandum of a conversation between Vyshinsky and Cripps—"Another British provocation."

They talked about the period before the war, and Churchill con-
ceded that the British-French delegation at the Moscow negotiations
in 1939 was neither representative enough nor duly authorized to conclude a serious agreement. Stalin briefed Churchill in general terms
about Molotov's trip to Berlin, his talks with Hitler and Ribbentrop,
and told him how during Molotov's last conversation with the German
foreign minister in the Reich's capital an air alert had sounded.

"Why did you bomb my Vyacheslav at that time?" he asked his guest
jokingly.

"I've always believed a golden opportunity should never be passed
up," the British PM riposted.

It was getting on toward midnight. Early the next morning Churchill was to leave for the airport. But Stalin didn't want to let him go yet.

"Why don't we stop in at my Kremlin apartment for a drink?" he suggested.

"I never refuse offers like that," Churchill replied.

They immediately set off on their way along the Kremlin passageways. They came out into a small yard, crossed a street, and finally found themselves in Stalin's apartment, which the British prime minister later described as "modest in style and size": a dining room, a living room, a study, and a large bathroom. Stalin made no mention of the fact that the place had previously belonged to Bukharin. They switched apartments after Stalin's wife, Nadezhda Alliluycva, committed suicide.

By inviting Churchill to his apartment, Stalin was extending a special courtesy to him. No foreign politician had ever been granted that privilege before. Thereby Stalin clearly wanted to emphasize that, despite their clash over the second front, he valued cooperation with Britain and was grateful to London for its readiness to treat the Soviet Union as an equal partner. As a further sign of deference to his distinguished foreign guest and in an effort to end the evening on an intimate note, Stalin invited his school-age daughter, Svetlana, to join them, and she hovered around the table as if she were the mistress of the house. A little later Molotov arrived and, assuming the role of toastmaster, began making one toast after another.

"Molotov has one thing going for him," Stalin remarked gleefully. "He is great at running parties and is an expert drinker himself."

More and more dishes appeared on the table, along with various drinks. Churchill understood that he was in for a long and hearty dinner.

Among the other topics discussed, they touched upon collectivization in the Soviet Union.

"Tell me," Churchill inquired, "for you personally is this war as much of a stress as was the burden of collectivization?"

"Oh, no," the "father of the peoples" replied. "The campaign of collectivization was a terrible struggle."

"I thought you would have found it rough going. You were not dealing with a few score thousands of aristocrats or big landlords, but rather with millions of small landholders."

"Ten million!" Stalin exclaimed, raising his hands. "It was fearful!

For four years it went on. But it was absolutely necessary for Russia if we were to avoid periodic famines and to supply enough tractors for the countryside."

Stalin's figure for the number of farmers repressed during collectivization roughly tallies with the one recently published in the Soviet press. If we assume that about half of the uprooted villagers, after drifting around the country, eventually joined the kolkhozes or ended up working at construction projects, then about 5 million people perished or were purged, a number close to the 6 million that is a figure accepted by most researchers. We should bear in mind that they were the most hardworking, efficient, and capable farmers and cattle raisers, who had flourishing farms, and that was why their resistance to the expropriation was so fierce—for which they paid with their lives. After such devastating losses, it is easy to understand why our country is still unable to get over its agricultural crisis. The farms where there are plenty of tractors but where the land has no real master will not be able to feed the country's population.

"Were they all kulaks?" Churchill asked.

"Yes," Stalin replied, and after a pause repeated: "It was very hard, but necessary."

"And what happened to them?"

"Well," Stalin continued, somewhat vexed, "many of them agreed to join us. Some got plots of land in the area of Tomsk and Irkutsk or even farther north. But they didn't put down new roots there. They didn't get along with the local people. Eventually, their own farmhands finished them off."

Of course, neither the local people nor the farmhands had anything to do with the tragic end of our poor farmers. Victims of forced collectivization, they were exterminated by special units of the People's Commissariat of the Interior. Did Churchill believe Stalin's account of the events? He did not challenge anything in it. And in his memoirs he only wrote that after listening to Stalin's tale he shuddered at the thought that millions of men, women, and children perished in the freezing stretches of Siberia.

Stalin and Churchill spent a total of almost seven hours together. The British prime minister returned to his villa only after three A.M., and at five-thirty A.M. on August 16 his plane took off from Moscow's Central Airport and headed for Teheran.

The visit of the head of the British government ended on a conciliatory, even friendly note. The communiqué published immediately afterward stated that "the cordial and very frank discussions demonstrated once again that there was close cooperation and mutual understanding among the Soviet Union, Great Britain, and the United States, fully in keeping with their allied relations."

Commenting on the Soviet reaction to the news of no European landing in 1942, Churchill telegraphed to Roosevelt on April 17: "In the upshot, they have swallowed this bitter pill."

Nevertheless, the refusal of the Western powers to keep their promise to open the second front in northern France in 1942 left a bad feeling in Moscow. Stalin's distrust of Churchill did not disappear. He became even more distrustful in 1942 when the number of convoys carrying military supplies for the Soviet Union via the northern route decreased sharply.

At the Teheran conference in November–December 1943, Stalin and Churchill did not manifest the degree of trust that developed between the Soviet leader and President Roosevelt. True, it was Churchill who came up with the proposal to "move" Poland westward and to establish the Soviet-Polish border along the Curzon Line, an idea that was to Stalin's liking. But the head of the British delegation put up a fierce fight against the decision to land the Allied forces in Normandy and pushed hard for an invasion in the Balkans. Stalin read Churchill's mind: he didn't want to let the Red Army into Eastern Europe. Even after the Soviet delegation, supported by Roosevelt, was able to secure a commitment for an invasion of France, Churchill tried to drag Turkey into the war, hoping thereby to wreck the agreement worked out in Teheran.

The British prime minister's thinking was that after Turkey's declaration of war on Germany, the Germans would attack Istanbul and maybe even take that city. In that case the Allies would be forced to take urgent measures to save Turkey, and the landing in France would be called off automatically. At the same time, hostilities would break out in the Balkans, a development Churchill was trying to trigger. However, Turkish president Ismet Inönü, whom Churchill met on his way home from Teheran, didn't want to declare war on Germany, and the PM's Balkan plot unraveled.

Stalin was also leery of the British delegation's position at the conference in Dumbarton Oaks, convened in the summer of 1944 to draft the charter of the future international security organization. The British initiated a proposal under which the great powers, i.e., the permanent members of the Security Council, were not to vote with regard to disputes in which they were involved. They managed to persuade the Americans to support them. But since the Soviet Union was the only noncapitalist country at that time, that formula could be used to attempt to impose unacceptable decisions upon Moscow. The United States and Britain expected to have an absolute majority in that organization that they could use at any moment against the Soviet Union. The USSR successfully defended the right of veto in the Security Council. But Stalin, of course, never forgot London's attempt to put the Soviet Union in a vulnerable position.

A Silent Scene With Follow-up

IN OCTOBER 1944, it seemed that a new era had begun in the relations between the Soviet and British leaders. The main topic discussed during Churchill's second trip to Moscow was the Polish problem. The British prime minister assured the Soviet leader that he was doing his utmost to convince the Polish government in exile, which had found a safe haven in London, to accept the Soviet demands. That could pave the way to a mutually acceptable agreement and create the conditions allowing a reorganized government of Poland to move to Warsaw after its liberation by the Red Army, prepared to establish good-neighborly relations with the USSR and to recognize the Soviet-Polish border along the Curzon Line.

We cannot state with full confidence that if that had happened, the development of Poland would have followed the path of Finland or Austria. However, one cannot rule out such a possibility either. But the premier of the exiled Polish government, Mikolajczyk, who was also in Moscow during Churchill's visit there, did not use that opportunity to reach agreement with the Soviet leadership. Was the British PM telling the truth when he said that he was urging the Polish émigré politicians to conclude an agreement with Moscow? Or was he, like the Americans, advising Mikolajczyk behind the scenes not to make any concessions? It would appear at the time, however, that Stalin was inclined to believe Churchill. In any case, the informal atmosphere of their last Moscow meeting suggested a high degree of mutual trust.

It was in that atmosphere that the British PM broached a subject that to this day remains a source of controversy among historians and journalists. That is why it is important to reproduce in greater detail what actually happened in Stalin's office on October 9, 1944.

By that time Harriman was already U.S. ambassador to the Soviet Union, and Roosevelt had asked him to act as an observer at the meeting between Churchill and Stalin. In a letter to the Soviet leader the president stressed however that Harriman would not participate in the talks and that the United States would not consider itself party to any agreements that might be reached at that meeting. That was why Harriman didn't attend all the negotiating sessions, even though the British PM kept him abreast of developments.

The meeting I am referring to took place not only without the U.S. ambassador, but the British foreign minister, Anthony Eden, who was accompanying his prime minister on that trip, was also absent. Stalin and Churchill met one-on-one with only their interpreters present.

Churchill led off by saying that he thought it was important to clarify certain questions they had been discussing in their recent correspondence.

"I am ready to discuss any questions," Stalin replied.

"We have to talk about two countries," Churchill said as he began to elaborate his idea. "One is Greece, the other—Romania. We are not too worried about the latter. However, Greece is another matter. Britain must be a leader in the Mediterranean, and I hope that Marshal Stalin will recognize our central role in Greece, just as I am prepared to recognize Marshal Stalin's central role with regard to Romania."

Stalin showed understanding for the position of the British government, saying that Britain would have a serious problem if it didn't control the Mediterranean.

"I think," the British prime minister continued, "we should couch these ideas in diplomatic terms, avoiding phrases like 'division of spheres of influence,' since that would shock the Americans. But when you and I arrive at a mutual understanding, I will be able to explain the situation to the U.S. president."

Stalin reminded Churchill that Roosevelt had expressed a wish that any decisions reached at that meeting be adopted *ad referendum.*

"We have no secrets from the president," the PM hastened to say. "I welcome Harriman's presence at some of our negotiating sessions. However, this shouldn't prevent us from holding private conversations, too."

"In my opinion, the United States claims too many rights for itself, leaving limited opportunities for the Soviet Union and Great Britain," Stalin observed understandingly. "Yet our two countries have a treaty of mutual assistance, do we not?"

After such a confidential exchange where more was implied than actually stated, Churchill went on to say, "I have this naughty document here with some ideas of certain people in London." He pulled out of his breast pocket a sheet of paper folded four times. He smoothed it out on the table and pushed it toward Stalin.

The text needed no translation. The sheet contained only these few lines:

Romania
    Russia 90%
    The others 10%
Greece
    Great Britain 90%
    (in accord with USA)
    Russia 10%
Yugoslavia 50% 50%
Hungary 50% 50%
Bulgaria
    Russia 75%
    The others 25%

There was a long silence. Stalin looked at the numbers carefully without saying a word. Then he took one of his favorite thick, two-color pencils from the bronze pencil-holder on his desk and put a little blue checkmark in the paper's top left corner. Then, without saying a word, he pushed the sheet back to Churchill.

A long pause again ensued. Churchill was the first to break the silence: "Might it not be thought rather cynical if it seemed that we had disposed of these issues, so fateful to millions of people, in such an offhand manner? Let us burn the paper."

"No. You keep it."

Churchill folded it and put it away in his pocket.

There was another long silence.

Much has been written about that "silent scene." The Soviet side flatly denied that any agreement was reached at that meeting to divide up spheres of influence in Eastern Europe. Our top government authorities assured the world that "a socialist state could not be involved in any shady deals with imperialist Great Britain" as this would "run counter to the basic principles of Leninist foreign policy of the Soviet Union." I also followed roughly that same line of argument in one of my own articles. It was hard to dig out the truth because Soviet archival materials remained inaccessible. The 1983 USSR Foreign Ministry publication entitled "Soviet-British Relations During the Great Patriotic War 1941–1945," which is a compilation of documents of that period, does not contain any protocols on the conversations between Stalin and Churchill on October 9, 1944. Although the events that followed their meetings seemed to suggest some kind of sub-rosa agreement had been concluded, it was impossible to find out what it was.

Today, the situation is becoming clearer.

The conversation the two leaders had before Churchill showed the sheet to Stalin indicates that both were ready to define their countries' share of influence in Greece and Romania as well as in other Eastern European countries. The following day's conversation between Molotov and Eden lends further support to that. I was not present at that meeting: Pavlov was the interpreter for the Soviet side. The memorandum of this conversation is also absent from the above-mentioned USSR Foreign Ministry publication. Recently, however, it appeared in the Western press.

Making a reference to the meeting between Stalin and Churchill, Molotov told his British counterpart that the percentage proposal deserved further consideration.

"Can we agree," Molotov went on to say, "that not only with regard to Bulgaria, but for Hungary and Yugoslavia, too, the percentage ratio will be seventy-five by twenty-five percent?"

"But that is much worse for us than what was agreed on yesterday," Eden objected.

"Then let the percentage for Bulgaria be ninety and ten, for Yugoslavia fifty-fifty, and as for Hungary, we'll work out an agreement at a later date."

"We are prepared to accept your proposal for Hungary, but we would like to have more influence in Bulgaria."

"If the ratio for Hungary is seventy-five by twenty-five, let the same ratio apply to Bulgaria, too. But then it must be sixty by forty for Yugoslavia. This is our limit and we won't go down any further."

Eden proposed eighty and twenty for Bulgaria, but continued to insist on a fifty-fifty ratio for Yugoslavia. In his turn, Molotov declared that if the British proposal for Yugoslavia was accepted, then the ratio for Bulgaria had to be ninety by ten. In this connection he clarified that while offering sixty and forty for Yugoslavia, he wanted to indicate that the Soviet Union had little interest in the coastal areas but would like to have more influence in the center of the country. Interestingly enough, Greece was not touched upon in the discussion at all, which demonstrates that the Soviet side had no objections to the initial British proposal for that country.

Tired of haggling, Eden finally declared that he didn't care much for numbers. He said he understood perfectly well the Soviet interest in Bulgaria and that Britain was prepared to accept it. As for Yugoslavia, it was important for the Allies to pursue a common policy there regardless of whether Tito and the Yugoslav government in London reached agreement or not.

During dinner with Churchill at the prime minister's country residence, Eden briefed him on his talks with Molotov and said that it had been a real battle in which he didn't sacrifice British interests. Everything appeared to indicate that in principle agreement had been reached on the spheres of influence in Eastern Europe.

Waking up late the following morning after enjoying his usual long stay in bed, Churchill dictated a letter to Stalin, recapping the agreement these two had reached on the percentage ratios. Probably feeling uneasy over the fact that the deal had been concluded behind Roosevelt's back, he prepared a draft letter to show Harriman, who stopped by to see the PM.

The U.S. "observer" was categorically opposed to sending this letter, saying that the president would be displeased with the whole affair.

Harriman's reaction was understandable. Churchill's sheet, which had set the entire process in motion, had outlined the U.S. shares in vague terms, and that, of course, would not be to Washington's liking. After listening to Harriman's arguments, Churchill decided against sending the letter after all, and the joint telegram that Stalin and Churchill signed and dispatched to President Roosevelt only stated: "We have to consider how best to coordinate our policies with respect to the Balkan countries, including Hungary and Turkey."

Turkey was probably mentioned in the context of an exchange of views that Stalin and Churchill had regarding the regime of the straits. The British prime minister was favorably disposed to the wish expressed by the Soviet leadership to revise that regime in favor of the USSR.

The issue of the straits was always on Stalin's mind. Stalin remembered that during World War I, Russia's Western allies had promised they would give the Dardanelles and Bosporus, including Constantinople, to the czarist empire after the defeat of the enemy coalition, which included Turkey. Having already annexed to his empire the Baltics, Bessarabia, and a part of Poland, Stalin continued to dream of the straits. He didn't have any success presenting that demand to Hitler and was now hoping to get what he wanted with the help of his allies in the anti-Hitler coalition.

But Stalin's dream never came true. He never got the straits.

The events that followed in Greece, where the British ruthlessly crushed the Communist-led units of the Resistance, give reason to believe that the two sides were honoring the secret Moscow agreement. All pleas for help from the Greek Communists fell on deaf ears as Stalin tranquilly followed London's campaign of repression against them. For his part, Churchill ignored the Foreign Office demand to react vigorously to the situation in Romania, where, in the opinion of the British diplomatic service, Moscow was riding roughshod over the Romanians. In light of the Moscow agreement we can also understand why Stalin was so exasperated when later the Western powers tried to interfere in the events unfolding in Hungary.

"Cordial Accord"

THE SPECIAL HONORS lavished upon Churchill during his stay in the Soviet capital proved that Stalin was quite pleased with the agreement reached with the British prime minister. Not only did he invite Churchill to dinner in his Kremlin apartment again, but he continued generally acting completely out of character. I remember the commotion in Molotov's secretariat and especially at the British embassy in Sofiyskaya Embankment (later renamed after Maurice Thorez) when Stalin accepted Churchill's invitation to dine there with him. It was not to be believed. The "father of the peoples" had never set foot in any foreign embassy before. Molotov sent me to the embassy well in advance with a list of principal guests so that the

British could prepare invitations. Apart from Stalin, the Soviet leadership at the dinner was represented by Molotov, Vyshinsky, Litvinov, and Kaganovich.

Molotov, who took both Pavlov and me along, arrived before all others. We stood behind Churchill, who was welcoming his guests. For some reason Molotov decided to introduce me, too. As he was giving Churchill my name, he said: "You haven't heard about him yet, have you? That's all right, you soon will."

I was never able to find out what he meant by that. Maybe there were plans to promote me from assistant to the people's commissar for foreign affairs to a more visible position or to post me abroad as a ranking diplomat, and he wanted to draw the attention of the people present there to a young man, unknown to them, who was already within Stalin's inner circle. Be that as it may, nothing came out of it—maybe because of a memo Beria wrote to Stalin. But I will talk of that later.

Before dinner was announced, waiters served cocktails and everyone was soon engaged in lively conversation. Churchill was making his way through the crowd, exchanging remarks with his guests, and his interpreter, Major Birse, and I followed close behind him. Pavlov stayed with Stalin and Molotov, who were surrounded by British and U.S. diplomats. Coming up to the people's commissar for transportation, Kaganovich, the prime minister asked him how he managed to ensure the effective functioning of Russia's transport system.

"If a locomotive engineer does not fulfill his responsibilities, he gets this," Lazar Moiseyevich answered, slashing his finger across his throat, a wry smile on his face.

In fairness, it should be admitted that during the most difficult period of the war, in spite of the bombings, the shortages of cars and engines, and a lack of fuel and qualified personnel, the railway transport system passed the test, even though it was pushed to the limit. I believe that the railway workers were driven not only by fear but also by their sense of duty to those who fought at the front or worked in the rear.

During dinner, gun salvos could be heard: Moscow was saluting the Red Army units who had taken the Hungarian city of Szeged. In the course of his stay in Moscow, Churchill had a number of occasions to see joyous Muscovites gather in Red Square to celebrate another victory. The Soviet forces had liberated Riga and were advancing toward East Prussia. In the West, the Allied forces, after liberating

Paris, were moving toward the Rhine. Those developments put people in an upbeat mood, which brightened the atmosphere at that memorable dinner at the British embassy.

With much fervor Churchill told Stalin about his recent trip to Italy and the enthusiastic reception he got there.

Stalin cast a damper on the PM's ardor by observing that only a short while ago the same crowd had been cheering Mussolini. Churchill didn't like the analogy and changed the subject.

He began talking about how important it was to preserve cooperation among the Big Three in the postwar period. Was he sincere in saying that? I believe he was not. After all, he was the one who—in his 1946 speech in Fulton, Missouri—proclaimed the beginning of the Cold War.

In a conversation with Lord Moran (Churchill's personal doctor) that same year, Churchill advocated striking before Russia had the bomb.

> We ought not to wait until Russia is ready. I believe it will be eight years before she has these bombs. America knows that 52% of Russia's motor industry is in Moscow and could be wiped out by a single bomb. It might mean *wiping out three million people*, but they would think nothing of that. (He smiled.) They would think of erasing an historical building like the Kremlin.

But in 1944, when the Soviet Union was bearing the brunt of the struggle against Hitler's Germany, Churchill believed that it was important to make Stalin feel that he had been admitted into the company of the Western democracies.

"In that future world, for the advent of which our soldiers are shedding blood on countless battlefields," the British prime minister held forth in his usual grandiloquent style intended for history, "our three great democracies shall demonstrate to the whole world that in time of war and in time of peace they have remained committed to the lofty ideals of freedom, human dignity, and happiness. That is why I attach such great importance to good-neighborly relations between a reborn Poland and the Soviet Union. Britain went to war to preserve Poland's freedom and independence. The British people have a sense of moral responsibility with regard to the Polish people and their spiritual values. It is also important that Poland is a Catholic country. We cannot allow internal developments there to complicate our relations with the Vatican."

"And how many divisions does the pope have?" Stalin suddenly asked, interrupting Churchill's train of oratory.

The British prime minister stopped short. He hadn't expected that question. He was talking about the moral influence the pope exercised not only in Poland but throughout the world. Stalin's remark, proving one more time that the only moral force he believed in was the right of might, brought Churchill back to reality.

They touched upon the problem of Yugoslavia. Stalin warned that, in Tito's opinion, the Croatians and the Slovenes would never agree to cooperate with King Peter and his government in exile in London. Eden remarked that King Peter was highly educated, and Churchill added that he was still young but would gain experience as time went on.

"How old is he?" Stalin asked.

"He's twenty-one," Eden replied.

"Twenty-one!" Stalin exclaimed. "Peter the Great became the ruler of Russia at seventeen."

Our leader liked making references to the imperial rulers of the Russian Empire. Before the Potsdam conference, Harriman, who was in the receiving line for the Soviet delegation at the railway station of the fallen capital of the Third Reich, asked Stalin whether he liked being in Berlin as a victor.

"Czar Alexander got as far as Paris," Stalin replied, unabashed.

Was it just a joke or did his remark have some hidden meaning? Soon after the liberation of France, the leader of the French Communist Party, Maurice Thorez, came to Moscow and asked Stalin when they met:

"De Gaulle is demanding that the Resistance fighters hand in their weapons to the authorities. What shall we do?"

"Hide your weapons!" was the response of the leader of the peoples. "It may happen we will need your help."

What could Stalin have meant by that? Was he afraid that his former Western allies would start a war against the Soviet Union and then French Communists would instigate an uprising in the rear of the American troops in Europe? Or was he dreaming of leading the Red Army to the Atlantic?

The conversation drifted on to Britain's parliamentary elections scheduled for the following year. In an attempt to flatter Churchill, Stalin said, "I have no doubt in my mind that the Conservatives will win."

He said the same thing at the Potsdam conference as he was saying goodbye to Churchill when he was about to depart for London. When the PM sounded uncertain as to whether he would be returning to Downing Street or be replaced by Attlee, Stalin stated with confidence that a winner couldn't lose and that the electorate would support Churchill, who had led Britain to victory. What was it—a wrong assessment of the situation, lack of information, or just a desire to say something nice to Churchill?

Churchill's visit to the Bolshoi Theater was also turned into a big event. The interior of the theater was decorated with British and Soviet flags. The orchestra played the British anthem. When Churchill appeared in the "czar's" box, the audience burst into thunderous applause and cheers. On that occasion, too, Stalin broke his rules and also came to the theater—arriving five minutes after the British prime minister. He went up to Churchill, who was seated in the box, and the audience, undoubtedly handpicked earlier, went into raptures at seeing the two leaders together. A few minutes later Stalin stepped back into the shadows so that the prime minister could bask in the applause alone. The ovation continued. Churchill, noticing his host's courteous gesture, turned to Stalin and beckoned him forward. Stalin approached the railing of the box again, which brought a new deafening salvo from the audience.

The lights faded away and the hall filled up with the sweet sounds of an overture. The evening's program had two parts: first, the opening act of the ballet *Giselle*, and second, a performance by the Red Army Song and Dance Ensemble.

During the intermission a light dinner was served in a small room adjoining the czar's box: cold cuts, caviar, crabmeat, *satsivi* (a Georgian dish of chicken and nuts), suckling pig, vodka, cognac, wines, sweets, fruits, tea, and coffee. The atmosphere at the table was very informal. The people made toasts, told jokes, and shared funny stories. Somebody, speaking of the Big Three, compared them with the Holy Trinity. Stalin quickly seized on that comment to crack a joke:

"If that is so, then Mr. Churchill is, of course, the Holy Ghost—he is flying all over the place."

After the meal, Churchill and Eden asked to be escorted to the bathroom. The bell had already rung three times announcing the beginning of the second part of the show, but the distinguished guests were not back yet. Stalin was getting worried and he sent me after them. When we came back, Eden, noticing Stalin's questioning look, explained, "The prime minister had some new ideas in there regarding Poland. We got carried away talking and didn't hear the call."

The explanation tickled all those present, and they returned to their seats in an even more cheerful mood.

After the concert, Stalin invited Churchill and Eden to his Kremlin apartment for dinner. He welcomed his guests in the hall, and then, pointing to a door, said, "Here is the bathroom. You can use it whenever you want to discuss important political issues."

Each time the two leaders met, Stalin never let the opportunity pass without showing Churchill his respect for him. Maybe he thought that the leader of the British Tories was finally ready to start building relations with the Soviet Union on a basis of mutual trust and was prepared to treat him, Stalin, as an equal. A good number of statements and moves that Churchill made seemed to support that conclusion. The British visitor became especially soft after their usual lavish meal in the Kremlin when the two leaders withdrew into a small, elegantly furnished "green" study adjoining Catherine's Hall where banquets were usually held. Sipping brandy and coffee and puffing on his Burmese cigar, Churchill often engaged in self-flagellation, asking Stalin not to bear Britain any grudge for its participation in the intervention against the young Soviet state.

"Let bygones be bygones," Stalin said in a conciliatory tone of voice.

"But can you forgive me personally for organizing the Entente intervention campaign?" Churchill insisted.

"I don't have to forgive you," the leader of nations responded magnanimously. "Let God forgive you."

On the morning of October 19, when Churchill was getting ready to go to the airport, he received two large cardboard boxes and a personal note from Stalin. The boxes contained vases with an intricate design: one, intended for the PM's wife, portrayed "a sternsman in a boat," the other was entitled *A Hunter With a Bow Against a Bear*. Was there some hidden message in those gifts? In the letters Churchill and his wife exchanged during the Moscow talks, they referred to Stalin as "the old bear." But how could the Kremlin's Boss have known about that?

Thanking his host for the presents, Churchill wrote to Stalin:

My hope for the future alliance of our peoples never stood so high. I hope you may long be spared to repair the ravages of war and lead all the Russians out of the years of storm into glorious sunshine.

> Your friend and war-time comrade,
> Winston Churchill

I left well in advance for the airport where a farewell ceremony for Churchill was to take place. The weather was dreadful. It had suddenly turned cold with heavy rains. The canopy at the airport building was too small to provide shelter for all the people assembled there. I was surprised by the great number of government security agents, both in uniform and out. Before five minutes had passed I found out the reason. A motorcade pulled up to the canopy. Officers in long coats jumped out of the first and third cars. One of them opened the door of the second limo—and we saw Stalin. He had on a light green overcoat with shoulder straps and a marshal's cap. He was wearing trousers with the bright red marshal's stripes, loose over his boots and visible under his coat. His sudden appearance at the airport was one last gesture of hospitality he wanted to make to Churchill before he left.

The British contingent hadn't yet arrived, and Stalin, declining to seek shelter inside the building, waited outside, standing in the rain. Finally, Churchill and his party arrived. Molotov and Harriman were with them.

Churchill was pleasantly surprised to see Stalin there. The two leaders made short speeches after which the British PM decided that it was his turn to make a nice gesture and invited Stalin and Molotov to take a look inside the cabin of his plane. It was fully fitted out and very comfortable. Stalin couldn't help remarking that now he knew why the prime minister enjoyed flying around the world so much.

Stalin made another attempt to preserve his special relationship with Churchill in late December 1944. At that time, the British and U.S. forces were in difficulties in the Ardennes. The Germans were mounting the large-scale counteroffensive that came to be known as the Battle of the Bulge and were rolling the Allies back to the west. There was the danger that the enemy would break through the front and rout the units under the command of General Eisenhower. Churchill appealed for help. He dispatched to Moscow Chief Marshal of the Royal Air Force Tedder to transmit a letter to Stalin describing the plight of the Allied forces and to find out whether the Red Army could start its winter offensive earlier than had been

planned. "The fighting in the West is very heavy," Churchill wrote to
Stalin. "Can we count on a large-scale Russian offensive at the Vistula
River or in some other area in January? I consider this to be very ur-
gent."

The Soviet command had not yet completed all the necessary
preparations. The weather was unfavorable. Moving up the offensive
could cause further difficulties and more losses. But Stalin decided
to demonstrate his goodwill to the Allies and, at the same time, to remind them that when the Red Army was in a similar situation in the
summer of 1942, Britain and the United States had not rushed to its
rescue. "Taking into account the situation in which our allies on the
Western front find themselves," he wrote in a wire to the British
prime minister, "the General Headquarters has decided to step up its
preparations and, in spite of the bad weather, to launch a large-scale
offensive operation against the Germans along the entire central
front no later than the second half of January. You may rest assured
that we will do all that is humanly possible to provide assistance to
our valiant allied forces."

Stalin kept his word. In the period between January 12 and 15, the
Red Army began advancing to the west along a wide area of the front
spanning over seven hundred kilometers. By February, in the main
direction of the attack the Soviet forces had advanced five hundred
kilometers, liberated Warsaw, and reached the Oder River, that is to
say, the future eastern border of Germany. By February 4—the day of
the opening of the Yalta conference—the Soviet forces were within
sixty kilometers of Berlin. The Allied units were no closer than five
hundred kilometers from the German capital.

At the first plenary meeting in Livadia Palace, Churchill thanked
Stalin for the readiness to help Eisenhower and informed him that
the situation in the Ardennes had improved. But the subsequent discussions at Yalta showed Stalin that his hopes for continued understanding with the British leader were in vain. With regard to the main
issues—German reparations, the Polish problem, and the draft
United Nations charter—the positions of Moscow and London soon
diverged to the point of turning confrontational. Stalin found it easier to deal with Roosevelt than with the stubborn leader of the British
Conservatives.

On the eve of Germany's capitulation the relations were aggravated by the behind-the-scenes talks the British and Americans had
held in Berne with Himmler's emissary, SS general Wolf.

As described earlier, Stalin and Roosevelt clashed sharply over this in their letters. But Stalin believed that the whole thing had actually been started by the British and that there was a reason for Churchill's silence about it.

At the Potsdam conference Stalin felt that President Truman, who made no secret of his hostile attitude toward the Soviet Union, had found a like-minded ally in Churchill. Stalin became especially worried when in Potsdam the two attempted to blackmail Moscow with the atom bomb. Stalin's response to that threat was increased pressure on the Eastern European countries, which, in turn, provoked a hostile reaction from the Western powers. When Churchill made his Fulton speech, applauded by Truman, it became clear to Stalin that his hopes for postwar cooperation with Britain had all along been nothing but an illusion.

Litvinov's Death Sentence

AT FIRST I WAS SURPRISED that the Chinese province of Sinkiang was listed in the Soviet Foreign Ministry's register as a "special entity" and that Deputy Foreign Minister Dekanozov was placed in charge of it. But I soon learned that the province was effectively governed from Moscow. The person largely responsible for that situation was the Soviet consul general in Urumchi, Apresyan. He had developed friendly relations with Sinkiang's Zupan (Governor) Shen Shi-tsai, getting him to turn that Chinese territory into a Soviet "province." When Shen Shi-tsai, together with his family, came to the Soviet Union for medical treatment and rest, he met Stalin on a number of occasions. The *zupan* asked the Great Leader to be admitted into the All-Russian Communist Party of Bolsheviks.

"You may consider yourself to be a member of the All-Russian Communist Party of Bolsheviks," Stalin declared magnanimously. "However, for political reasons, we should not tell this to anyone now."

The *zupan* indeed regarded himself as a Soviet citizen. And as a disciplined member of the Party, he never questioned Moscow's orders, handing over to the Kremlin control of the rich natural resources of his region. But at that time this deal was kept completely under wraps.

Stalin thought highly of Consul General Apresyan in Sinkiang. He showered him with favors and praised him for instilling love for the Soviet Union among the peoples of that province. Later Mikoyan told me that when our relations with Kuomintang China changed and Sinkiang had to be returned to Chungking, Stalin was heard to say in the company of some close followers, "Apresyan knows too much." That was the signal, and the esteemed consul fell into disgrace. His fate was already sealed. But the boss didn't want to make too much noise about it. He decided to remove Apresyan quietly. Events soon followed an established pattern.

When Apresyan arrived from Urumchi on his regular leave, he went to Abkhazia for a vacation. There, on a mountain road, he was killed in a car accident. None of the people around the Great Leader had any doubts that Stalin had arranged the accident. They had heard the sentence: "He knows too much!"

In the first years of the war, Dekanozov went to Urumchi a number of times to see the *zupan*. A new consul general was already there, a typical party bureaucrat named Bakulin. During that consul's tour of duty, relations with Shen Shi-tsai began to deteriorate, and the visits of the deputy people's commissar failed to restore them.

Soon after that, Chiang Kai-shek took care of the *zupan* in his own way: he ordered his head chopped off and Sinkiang was fully restored to China.

Years later, I had a number of private conversations with Anastas Mikoyan. They happened as if by chance, when I came to see him on some specific business. After the questions I had come to discuss had been resolved, he would usually ask me to stay and sit and talk about the past. He would order tea and crackers. We would sit in armchairs opposite each other and he would begin telling me a fascinating story involving Stalin. In the 1960s, Mikoyan was chairman of the Presidium of the Supreme Soviet, and whenever I came to see him, his secretary would warn me that Anastas Ivanovich had no more than five minutes for me. I tried to complete my business within that time and was ready leave as soon as I was done. When Anastas Ivanovich asked me to stay, I would tell him about his secretary's warning. On hearing that, he would smile at me slyly and say, "It's all right. Nothing's going to happen. They can wait," as if telling me that he knew only too well the ceremonial nature of his position. When at long last I would leave his office, the visitors cooling their heels in the waiting room would look daggers at me.

The conversation I want to speak about here was longer than usual, and Mikoyan was frank in his comments. It took place in 1972, when Mikoyan had already been relieved of his post as chairman, but was kept on the Presidium of the Supreme Soviet. At that time, working as editor in chief of *USA—Economics, Politics, Ideology* magazine, I was preparing for publication an article of Mikoyan's recollections about his business trip to the United States in the mid-1930s. I came to see Anastas Ivanovich to discuss some editorial changes proposed by the magazine. When we were through talking about that, Mikoyan, as was his wont, suggested that I stay and we "talk about the past." On that occasion he spoke about Litvinov and Chicherin.

"Litvinov," Mikoyan began, "was a bright and sophisticated diplomat and was highly regarded by Stalin—until a certain point in time, that is to say. Molotov, on the other hand, couldn't stand Litvinov. He was jealous when Stalin praised him, and he was, in fact, responsible for Litvinov's removal in the late 1930s, although he could still have been quite useful to his country and the Party. Molotov didn't like Chicherin, either. He persuaded Stalin to dismiss Chicherin who had been appointed commissar for foreign affairs by Lenin. It was a pity that the experience and knowledge of that man were no longer to be utilized. At least he could have remained deputy people's commissar for foreign affairs or a consultant to the Commissariat for Foreign Affairs. Instead, Chicherin spent his lonely days at his dacha on the Klyazma River, playing the piano. Depression and inaction probably precipitated his early death. But at least he died of natural causes. Litvinov wasn't so lucky."

At that last remark I pricked up my ears. What did he mean "wasn't so lucky"? According to the official report, Litvinov had succumbed to an illness at his dacha. Mikoyan went on with his story:

"It was true that it was decided to replace Litvinov when the pact with Hitler began to take shape. Litvinov, a Jew and a man who personified our struggle against Hitler's Germany at the League of Nations and in the international arena in general, was of course at such a moment an unsuitable candidate for the post of people's commissar for foreign affairs. But he could have been kept as a deputy. His experience could have been used. But Molotov saw to it that he was removed from office altogether. Molotov didn't know

much about international affairs and he didn't want to have a man
at his side who was more experienced and knowledgeable than he
was. As a result, until the fall of 1941, Litvinov lived in idleness.
Only when our situation became catastrophic and Stalin was prepared to grasp at any straw did he decide to use Litvinov's experience again and sent him as Russia's ambassador to Washington. In
that job Litvinov did much useful work. It can even be argued that
he actually saved us at that critical juncture by getting the Americans to extend lend-lease and a billion dollars in credits to the Soviet Union. Today it is easy to say that the lend-lease didn't mean
anything. It lost its significance much later. But in the fall of 1941
we had lost everything, and had it not been for lend-lease—the
weapons, the food, the warm clothes for the army, and other supplies—it is anybody's guess what could have happened. Litvinov
gets the credit for this. Thanks to his good personal relations with
Roosevelt and other American personalities, he managed to get the
military supplies going, just as much earlier he was successful in
getting the United States to recognize the Soviet Union and establish diplomatic relations with our country. But as soon as things
began to run smoothly, Molotov again began weaving a web of in-
trigue around Litvinov, which resulted in his recall from Washington. My opinion: they shouldn't have done that. Litvinov could still
have been useful and he shouldn't have been replaced by a
mediocre man with no initiative. Upon his return to Moscow, although officially he was offered the job of deputy foreign minister,
he was in fact left with nothing to do and was soon retired altogether. His life had a tragic end. The car crash he was killed in was
not an accident but a plan hatched by Stalin."

What Mikoyan said about the car accident was complete news to
me. I was so badly shaken by this story that I exclaimed involuntarily,
"Anastas Ivanovich, it just can't be, I just can't believe this," and I immediately apologized for interrupting him.

Mikoyan continued, unperturbed. "I know the place where it happened very well, not far from Litvinov's dacha. There is a sharp turn
there, and when Litvinov's car came barreling around it, a truck was
parked across the road. It had all been prearranged. Stalin was an unsurpassed master at things like that. He would call in the NKVD people and instruct them personally, one-on-one, and then a car crash
just happened, and the person Stalin wanted to get rid of was killed.
There were a number of cases like that. The well-known actor of the

Jewish theater, Mikhaels, the Soviet consul general in Urumchi, Apresyan, and others died in such tragic accidents.

"Stalin had a reason for getting rid of Litvinov. In the last years of the war, when Litvinov was effectively relieved of his duties and was living at his dacha, he was often visited by high-ranking Americans when they came to Moscow and who invariably paid him a visit for old times' sake. They talked about all kind of things, including politics.

"During one such conversation the Americans complained about the Soviet government's intransigence on many issues and that it was difficult for the U.S. to deal with Stalin because of his stubbornness. In response to that Litvinov said that the Americans shouldn't despair, that intransigence had its limits, and that if the Americans were firm enough and applied sufficient pressure, the Soviet leaders would make concessions. That conversation, just as the others that Litvinov had at his dacha, was overheard and recorded. It was reported to Stalin and the other members of the Politburo. I also read it. We were all furious at Litvinov. It amounted to a crime against the state. It was treason. Litvinov had coached the Americans on how to deal with the Soviet government so as to realize their objectives to the detriment of the interests of the Soviet Union. At first Stalin wanted to put Litvinov on trial and have him shot. But then he thought that could create an international scandal and complicate our relations with the Allies, and he put off the decision for the time being. But he didn't forget. He never forgot things like that. And many years later he decided to carry out his sentence, but quietly, without too much noise. And Litvinov died in a car accident."

Considering the importance of what Mikoyan disclosed to me, I asked him if I could use his account of those events in one of my articles, of course with an appropriate reference to him.

"I had hoped," Anastas Ivanovich replied, "to tell the whole story myself when I get to that period in my memoirs. But if I don't have the time, you may use that information, taking into account the circumstances and guided by common sense."

When I got back to my office, I wrote down my conversation with Mikoyan in every little detail, and all through the years I have kept a record of it in a safe place. Mikoyan didn't have the time to write it himself as he wanted to do. Today, in making our conversation public, I do not go against his last wish.

As for the substance of the matter, I don't think there is any reason to question the truth of Mikoyan's story. If it was indeed the case, then another name can be added to the martyrology of Stalin's heinous crimes. One more such crime comes to light.

I should add that there is a somewhat different account of what caused Litvinov's removal as Soviet ambassador to the United States. Essentially, it goes like this. During Molotov's trips to London and Washington in the spring of 1942, the Western powers, as was mentioned above, promised to open a second front in Europe that same year but subsequently refused to carry out their pledge. That caused a wave of protests among the public in Britain and the United States, and Litvinov was invited to speak at protest meetings in America. Naturally, he criticized the policies of the U.S. government. In one of his conversations with Stalin, U.S. ambassador Harriman hinted that President Roosevelt was not happy with such statements by the Soviet ambassador. An ambassador, Harriman observed, shouldn't attack the government to which he is accredited.

That sounded like a declaration that Litvinov had become persona non grata. And Stalin, who didn't have any special liking for Litvinov anyway, was given a pretext to recall him to Moscow. Maybe Molotov's intrigues had also played a role in that, as Mikoyan had suggested. At the same time, Stalin was annoyed by the fact that the Americans were showing the door to his ambassador. Washington probably believed that Moscow would send a high-ranking official there to replace Litvinov. But Stalin decided to take the Americans down a peg and made an unprecedented move: he put in Litvinov's place the Soviet embassy's counselor, Andrey Gromyko.

"All Clear: No Mines!"

ON NOVEMBER 6, 1943, the Red Army liberated the capital of the Ukraine. When I learned about that, I immediately asked Molotov for permission to fly to Kiev to find out what had happened to my parents. I hadn't had any news from them since the city was occupied by the Germans.

"Go," Molotov said. "Let Kozyrev find out when the situation warrants and let the military pilots take you along on their next flight there. Of course, you acted recklessly in 1941 when you didn't take appropriate measures to evacuate them in time."

I had already explained to Molotov on a previous occasion why it had happened that way. When I returned from Germany, I immediately informed my parents about it and we wrote to each other on a regular basis. In the first weeks of the war, no one expected that the Germans would capture Kiev. Father also sounded confident in his letters that the capital of the Ukraine would not be surrendered. General Tupikov, who was with us when we got out of Berlin, was assigned to the southwestern front and made chief of staff of the army defending Kiev. I asked him to watch out for my parents, if need be. The only note I received from him stated that they were doing fine and that, generally speaking, I shouldn't worry because Kiev's defenses were secure and impregnable. That turned out to be unpardonable presumption. Events unfolded much faster than could have been expected. Guderian's tank divisions were rapidly encircling Kiev from two sides. For a time it was still possible to take the army out of the encirclement. Maybe Tupikov could have gotten my parents on the last transport out of the city. The commander of the units there, General Kirponos, was imploring General Headquarters to allow an orderly evacuation of the Ukraine's capital. But Stalin banned a retreat and ordered the units to fight till the last man. Hundreds of thousands of soldiers and officers found themselves surrounded by the enemy and were either killed or taken prisoner instead of going on to fight on other fronts—which would have been possible if only they had been permitted to retreat. When German tanks roared into the area where the front headquarters was located, Kirponos and Tupikov shot themselves. My last link to my parents was broken.

On November 11, 1943, a military transport plane was scheduled to leave for Kiev, and the crew agreed to take me along. I had laid up some food—white bread, butter, bacon, sausage—which I packed into a small suitcase, thinking that I would probably have to foot it part of the way. I was issued a travel document signed by First Deputy People's Commissar for Foreign Affairs Vyshinsky and Deputy Chief of the Soviet Army's General Staff Antonov. It requested the military and civilian authorities to extend to the bearer, Assistant to the People's Commissar for Foreign Affairs Berezhkov, every facility during his mission to Kiev.

It was already fairly cold in Moscow in November, and I decided to wear my winter coat. I had bought it in a thrift shop right after my return from Germany, since I had left all my warm clothes in Berlin. The coat was gorgeous. In Russia before the Revolution, only wealthy people wore coats like that; made out of thick black wool, it had a sable lining and a huge beaver collar. It was sold together with a beaver hat with a black velvet top. That whole set, exactly like the one worn by Chaliapin in his famous portrait by Kustodiyev, cost very little—only 1,100 rubles when I was making 1,800 a month. The curious thing was that Moscow thrift shops were crammed with such fur coats and lady's fur stoles. The people who had evacuated the capital early had sold off everything, unable to take things along. As was now evident, the Muscovites, even after the Revolution, the Civil War, and the famine of the early 1930s, still had a fair number of personal belongings left.

But I had made a mistake dressing up like that. After the plane landed on the left bank of the Dnieper, in Brovary, I had to travel on trucks or carriages going my way or simply wade along in the human river of refugees, haphazard groups of wounded soldiers, guerrillas coming out of the woods, or just some wretched ragged people turned into nomads by the war. The people, looking suspiciously at my nouveau riche getup and probably thinking I had grown fat on other people's misery, were hostile to me, and every soldier with a gun and every guerrilla with a red ribbon across the visor of his hat and his quilted jacket crisscrossed by machine-gun cartridge belts, thought it was his duty to stop me and check my papers. In most cases, my travel documents had the desired effect. But some doubted their authenticity and took me to their superiors for a further check. I have to say that many people had great respect for my boss. After looking at my papers, they would ask, "Do you really work for Vyacheslav Mikhailovich?" and they would try to help me in any way they could.

But the countless checks took a lot of time. By about ten o'clock in the evening, I reached the Dnieper. Down below I could see wrecked and twisted military hardware scattered around on a sandbank, both German and our own. I could see the smoldering remnants of houses and smell the smoke in the air. A full moon was beaming down on that sorrowful scene of recent battle. Kiev's famous Chain Bridge had caved in and looked helpless, its steel spans collapsed into the river. Its brick piers rose out of the water as if lone geodesic marks, punctuating the waterway in the direction of the other bank and disappearing in the fog.

As I stood there, a scene from a freezing December day in 1920 replayed in my mind. Together with my father and mother, I had stood at exactly the same spot, peering at the girders of the Chain Bridge, which had been blown up by the Poles and was sticking out of the ice-bound surface of the river. Kiev had been the destination of our long and arduous journey across the war-ravaged country from hungry Petrograd, where I had been born, to the Ukraine that seemed like a country blessed by God. I was only four years old at the time, but many episodes from our wanderings, like the sight of this blown-up bridge, had become so firmly etched in my memory that I see them clearly to this day. With great difficulty we crossed the frost-bound river by climbing onto the icy steel beams. In 1923, when we returned to Kiev again after more wandering, the reconstruction of the Chain Bridge had begun. As chief engineer at the Bolshevik factory where the bridge girders were riveted together, my father was participating in this project. And now, twenty-three years later, here I was again standing in front of the ruins of the Chain Bridge. How many hardships did our people have to endure? Again and again they had had to rebuild what had been destroyed.

I asked a passing soldier how I could get to the other side.

"Further down, about two kilometers from here, there is a pontoon crossing."

Finally I reach the well-beaten track leading to the crossing. The vehicles form an endless line. Many of them are crowded on the bank, waiting their turn. The pontoons rock in the water and hoarsely moan under the weight of Studebaker trucks loaded to capacity. I hitch a ride on one of them.

Here I am now on the right bank of the Dnieper. To all intents and purposes this is Kiev. The column of trucks is turning left. I jump out of the vehicle and head right. Somewhere near here the road must turn and then wind on toward the Lavra Monastery.

The night is warm, filled with the smells of moist leaves and bark. I am surprised it is so quiet and there isn't a soul around. The place looks dead. I am getting hot in my coat and I take it off. I climb up a hill and walk along the Mariinsky Park. The ground is covered with a thick carpet of unswept leaves. Chrysanthemums, now slightly wilted, are planted along the sidewalk. Someone went to that trouble in the occupied city. This is Lipki, which before the Revolution had been Kiev's aristocratic suburb. No visible signs of destruction here.

I walk past the Arsenal. In 1938, I left to serve in the Pacific Fleet from here. To the right stands a monument to the victims of the Mazepa's betrayal*—Iskra and Kochubei, who remained loyal to Peter the Great during the war with Sweden's King Charles XII. Soon after the Revolution, the monument was toppled and sent for remelting. In its stead a Maxim machine gun had been mounted to commemorate the Arsenal workers' uprising. The Germans left the machine gun intact. Everything looks so familiar! How many times did I walk along this road to my work at the Arsenal! Here is the House of the Red Army, the former officers' assembly hall; a little farther on, the residence of the sugar manufacturer Zaitsev, an elegant building, as white as a sugar cube. In the 1930s, it was occupied by the secretary of the Ukrainian Communist Party, Postyshev, an old-time Bolshevik. He was shot on Stalin's orders a short time before the war.

At the corner of Levashovskaya Street (later renamed in honor of Karl Liebknecht) is the building of the former Polish consulate general. I will have to speak about it again when I will be answering Molotov's questions about Beria's memo to Stalin. I turn left and walk toward Institutskaya Street. There, at the street corner, is our house. What will I find there? I hold my breath in anticipation. The street, which used to be so familiar, looks strange and hostile in the uncanny moonlight. Only a few days ago, German boots pounded this sidewalk. Now they are gone, not even a bootprint left.

The power is out throughout the city, but I hoped to see the flicker of a candle in at least one window of our apartment, located on the ground floor. But it is pitch-dark behind the windows. I pause before the entrance. The door is wide open. Next to it, on the wall, there is a sprawling inscription: "All clear: No mines!"

With trembling fingers, I tap our old-time code message on the window pane: *ta-ta-ta, ta-ta-ta, ta-ta.* Silence. I walk over to the other window. Behind it is my parents' bedroom. I tap on the window again. Again not a sound. I enter the house. A small corridor, two steps up and it is the leatherette-covered door on the left. Automatically, I press the buzzer. Nothing—the power is down. I knock, but there is a thick layer of cotton under the door's leatherette upholstery. I knock on the doorframe, first gently, then harder and harder.

Hetman Mazepa, the governor of the Ukraine, betrayed Peter the Great and joined forces with the Swedish King Charles XII. Defeated by Peter the Great at Poltava (Ukraine), Charles XII and Mazepa fled to Turkey. Iskra and Kochubei warned Peter about the treason, but were executed by Mazepa.

Still no answer. I pull the door handle—and the door opens. I call, "Mother, Father." No one answers my calls. I walk into the living room, using the pocket flashlight I have with me. The beam of light illuminates the vandalism: the broken-off top of the piano is lying in a corner, cracked, empty picture frames, the glass doors in the china cabinet shattered, human feces, already dried up, all over the place. It must be at least some weeks since the inhabitants of this apartment left—after which the Wehrmacht soldiers, just before they fled the city, or some marauding savages during the short break in authority, must have run wild in here.

I walk inside the bedroom—here it has also been turned upside down. My room isn't any better. The books I have been collecting so lovingly have been dumped out of the bookcases onto the floor. In fact, few of them are left. Most are missing.

I use a broom to sweep out an area of the floor, spread out torn newspapers, and place my gorgeous coat over them. I lie down, feeling drained. But I can't go to sleep. The shock of the last few hours is too overpowering. One thing is certain—my parents have been gone from here a long time. Could they have been killed? Father hadn't been feeling too well for quite some time. He had complained of chest pains. The fresh hardships of the Nazi occupation could have been too much for him. But Mother wasn't old. She was full of energy. She was sure to have made it. If she had been thrown out of the apartment, she might have left me a message. In the morning, when it becomes light, I look all around the apartment carefully, I search under the beds and furniture, examine the windowpanes and the entrance door. Maybe a message is scratched somewhere that will give me a clue to what happened to them. But I find nothing and I leave the apartment to continue my search in town. I make the rounds of all the people I know in Kiev. Some saw Father, some met Mother. But that was months ago. Therefore, I could presume they were still alive. A heavy load off my mind! But where are they?

Gradually, I become more and more certain that my parents are not in town and that they are not even on our side of the front. Have they been deported by the Germans or have they decided to go over to the West, knowing that after their stay in occupied territory they were in for more troubles after the restoration of the Soviet regime? But that was actually beside the point. The point was that I was sitting on a time bomb.

All too aware of the way things were done in our country, I had no doubt that sooner or later I would be fired from the Commissariat for Foreign Affairs and given a job in some obscure agency. That is to say, if I was lucky. If I wasn't, I would be bundled off to a distant labor camp or, worse still, would be framed and eliminated altogether since I "knew too much." Stalin would not allow the likes of me to walk the face of the earth.

What can I say about my parents' life? One thing only: it was full of suffering. My father, who had fought his way up from an orphanage to become a talented shipbuilder, could practice the profession he loved for only a limited number of years. Then came the Revolution, the Civil War, the famine, the wanderings around our devastated country, and the hardships that drove him to make his own soap and boots. A few happy years in the 1920s with work on the construction of a shipyard in Kiev. Then the humiliation in the GPU prison and, after he got out, a transfer to work at a small factory. Another terrible famine in the Ukraine, anxieties about his malnourished family. And finally, the war. So when an opportunity presented itself to go over to the West, why wouldn't they take it?

When I understood that I would not find my parents, I felt no fear for myself. Each time I entered a "danger zone," for some reason or other I remained totally calm. I noticed that for the first time when I was still a little kid and found myself alone on the platform of some small railroad station. I was watching the cars roll by, packed with fleeing refugees, taking my parents, from whom I had been separated in the crush on the platform, into the unknown. Then, some years after, choking on a huge abscess in my throat, I remember calmly hearing somebody say to my parents, "Take courage. He is not going to live through until morning." But by the next morning the boil had burst and I was still alive.

But my heart was heavy. On the one hand, I was worried about what had happened to my parents, and on the other, I understood perfectly well that I had to inform Molotov about everything as soon as possible. But as it turned out, it wasn't easy to get out of Kiev. There was no regular service to Moscow and I had to wait for some special arrangement.

The papers I had with me came in handy. The military commandant gave me a Willis to take me to the left bank, to Brovary, where an airborne unit of Hero of the Soviet Union General Lakeyev was deployed. He had a transport plane that occasionally flew to Moscow.

But low clouds and a thick fog kept all his aircraft grounded. Even the fighters had to stop flying combat missions.

Lakeyev invited me to stay with him. We played chess late into the night, drinking a home brew that the mistress of the house made from beets, then went to sleep on benches in the large living room.

A whole week went by like that. I wasn't happy with that forced delay. I knew that the Big Three were to meet in Teheran, and that Molotov could leave Moscow before my return. At the same time I understood that the sooner I told him the whole story the better it was for me. If he learned about it from someone else, it would look as if I were trying to hush everything up. And that was the deadliest of sins by our ground rules.

The weather was not improving, but we got word that the clouds had lifted in the area of Kursk. Of course, I couldn't tell Lakeyev why it was so important for me to return to Moscow before our delegation left for Teheran. But he probably sensed that it was indeed urgent. And so, at his own risk, he ordered a fighter plane to take me to a military airport at Kursk. From there I was able to take off for Moscow on the following day.

No matter how hard I tried, I was still late. Two days prior to my arrival, Molotov, together with Stalin and Voroshilov, had left by train for Baku, whence they were to fly out to Teheran. At the same time, I also learned that my diplomatic passport was ready for me and that same night a transport plane was leaving from Vnukovo to Baku, the capital of Azerbaijan, and a place had been reserved on it for me. And so, without saying a word to anyone, twenty-four hours later I arrived in the Iranian capital. I decided to break the story to Molotov after the conclusion of the Teheran conference, after completing my last interpreting assignment, so as not to disrupt the work. There was no doubt in my mind that immediately after that I would be fired.

Throughout the days of the conference I was so busy attending the plenary sessions, the bilateral talks between Stalin and Roosevelt, interpreting at the dinners of the Big Three, writing up my notes, and preparing all kinds of documents that at times I forgot the whole thing. But in the few hours we had to get our breath back, I couldn't go to sleep for a long time, visualizing the way I would be "banished from paradise."

When the conference was over, our delegation flew to Baku on separate planes. From there we set off for Moscow by train. I was riding in Molotov's car and, at a suitable moment, told him I hadn't found my parents in Kiev. Contrary to what I had expected, Molotov took my story calmly.

"You did the right thing by informing me right away," he said after a brief pause. "One doesn't put off things like that. Under what circumstances did they leave Kiev?"

"I don't know. Maybe they have been taken away by the Germans? This happened to many people."

"That cannot be ruled out. I think they will be found. As for you, just go on working as before and don't tell anything to anyone else. You informed me, and that's enough."

And so I went on working. I was still called in to interpret for Stalin. In the summer of 1944, I was made a member of the Soviet delegation to the Dumbarton Oaks conference to draft the United Nations charter and spent a few months in Washington. It looked as if things had blown over.

But it only looked that way.

CHAPTER SEVEN

Beria's Memo

AT THAT TIME, the Politburo members, in addition to their offices in their respective commissariats, also had office space in the Kremlin. All their rooms were located on the second floor of the building of the Council of People's Commissars. Stalin's and Molotov's offices were also on that floor, but they were in a different corridor. The office suite closest to the boss's was that of Beria. In mid-October 1941, when the People's Commissariat for Foreign Affairs was evacuated to the city of Kuibyshev, where all the diplomatic missions were also relocated, Beria left for the Caucasus, ostensibly to coordinate the supplies of oil products for the army. In reality, he probably wanted to sit out the time of danger far away from Moscow.

In early November 1941, when Pavlov and I, on Molotov's orders, returned to the capital from Kuibyshev, we found our office occupied. Since Beria's Kremlin offices were still vacant, Molotov suggested that we move in there on a temporary basis.

The commandant of the Kremlin was called and, without any enthusiasm, carried out Molotov's instructions and opened the empty place for us. It had an un-lived-in look and was in perfect order: not a file or a piece of paper anywhere, as if its occupant had no intention of coming back. But all the phones were working, including the Kremlin switchboard and the government intercity high-frequency link.

When we were by ourselves, we couldn't resist the temptation to investigate the offices of the all-powerful chief of Stalin's secret police.

A visitor first entered a reception room, where the guards were posted. A door to the right led to the secretariat, which comprised two relatively small rooms. The door on the left opened into a spacious meeting room with a long table. Then followed Beria's study, which connected with a relaxation room; a little farther on was a bathroom and a small kitchenette with a sink and a gas stove. Molotov's relaxation room was more modest, probably because he, like Stalin and other Politburo members, had his apartment within the Kremlin. I visited him there on occasion when the people's commissar was indisposed and some issue required his immediate attention. In 1918, when the Soviet government relocated from Petrograd to Moscow, the leaders of the Revolution moved into rather unimpressive apartments with low ceilings and small rooms furnished with old, pre-Revolutionary furniture. Before the Revolution, these had been occupied by the servants who took care of the czar's quarters in the Kremlin and looked after the royal family during their infrequent visits to Moscow.

The young leaders of the Revolution were unpretentious and quite content to live in the former lodgings of the czar's domestics.

When Beria was transferred from Tbilisi to Moscow, he didn't move into an apartment like that. Rumor had it that he managed to convince Stalin that the chief of state security should live outside the Kremlin so that in case of a terrorist act or an uprising he could coordinate the operations to rescue the Politburo members. Either that or some such argument worked and the boss allowed him to move into a residence at the corner of Kachalov and the Sadovoye Koltso (Garden Ring) streets. Therefore, while the other leaders were almost constantly inside the Kremlin, Beria enjoyed relative freedom and stayed out of their sight. Turning that situation to his advantage, he handpicked a group of trusted KGB officers who cruised the streets looking for attractive girls and young women. His people acted unceremoniously. A car would pull up in front of an unsuspecting woman going about her business. An officer wearing the uniform of the secret police would approach her and politely invite her to get inside the car to discuss an important matter. Then the door would slam shut and yet another victim of Beria's lust soon found herself getting out of the car in the enclosed yard of his residence. She would be escorted into the dining room, where she was offered food and drinks, and then she was left alone.

Her bewilderment wouldn't last long. A toadlike, bespectacled man, seen in many portraits, would enter the room, wearing a bathrobe. He would make her an indecent proposal, and if she refused, he would simply rape her. When everything was over, a security officer would walk her outside, warning her that if she divulged "this secret," she and her family would be sent to Siberia.

And the women kept their mouths shut. They began talking only after Beria was shot.

Beria was a collector of sorts. A record was found in his bedroom with the names of over five hundred of his victims.

When Stalin died, Khrushchev immediately saw that the existing housing arrangement was dangerous for the top leadership. At any moment they could become Beria's prisoners behind the Kremlin wall. So, in one of his first decisions, Khrushchev decreed that Politburo members move out of their Kremlin apartments. Private residences were built for them in the Lenin Hills. But before long, the leaders decided to move out of these residences, too. The empty houses remained there as monuments commemorating the exodus from the Kremlin.

Under Stalin, the country's top leaders didn't have any housing problems. They lived in their Kremlin apartments as long as they held on to their jobs. When somebody fell out of Stalin's favor, having an apartment in Moscow didn't make sense anymore because the disgraced leader would first spend some time in prison and, before long, go to his last home. At the same time, his family would be moved to a labor camp in Kolyma.

After Stalin died the situation changed. A leader who lost his job was no longer shot, but he had to vacate his residence in the Lenin Hills. From that the idea was born to organize a construction company solely to erect luxury apartment houses for the ranking party and government officials in the capital's prestigious neighborhoods. Now if they were retired or demoted to a position of lesser responsibility, they no longer had to move out of their apartments, which were designed to their specifications and tastes.

This is by way of a brief historical note on the housing problem of the leaders of the workers' state.

We didn't feel comfortable in Beria's Kremlin office suite. The only thing we liked there was its bathroom with its constantly running hot water and the government intercity telephone. Quite often we had to call Kuibyshev, where Vyshinsky and our colleagues on the

U.S. and British desks of the Commissariat for Foreign Affairs were still staying, to get information on a specific issue. Sometimes, we were able to call our wives, who also stayed on in Kuibyshev. One time, when I was on the phone talking to Galina, I sensed that someone had tapped into our line. I quickly said goodbye to Galina and hung up. Almost immediately, the government phone rang.

"Hello . . ."

"Who gave you permission to use Lavrenty Pavlovich's phone?" a gruff voice asked brusquely.

"Who is this speaking, please? Maybe we should first say hello to each other."

"I have no time for niceties with you. Who allowed you to enter that office? Who are you?" The voice became threatening.

I felt uneasy but I refused to be intimidated since I had official authorization to be there.

"First you tell me who you are and why you are hooked up to a government line?"

"This is General Serov speaking. I am in charge of government communications. I am informed this is not the first time you have used the government communication system to make personal calls."

That was true: I had called Kuibyshev a few times to discuss personal matters. Galina was in the early stage of her pregnancy. We were expecting our older son, Sergei. And she was not feeling too well. I was trying to get some medicines for her and sometimes to send her some food. And so I called to tell her who would be carrying my parcel and, in general, to find out how she was. Our conversations didn't last more than a few minutes and I didn't think it was such a terrible thing to do.

There I was again, just as back in Lvov, having a confrontation with General Serov. But he must have forgotten me. And so I replied: "Berezhkov speaking here. We met in Lvov, you may recall. And I work in this office because Vyacheslav Mikhailovich instructed me to, while Comrade Beria is away. I am Molotov's assistant. How come you don't know this?"

"I am in Kuibyshev at present and I guess I haven't been brought up to date," Serov said, somewhat flustered, and hung up.

The general probably reported the incident to his chief, and I knew perfectly well that, if Molotov hadn't cleared the question with Beria before we moved into his office, someday he would remember it. Understandably, we were glad when we finally got back our old office next to Molotov's.

On the surface at least, Beria was nice to me on the few occasions we met. The first time this happened was at the Teheran conference, where officially only Stalin, Molotov, and Voroshilov were on the Soviet delegation. But Beria was also with them at the Soviet embassy. Every morning as I headed for the building where the plenary sessions were held, I saw him cruising around the embassy park in a Buick with tinted windows. The collar of his overcoat was turned up and his felt hat was pulled down over his eyes. Only his glasses twinkled. Once we came face-to-face at the door of the security room, which was close to our cafeteria. He greeted me pleasantly, inquired about the situation at the conference, and then gave me a piece of advice similar to the one I had recently received from Voroshilov at a meeting of military experts: "Stalin seems to like you, and you should use his favorable disposition to further the interests of your career." I thanked him, saying that I valued highly my present job and couldn't dream of anything better.

At a Kremlin banquet, the seating arrangements were usually as follows: Stalin would sit in the middle of the table, the principal guest to his right, then an interpreter, who had Beria to his right. As a result, I often found myself sitting next to the security chief. He ate almost nothing. But in front of him he always had a plate of little red peppers, which he popped into his mouth one after another, as if they were peanuts. Once he offered one to me. The moment I put it to my lips I felt as if they had caught fire. Beria laughed and insisted that I swallow it. I pretended to swallow, but later, when he wasn't looking, spit it out and threw it under the table.

"It's very good for your health. Every man must have a plateful of these peppers every day," he announced professorially.

He also always asked me why I was so skinny.

"That's the way I'm built," I would reply. I couldn't possibly tell him that the two sausages we had for the whole day in the Kremlin guards' cafeteria wasn't the kind of food that helped one put on weight.

I felt uncomfortable in Beria's presence. I knew that at any moment he could hint to Stalin that I "knew too much." Eventually, something like that happened.

Sometime in the fall of 1944, I was briefing Molotov on a cable we had received from Washington. The people's commissar listened while he continued going through the papers on his desk. Suddenly, he looked up at me intently and asked: "What were you doing at the Polish consulate in Kiev in 1934?"

I was baffled by the question, wondering why he had asked it. Molotov didn't take his eyes off me. I saw that I'd better give him an answer.

"At the Polish consulate?" I spoke up, trying to remember. "Indeed, I had occasion to go there. At that time I worked as a guide at Kiev's Intourist. Tourists usually returned home through Poland. I collected their passports and took them to the consulate to get transit visas."

"We know that," Molotov said in an icy voice. "But the visit in question to the Polish consulate did not take place during the tourist season. It occurred later, in the fall, and you didn't enter the building through the front door, but used the back entrance. What were you doing there?"

Just to think about it—ten years had gone by! Kiev had been through an occupation and seen heavy fighting during its liberation. Old Kreshchatik had been destroyed, the Assumption Cathedral in the Monastery had been blown up, priceless works of art had perished, and thousands of Kievites had died, but some worthless piece of paper, filed by someone who had tailed me back in 1934, had survived and was now becoming a dangerous piece of evidence.

"I went to see my friend there. He had worked as an Intourist driver and drove my tourists around town in his bus. Then he went to work for the consulate, most likely after getting an appropriate security clearance. I ran into him in the street one day, and he invited me to see him in his garage. We sat and talked there for a while, smoked Pro Patria Polish cigarettes, drank some German beer—and that was it."

Molotov's look softened a little, and he said, "I accept your explanation. Beria wrote a memo to Comrade Stalin about your visit to the Polish consulate. You may go now."

It looked as if I was off the hook. I could easily have been declared the one spy for the White Poles who had penetrated into the holy of holies—Stalin's very office! Today, when I recall that episode, I sometimes think to myself: It's true that this is a small world. The Polish consul in the Ukraine at that time was a man named Brzezinski, the father of the U.S. Sovietologist Zbigniew Brzezinski, who became national security adviser to Pres. Jimmy Carter. To expand coincidence,

Zbigniew's son Ian is today an adviser in Kiev to President Kravchuk of the Ukraine. If at that earlier time an action had been brought against me and I had been made "to confess," I would have had to say that I had been recruited as a spy by Brzezinski senior.

My conversation with Molotov had a follow-up.

As 1944 was drawing to an end, fireworks displays lit up the sky in celebration of our victories. Galya and I lived in a two-room apartment in Moskvin Street, where we moved in the spring of 1942, a short time before Sergei was born. We were lucky to find a baby-sitter. It was especially important for Galina, who didn't want to quit her job at Tass. We decided to stay at home to ring in 1945 and invited many friends and colleagues to join us. There was a lot of noise and a lot of fun. The guests began leaving only in the dawn.

On January 1, Pavlov was to go on duty in the secretariat, and he left for the Kremlin right from our place. I had the day off. We tidied up the apartment, went out for a walk, taking Sergei for a sleigh ride with us, and went to bed early. Around three o'clock in the morning of January 2, the phone rang. Molotov was requesting me to report to the Kremlin immediately. Not suspecting that anything was wrong, I called a car and a few minutes later was already entering our secretariat. I wished everyone a happy New Year and noticed immediately that the people there were taciturn and gloomy. I wanted to walk directly in to Molotov as I usually did, but Kozyrev asked me to wait and went inside our chief's office himself. Somehow it all seemed strange. Finally, Kozyrev came out and, turning to me, said very officially: "Comrade Berezhkov, Vyacheslav Mikhailovich is expecting you."

All of a sudden everything looked alien to me: the large reception room with the long table and rows of chairs and the people's commissar's room. As if I hadn't gone there every day for the past four years.

Just as back in 1940, when I saw him for the first time, Molotov was bent over his desk illuminated by a lamp with a green shade. I stopped in the middle of the room, hesitant.

Molotov raised his head and looked at me closely. Finally, he broke the silence: "Come closer and sit down."

I took the chair next to his desk, still wondering what I could have done wrong. But it was already clear: something had happened.

"Have you had any news of your parents?" Molotov asked.

"As I have already reported to you, I went to Kiev in November

1943 but didn't find them there. Maybe they died or were taken away to Germany by the Nazis, as were many other Kievites. I have not been able to get any further information."

"Beria believes they defected to the West."

"Does he have any evidence for that?"

"He says he has information from his agents. Beria has submitted a memo to Comrade Stalin where he again writes about your contacts with the Polish consulate. He believes that, coupled with the disappearance of your parents, a new situation emerges that calls for additional investigation. Under the circumstances he questions the advisability of keeping you in your present job."

Molotov paused, looking at me questioningly. I was petrified. It was not hard to understand what Beria meant by "additional investigation." First he had advised me to take care of my career while I was in Stalin's favor, and now he had my future in his hands. Suddenly, I felt absolutely indifferent. Whatever happened, it was pointless to put up a fight.

Meanwhile, Molotov continued, "We conferred with Comrade Stalin about what to do with you. He is also of the opinion that under the present circumstances you cannot stay here, at the very top, as it were. Give your files and the key to your safe to Kozyrev and Pavlov immediately and stay at home until we come to a decision about your situation. Goodbye."

That was it. I groped my way out, as if I were walking in a fog. Mechanically, I opened my safe, took out the folders with my files, put them on my desk, and made an inventory. I got Kozyrev and Pavlov to put their initials on it next to mine. Immediately after that both of them vanished somewhere without even saying goodbye.

I remained alone in the room. I sat down on a chair, trying to collect my thoughts, which were scattering like cockroaches under a bright light. I put on my military-style coat with a major general's big star on the shoulder boards, the insignia of an assistant to the people's commissar for foreign affairs. Then I put on my gray fur hat and headed for the door.

The duty officer at the Spassky Gate took my blue all-area Kremlin pass, looked at it longer than usual, and then said, "I have orders to take your pass."

The words sounded like a door slamming on my past.

I left without saying a word, crossed Red Square, and set off on an aimless walk around town. I couldn't go home right away. I spent a few hours roaming the empty streets like a sleepwalker. When I finally found my way home, my wife had already left for work. Sergei was asleep and the baby-sitter was busy in the kitchen. In the days that followed I couldn't just sit at home. Every day I spent many hours wandering around town, sometimes late at night. For two long weeks I had no news whatsoever. My colleagues and numerous "friends" of yesterday were all gone. At night, I waited for a knock on the door, recalling Beria's promise to carry out an "additional investigation."

Finally, on January 17, the phone rang. They were offering me a job on the staff of *War and the Working Class* magazine. I could breathe a little easier. I knew that magazine and the people who worked there. Molotov, who was actually its editor, had occasionally requested me to prepare materials for the editorial board, to read articles, and to take edited proofs back to the magazine's offices. I also knew the deputy editor in chief there, Lev Abramovich Leontiev, the man who managed all the practical aspects of the publishing process.

He gave me a hearty welcome as he sat me down in an armchair behind a coffee table in his office in Kalashny Street where the magazine was then published.

"We have just received an excerpt from a decision by the Central Committee's secretariat, signed by Comrade Stalin, stating that you have been relieved of your duties as assistant to the USSR people's commissar for foreign affairs in connection with your transfer to work on *War and the Working Class*. In fact, I had known about that decision earlier, but I wanted to get an official document before inviting you in."

I thanked Leontiev for that information and said that, although I hadn't had any experience working as a journalist, I would make every effort to carry out my responsibilities as best I could.

Leontiev then told me, "Vyacheslav Mikhailovich asked me to pass on a few recommendations to you. In your private conversations don't talk too much about your work in the Commissariat for Foreign Affairs. Don't tell anyone what you did in Molotov's secretariat. Just simply say, 'I worked in the Commissariat for Foreign Affairs'— that's all. Avoid contacts with the foreigners you met in your previous job. If you want to write articles, use a pen name."

It was clear to me that by giving me those instructions, Molotov was trying to save me from Beria. I had to lay very low, and even my name shouldn't appear in public so as not to invite reminders about my pending investigation.

"And now about your job on our staff," Leontiev continued. "A decision has been taken to publish our magazine in English and German, and Molotov suggested that you should start by getting involved with these translations. What do you think about that?"

"Well, this is certainly very familiar ground for me. I accept your proposal with gratitude."

"I think you should also start thinking about eventually writing your own stuff, too. Under a pseudonym, of course."

On the way back home, I was mentally thanking Molotov. He rarely intervened on other people's behalf. He did not hesitate to put his initials on the lists of people condemned to death. Quite often his initials *V.M.*—Vyacheslav Molotov—were followed by another abbreviation with the same two letters but with a sinister meaning in Russian: *vysshaya mera*—"capital punishment." Molotov's four assistants before me had died unnatural deaths, three of them shot by the NKVD and the fourth driven by torture to jump down an elevator shaft in the Lubyanka prison. Molotov didn't plead on their behalf. But for some reason he had decided to save me and even make provision for my future. I also had reason to believe that he had talked Stalin into signing the decision about my transfer to work on the magazine. That move probably blocked Beria's further probe into my case. Much later, after Stalin had died and Beria had been executed, after he hadn't spoken to me once in ten years, Molotov remembered me and removed the brand of the "untouchable" from me. But the period from the end of the 1940s until Stalin's death was a time when Molotov himself was threatened—to escape only by the skin of his teeth.

"Paulina Is Still Alive . . ."

THE LAST TIME I MET Ivan Mikhailovich Maisky, the Soviet ambassador to London during the years of the war, was a short time before he died. By then he was spending almost all his time at a dacha in Mozhenka outside Moscow belonging to the Academy of Sciences.

I went to see him on a warm summer day. His house stood deep inside a well-tended garden bright with flower beds and blossoming rose bushes. The silence was broken only by the low humming of the bees, flying from flower to flower, and the distant drumming of a woodpecker, hiding in the branches of a tall pine tree.

Maisky was sitting out on an open veranda in a wheelchair, a thick book in his hands. His legs were wrapped in a Scottish plaid with a bright tartan pattern. We were served tea with raspberry jam. Maisky himself poured the tea into exquisite bone-china cups and put the jam in little saucers.

We usually began our conversations by recalling the distant days of the war. I first met Maisky at the Yaroslavsky Railway Station when he, together with the British foreign minister, Anthony Eden, arrived in Moscow in the second half of December 1941. They had flown from Scotland to Arkhangelsk, then traveled the rest of the way by train. A short time before their arrival the Red Army had scored its first major victory in the Battle of Moscow. But Hitler's Luftwaffe was still active around the capital. Eden and Maisky were wearing fur hats and white sheepskin coats with huge collars. The winter that year was bitter and they were dressed for it, wearing clothes they had bought before departing from London. Subsequently, Maisky and I met on numerous occasions—during Churchill's visits to Moscow, at the Moscow conference of the three foreign ministers in the fall of 1943, and later when he returned from Britain to become deputy foreign minister. But then I was expelled from the Foreign Ministry and Maisky ended up in the Lubyanka prison.

"It was terrible," Ivan Mikhailovich recalled, sounding a little distant. "Beria personally interrogated me. He hit me with a chain and a lash, trying to get me to confess that all that time I had been working for British intelligence. Eventually I owned up to having been a British spy for a long time. I was thinking to myself, if they don't put me before a firing squad, they'll send me to a labor camp and leave me in peace. But they continued to detain me in a Lubyanka basement cell. They also kept interrogating me and it was from the cross-examinations that I soon learned that they weren't only after me, but that Beria was trying to get at Molotov."

By the late 1940s Molotov's position had weakened. He was replaced by Vyshinsky as foreign minister. His wife, Paulina, the woman in charge of the perfume industry, someone who had done much to ensure that the fair sex got fair treatment, had been arrested. Rumor had it that she was an Israeli spy. When the Soviet Union established diplomatic relations with Israel, after having played a major role in its creation, Tel Aviv posted Golda Meir as its ambassador to Moscow. It turned out that the new ambassador and Paulina Zhemchuzhina-Molotov had gone to the same gymnasium together, and naturally they met in Moscow as old friends. They often had each other over for tea and spent much time together. That gave Beria an argument to persuade Stalin that Paulina Zhemchuzhina had long been working for the Zionists. And so, although Molotov still remained a Politburo member, his wife, whom he, of course, loved, found herself in the Lubyanka prison. As far as is known, Molotov had the guts to ask Stalin why Paulina had been arrested. Stalin answered tongue in cheek:

"I haven't the slightest idea, Vyacheslav. They have put all my relatives in prison, too."

It was true. Almost all the relatives of Stalin's first wife, Svanidze, and his second spouse, Alliluyeva, were either in prison or had been shot. Molotov had nothing to answer to the quip of his all-powerful boss. All the more so since the wives of our president, Kalinin, and Stalin's main assistant, Poskryobyshev, were also in prison. Molotov later recalled that when he ran into Beria in the Kremlin corridor, the security chief would whisper into his ear as they were passing each other by:

"Paulina is still alive . . ."

Molotov could trust that information since his dear wife was in Beria's custody. Molotov also recalled how happy he was when immediately after Stalin's death, Beria, graciousness incarnate, brought Paulina to him. At about the same time, Maisky was escorted from his prison cell to Beria's office. When he walked in, he saw a table in the middle of the room with a vase filled with fruit, a bottle of Georgian wine, and wineglasses on it. Lavrenty Pavlovich was going out of his way to be nice to him.

"Ivan Mikhailovich," Beria said, turning to the accused. "Why do you tell stories about yourself? You're not a spy! This is utter nonsense!"

Maisky didn't know anything about what had happened. He thought Stalin's henchman was just trying one of his dirty tricks on him. "If I say I am not a spy," he was thinking to himself, "they'll beat me up again for sure."

"No, Lavrenty Pavlovich, I am a spy, I have been recruited by the British, and that is the fact."

"Enough of that nonsense, Ivan Mikhailovich! You are not a spy. You have been framed. We've gotten to the bottom of this. Those who are responsible will be punished. And as for you, you can go straight home."

Maisky couldn't believe his ears. What had happened in our country? Or was Beria just testing him before starting to humiliate him all over again?

An officer walked in. He spread out clothes before the accused, the same clothes that had been taken away from him when he was thrown into a cell.

Beria walked Maisky to his relaxation room to change.

"Well, that's it," he said, putting out his hand to Maisky. "Please forgive us, there has been a mistake. A car is waiting for you downstairs." He turned to the officer. "Escort him out," he ordered.

In the short period between Stalin's death and his own arrest, Beria took on the role of a denouncer, accusing his henchmen of wrongdoing, of overstepping their authority and of treating their prisoners brutally. In an effort to shield himself, he arrested and summarily executed the chief of the NKVD interrogation department, Ryumin, as well as several others.

But before that, Beria had needed both Maisky and Paulina in order to frame Molotov as a British spy. From Maisky's accounts of his interrogation sessions, Beria seemed to be working on the following scenario:

Molotov was allegedly recruited by the British during his trips to London and Washington in the spring of 1942. On his trip to London, he was accompanied by a number of his security officers and by Pavlov as his interpreter. They had flown to Scotland in a hastily converted Soviet long-range bomber. From Glasgow they took a special night express to London. At the airport in Glasgow, the Soviet delegation, code-named Mr. Brown's Mission for security reasons, had been met by Anthony Eden, who accompanied his guests on the ride to the British capital. Molotov and Eden had separate cars on the train. In addition to living rooms and spacious compartments for the ministers, each car had several sleeping compartments—for interpreters and security guards.

Late at night, Eden, accompanied by his interpreter, came to Molotov's compartment. He knocked on the people's commissar's door; the door opened and the two men went inside.

At that time a stringent regulation was in effect for all Soviet officials. Anyone negotiating with foreigners, even if he was a member of the Politburo, had to have at least one, preferably two Soviet "witnesses" at his side. This role was usually performed by the interpreter. But on that particular night, Molotov stayed alone with Eden and his interpreter for almost one hour. What did they talk about? "Working out an agreement," to be sure. The episode was duly recorded by someone in Molotov's entourage. The report reached Beria, who kept it, biding his time. Now that report was produced as evidence in support of charges that on that very night Eden had recruited Molotov as a spy, a priceless acquisition for the British intelligence service. Only the "confidentiality" of the conversation in the compartment of the speeding night express could explain why Molotov disobeyed so willfully Stalin's peremptory order—never to be alone with foreigners.

For many years, Molotov had been the country's number two man, enjoying enormous respect among government officials. And although Stalin didn't care any longer what the people around him thought about his actions, in Molotov's case he had to take some steps to prepare public opinion. The arrest of Molotov's wife was a start but was still not enough to convince the country that Molotov had "defected," since the wives of others were also languishing in prisons. And so, in the last years of his life, Stalin was constantly trying to discredit Molotov. At the Central Committee's plenary meetings and in more restricted forums, he spoke about Molotov's "mistakes," his inability to resist the pressures of the imperialist forces, and his "capitulations" to the West. At the same time, he was gradually pushing Molotov into the background, eventually removing him from the Politburo. Everything seemed in place for the final strike— arresting Molotov and denouncing one of Stalin's closest colleagues as a spy and an enemy of the people with all the ensuing consequences. But at the last moment something got in the way—Stalin died.

Molotov spent the last years of his life, a widower, at his dacha in Zhukovka, near Moscow. In the company of his friends he invariably raised three toasts: "To Comrade Stalin! To Paulina! To communism!"

When asked "How come, Vyacheslav Mikhailovich? Stalin arrested Paulina, didn't he? And he nearly bumped you off, too, didn't he?" he had a pat answer: "Stalin was a great man."

New Times

By MARCH 1945, we were able to put together a group of translators and editors. Work got under way publishing the first issues of the English- and German-language editions of *War and the Working Class*. Soon it was decided to publish the magazine in French, too. I became the editor for the English and German editions, but my knowledge of French was not good enough to meet the required standards for quality and accuracy of translation. And so I had to look for a suitable person to do that job. At the Foreign Ministry a woman named Nina Chegodayeva, who had worked at the Soviet embassy in France before the war and who had an excellent command of French, was recommended.

After the defeat of Germany and the end of the war in Europe, the title of our magazine had become obsolete. Leontiev proposed that we all think about another title.

Pretty soon we had a whole list of names. Working through that list and discarding some suggestions, we came up with a short list, which Leontiev sent to Molotov, who, in turn, forwarded it to Stalin for final approval.

Admittedly, our ideas revolved around a rather limited set of titles, all of them for show. We had on our list *Peace and the Working Class, International Life, International Review, Periscope of International Life, World Orbit, Politics and Life*, and some others. Two weeks went by and we still had no answer. The date for printing our next issue was drawing nearer, and all the staffers were getting jittery, aware that it was inappropriate to keep the old title now that the war was over.

Finally a messenger arrived at our offices in Kalashny Street (the building was later transferred to the Japanese embassy). He delivered a large red envelope with five sealing-wax seals. We saw right away that it was from Stalin's secretariat. After signing the receipt for the package, Leontiev opened the envelope and pulled out the list with our suggestions. The first page had the familiar crisscross mark in a thick blue pencil all across it. In the bottom right-hand corner was the phrase, scribbled in large letters, *New Times* and the initials

J.S. The Great Leader hadn't liked any of our suggestions and had given the magazine a name of his own.

The issue was settled. Leontiev, however, was unhappy with Stalin's choice. Many people still remembered the extremely reactionary newspaper *New Times,* published before the Revolution by Suvorin, a member of the Black Hundred. Lenin had bitter disputes with it, calling it all kinds of bad names. As is well known, Lenin generously showered his opponents in debate with insulting invective and spiteful labels. For a brief period, the Moscow correspondent of the U.S. magazine *Time* was a Russian American named Amfitreatrov. Once he came to see me and proudly announced that Lenin frequently mentioned his grandfather in his writings. I got curious and checked the pages where the American journalist's grandfather was cited in Lenin's *Complete Works.* It turned out that the one name Lenin had for the *Time* correspondent's ancestor was "prostitute Amfitreatrov." As a writer, he had published many of the articles in *New Times* that had made Lenin spit polemical fire. However, what got our chief most worried was the fact that the editor in chief of Suvorin's publication had also been named Leontiev.

A draft cover design for the Russian, English, and German editions had already been commissioned, but Lev Abramovich was still troubled by doubts. He couldn't go against Stalin's decision, but the analogy was unacceptable. What if, after the next issue came out in print, somebody brought the unfortunate coincidence to the attention of the boss, who would then come down on the editorial board like a ton of bricks, demanding why we hadn't warned him about it earlier.

After painful hesitations Leontiev decided to raise the matter with Stalin after all. Technically this was easy since the magazine was connected to the Kremlin switchboard. When the phone linked to that system rang, Stalin usually picked it up himself. But it wasn't easy to pluck up the courage to disturb the Great Leader, let alone to question his decision.

Stalin listened to Leontiev's arguments, remained silent for a while, and then said:

"Well, it was one new time then, it's another one now. We won the war. The enemy has been defeated. Friends are all around us. New times have come."

And he hung up.

Leontiev's doubts were allayed.

Did Stalin really believe at that time that a new era had begun, that cooperation with the Western countries could be preserved, that there would be no more witch-hunts in our country, and that better times had indeed arrived for the Soviet Union and the rest of the world? Vast stretches of our land lay in ruins. Millions of people lived in the squalor of dugout huts, lacking the essentials. The Soviet Union had yet to make good on its promise to join the war against Japan. But that was regarded as a short-term operation. The priority task on the national agenda was to create conditions of life worthy of human dignity and to rehabilitate the devastated countryside. It is possible that at that time Stalin still believed that the Americans would help in this. Maybe he was even prepared to curb his appetite and to work out a compromise? After all, hadn't President Truman, after his recent move into the White House, provided assurances that he would continue Roosevelt's policies in international affairs?

Who was to blame that the relations between yesterday's allies deteriorated so quickly? Some Western scholars believe that the leaders of all three of the principal countries in the anti-Hitler coalition were equally interested in not keeping up good relations. In my opinion, right after the end of the war, the Soviet leadership tried to preserve an atmosphere of trust, while undermining it in a number of cases by its actions. Part of the blame is attributable to Stalin's suspiciousness, his tendency to think in terms of the past war, his preoccupation with creating around the Soviet Union a zone of buffer states with regimes he could totally rely on.

All that, of course, provoked an appropriate reaction from the United States and Britain. But then those countries didn't go out of their way to preserve a favorable climate, either. Truman's rude outbursts in conversation with Molotov, who was on his way to San Francisco to sign the United Nations charter, gave Stalin reason to believe that the new U.S. administration was departing from Roosevelt's political course. When later, at the Potsdam conference, Truman attempted to blackmail the Soviet Union with the A-bomb, Moscow perceived this as a serious threat. In turn, Stalin's subsequent moves were interpreted as a Soviet threat to the West. The level of confrontation heightened and the Cold War broke out. There was even a danger that the situation could escalate into armed conflict.

The United States mounted an internal campaign against communism. The Soviet Union responded with a no less virulent anti-imperialist drive. Both sides were readying their nations for a confrontation, while their people still preserved the warm feelings of friendship forged over the years of their joint fight against the common enemy. In the second half of the 1940s, a campaign to condemn "cosmopolitanism" and "foreign lifestyles" was launched in our country. I believe that it had two objectives: to promote hostility toward the "new aggressor," the United States, and to revive an atmosphere of fear at home.

I am sure that Stalin must have been haunted by the "specter of the Decembrist conspiracy." In the Patriotic War of 1812, the great struggle against Napoleon, hundreds of thousands of Russian officers and soldiers marched all the way to Paris in victory. Along their way they saw how differently people in Western Europe lived and how sharply their life contrasted with Russia's system of serfdom. Even after the defeat of Napoleon, France continued radiating the ideals of freedom, equality, and fraternity, and these the Russians eagerly absorbed and brought back to St. Petersburg. A few years went by and the Decembrists walked out on the Senate Square in open revolt against the czarist authorities.

Now multitudinous Soviet armies were marching through Berlin, Vienna, Prague, Budapest, crossing into the territories of Western European nations. They could see with their own eyes that even after five years of devastating war and Hitler's occupation, life there wasn't as bleak as it had been portrayed by Soviet propaganda and that the people in general had a better life than the Soviet people. Not only in East Prussia, but in Bohemia, Slovakia, and Hungary, the basements of the farmers' houses were well stocked with hams, sausages, and cheeses, all delicacies that our farmers, living under Stalin's institutionalized serfdom, had long forgotten. The Great Leader was getting apprehensive. What would happen when all those people, whom he had kept in isolation and ignorance for almost twenty years, returned home and began making comparisons?

He also had another concern. The war had freed people from their inferiority complex and the bureaucracy-conditioned reflex to wait for instructions from the top. During the war even a simple soldier, in order to survive, often had to make decisions and act as the situation warranted. That assumed a sense of freedom that Stalin had been trying to eradicate in his subjects. The war also freed people from fear, that mainstay of Stalin's system. Therefore, the system was in jeopardy and measures had to be taken to save it.

A campaign was launched to disparage all things foreign. The overzealous bureaucrats went so far as to rename the French roll, known under that name since before the Revolution, as a "city roll," and the famous Leningrad coffee shop Nord became Cafe Sever, Russian for "north." Soviet preeminence was to be demonstrated in everything, and where it was impossible to prove, the item had to be flatly rejected. Genetics and cybernetics were declared "bourgeois pseudo-sciences." If somebody dared speak favorably of some Western discovery, that person was branded a "cosmopolite without kith or kin" and an "idolater of foreign things." People who had remained in the territories occupied by the Germans were treated with suspicion. Information about this had to be provided on job applications, as if the people had deliberately chosen to stay under the Germans and were therefore somehow to blame. As if the Soviet leadership had not promised to defeat the aggressors on their own territory but had then allowed the Red Army to retreat as far as the Volga River and the Caucasus Mountains. Scores of thousands of POWs went to labor camps, blamed for not having retreated in time and for ending up surrounded, as if they hadn't stood fast under Stalin's direct orders. Arbitrary arrests resumed and "legal" proceedings were instituted against totally innocent people, as in the infamous "Leningrad case" and "the doctors' plot."

Stalin had reason to be pleased. Again he had the country gripped by fear. But his triumph became his personal tragedy. When he suffered a stroke, no one was there to help him. He had sent all his physicians to the dungeons.

Stalin's Death

THE YOUNG PEOPLE OF MY GENERATION didn't know about Stalin's atrocities. On the contrary, we thought he was like a wise, just, caring, if strict father of the peoples of our country. Why did we have to be afraid of him? We admired and worshiped him. To be next to him was the pinnacle of happiness, an honor that no one would ever be able to repay. I regarded the opportunity I had to interpret his words as a manifestation of full confidence in me, something that filled me with pride and a tremendous sense of responsibility. I wanted to do my job so that he would be pleased. His smile of approval was a priceless gift. I didn't identify the things that happened to my father with Stalin but rather with the bad people who had penetrated his inner circle. Was it not Stalin who with his article "Dizzy With Success" had tried to put the brakes on the runaway forced collectivization? He didn't hesitate to remove or execute the people who violated "socialist law." Yagoda, Yezhov, and other butchers paid with their lives for their hideous crimes. He was also ruthless to those who departed from or perverted Lenin's teaching.

Millions and millions of Soviet people shared that thinking then. I was one of them who just happened to have the good and rare fortune to be near the Great Leader.

During the war when I was often summoned to Stalin, the wave of repressions was on the wane. Few people I knew personally disappeared. The sacrifices and hardships of those terrible years brought the people together, made them more devoted to their homeland—and more committed to the cause of socialism. We believed that the nightmares of the past, with enemies and saboteurs all around us, would never come back to haunt us. The new arrests and show trials of the late 1940s appeared preposterous and unintelligible. It was hard to believe that new enemies had appeared. We had won, hadn't we? The Soviet system had endured, hadn't it? Hitler's formidable war machine had been incapable of destroying it. Who was going to carry out acts of sabotage anyway? It didn't make any sense.

It was at that time that many people, including me, began to have doubts. Something was wrong somewhere. Somebody was again trying to hurl the country into the abyss of repression and violence. Somebody, but, of course, not Stalin—the Generalissimo, the Supreme Commander, the Great Leader at the pinnacle of his success and fame.

Stalin's death hit me hard. For me he was not just the leader of our country, a faithful follower of Lenin and the alpha and omega of all we lived by before, during, and after the war. For me he was someone I had known personally, someone I had sat next to, hanging on his every word in an effort to get across to his interlocutor the tone and tenor of his every thought. When he died, I no longer felt heartbroken over the fact that he had spurned me. What was my puny pain compared to the irreparable loss for our people and for humanity as a whole! I didn't grieve over the fact that I hadn't gained his affection, unaware that this lonely and morbidly suspicious man wasn't attached even to the people closest to him, not even to his sons. We all felt orphaned by his death. I thought I would cherish as a precious relic my memory of the demigod who bestowed the ultimate honor upon me by allowing me, from time to time, to be in his presence in the course of four years that had flashed by like lightning.

The 20th Party Congress shattered the graven image my mind had fashioned. When I first heard Khrushchev's secret speech, I didn't want to believe it. But going over its details and recalling the gruesome accounts of the victims of Stalin's repressions, I felt cruelly betrayed by my fallen idol.

My reaction to the 20th Party Congress was already more calm and realistic. All of us, both the Party and the Soviet people, had fallen victim to horrendous lies and mystification. The object of our worship had duped his credulous followers into believing his pipe dreams. Later, when I began putting down on paper my recollections of what I had witnessed during the war years, I tried to present as objectively as possible what I had seen and heard, without excessive emotion, going only by the facts as I knew them.

Today, when an avalanche of new disclosures of Stalin's atrocities descends upon us and new crimes of his system against our country and other states come to light every day, I believe it is important, while condemning and castigating the bloody iniquities of Stalin's regime, to continue to write an objective story about the past.

My observations led me to conclude that Beria was not the only one who had a pathological obsession with the fair sex. Unbridled sexual appetites also caused Dekanozov's first fall from grace. After the war, he seduced a girl who turned out to be the daughter of a ranking government official close to Molotov. When that happened, Stalin didn't step in to cover his protégé. Dekanozov was reprimanded by his Party cell and was fired from the People's Commissariat for Foreign Affairs.

However, as always was the case with the Party *nomenklatura*, Dekanozov was not allowed to fall too low. He landed on his feet with a job as deputy chairman of the State Committee on Radio Broadcasting. And soon he began to rise again. One of his buddies, Merkulov, the chief of the Main Directorate for Soviet Property Abroad, known under its Soviet acronym Gusimz, made Dekanozov his first deputy. Gusimz not only managed our vast spoils of war, but effectively directed the organized plunder of the countries of East-

ern Europe. Entire mansions and palatial residences were moved out
and brought into our country for the enjoyment of our top government and military elite. The buildings were taken apart before the
transfer and then reassembled on Moscow's suburban estates. Automobiles, sculptures, paintings, etc., were moved by the trainload.
That was how some "proletarian" bureaucrats started their "private
collections." Gusimz's activities also laid the groundwork for cataclysms that would shake Eastern Europe.

Gusimz, however, was not the highest rung of the career ladder
that Dekanozov reached. Right after Stalin's death, Beria made him
the KGB chairman in Georgia. In the summer of 1953, he was arrested in the republic's capital, Tbilisi, along with the other members
of Beria's group, including his former sponsor Merkulov. They were
all tried by a military tribunal and then shot by a firing squad in December of that same year.

The tribunal hearing was closed, and to this day we do not know the
charges brought against those accused. According to the grapevine,
Beria allegedly assigned Dekanozov the task of putting together
groups of hit men to be secretly dispatched to Moscow for a coup he
was preparing. In this connection Khrushchev writes in his memoirs:

> By the 1950s, I had come to the conclusion that, when Stalin
> died, it was critical to do everything possible to stop Beria from
> securing a leading position in the Party because that would
> mean the end of the Party. I even thought that, were this to hap-
> pen, we could lose the gains of the Revolution and that he
> would put the country not on the Socialist but on the Capitalist
> track.

After Beria's arrest there were rumors that he had been planning
to disband the kolkhozes and to set up private farms. The plotters
were accused of advocating a market-oriented economy in the Soviet
Union and joint ventures with capitalist companies. Beria, born in
the village of Merkhiuli, close to Sukhumi, patronized that city and
gave his blessing to the construction of a stunning embankment
there and places of entertainment in an area known as Stalin's Hill.
It was claimed that his ultimate objective was to turn Sukhumi Bay
into the Nice of Abkhazia, the Riviera of the Caucasus, by selling it
off to foreign capital to construct international hotels and gambling
casinos. A secret letter, drafted by the Party's Central Committee and

read out at closed meetings, informed Party members that Beria wanted to withdraw the Soviet forces from Austria and to normalize our relations with Yugoslavia by sending his secret envoy to Tito.

Back in 1953, those allegations were crimes of sedition whose perpetrators deserved capital punishment. But by 1955, a state treaty with Austria was signed and all foreign forces, including the Soviet troops there, departed. That same year Khrushchev himself traveled to meet with Tito and declared that the break with Yugoslavia, provoked by Stalin, had been a mistake.

Generally speaking and on the basis of information that is mainly hearsay, much of what the plotters were accused of appears in an entirely different light today. It turns out that we had a chance to set up private farms forty years ago. Maybe that would have spared us at least one problem, that of food shortages. When Khrushchev committed himself to leading our country along the socialist path and promised to "bury" America, the Soviet farmers lost even the tiny private gardens they had had under Stalin.

Beria, of course, was a bloody butcher, a rapist, and a revolting pervert. But now we know that other Soviet leaders also had the blood of innocent victims on their hands. Before Beria, there were Yagoda, Yezhov, and all the others who had not hesitated to shoot innocent people or who derived sadistic pleasure from torturing millions of victims of Stalin's purges in interrogation rooms and maximum-security labor camps. The records of Beria's trial should be made public to determine whether it was just a power struggle at the top or whether fundamental differences over the future of our country were at issue.

Recommendations of Josef Wirth

WHEN I RECALL my early work at *New Times* magazine, I have to admit that, all in all, it was an interesting period for me. I was soon co-opted as a member of the editorial board and made its executive secretary. The foreign-language editions now had new editors, and I only had to keep track generally of what they were doing. The executive secretary had varied responsibilities, ranging from those relat-

ing to journalism and publishing as such, to administrative, personnel, and financial matters. While it was a well-paying job, I was also
able to make some extra money by publishing my own articles.

In 1947, my first book, *The Deceived Generation*, came out from
Molodaya Gvardiya Publishers. It was a study of the problems facing
the youth in Great Britain. At that time we broke our hearts thinking
about the hard life of the young men and women of Britain, blissfully
unaware that in actual fact successive generations of our own people
had been brainwashed into believing that two or three five-year plans
down the road they would all live happily ever after while the capitalist countries would be left trailing in the dust.

Now we have awakened to broken promises and shattered dreams.
But at that time I was proud of my first major work, which was subsequently translated into English.

All our magazine staffers were allowed to stock up on food at a special store for the government elite that offered a wide range of quality foodstuffs. In that respect I was much better off working for the
magazine than in Molotov's secretariat. But I wasn't completely
happy. I was haunted by my still vivid memories of the past. I missed
my involvement, albeit indirect, in big-time politics, being privy to
the political decisions taken at the top government level and the special feeling I had had of being close to the two leaders, Stalin and
Molotov. Every night I had the same painfully tantalizing but, more
often, frightening visions in which the joy of light was whimsically in-
terwoven with the despair of falling down a dark abyss. On sleepless
nights I relived again and again the unforgettable moments of thrill
I experienced each time before going to see the Great Leader. Here
I am walking along that unforgettable corridor leading to his offices.
I am going past a security guard who salutes me. Here is that door
next to which General Vlasik is taking his usual nap. I am trying to
open the door but it doesn't give. Vlasik gets up to his full height and
brushes me aside with his arm. "You are not allowed to go in there!"
I hear a voice reaching me from somewhere far below. The floor
cracks open and I am falling into a black hole. . . . This scene or similar variations on the theme "the fall of the interpreter" play out in
my mind night after night.

The habit of many years of working until the crack of dawn keeps
me at my desk after regular office hours. When all leave, I stay in my
office to read Tass information bulletins or the U.S. and British newspapers we subscribe to. As I read, the names of U.S. and British politi-

cians come alive and serve as a painful reminder that I have been expelled from their midst. Maybe I should throw the papers away and forget about them, but my hand keeps reaching out for them, as if I needed to scratch an itching wound. My Foreign Ministry colleagues of yesterday, whom I encouraged as they made their first tentative steps in their diplomatic careers, are becoming consuls general, envoys, or ambassadors, while for me this path is forever closed. They all turned their backs on me the moment I was fired. On Victory Day, nobody came to see me or even called to share the joy. To think that only recently they were jostling to have me over as their guest. On May 9, 1945, only two men, my former fellow servicemen in the navy, stopped in at the office with a bottle of champagne, and we headed for Red Square, packed with jubilant crowds.

It was especially hard to read the bulletins about the Yalta conference. It seemed that only yesterday I was near all its participants. I was to travel with them to the Crimea, to walk inside the Livadia Palace and to interpret Stalin's conversations with Roosevelt and Churchill. Over the four years I had grown used to the idea that I was always needed on such occasions. I felt so hurt, so humiliated, that I could cry. What's an interpreter? The negotiators are deaf and dumb without one. The interpreter is needed, necessary and irreplaceable. But now I see that he is needed only in his professional capacity—and not as a person. The person may vanish, but the professional will take the shape of another person. The former person is gone, but nothing has really changed.

I could understand that in my mind but could not accept it in my heart. Reopening the old wound, I kept reasoning with myself: I was not just an interpreter; I was an assistant to the minister of foreign affairs. But even in that capacity I didn't amount to much, although I tried to perform my functions efficiently and conscientiously. I overrated myself then, thinking that I had some special abilities and that therefore I couldn't be kicked out just like that. I remembered a pronouncement by the Great Leader—"Our cadres are our greatest asset"; but then another aphorism was attributed to him: "No person is irreplaceable." Even more capable people, whom the country needed, were dumped "on the dust heap of history" or physically eliminated. I should be grateful to be alive and have a fairly good job! But my wounded pride kept gnawing away at my heart. I felt as if my life was finished. My body was aching all over. More and more often I was gripped by a paralyzing indifference. At thirty, I felt old and feeble.

My night vigils took a toll on my family life. The birth of our second son in 1947 did not save our rocky marriage. Then came another woman, an infatuation verging on insanity, with wild scenes of jealousy and reconciliation, of patching up and breaking off. It was all a sweet and horrible nightmare. However, the woes of my heart cured my depression and numbed my grief over my "paradise lost."

In March 1953, when Stalin died, I was crying together with millions of other Soviet people, but no longer feeling hurt at being disdainfully thrown out.

In early April 1954, soon after Beria's execution, the phone in my bachelor's apartment rang. Kozyrev, whose voice I hadn't heard in ten years, said matter-of-factly, "Vyacheslav Mikhailovich would like to see you on an urgent matter."

After the death of the Great Leader, Molotov, who had just escaped disaster by a hair's breadth, was reinstated on the Politburo and again became first deputy to the chairman of the Council of Ministers and minister of foreign affairs. Malenkov was made chairman of the Council of Ministers. Beria became his deputy and also got the job of the minister of the interior. Khrushchev was given the duties of secretary of the Party's Central Committee, which in those days was not regarded as a key post.

Over the last years, a number of high-rise buildings, resembling the Kremlin towers, had gone up around Moscow. Stalin had a liking for them. The Ministry of Foreign Affairs had moved into the high-rise in Smolenskaya Square. My pass was left with the security guard at the main entrance. All excited and at a loss over the reason for the sudden call from the minister, I went to the seventh floor where his secretariat was located. "It's a good thing the ministry has moved from Kuznetsky Most Street and that I'm not going to see Molotov in his only too familiar office in the Kremlin," I was saying to myself. "I wouldn't want to break my heart again. Here, at the Foreign Ministry building in Smolenskaya Square, everything is different."

When I walked into the secretariat, Kozyrev told me to go right in since the minister was expecting me.

Molotov remained seated at his desk. He nodded at me and invited me to take the chair in front of him. Everything looked exactly as it had during the four years I had worked for him, as if a full decade had not gone by. I felt as if I had seen him only yesterday or maybe even that morning. He didn't ask how I was doing or where I had lived all those years but came directly to the point:

"A session of the World Peace Council will open in Vienna tomorrow. We want to send you there on a mission. According to our information, the chancellor of the former Weimar Republic, Josef Wirth, will attend the conference. You will have to meet him. It is best that you travel there as the *New Times* correspondent covering the meeting. You will introduce yourself to Wirth in that capacity. You will ask him to give you an interview for the magazine on the peace movement. However, we also have another interest. We are currently reviewing the international situation. We feel that we have become isolated. Something needs to be done to break out of it. We also think it is important to formulate a new European policy. Wirth, who as far back as 1922, during the Rapallo period, spoke favorably of the cooperation between Germany and Soviet Russia, may have interesting ideas about what approach we should now take to European problems and, more specifically, how we should deal with West Germany. I hope you understand what we have in mind?"

"Yes, Vyacheslav Mikhailovich. I will do my best."

As I was listening to Molotov speak, a thought crossed my mind: once again my life was taking a new turn. Of course, he could have assigned that mission to any officer in the Foreign Ministry, but for some reason, he had decided to call on me. Maybe because I had had experience working with the Germans before the war? In recent years, Molotov had been kept away from the formulation of foreign policy and from the Foreign Ministry staffers. And I was somebody he knew personally. That was probably why he was entrusting me with this delicate mission. I was particularly struck by the fact that it involved a trip abroad. It was true that Soviet forces were then stationed in Austria; but there were also U.S., British, and French units there, and there were no barriers between the four occupation zones in Vienna. Once in Austria, a person could head in any direction, including west. At that time, such a trip abroad, given my specific situation, was a sign of special trust. And Molotov, who hadn't seen me all those years, was giving me a clear signal that he trusted me. I found that show of confidence, coupled with the fact that he had actually wrenched me from Beria's clutches in 1945, totally incredible and out of character for a man who had been, let's face it, ruthless and who prided himself on being "as solid as a rock." He had never been sentimental. Maybe he thought the time had come to right the wrong that had been done to me. Or maybe he had become softer at heart after the injustices he and his wife had suffered.

"Of course, Wirth must not be aware that you are acting on instructions from our government," Molotov went on. "Just drop a hint that certain influential people in Moscow would like to know his opinions and that his views will be treated with respect. When you get back, give me a detailed briefing. You will now be given special papers valid for the trip to Austria. You are leaving tomorrow morning. A hotel in Vienna has been booked for you. Good luck!"

"Thank you for the trust you place in me," I rattled off from force of long-established habit of thanking the Party for everything, even when, on extremely rare occasions, it was merely atoning for its sins.

It is really incredible with what lightning speed our system can sometimes function! The moment I stepped outside Molotov's office, Kozyrev handed me my purple-colored photo ID with the Ministry seal and an exit visa. As it turned out, my personal file, with a few photos in it, had been kept in the secretariat all through those long years. In addition to my papers, I also got my plane ticket.

The plane was leaving from the Vnukovo at seven A.M. I didn't even have time to tell the people at the office about my trip. As I learned later, Leontiev had been informed by Molotov. At the Vienna airport I was met by a Soviet embassy representative who had been advised about my arrival by coded cable. I got a room in the Hotel Imperial, commandeered by the Red Army and managed—or maybe *mismanaged* was the more appropriate word—by the army's administrative branch. After several years of the occupation, a once posh hotel presented a sorry sight. One of its two elevators was out of order, room service was erratic, and the washbasins and baths had rusty spots from the leaking faucets. The restaurant and the cafe were closed— there wasn't even a place to boil water to make tea. But I found all those discomforts trifling. The important thing was that, after having been grounded for ten years, I was in Vienna and, on top of that, entrusted with an important government mission.

That evening, I went to the opening session of the World Peace Council. The corridors were already filled with the participants, guests, and correspondents. The fragrance of freshly brewed coffee, expensive cigars, and some intoxicating perfume floated in the air. Later I learned that the dizzying smell was the French perfume Chanel No. 5, still unknown in our country. In those years, world-renowned political figures, scholars, and writers participated in the peace movement. At the conference I met Bertrand Russell, Irène Joliot-Curie, Ilya Ehrenburg, and, of course, Josef Wirth. I decided not to rush things and not to impose myself with my interview right away, but first to get my bearings in the unfamiliar situation and to make contact with as many participants as I could.

I also met there a popular playwright of the time, Aleksandr Korneichuk, whom I had known in Kiev. He had been a frontline correspondent since the beginning of the war, but often came to Moscow since his wife, the Polish writer Wanda Wasilevskaya, was a member of the Moscow-based Polish Liberation Committee. She was a tall woman, no longer young, wearing a military-style jacket, riding breeches, and high boots. By her side, Korneichuk looked diminutive and young.

At that time, a humorous verse about the couple could be heard at the front line:

> We got a strongly worded wire
> That gave our headquarters quite a shock:
> "Welcome Wanda Wasilevskaya,
> Husband of playwright Korneichuk."

By the end of the war Aleksandr Korneichuk was appointed deputy commissar for foreign affairs in charge of the Slav countries' desk, and I often saw him at Molotov's office where he attended the meetings of the Collegium of the People's Commissariat for Foreign Affairs. He usually sat at the end of the long table and mostly kept silent. Molotov would sometimes comment, a twinkle in his eyes:

"Look at Korneichuk. He is sitting here making mental notes of everything that's going on, and then he will make us characters in his next comedy."

The Vienna conference had morning and afternoon sessions, while in the evening a cultural program was offered. The city authorities invited us to the Vienna Opera to hear Mozart's *The Abduction From the Seraglio*, to a performance of works by Johann Strauss, and to see a political satire at a cabaret. One of the three sketches at the cabaret stuck in my memory. An actor was sitting on a Viennese chair placed in the middle of the stage. He was wearing a strange uniform—on his left leg he had on Red Army khaki pants tucked into a soldier's boot, while his right leg was wrapped in American leggings, a GI boot on his foot. Half of his jacket and the shoulder board were part of the British uniform, while the other half was French. An Austrian in an Alpine cap would run out onto the stage and shout something to which only one part of the body, let's say the Soviet leg, would react, while the rest of the body remained motionless. Then the same thing happened with the American leg, the French or British hands. The parts of the body moved separately, but the soldier wearing the four-uniformed costume stayed put. Finally, the despairing Austrian ran out on the stage again and shouted at the top of his voice, "The Chinese are coming!" On hearing that, the actor jumped up from his chair and, to laughter and applause from the audience, dashed off the stage. All those present clearly got the message: the Austrians wanted to be rid of the four occupying powers as quickly as possible.

One night, the Soviet political commissar in Vienna invited the journalists accredited to the Peace Council to his residence to watch a documentary about the capture of Berlin. During the break a small reception was held with chilled vodka and all kinds of snacks. A uniformed waiter was serving drinks. I looked at him and was startled. It was Lakomov, Ambassador Dekanozov's cook in Berlin before the war. We were glad to see each other—for the first time in thirteen years!—and gave each other a hug and a kiss. We talked about the past, recalling the time in late June 1941, already after Hitler's invasion of Russia, when we were locked inside the Soviet embassy in Berlin and arranged a lunch for SS Hauptsturmführer Heineman, who helped me to get Sasha Korotkov out of the embassy compound to meet with the German underground fighters.

Josef Wirth immediately accepted my request for an interview for *New Times* magazine. We met at the Ambassador Hotel where he was staying. Unlike our Hotel Imperial, his place was in perfect order since it was maintained by Austrian personnel. Everything was sparkling clean, the lobby had carpets and exotic plants, a uniformed operator stood motionless by the elevator ready to spring into action. He took me to my floor in a noiseless, high-speed car. In general, in a few years after the war, the Austrians managed to create a decent living in their country. The well-arranged store windows displayed an abundance of food and goods. The people in the coffee shops and in the street were tastefully, if somewhat extravagantly, clothed. Flowers were everywhere. There were still few automobiles in the streets, but the city was filled with relatively cheap motorbikes, which had become quite fashionable. Young men with their girlfriends riding behind them, their hair streaming in the wind, added a special charm to the city.

It was a sunny, cloudless day. Through the open window of Wirth's room we could see the kaleidoscopic roof of the St. Stephen's Cathedral. My gracious host ordered coffee and we made ourselves comfortable in the wicker chairs by the low round table. First we talked about the Vienna meeting of the World Peace Council. Wirth spoke at length about how important it was to fight for peace and to have prominent public figures involved. He expressed regret that the struggle for peace had not become a mass movement. That was why national leaders could ignore calls for disarmament and continue the arms race. In his opinion the press could play an important role, but for the time being it was distorting rather than bringing into sharper focus the objectives of the movement. Wirth believed that the international situation was quite complicated and that the Cold War had hamstrung a Europe that was still unable to overcome the trauma of World War II. That comment gave me an opening to ask my main questions.

"I believe that one of the key issues in Europe is the problem of Germany," Wirth explained. "At present there are two Germanys, and I think Washington will not accept any of your proposals about a confederation or some other form of a union between the German states. The United States has a firm grip on the western part of the country and it won't let go. Your current relations with Bonn are awful. Your propaganda machine is portraying Adenauer as a militarist, almost a neofascist. This is factually wrong and only complicates matters. In reality, Adenauer himself was a victim of the Nazi persecutions in the past and is a person not easy to define in simple terms. Of course, he is anticommunist, but he is also a German patriot in his own way. And in his way, he finds his 'friendship' with the Americans somewhat burdensome and would like to establish a dialogue with Moscow. But you must also show readiness for this."

"What do you think we should do, Mr. Chancellor?" I asked.

"The Soviet government has a number of trump cards it could play. First of all is the thousands of POWs whose fates are a cause of concern for all the Germans. The question of the burials of the German soldiers killed on Soviet territory is also of considerable significance. It is, of course, mainly symbolic. Many burial sites have already been leveled to the ground. But a move in this regard would be very important for Adenauer in moral terms. Finally, the question of the second Germany—which Bonn still regards as a zone of Soviet occupation. A number of issues arise here: family reunification, property claims, etc. I think you should sound out West Germany about the prospects of reestablishing relations. Maybe you should start with the question of the return of the POWs. In parallel with this, you could discuss establishing diplomatic relations between Moscow and Bonn. I believe that when things get off the ground as a result of the initial contacts, Adenauer will be prepared to come to Moscow, which would be an important event both on practical and symbolic levels."

I found all those considerations quite reasonable. The problem of the POWs, for instance, was ripe for solution. Over ten years had gone by since they had been captured. Recently, I had had occasion to meet many of them. In the village of Pavshino, outside Moscow, shops had been set up for the German POWs, who had practiced a variety of trades in their previous civilian lives: they had been tailors, carpenters, plumbers, and so on. People on the staff of a number of magazines got special coupons they could use to order all sorts of things in those shops. Some people bought plumbing items or wood-work or even whole sets of furniture for their living rooms or their kitchens. I had a few suits made to order and the quality was excep-tional. During the fitting sessions, my tailor and I spoke German and even became friends.

On the whole, the life of the POWs wasn't too bad. They could practice their trades and seemed to be doing it with inspiration. Their village of small cottages was kept in excellent condition; it had a community center, sports grounds, flower beds, and yellow sand-strewn paths planted with young trees on both sides. Compared to the inhuman conditions of the Soviet POWs who had been captured by Germany, they lived in paradise. Nevertheless, after the long years of captivity, they were terribly homesick—which was indeed under-standable.

"And what do you think about the European policy of the Soviet Union, Herr Wirth?" I asked.

"Here, too, you have to break out of the circle of isolation and hos-tility. In the years after the war, an enemy image has taken strong hold over the minds of millions in the West. The Soviet Union has to try to convince Western Europe, backing its words with appropriate actions, that it poses no threat. The first question to be addressed is the withdrawal of all the occupation forces from Austria. It is also im-portant to relaunch the process of consultation among the foreign ministers of the victorious powers. And although Indochina is far away, a settlement in that region will promote an effective policy to normalize the situation in Europe. The French have bogged down in Indochina and want out—if possible, without losing face. Your friends the Chinese can be helpful in this regard. An international conference on Indochina would perhaps be the best way to proceed. That meeting would also be important for contacts between the leading politicians of the major international players. In brief, there are at present many problems that call for Soviet initiatives."

Wirth gave me a whole set of recommendations. Now I had things to report to Molotov. But I also wanted to talk to Josef Wirth as a man who had been witness to the landmark events of the recent past. For me he personified history itself! Rapallo . . . the spring of 1922. Chicherin, the Soviet commissar for foreign affairs, carrying the instructions signed by Lenin, is conducting negotiations in Italy with the leaders of the Entente. The Allies are insisting that Soviet Russia, an entity they still do not officially recognize, pay the outstanding debts of the czarist and provisional governments. Only after that can there be talk of recognition. Chicherin categorically rejects these demands. The shadow of defeated Germany is lurking behind the backs of the negotiators. The political leaders—British prime minister Lloyd George, French foreign minister Louis Barthou, German chancellor Josef Wirth, German foreign minister Walther Rathenau—all have official and unofficial contacts. Chicherin, fluent in English, French, German, and Italian, also conducts informal talks. The Western nations are trying to keep Soviet Russia isolated. But Chicherin manages to make a breakthrough. He puts forward attractive proposals to the Germans, who are getting rough treatment from Britain and France. The head of the Eastern Desk at the German Foreign Ministry, Malzahn, talks Rathenau into accepting the Soviet proposals. Wirth also concurs with them. Diplomatic and consular relations between Germany and Soviet Russia are immediately reestablished.

I ask Wirth to tell me how it actually happened then.

"The situation was indeed critical. We reached agreement with the Soviets on all points in the course of one night and signed the accord before dawn. The following morning it was as if a bomb had exploded. The British and the French were furious and demanded that the agreement be canceled. We found ourselves in a very difficult situation. President Ebert was leaning toward an agreement with the Western allies and we had a tough job talking him out of it. On the whole, it was a good and proper agreement, and it eased the situation for Germany."

"You are very highly thought of in our country, Herr Chancellor, precisely because of the role you played in concluding the Treaty of Rapallo," I said.

"Well, I am very pleased to hear that."

We said goodbye to each other, and I headed back to the Imperial to make a detailed record of our conversation.

The day after my return to Moscow I briefed Molotov on my meeting with Josef Wirth and handed him a memo of the conversation.

After a cursory glance at my report, Molotov said, "I can see you have done a pretty good job. What are your plans now? Maybe you want to return to work at the Ministry?"

I hadn't been sure I would get that offer. But I had thought it over anyway—just in case. By that time I was already quite content to work as a journalist. Compared to the Foreign Ministry, I had much more freedom, independence, and room for initiative. From a financial point of view, too, no matter what I was offered, my job on the staff of the magazine was a far better deal. Neither was I too thrilled at the prospect of going back to the past after many years of disfavor. I thanked Molotov and said that I wanted to stay a journalist.

"Well, you have the right to decide," Molotov said, not pressing the issue.

I had to prepare an article for publication in our magazine about the Vienna sessions of the World Peace Council and my interview with Josef Wirth. Previously, I had published my material under a pen name; however, when I traveled to Vienna and interviewed the former German chancellor, I used my real name. I had to seek Molotov's advice.

"You can use your own name now," he said firmly. "There is no need to use a pseudonym any longer."

Molotov no longer feared for my life. Beria had been executed. But still, aware of the ways of our bureaucrats, Molotov thought it necessary to protect me a little longer. He included me in the group of correspondents who covered the 1954 Geneva conference on Indochina and the Geneva summit in the summer of 1955, and he recommended me to be among the seven Soviet journalists who, in the fall of 1955, toured the United States, the first Soviet journalists to do so since the beginning of the Cold War.

It was a spectacular journey. For the whole month the U.S. press carried front-page reports on our travels and on our meetings with U.S. political figures. It was on that trip—in the city of New York—

that I met John F. Kennedy, who was a senator from Massachusetts at the time.

From then on things took on a momentum of their own.

As for the recommendations of Josef Wirth, much of what he suggested was soon realized. In early 1954, the foreign ministers of the great powers met in Berlin. In the summer of that same year a conference on Indochina took place in Geneva. And in 1955 a treaty with Austria was signed, soon followed by the withdrawal of the occupation forces from its territory. Then Adenauer came to Moscow. Diplomatic relations between the Soviet Union and West Germany were established, and the German POWs went back to their homeland.

Meeting With Chou En-lai

MY WORK ON THE FOREIGN-LANGUAGE EDITIONS of *War and the Working Class* had begun with a search for qualified translators. At that time the best language specialists in Moscow were to be found in two places: the Inostrannaya Literatura (Foreign Literature) Publishers, later to become Progress Publishers, and the weekly *Moscow News*. The newspaper published only a limited number of copies in Russian, just enough so that the bosses in the propaganda department in the Communist Party's Central Committee could monitor its contents. Few people were even aware that a Russian-language version existed. The Russians themselves referred to the newspaper by its English name, *Moscow News*, in the belief that it came out only in English. The newspaper's editor in chief was Michael Borodin, and I turned to him for help.

At first I didn't know a thing about the business of producing a periodical. But Borodin and his staff were encouraging and ready to help me learn all the intricacies of what was for me a new field. So much so that over a number of weeks I took what amounted to a hands-on training course at the *Moscow News*. The arrangement suited me perfectly since the newspaper offices were located in the same building in Moskvin Street where I had my apartment.

Borodin and I became good friends. I found him especially interesting and informative after I learned that he was the same Borodin
whose name had often been seen in the world press in the late 1930s
and early 1940s. At that time he was a Soviet adviser to the Chiang
Kai-shek government in China and played a major role in resolving
the disputes between the Communist Party of China and the Kuomintang, helping organize their joint resistance to the Japanese invaders. When the Chinese government moved to Chungking, after
the Japanese occupied much of China, Borodin followed it there.
His residence was close to the mission of the Chinese Communist
Party, headed by Chou En-lai.

Borodin told me a lot about that man, whom he described as a talented politician, a well-educated, sober-minded, even-tempered
leader, and a strong and vigorous man. Borodin shared with me the
details of the "Sian incident," which at the time created quite a stir,
when two Chinese warlords—Chang Hsüeh-liang and Yen Hsi-
shan—invited Chiang Kai-shek to their headquarters for negotiations but then arrested him and were preparing to kill him. The leadership of the Communist Party understood that dissension within the
Kuomintang would undermine resistance to the Japanese invasion.
Although the Communists suffered much at the hands of the Kuomintang, they couldn't allow the elimination of the country's recognized leader. The delicate mission to resolve the situation was entrusted to Chou En-lai.

While Chiang Kai-shek was kept under arrest in an adjoining
room, Chou En-lai spent many hours trying to persuade the warlords
to abandon their plot and to release their prisoner in the interests of
China. Eventually, the generals agreed to set Chiang Kai-shek free.

Borodin had many interesting stories to tell me about China, kin-
dling my interest in a country I had never visited. However, our contacts were abruptly broken off. One day when I stopped by at the
Moscow News, I didn't find Borodin there. I was told that he hadn't
showed up at the office for the past few days and was probably sick.
A week later we learned that Borodin had been arrested. He was declared a Japanese spy and we never saw him again.

Many years later I traveled to China on assignment. Among other
cities, I visited Chungking. The city has turned the apartments of
Chou En-lai and Borodin into museums of sorts. Photos are hung on
the walls, their household articles and personal things are laid out on
tables and stands. Borodin's portrait is in a metal frame—a manly

face with a twinkle in his smiling eyes. This is how I remember him, a committed fighter, one of the many slaughtered by Stalin's butchers.

I also visited Sian. In actual fact, the Sian incident didn't take place in the town itself but at a little place called Huatsi, located near some hot springs about forty kilometers away. Over a thousand years ago, under the T'ang dynasty, here on the slopes of the Tsinling Mountains was an exotic park and right by the spring itself the imperial palace, where Emperor Ming Huang kept his lovely concubine Yang Kuei-fei, one of the five legendary beauties of ancient China. Next to Yang Kuei-fei's arbor, which has survived to this day, was a garden house where Chiang Kai-shek stayed. The warlords decided to seize him there at night. The premier's bodyguards put up a fight and shooting broke out. Chiang was awakened by the uproar and jumped out a window. He tried to climb the mountain but got trapped in a crevasse where his pursuers found him.

In early 1957, when I arrived in Beijing as a *New Times* correspondent, I immediately turned to the Foreign Ministry for help in arranging an interview with one of the Chinese leaders. I couldn't possibly count on a meeting with Mao Tse-tung, and that was why in the letter I wrote I mentioned the names of Chou En-lai, Liu Shao-ch'i and Marshal Chu Teh. I sent the letter and set off on a trip around the country. After my visit to Chungking, which brought back memories of my conversations with Borodin, I felt a strong urge to meet Chou En-lai. But when I returned to Beijing, I found no reply to my request. Before leaving for Manchuria, I decided to spend a few days in the capital. I asked the hotel administrator to get me two tickets to the Chinese opera (one for me and one for my interpreter).

As usual, the house was packed. Before the show began, ushers in white gowns poured hot green tea from huge zinc-coated kettles into the spectators' cups. Our seats were in the fifth row on the right. I noticed that one chair, the one to my right, was empty. The lights went out leaving only the footlights dimly lighting the hall. At that moment a Chinese sat down next to me. I had time to notice only that he was wearing, like everyone else in the audience, a blue military-cut jacket, a cap of the same fabric, and cloth slippers. The curtain went up and the faces of the people in the audience lit up. I squinted my eyes and saw that the man sitting next to me looked very much like Chou En-lai. "This can't be," I thought to myself. If it were, the audience would be going wild. There would be applause and cheers. And

how could he possibly show up at the theater just like that—with no
bodyguards and no special box but seated with the simple folks? But
I still leaned over to my interpreter on my left and asked if he knew
who the man sitting next to me was. He answered matter-of-factly,
"That is Chou En-lai."

I was staggered. The people in the audience riveted their eyes on
the stage as the plot unfolded. They were oblivious of the presence
in their midst of the chairman of the country's State Council, the famous and popular leader of the still young Chinese Revolution. They
were completely absorbed in the struggle of the King of the Monkeys
with the Monster, the story about the love of a lass named Peach
Flower for a simple lad and how she was kidnapped by robbers. While
following the antics of the actors on the stage with half my mind, I
tried to figure out what the presence of the Chinese leader by my side
could possibly mean. Would I be able to talk to him? Was he going to
stay during the intermission or would he fade away into obscurity as
mysteriously as he had materialized from it?

The curtain fell and the lights came up. Normally, Chinese theaters do not have lobbies. During intermissions, the audience walks
right out into the street. The hall was quickly emptying. Nobody was
even looking our way.

"He hasn't been recognized!" flashed through my mind.

Chou En-lai remained seated. I was tense. How could I start the
conversation? What could I start with?

Before I made up my mind, he said to me in good English, "And
from where are you coming to our country?"

Of course, he knew everything about me. I had ordered my tickets
at the hotel in advance and his sitting next to me was no coincidence.
But he also had to start off the conversation somehow. By that time,
I was already deputy editor in chief of our magazine, and I had come
to China on a six-month assignment as its special correspondent.
That was how I introduced myself to Chou En-lai.

"And who is your editor in chief now?"

I told him that the job had recently been given to Leontiev, who
had been its deputy editor when the magazine first came out.

"Lev Leontiev, the prominent economist. I know him quite well. In
the 1920s I attended his lectures at the Moscow Institute of the Peoples of the East. Please give him my regards and very best wishes."

"I certainly will. Thank you."

"Do you know what happened to Borodin? Where is he now?"

I was prepared for that question, yet I jumped when it came. Did he know about Borodin's tragic fate? I told him about my meetings with Borodin at the *Moscow News*, the stories he had told me about his work in Chungking, and what he had to say about the Sian incident.

"Yes, it was a hard time. If they had killed Chiang Kai-shek, internal strife would have broken out in China again. And the Japanese would have used it to their advantage. And that would have been very bad for our Communist Party. . . . But still—what happened to Borodin?"

"I don't know exactly. He disappeared, as many others did, in the mid-1940s."

"Pity. I am very sorry for Borodin. He was a wonderful man, a loyal friend, and a true Communist. We often found ourselves in tough spots together. He was a man who knew no fear. He had a great force of character."

So many wonderful people and men of forceful character had been gobbled up by Stalin's mincing machine! We talked until the end of the intermission. But even after the second act Chou En-lai didn't leave. He began talking about how hard it was to build a new life in China.

"We had our own 'Hungarian events' at different times. In the Oukhan, Sian, and Ch'eng-tu there were serious disturbances, involving not only bourgeois elements but also workers and peasants. Of course, we managed to get these situations under control ourselves. But the problems cannot be resolved by force alone. We have to make a thorough analysis to understand why this is happening in Hungary, in Poland, in East Germany, and here in China. There is something wrong in the relations between the leaders and the led, contradictions emerge within society, between the Party and the people and even within the Party itself."

Chou En-lai told me that he had discussed this issue with a Soviet delegation comprising Voroshilov and Rashidov, who had recently visited China.

"But they made light of it," he continued. "Voroshilov said, 'Your Forbidden City, just like the Kremlin, has high walls.' I told him that these same walls didn't save the Chinese emperor. We all have to think about what needs to be done so that there is no discontent among the people."

The premier asked where I had visited in China and whether I had any special requests. I told him that after a trip to the northeast to visit Dairen and Port Arthur, I wanted to travel south, to Yunnan province and Hainan Island. I wanted to live for a week or two in a Chinese village. It would also be interesting to go to Lanchow where China was building its nuclear energy industry. But, I observed, foreigners were probably not welcome in a place like that.

"I will take a look at your itinerary. I believe your requests can be met."

And indeed he kept his word. I didn't have any problems during the rest of my trip around the country.

After the third and last act the lights came back on, but no one in the audience moved.

Chou En-lai got to his feet, shook my hand, wished me a pleasant stay in China, and left the theater. Only then did the people come back to life, as it were, and begin leaving the theater. And then it dawned upon me: They had known about everything all along. They had seen us talking together through the two intermissions. But no one had let on, no one had made any sign or said any word that could disturb our conversation.

Later I learned that Chou En-lai was a frequent visitor to the theater, where he sat in the stalls among the people, and that the audience was used to it by now. For me, familiar with our scene, it verged on the fantastic. When Stalin or Molotov was planning to go to a theater, all the tickets for the show were distributed beforehand among trusted people. The leaders were taken to a special entrance and up a special elevator. Their box was draped with curtains in such a way that they could not be seen from the hall. In a room next to their box, snacks, sweets, and drinks were awaiting them. And no contacts with the people in the audience, even after they had been handpicked. Security, both uniformed and plainclothes, were all over the place.

I was somewhat intrigued by the fact that I didn't see any bodyguards around Chou En-lai. Most probably they were somewhere very near. But they kept such a low profile that I was unable to pick them out.

The following day I received a message from the Foreign Ministry's Department of Information that I would be interviewing Marshal Chu Teh for the magazine. By this I was given to understand that my conversation with Chou En-lai was unofficial and off the record.

I was dying to know why he had arranged that meeting in the first place. Some local sinologists explained to me that since I had the premier at the top of the list of people I wanted to interview, the encounter was a special Chinese courtesy to compensate for their refusal. That sounded like a plausible explanation. But I also wondered if maybe Chou En-lai wanted to show his respect for his friend and comrade Borodin.

After I returned from China, where I had spent almost six months, I locked myself up in my office and from early morning until late at night, with Editor Leontiev's blessing, hammered away at my typewriter, writing up my travel log. Apart from me, the magazine had one other deputy editor, Natalya Sergueyevna Sergueyeva. While I was busy working on my project, she took over the preparation of every issue of the magazine, although usually we alternated.

One day I stepped out of my office to fill my thermos with hot water. As I headed down the corridor, I saw a young girl walking toward me. Strikingly beautiful—tall, slim, her chestnut-colored hair falling down on her shoulders—she attracted me immediately. I had never seen her in the office before. I greeted her and, keeping to my rule never to turn around to look at a woman, walked on toward the boiler that always had hot water in it. But some ten steps farther down the corridor I couldn't help it and turned around. At that same moment the mysterious stranger also looked back. For a second, our eyes met.

Of course, it wasn't hard for me to find out that, while I had been away, the girl of my fancy had joined our staff as a proofreader. Then, after I finished writing my travel stories, I left on business for Britain. After that I went to cover the 1958 World's Fair in Brussels. But I couldn't forget the girl I had met in the corridor and her eyes followed me wherever I went.

Early in 1960, when she turned twenty-five, Lera (she still doesn't like to be called Valeriya Mikhailovna) moved in with me. In 1966, we were married, and the next year after that we had a son, Andrei, who was to bring us much joy—and also sorrow and grief.

At the time of this writing, after two granddaughters from my older sons, I have also been blessed with a grandson, Daniel, from Andrei.

The Shattered Dream

TO LIVE A LIFE is not just crossing a field. This Russian saying encapsulates popular wisdom. Indeed, there are ups and downs in the life of every person. A journey along the road of life is not a walk on a smooth parquet floor. Every now and again, cracks and roadblocks appear, walls of rock and gaping holes. The longer the journey the more you can be certain that after a smooth stretch there will be bumps on the road—and this will happen again and again. Life is often judged in terms of how smooth or bumpy your road has been. However, it is human nature, when thinking about the past, to recall bright, sunshiny days, even though there must have been spells when dark clouds covered the sky, with periods of storm and blizzard. Today, casting aside my rose-tinted glasses and taking a hard look at the years I've lived, I can see that I tripped and fell so many times and met with so many disasters that sometimes I wonder how I was ever able to get up again. You are never ready for calamities, and in most cases they hit you like a bolt from the blue. Yet, whereas you can forgive or forget a slight, right the wrong and start from scratch after what seemed an irreparable disaster, only one thing cannot be mended—death. Death is final. And the death of a person who was close to you inflicts a wound that can never heal.

After I miraculously escaped the bandit's bullet in the Hotel Hay-Adams, it seemed that fortune was on the side of our family again. In 1978, I was invited to the Soviet Foreign Ministry and was offered a job in Washington, D.C., as First Secretary of the Soviet Embassy and a representative of the USA and Canada Institute of the USSR Academy of Sciences. My work at the embassy, where I was liaison officer with the U.S. academic community, was interesting and instructive. I received invitations from people all across the country to visit them and to speak. Lera and I traveled everywhere and made many friends among the Americans. We tried not to miss any of the shows at the John F. Kennedy Center and went to see most of the new movies. Andrei, the son we had had together, went to the embassy school and already had a good command of English. We were a little worried by his passion for rock'n'roll, but then he was just doing what other kids were doing at that time and at that age. We bought him a guitar as a present and he became quite good at it, studying from a teach-yourself manual.

We were renting an apartment in Chevy Chase, Maryland, just outside the District of Columbia. Our neighborhood was very green, with lots of parks and sports grounds where Andrei played with the local kids. During amateur rock concerts near our place he struck up an acquaintance with a young man named Sulhan, a dark-haired twenty-year-old with a touch of something oriental about him. They began meeting regularly. Sulhan shared our sixteen-year-old's craze for rock'n'roll and its superstar Mick Jagger. The difference in age of the new friends troubled Lera a little, but I didn't pay any attention to it.

One day in early August 1983, I came home for lunch, parked my car in the underground garage, and while Lera was setting the table, went to take a swim in the pool, as I always did. The pool was on the roof of our twenty-two-story apartment building. As I was changing into my robe, I heard Andrei call me:

"Dad, can I borrow your car keys? I need to get a tape from the glove compartment."

"Go ahead! And then come join me on the roof for a swim."

The roof gave a fine view over the city and the green-clad, rolling hills beyond. Folding chairs, sunning pads, and brightly colored umbrellas stood around the pool with its blue water. I basked in the sun for a while, did a few laps around the pool, but still there was no sign of Andrei. Thinking that Lera had probably sent him to pick up something at the store, I went down to the fifth floor where we lived.

"Where's Andrei?" I asked Lera, who was bustling about in the kitchen.

"What do you mean? Wasn't he up there with you?"

"He didn't show up at the pool. He was down here with you, wasn't he?"

"No, I haven't seen him. Go check the garage. Maybe he is listening to that stupid music of his on your car radio. The kid is going crazy with that music."

I went down to the garage. I didn't find the car where I had parked it. Maybe Andrei, who already knew how to drive a little, had decided to take it for a spin around the garage and was on another level. I searched all four underground parking levels but didn't find Andrei or the car anywhere. I became worried, fearing that something had happened to him. A criminal could have been hiding in the garage. Seeing a boy by the car, he could have hit him on the head, gagged him, thrown him in the trunk, and taken off. I had this big new Oldsmobile purchased for me by the USA and Canada Institute. But the car wasn't the point. It was insured and I would get my money back if it had been stolen. What had happened to Andrei? Where was he? I left the garage and walked all around the block. Not a sign of Andrei. What would I tell Lera?

I am not going to describe how she took the news that our son had disappeared. We were both in despair. After she calmed down a little, she began leafing through Andrei's notebook and found Sulhan's phone number. It turned out that he lived in the building across from us. I dialed his number and a voice at the other end answered, "Sulhan speaking."

"I am sorry to disturb you. I am Andrei's father. You have been seeing each other recently."

"Yes."

"He's disappeared. Maybe you know something that can help?"

"I saw him today. I think he was planning to go to New York."

Now what was all that about! Andrei and I had gone to New York only last week, and there were no plans to go there in the near future. I said as much to Sulhan.

"Well, then I don't know what to think," he replied. "He must have just been daydreaming. Sorry, I can't help you."

And what if Andrei had gotten it into his head to go to New York? I had heard that Mick Jagger was going to give a concert there. But that was impossible! Andrei didn't have a driver's license. He didn't know the way to New York and had no driving experience. How could he maneuver on a congested highway with hosts of intersections, exits, tunnels, and bridges? Moreover, every so often you have to pay a toll. Where would he get the money? I decided to call the police. Some ten minutes later a Maryland county traffic patrolman was at our door. I explained the situation to him, saying that, incredible as it might sound, Andrei could be on one of the roads to New York.

"How old is he?" the officer asked.

"Sixteen."

"Oh, kids that age do even worse things. They have these crazy ideas in their heads. But don't worry. We'll find him. Your car is easy to spot, with its diplomatic license plate. There's a special patrol vehicle keeping an eye on them. I'll get your runaway home before you know it."

That cheered us up a little. Indeed, it shouldn't be a problem to track down a car like that, especially with a teenager at the wheel. But one hour went by, then another, and still there was no word from the police. I called the precinct again.

"We're working on it," was their answer. "Don't worry. You'll be notified right away."

So much time had already gone by and still no news of Andrei! No matter how much I hated it, I had to inform my consul. Of course, there would be a great commotion there. Just think of it: a Soviet boy disappeared!

The consul said he would be right over and asked us to stay at home. Another hour went by. The bosses at the embassy were probably discussing the Berezhkov family "incident."

"Andrei back yet?" the consul asked cheerily when he finally showed up.

When he learned that Andrei wasn't, he began calming us down, recalling similar incidents and assuring us that after a joyride around town Andrei would be back. We were grateful to him for his concern. Lera told him about our son's friendship with Sulhan and the latter's strange idea about Andrei's going to New York.

"Let me talk to this Sulhan," the consul suggested.

I dialed the familiar number. This time a woman answered the phone.

"May I speak to Mr. Sulhan?" I asked.

"Mr. Sulhan doesn't live here anymore."

"But I spoke to him only an hour ago."

"I repeat, Mr. Sulhan doesn't live here anymore. He left the country." And she hung up.

"This is very strange," the consul said pensively. "If this man Sulhan is indeed connected to Andrei somehow, then this whole thing doesn't look too good."

He didn't have to tell us it looked bad. We knew it only too well. Why hadn't the cops been able to locate the car? Could it be that Sulhan was a gangster who had kidnapped our son and hidden him somewhere well out of sight? Or maybe some higher authorities were involved in this? But why would they want our boy? What was the point of playing hide-and-seek with us?

The embassy office hours were over. The consul stayed with us a little longer and before he left asked us to call him at home if there were any developments. We were left alone and felt completely lost.

I was trying to calm Lera down as much as I could, although it was perfectly clear to me that we were in deep trouble.

All our plans had crumbled. The last year of my five-year tour of duty in the United States was drawing to a close. Andrei had completed the eighth and last year at the embassy school and was to start his ninth year at a school in Moscow. Since the USA and Canada Institute had not yet found a replacement for me, we had been planning that Lera and Andrei would leave for Moscow, where she would get him into school and then come back to Washington to wrap things up before we finally left for home. I had already booked air tickets for them for the middle of August. Now everything was up in the air until we found Andrei. We sat in our living room facing each other, waiting. What were we waiting for?

Around two o'clock in the morning the phone rang.

"I'm downstairs in the lobby. Come down here, will you?" I heard the familiar voice.

"It's Andrei," I hastened to tell Lera the good news. "He's downstairs."

"Give him hell!" She sighed with relief.

I hurried toward the elevator. Andrei stood in the middle of the lobby; he looked haggard and, I thought, swollen.

"The car is outside by the entrance. I haven't cut the engine. It's hard for me to get it into the garage," he said.

We went out to the car. The odometer showed that it had covered a couple of hundred miles in the past twelve hours. I didn't ask any questions, seeing the sorry state Andrei was in. We parked the car in the garage and went up to the apartment. Lera, forgetting about "giving him hell," clung to him and began kissing him. But he stood there indifferently and didn't say a word.

"Are you going to tell us what's happened to you?" I finally asked.

"Tomorrow. I'm too tired. Can I have some water?"

He downed two large cups in two gulps, wiped his lips with his hand, and said, "I'm terribly sleepy."

He walked over to his room, swaying a little, fell down on his bed with his clothes on, and was asleep at the same moment.

Of course, we didn't sleep a wink that night. I called the consul. He was also up. One thing he said jarred me: "Let's hope this is the end of it."

In the morning, no matter how hard I tried to get out of Andrei what had happened, he either kept his mouth shut or said he didn't remember anything. It was time for Lera and me to go to the office, but how could we leave Andrei alone? So I took him along. I left him in the embassy buffet and went to brief the embassy's chargé d'affaires, Oleg Sokolov, on the situation. (Ambassador Anatoly Dobrynin was away in Moscow.)

Oleg also wasn't sure we'd seen the end of the story. Everything looked too strange. We decided to speed up Andrei and Lera's departure. Fortunately, there was an Aeroflot flight the following day. Oleg and I were friends, and I knew he was sincerely trying to help.

The phone rang. Oleg picked it up, listened for some time, and I saw the expression on his face change. He hung up and looked at me sympathetically.

"That was our mutual friend Leslie Gelb from the *New York Times* Washington Bureau. He just got a copy of Andrei's letter addressed to President Reagan. Andrei has requested asylum in the United States. The letter will be published in the paper's late edition tonight."

That was the blow I feared, but I still couldn't believe it was true. Why hadn't Andrei told me about it? And who needed him here in the United States anyway? They would make a big hullabaloo about the defection of the son of a Soviet diplomat and then forget all about it. It was absolutely crazy for a Soviet teenager to expect anything here.

"I think it's better if you left Chevy Chase right away," Sokolov continued. "There will be reporters all over the place. Why don't you move to the embassy compound?"

"It looks like we'll have to," I agreed reluctantly. The consequences of what had happened still hadn't fully sunk into my mind.

I went down to join Andrei in the buffet. He sat there sipping Coke as if nothing had happened. It was hard for me to keep harsh words back, but I managed to control myself. I had to stay calm. The next thing to do was to pick up Lera at the office of *Soviet Life* magazine, go home, pack the things we needed most, and move to the embassy compound. We walked to the car in silence. There I let my anger spill out. But Andrei didn't react in any way to my outburst.

"Tell me the truth. Did you write that letter or didn't you?" I asked when I ran out of epithets.

"I don't remember. But I really want to stay here. I don't like Moscow. Life's much more interesting here."

"Well, you could finish school, go to college, and get a degree. Then you could come back and work here."

"And who would let me? This is my only chance."

"But who needs you here without qualifications? They have enough people of their own out of work."

"I'd give it a try. Either I make it and become successful or I fail and perish. This is still better than wasting my life away at home. You were lucky to come here. No such luck for me."

"Have you thought about Mother and me?"

"I have. That's why I'm back."

What could I say in reply? Of course, the situation in our country was getting worse and worse. We, the people of the older generation, had grown used to living according to the formula "Right or wrong, my country." But even we, when we were among trusted friends—and preferably somewhere out in the open air—complained that our leaders were not thinking about the people, but were only concerned about themselves and their offspring. But the time hadn't come yet for us to speak out, and we continued to accept black for white, especially when we were abroad. It was harder for the young people. They still believed they had to tell the truth.

At home we quickly packed the things we needed to take with us and immediately left for the compound, where we found temporary quarters in a two-bedroom apartment.

The handwriting of the letter reproduced in facsimile in the *New York Times* bore only a vague resemblance to Andrei's. It was signed "Berzhkov" and not "Berezhkov," which raised questions, and the text was too harshly critical of the Soviet Union. I found it hard to believe that Andrei could have written it:

August 9, 1983

I'm a Russian kid. My father works at the Soviet Embassy. He is the 1st secretary. I hate my country and it's rules and I love your country. I want to stay here. I wrote to Mr. President and I hope he will help me. I'm afraid if my parents find that out they'll put me in Siberia. So I'm running away. On 11 of August at 11 o'clock I'll drive up to the US mission in New York. If the letter doesn't get to the President in time I hope you will help me. I love your people and country. I hope you understand me. We children are treated like prisoners here. We can't say anything good about your country

in school and anything wrong about our country. I know you are a free press not like ours and I hope you'll help me too.
Thanks for reading the letter.
Andy Berzhkov

I showed the newspaper to Andrei. "Take a good look. Did you write this or didn't you?"

This time he admitted that he did.

"And why is the family name misspelled?"

"I was nervous and made a mistake."

I was itching to give him a spanking, but I controlled myself.

"Let's sit down and talk calmly," I suggested, knowing that if I was tough on him again, he would only withdraw into himself.

Meanwhile, some decision had to be taken fast. But the first thing to do was to talk Andrei out of his crazy idea to stay alone in a foreign country and to get him to give a firm promise that he would return to Moscow with us. Only after that could I propose a plan of action to the embassy. I advanced different options. Andrei was mostly silent, although he listened attentively.

"Mind you," I cautioned him, "we can get out of this respectably only if we agree on every detail and you keep your word, no matter what happens. Agreed?"

"Agreed."

"Very well. Think everything over one more time. We'll talk some more tomorrow. And now go to sleep."

We had left our apartment in Chevy Chase not a moment too soon. Sometime later at the compound we met our neighbor, a Novosti Press Agency correspondent, who said, "There are some people in plainclothes and a whole bunch of journalists with video cameras hanging around in the lobby and on your floor. They are waiting for you, unaware that you have moved."

I would have had to answer their questions and I still didn't have the slightest idea how we had ended up in this incredible mess. The first priority for our family, including Andrei, was to decide what to do. Supposing the U.S. authorities blocked Andrei's departure. What were we to do then? Go without him and leave an immature adolescent behind in a foreign country? Or stay with him and become defectors ourselves? This was 1983 and still a long way from perestroika. When Andropov came to power, some things did change, but essentially the old rules were still in place. And then Lera and I were not

prepared psychologically to take that step. We had friends in the Soviet Union, we were attached to certain things, I had my name to
think about. I was already fairly well known because of my writings.
What would happen to my two older sons, working in Moscow, and
to their families? Our country had not yet abandoned Stalin's practice of holding one's relatives hostage. No, we couldn't possibly stay.
I think that if Andrei had been detained in the United States, Lera
and I would have returned to Moscow without him. Today, many people would probably consider such a decision inhuman, but at that
time we, like most Soviet people, remained prisoners of our minds.

In any case, I concluded that for the time being we shouldn't be
talking to correspondents.

All evening, news shows carried reports about "the son of a Soviet
diplomat" appealing to President Reagan to grant him asylum in the
United States. Pictures of Andrei and me were shown, as well as the
letter that had appeared in the newspaper.

A fiery propaganda campaign was getting under way to add substance to President Reagan's statements about the "evil empire." The
case of our family was to add fuel to the flames.

But a number of things in this whole story were very strange. The
letter had been sent by Andrei the day before he disappeared. How
could it have reached the newspaper by the following morning? Who
delivered it there? I knew from personal experience that it usually
took two days or more for letters to travel from one part of Washington, D.C., to another. And then that letter to the president. There
must be thousands of letters arriving at the White House every day.
How could that letter have reached there in only a few hours and
then have been picked out of that flood of correspondence?

What explanation of what happened did I have? I thought that
somebody probably knew about Andrei's plans from his telephone
conversations with his school friends and decided to use the opportunity as it presented itself. But why would somebody do that? Probably to discredit his father. He was hopping from one speaking en-
gagement to another all around the United States, defending
Moscow's line, while his son was falling in love with the American way
of life. How could anyone possibly believe this Soviet propaganda if
his own son didn't buy it?

The following day Andrei and I had a serious talk. The embassy insisted that he deny the authenticity of the letter. It took a lot of per-
suading on my part to convince Andrei that this was necessary. Fi-

nally, he reluctantly agreed and promised to return home with us. Before going to the embassy, I asked him:

"Can I depend on you not to let me down?"

"Yes, Dad. I promised and I'll keep my word."

At a meeting with the top embassy officials we discussed what steps we had to take. I suggested that we immediately call a press conference at the compound so that Andrei and I could shed light on the situation. After that Andrei and his mother would return to Moscow while I would stay on to wait for my replacement, as had been planned. But my colleagues had their doubts about that course of action. What if Andrei changed his mind and declared that he wanted to stay in the United States? I tried to convince them. He had given me his word and would keep it. After all that had happened and our frank talks, he would not let his parents or the embassy down. Unfortunately, my arguments didn't hold sway with them. They decided to request instructions from Moscow and wait. I am sorry Ambassador Dobrynin wasn't in Washington. I believe he would have taken the responsibility upon himself and allowed us to hold a press conference without delay. If that had happened, the U.S. authorities would have had no basis for detaining Andrei and the whole propaganda brouhaha would have fizzled out. But the time for that was lost.

By nightfall, the whole housing compound was surrounded by beefed-up police units. A helicopter hovered over the roof of our house. A presidential adviser, Edwin Meese, appeared on television that night to declare that the U.S. authorities would not allow Andrei's forced departure from the United States. The president was reported to have issued a directive to seal all U.S. borders. This hadn't happened since the end of the war! In the morning, groups of demonstrators gathered outside the compound gates, carrying signs that demanded Andrei's release. The State Department, "on instructions from the president," officially notified the embassy that the U.S. immigration authorities insisted that Andrei be handed over to them to clarify his intentions. A statement by an embassy spokesman that Andrei had no intention of staying in America and wanted to go home with his parents had no effect. The U.S. authorities demanded that an interview with Andrei be arranged.

Every day all day, radio and television stations were broadcasting the story of the "runaway boy." To drive the point home, an animated cartoon was made for television showing a small figure running away from a menacing hammer and sickle. Live "scholarly debates" were held on TV to discuss the punishment Andrei and his father would get if they returned home. My colleagues at the embassy also painted a pretty gloomy picture. Some even suggested that upon our return home we change our name, leave Moscow for some provincial town, and, in general, drop out of circulation.

Finally, word came from Moscow giving the go-ahead for the press conference. Andrei did what he said he would do. He insisted that he hadn't written any letter and wanted to return home to Moscow with his parents.

Immediately after the press conference, accompanied by embassy, State Department, and police escorts, we were taken to Dulles International Airport in Washington. Our TWA plane took off and headed for Paris. From there we took an Aeroflot plane to Moscow.

Although the situation in the Soviet Union was then already slowly changing for the better, that didn't prevent many of the people we had known from turning their backs on us. My books were taken off the shelves in libraries and placed out of access—"just in case." My latest manuscript was returned to me from the printer. Still, we had no intention of changing our name or hiding in the provinces. True friends stayed by our side helping us through this difficult period.

I was again appointed editor in chief of *USA—Economics, Politics, Ideology* magazine. Together with Dr. Georgi Arbator, we had launched that publication in January 1970. For twenty years I was its editor, trying to give Soviet readers authentic information about life and politics in the United States. I felt proud when Averell Harriman called my monthly "a constructive magazine."

In the spring of 1985, Gorbachev came to power and launched his perestroika. Gradually, the life of our family got back to normal. Not without difficulties, we managed to put our rebellious son through college and help him find an interesting job.

But Andrei's love for America did not die, nor his dream of returning to the United States someday. He wanted to prove to all that he could have made it there. He was among the first of his friends to open his own business—a souvenir shop. Then he was invited to work with an American company out of Texas selling oil-drilling equipment in the Russian Federation. Before long he became one of the company's vice presidents. For over two years, he traveled to many oil-producing regions in Russia to sell the company's equipment. A number of times he went to Houston on business. He had plans to go to the United States with his family (in 1990, his son, Daniel, was born) and stay there for a longer period, making his longtime dream come true.

When I look back at what has happened over the years, more and more often I think that maybe, way back in August 1983, Andrei should have stayed in the United States. Given his abilities, he wouldn't have gone under. And then our family would have been spared the terrible tragedy that hit us—also in August but in 1993—when the bullet of a raving maniac, who posed as a friend while being consumed with envy and deadly hate, cut short our son's life. . . .

My Parents' Grave

ALL MY ATTEMPTS to find my parents had been in vain. The Berezhkov family had vanished without a trace. But somehow I still had the feeling that my parents were alive. And if they hadn't perished, I thought to myself, then they had to know about me from my articles, which were often reprinted in the West, as well as from my books, many of which had come out abroad and had been reviewed in periodicals. They could also see me on television in England, the United States, Germany, France, and other countries. Why then were they not giving me any signs that they were alive? They were probably thinking that because of the Cold War and the uncompromising confrontation between the Soviet Union and the West, it was best for us not to look for each other, especially since my work brought me close to Stalin.

Beria's intention "to investigate" my case was not the only indication that my parents might be alive. Another telltale sign was that from 1945 to 1954 I was not allowed to travel abroad. Furthermore, after my trips to Vienna, Geneva, and the United States in 1954–55, the Communist Party Central Committee's department in charge of personnel working abroad again slammed the door shut on me. Only after first Molotov and then Mikoyan intervened on my behalf, with great reluctance they lifted the Iron Curtain a crack.

At the same time I was getting some vague signals that, when I considered the situation as a whole, I interpreted as coming from my parents. For instance, during a trip to the United States in 1955, each member of our group received stacks of souvenirs from the Americans: books, brochures, postcards, guides, etc. At first I didn't notice that among the books on California, delivered to me at the Ambassador Hotel in Los Angeles, was a book by Karl May about the American Indians entitled *Vinetou*—which had been my favorite reading in childhood. Only later did I ask myself, who but someone very close to me could have sent me this book?

A few years later, in the flood of letters I was getting at the *New Times* from the magazine's foreign readers, I came across a letter from Switzerland signed by a Mrs. Norr. She was requesting—for translation—a book by one Dr. Kaminsky about the therapeutic effects of balneological (water) treatment. In the 1920s, when we lived in Kiev, Dr. Kaminsky had been our family physician, and he had practiced those very methods on his patients. Why had some Mrs. Norr now turned to me with a request like that? I was asked to send the book to an address in Geneva, a sanatorium, care of Mrs. Luise Perels.

A few more years went by and then another letter came from Geneva with the same return address. In this letter, Mrs. Norr made reference to episodes in my childhood that only my mother could know. In 1966, when I was on a business trip in West Germany, I sent a letter to Geneva asking Mrs. Norr where she had learned all those things. I also asked her whether she knew anything about my parents. The next letter I received two years later contained further details about my life but no answer to my questions. Mrs. Norr only mentioned that she was going to spend the summer of 1969 in Switzerland and that she could be reached at the address known to me.

In connection with the one hundredth anniversary of Lenin's birth, which was celebrated in 1970, the USSR Union of Journalists organized a number of trips to Switzerland, where Lenin had lived in exile before the 1917 Revolution. Lera and I enrolled for one such trip.

In the early summer of 1969 we arrived in Geneva and went to the address of the sanatorium, as given to me in Mrs. Norr's letters. Luckily, we found Luise Perels there without any problem. She said she knew Mrs. Norr, who frequently stopped by to pick up her mail. We gave Luise the address of the hotel where we were staying and went on a tour of "Lenin's sites" in Geneva. The following morning, as we left the hotel after breakfast, we met an elegantly dressed elderly lady. I immediately recognized my mother even though she had greatly changed in the thirty years we had been separated. We were overcome with emotion and for some time were unable even to speak. The three of us went to a cafe where we regained the gift of tongues. Mother told me that Father had died in the late 1950s in Germany and that my sister had vanished in Kiev during the German occupation. Mother had completed a training program to become a cosmetologist. But now she was retired, and although she hadn't saved much money, she had enough for travel, which was her passion. Most of the time, she lived in Switzerland.

I felt too uncomfortable to ask her why she had changed her name, assuming that she had probably remarried after Father's death. Nor did I get any information from her on how my sister had disappeared. I had my doubts about her story but accepted it anyway, seeing that she had found it necessary to conceal some things. Still, when I began writing this book, I decided not to mention my sister at all so as not to cause her any trouble in case she was alive and had a family. The ideological confrontation between communism and capitalism had taught us to be wary, especially about putting our relatives in jeopardy. For us, relatives in the West, just as for many Westerners' relatives in the USSR, could bring unexpected troubles.

Seeing Mother's reticence, I didn't ask her what passport she was carrying on her travels. I assumed she had the usual documents issued to "displaced persons." I assumed also that my parents had changed their name in order to protect me, knowing where I was working. That was why my attempts to find them had proved futile. However, plenty of people were around who had fled Kiev and who could have tipped off Beria's agents about their little "ruse," and this was probably what had happened. The KGB had long known what I had not been aware of.

Subsequently, during my trips abroad, Mother and I met again. Then for a long time, until the mid-1980s, I had no news of her.

One day I came into my office and saw a brown envelope on my desk, addressed to me. The secretary explained that it had been brought by a foreigner about half an hour ago. He hadn't given his name.

I opened the envelope and I found a school notebook filled out in Mother's even hand. Seized with emotion, I asked my secretary not to disturb me for the next half hour, locked my office door, and immersed myself in reading.

When you get this message, I will no longer be alive. That is why I can now tell you what I couldn't bring myself to tell you before.

In 1943, your old school companion Michel helped us get out of Kiev. He had become an officer of the German Navy and came to see us during his short leave hoping to get some news about you. We told him that you were missing. He suggested that we move in with his mother in Sonthofen in Bavaria, and that was where we stayed until the end of the war. Michel died when his battleship, the *Tirpitz*, was sunk by the British Air Force. Shortly after that, not without difficulties, we managed to move to America. At first, we were very poor but gradually settled in, obtained U.S. citizenship, and lived all that time in California.

So that was the secret Mother had been guarding from me so closely! They had become U.S. citizens! But what was so bad about that? Was it the fact that the parents of Stalin's interpreter were Americans? But was it not also a fact that Stalin's daughter, Svetlana Alliluyeva—and her daughter, too, that is, Stalin's granddaughter—were also U.S. citizens? But it is easy to say this today. In Stalin's time, if one had parents who were U.S. citizens, it was as good as getting a death sentence. In the United States, too, during the period of McCarthyism, congressional witch-hunts, and militant anticommunism, the careers of many Americans were wrecked because they had close relatives in the Soviet Union.

The information I received in my mother's posthumous letter, together with the book *Vinetou* by Karl May that I had received at the Ambassador Hotel back in 1955, prompted me to look for my parents' graves in Los Angeles.

In 1991–92, I was invited to teach as a visiting professor at two colleges in the city of Claremont located near Los Angeles. It turned out that the priest at the local Orthodox Church had known my parents. He told me that they had been buried at the Inglewood Cemetery. From that it was easy for me find their graves.

They had found their final resting place under a granite stone on a green hill in the shadow of a huge pine tree. That was where they had ended their long and arduous journey. I brought white chrysanthemums to put on their grave and saw some roses lying on their tombstone. Who could have put them there? The cemetery administration gave me a number to call. When I did, my sister picked up the phone. We had found each other again—after a separation of fifty years!

How many families have been split and scattered by our cruel, tragic, and bloody age? How many people close to each other, loving each other, failed to look for each other for fear of being ground down by an ideological confrontation? Only a few of them were as lucky as I—to know the joys of reunion after the many years of forced separation.

POSTSCRIPT

I began my story at a time when, against the backdrop of a bloody civil war, devastation, famine, and terrible hardships, the Soviet society was taking shape. I am concluding it as I witness the disintegration and disappearance of the great empire in which I lived all my life.

During a span of three-quarters of a century, the Soviet Union was a major player on the global stage. People the world over had highly mixed feelings about it, ranging from admiration for the audacity of those living on one-sixth of the planet's surface who deemed themselves capable of building a "perfect society" and setting an example for all to emulate, to a categorical rejection and condemnation of the very premise underlying the unprecedented experiment the "Kremlin dreamers" carried out on their own people.

Today, the world is shaken by the death of the Soviet regime just as it was by its birth at the beginning of this century. Again, the peoples of the former Soviet Union and of the countries seduced or induced by Moscow to adopt its misguided "model for the construction of socialism" are going through the same hardships they had suffered then.

Misery, despair, endless lines to get necessities, loss of faith in a "bright future," disillusionment, hopelessness, and fear give rise to violence in all corners of the former Soviet Union and create a volatile mix that can explode at any moment into an all-out fratricidal civil war.

Just as seventy-odd years ago the "children of Red October" pinned their hopes on imported canned beef and powdered milk, distributed throughout our starving Russia by the American Relief Administration, today our people are again forced to look for help from outside.

After the failed August coup, whose instigators wanted to "reinforce the ideas of Red October" with tanks that filled the streets of Moscow, the Soviet Union rapidly unraveled, and in late December

1991 it ceased to exist. Only a short while before, anything like that had been simply unthinkable. However, the 1917 Revolution and the demise of the Russian Empire had happened just as quickly. The factors that brought down the czar and the causes that brought about the collapse of the Soviet Union are different. Yet they share one thing in common: the foundations of a state built on force and fear, repressions and deceptive propaganda, crumble as soon as people lose their fear and gain access to truthful information.

All this once again proves that a state cannot enforce stability through repressive means, no matter how sophisticated they are. Stability cannot be ensured by military force, either. The strength of any state system depends on the degree of its public's consent. There was no such consent either in czarist Russia nor in the Communist Soviet Union, at least in the last decades of the Soviet regime. And when the old structures began to disintegrate, nothing was left to hold the artificial entity together.

Looking back at the unfolding drama of the receding century, with its historic events and mind-boggling cataclysms, a play in which I have been both a spectator and an actor, I find it hard to believe that I have lived to see the final episode of the bewildering and in many respects bewitching "Soviet era," an era that will undoubtedly go down in history as one more daring but doomed attempt to build a just society. Willingly or unwillingly, millions of people paid with their lives to give this idea a try. However, as Oscar Wilde once said, "If a man dies for a cause, it does not necessarily follow that he died for a just cause."

As our experiment unfolded, we lived through terrible sacrifices, ravages to body and soul, incredible suffering and losses. But at the same time we were full of hope, faith, and enthusiasm and were prepared to sacrifice ourselves in our desire to create a "better future" for ourselves and those who would come after us.

We could also boast some remarkable accomplishments in our lives. In spite of muddles, mistakes, and blunders, tens of millions of people became literate, general secondary education was introduced, higher education and health care were provided free of charge, formerly backward peoples on the outskirts of the czarist empire were introduced to the best in the national and world cultures. And the low rents, cheap city transport, low crime, and full employment—all this was taken for granted.

Our sacrifices have not been in vain. The development of society will not stop once we have "advanced technologies," "information systems," and other trappings of modern capitalism. The best minds will go on thinking about how to improve life on earth. And the experience of our country, our triumphs and tragedies, will serve as points of reference for humanity on the march toward the future.

The price we paid to build a new social system on the ruins of czarism was exorbitant. In 1917, the old regime or what was left of it took up arms to fight the new government. Today, the custodians of the old administer-and-command system are again trying to nip the new life in the bud. That was the goal of the instigators of the rebellion in October 1993. Their disruptive actions were largely responsible for the failure of Gorbachev's perestroika, its architect's personal drama, and his exit from the political stage. Nevertheless, Gorbachev's place in history is secure. He succeeded, if unwittingly, in bringing down the system that Hitler had been unable to overcome in four years of deadly combat.

Today the new threat of aggressive nationalism is emerging. Playing up to the people with promises of a better life, rampant nationalism is only bringing them more misery, suffering, and war.

If the fledgling democracy in Russia and other states of the former Soviet Union dies, it will be a great tragedy not only for our people but for the whole world. We can only hope that the developed countries will not repeat the mistakes they made early in this century when, after the 1917 February Revolution, they aided and abetted in the elimination of the Russian democracy by forcing the Provisional Government to continue the bloodbath of World War I instead of reaching out a helping hand to a hungry country driven to despair by its defeats at the front.

If today the West continues to pursue its wait-and-see policy, given the presence of nuclear weapons and nuclear power plants on the territory of the former Soviet Union, the consequences could be far more devastating than the havoc wrought by the Civil War and intervention of 1918–22.

We can only hope that the people of our country and of other countries will not have to pay a terrible price to know what will come in place of the defunct Soviet Union.

I was one and a half years old when the czarist empire crumbled. My grandson, Daniel, had reached that same age when the Soviet empire fell to pieces. May God spare him the experience of my generation!

INDEX